Applied Public Finance and Fiscal Analysis

Applied Public Finance and Fiscal Analysis

Guest Editors

Andrey Zahariev
Borislav Dimitrov Borisov

MDPI
Basel • Beijing • Wuhan • Barcelona • Belgrade • Novi Sad • Cluj • Manchester

Guest Editors
Andrey Zahariev
Department of Finance and Insurance
University of Insurance and Finance
Sofia
Bulgaria

Borislav Dimitrov Borisov
Institute of Economics and Politics
University of National and World Economy
Sofia
Bulgaria

Editorial Office
MDPI AG
Grosspeteranlage 5
4052 Basel, Switzerland

This is a reprint of the Special Issue, published open access by the journal *Journal of Risk and Financial Management* (ISSN 1911-8074), freely accessible at: https://www.mdpi.com/journal/jrfm/special_issues/HZ63D22233.

For citation purposes, cite each article independently as indicated on the article page online and as indicated below:

Lastname, Firstname, Firstname Lastname, and Firstname Lastname. Article Title. *Journal Name* **Year**, *Volume Number*, Page Range.

ISBN 978-3-7258-8149-9 (Hbk)
ISBN 978-3-7258-8150-5 (PDF)
https://doi.org/10.3390/books978-3-7258-8150-5

Contents

About the Editors

Andrey Zahariev

Andrey Zahariev is a professor of finance at the University of Insurance and Finance, Sofia, Bulgaria with a PhD in economics. He has scientific interests, conducts research and teaches academic courses in public finance, financial management, project finance, financial analysis, international finance, debt management, etc. He was elected to the rank of professor twice, in 2012 and 2025, with habilitation monographs in the field of financial management of municipalities and fiscal decentralization. For over ten years, he served as editor-in-chief of the journal *Economic Archive*. He is a member of the editorial boards of scientific journals in Bulgaria, the USA and Ukraine. He supervises doctoral students from Bulgaria, Japan, Kazakhstan and Albania and has held administrative positions including vice-rector, dean of faculty, director of a center and head of department. He has led a master's program in financial management and various national and international projects. In the public sector, he was elected chairman of the National Association of Chairpersons of Municipal Councils in the Republic of Bulgaria. He has served as a financial consultant on projects of the USAID, SDC and DANIDA. He participated in the Advisory Council on Management and Audit of the Financial System to the Minister of Finance of the Republic of Bulgaria. As the author of more than 280 scientific publications, he has been published in journals such as *Risks*, *Sustainability* and *Journal of Risk and Financial Management* and has prepared over 30 manuscript reviews for MDPI. He has been awarded the honorary titles "Doctor Honoris Causa" in Ukraine and "Professor Honorificus" in Romania.

Borislav Dimitrov Borisov

Borislav Dimitrov Borisov is a professor and researcher at the Institute of Economics and Politics of the University of National and World Economy, Sofia, Bulgaria with a PhD in Economics and a Doctor of Science in Administration and Management. His scientific interests are in the fields of strategic and business planning, capital markets, public administration, financial management and control, etc. Among his scientific outputs are the annual studies of the administrative capacity of the state administration in Bulgaria, the determination of the main risks facing the country for the next 10 years (Ten for Ten), etc. He spent most of his academic career at the D. A. Tsenov Academy of Economics, Svishtov, where he was also Chairman of the General Assembly. He taught academic courses in administration and planning at various Bulgarian universities and lectures at the Institute of Public Administration. He has served as Deputy Mayor of Varna Municipality, Chairman of the Svishtov Municipal Council and an expert in the 40th National Assembly. He specialized at the State Academy of Local Government, Washington, USA; the Institute for Training and Development, Amherst, Massachusetts, USA; the Santa Cruz Institute, Tucson, Arizona, USA; and the Higher School of Public Administration, Ludwigsburg, Germany. He served as editor-in-chief of the journal *Business Management* and is currently a member of the editorial boards of several scientific journals. He is the author of more than 200 publications and 240 scientific and applied studies, and has been the head and member of the teams of over 50 projects financed by the European Investment Fund, UNDP, USAID, SDC, PHARE, Tempus, Sixth Framework Program and the operational programs of the Republic of Bulgaria. He is the winner of the national award "Finance Officer of the Year" (2008).

Preface

This reprint edition collects nine peer-reviewed articles that collectively examine key developments in the field of applied public finance and fiscal analysis. Applied public finance is a rapidly developing field of scientific knowledge that bridges the gap between theoretical public economics and the implementation of public policies. Following years of multiple crises, unprecedented fiscal challenges are being observed due to pandemic recovery, surging energy prices, local military conflicts, climate change, and demographic challenges. All of these factors require rigorous empirical analysis of the mechanisms of public finance. Traditional public finance theory, while precise in its theoretical foundations, often suffers from empirical failure. There is ample evidence of the clash between theoretical axioms and the realities of practice. This Special Issue reprint expands the boundaries of applied public finance by collating cutting-edge research that combines sophisticated econometric methods with new data sources. The tools of fiscal analysis provide answers to fundamental questions in public finance. The presented studies use diverse methodologies, exploring new data sets and providing causal evidence on the effectiveness of fiscal policies, tax reforms, public spending programs, and institutional sustainability and efficiency. The Special Issue has achieved its goal: to search for and map the "philosopher's stone" of applied public finance—studies that successfully combine the methodological rigor of fiscal analysis with policy relevance. As a result, both theoretical insights and practical guidelines for designing fiscal policy in the 21st century, based on a balance between governments, businesses, and households that promotes sustainable economic growth, are presented. This reprint places in the hands of academic researchers, policymakers, analysts, and practitioners the most up-to-date research on the problems of contemporary financial theory in the field of its applied testing and fiscal metrication. The collaboration of scholars from different countries and continents has resulted in this reprint book, which will inspire future research on applied public finance and fiscal analysis in a fast-changing international environment with the global transmission of economic disturbances.

Andrey Zahariev and Borislav Dimitrov Borisov
Guest Editors

Journal of
Risk and Financial Management

MDPI

Article

House Price Determinants: Evidence from Bulgaria as a New Eurozone Member State

Andrey Zahariev [1,*], Galina Zaharieva [2], Larysa Shaulska [3,4] and Mykhaylo Oryekhov [5]

1 Department of Finance and Insurance, University of Insurance and Finance, 1000 Sofia, Bulgaria
2 Department of International Economics, Economic Research Institute at the Bulgarian Academy of Science, 1000 Sofia, Bulgaria; g.zaharieva@iki.bas.bg
3 Academic Affairs, State University "Kyiv Aviation Institute", 03058 Kyiv, Ukraine; larysa.shaulska@kai.edu.ua
4 Department of Business Economics, Taras Shevchenko National University of Kyiv, 01033 Kyiv, Ukraine; shaulska@knu.ua
5 Department of Management and Behavioral Economics, Economic Faculty, Vasyl' Stus Donetsk National University, 21021 Vinnytsia, Ukraine; m.oriekhov@donnu.edu.ua
* Correspondence: a.zahariev@uzf.bg

Abstract

This study examines the relationship between house prices and the factors driving their growth during the transition from a long-standing currency board regime to Eurozone membership. The main objective is to identify and quantify the key factors explaining the variation in house price growth in Bulgaria under conditions of prolonged currency convergence. The study applies a set of econometric techniques, including stationarity tests (ADF and KPSS), diagnostic checks for normality, serial correlation and heteroscedasticity, and robustness checks. The study is based on 40 quarterly observations covering the period 2015Q4–2025Q3 and 48 selected predictors of the General house price index. The final ARIMAX(0,2,1) model is estimated using second-differenced data. The model includes a first-order moving average component and three exogenous regressors: the owner-occupiers' housing expenditures, the actual rentals for housing in Bulgaria and the homeowners' utility expenses. The model explains 87% of the variation in house price acceleration, with a comparatively low mean squared error. The diagnostic analysis confirms model adequacy. The three exogenous regressors are statistically significant at the 1% level with strong and stable effects on house price dynamics. No statistically significant relationship is found for the set of traditional macroeconomic, demographic, financial, and sectoral factors. The results show that during Bulgaria's transition from a currency board to the Eurozone, the sustained house price growth was driven by country-specific factors. The three statistically significant determinants of the house price acceleration in Bulgaria reflect, respectively, the active investment behaviour of homeowners in improving existing properties, the rational assessment by housing market participants of the balance between mortgage and rental payments, and the burden of utility and maintenance costs borne by owners and tenants, depending on property size and energy efficiency. The first factor is most influential for homeowners, the second for tenants, and the third has a similarly significant impact on both groups.

Keywords: house price index; ARIMAX; Eurozone; Bulgaria; ADF test; KPSS test; Ljung–Box test; Shapiro–Wilk test; Kolmogorov–Smirnov test; ARCH LM test

1. Introduction

Bulgaria's accession to the Eurozone on 1 January 2026 completes a long process of currency convergence that began with the introduction of the currency board in 1997. This historical moment puts the country in a unique position to study the effects of currency integration on the housing market—a position that combines the characteristics of a small open economy with almost three decades of fixed exchange rates to the Deutsche Mark and the euro. While the literature presents numerous analyses of housing markets (Pagourtzi et al., 2003) in established Eurozone members and separate studies of the post-communist transformation of real estate in Eastern Europe, there is a significant gap in understanding how house prices are determined during a transition from a long-term currency board regime to Eurozone membership.

Existing research on real estate prices in Central and Eastern European countries (Marinković et al., 2024; Idirizov, 2025) typically focuses either on the period of post-communist privatization and liberalization (Egert & Mihaljek, 2007), or on the effects of EU accession (Ciarlone, 2015), or—for the few countries that adopted the euro—on the consequences of monetary integration (Dandashly & Verdun, 2021). What is lacking is a systematic analysis of a wide range of determinants of house prices in the context of prolonged monetary convergence that preceded formal membership. Bulgaria presents a unique case for such an analysis. Unlike countries such as Slovakia, Estonia, or Lithuania, which adopted the euro after relatively short periods of preparation, Bulgaria maintained a fixed exchange rate to the euro, initially through a peg to the Deutsche Mark in 1997, for nearly thirty years before entering the Eurozone. This long transitional state creates a specific institutional environment in which expectations of currency stability are already incorporated ex ante, while the institutional mechanisms of the monetary union are not yet operational. The question arises whether, in such a configuration, house prices move according to determinants characteristic of economies in transition, of countries in the process of convergence, or already reflect dynamics typical of Eurozone members. Secondly, the question arises whether accession expectations generate an anticipatory increase in the house price index (Liu et al., 2024), with fundamental factors such as GDP and wages lagging behind price growth. Thirdly, the possibility of an independent trajectory of house price dynamics, based on the convergence of household wealth across EU member states as a whole and the Eurozone in particular, is considered. The search for answers to these questions defines the research problem addressed in this study.

The study focuses on identifying the key factors that drive the house price growth in Bulgaria during the period 2015–2025, which covers both the phase of intensive preparation for Eurozone membership and the pandemic shock, that had a strong negative effect on the Bulgarian population, followed by approval for admission to the Eurozone through the publication of the convergence report on 4 June 2025 (European Commission, 2025). From a theoretical point of view, this period represents a natural experiment for studying the stability of determinants under changing institutional regimes. From a practical perspective, understanding these factors (Yordanova & Hristozov, 2025) has direct implications for macroprudential policy implementation and for monitoring financial stability under a new exchange rate regime following the introduction of a new currency (Atanassov et al., 2017).

The central research gap addressed in this study is the lack of empirical models that systematically test which of the many potential determinants of house prices retain explanatory power under conditions of prolonged currency convergence. While studies of housing markets in individual Eastern European countries exist, they rarely use a stepwise approach to selecting factors from a wide range of variables and even less often cover the period immediately before and during Eurozone accession. This methodological gap is particularly important because it limits the ability of policymakers and central bankers to

https://doi.org/10.3390/jrfm19040261

identify the benchmark indicators needed to monitor the housing market under changing institutional conditions. Eurozone accession may act as a psychological factor with a strong influence on buyers and sellers in the housing market (Visković & Čipčić, 2025). Comparisons of house prices before and after Eurozone accession support the existence of an accession effect, which in turn supports the convergence process, including household wealth accumulation. The methodological challenge is to explain how, under conditions of macroeconomic stability and a declining HICP in line with the Maastricht convergence criteria, a sustained increase in the *ad valorem* indicator of house prices is observed. In search of an explanation for this process, the authors build on classical models that assess a limited number of macroeconomic variables and extend them through an econometric assessment of the widest possible range of housing-related determinants monitored by statistical institutions and banks, for which continuous data are available for the relevant period.

The aim of the study is to identify and quantify the key factors that explain the acceleration of house price growth in Bulgaria during the period 2015–2025 under conditions of prolonged currency convergence, using a methodological approach for selecting from a wide range of macroeconomic, financial, demographic and sectoral variables.

To achieve this aim, the following research tasks are defined: (1) to identify, on the basis of a review of the academic literature, a broad set of determinants of house price dynamics and to examine the direction of their influence; (2) to identify, through the application of statistical and econometric methods, the factors most relevant to the Bulgarian housing market and to assess their impact on house price dynamics; (3) to interpret the results in the context of Bulgaria's accession to the Eurozone and to assess the potential impact of this process on house price dynamics.

This study has several inherent limitations. First, the analysis uses quarterly data over a ten-year period (2015–2025), yielding 40 observations—sufficient for a statistically valid assessment, but conservative in terms of capturing high-frequency dynamics in factors for which market price data are generated daily, weekly, or monthly. Second, the focus is on nationally aggregated data, which conceal regional differences in housing markets, where capital cities usually exert a leading influence on national trends. Third, the econometric procedure requires the exclusion of certain predictors from the final model due to methodological constraints such as multicollinearity and non-stationarity. These variables are discussed separately in the interpretive section to provide a more complete picture of the factors driving the General house price index (GHPI)—the total House price index published quarterly by the National Statistical Institute of Bulgaria, covering transactions in both new and existing dwellings. Fourth, the observation period includes only a short interval following the publication of the convergence report recommending Bulgaria's accession to the Eurozone on 1 January 2026, which limits the possibility of assessing the long-term effects of currency integration.

On this basis, the study is structured as follows. Following this introduction, which sets out the study's relevance, research gap, aim, objectives and limitations, Section 2 presents an analytical overview of contemporary research on the determinants of house prices and the rationale for their possible grouping. Section 3 focuses on international trends in the EU housing sector, the collection and grouping of national data on the predictors, the development of the methodological approach, and the model specification. Section 4 presents the results of the analysis, including the statistical characteristics of the final model and the estimates of the individual factors. Section 5 discusses the findings in light of theoretical expectations, the institutional context, and empirical evidence from other national residential real estate markets. Section 6 summarises the main conclusions, outlines the implications of the results for institutional policymaking, and suggests directions for future research. In this way, the study seeks to position the Bulgarian housing market on

https://doi.org/10.3390/jrfm19040261

a spectrum between moderate, EU-conforming growth and distinct national price dynamics that anticipate the effects of Eurozone accession.

2. Literature Review and Hypotheses

The literature on house price dynamics provides extensive evidence on the determinants of house price growth at regional, national, supranational and global levels. A characteristic feature of these studies is their emphasis on macroeconomic factors as the basis for models assessing house price dynamics. Within this group, GDP and/or its components (Algieri, 2013) are repeatedly confirmed as influential determinants of house prices. These studies provide evidence of the role of GDP as a universal fundamental factor (Li & Zeng, 2010), both in national analyses (Cohen & Karpavičiūtė, 2017; Ubarevičienė & Aidukaitė, 2026; Mazáček & Panoš, 2025), and in studies of leading urban agglomerations (Sivitanides, 2018; Reichle et al., 2023), where the focus is on the problem of housing affordability in capital cities (Haandrikman et al., 2023), regional differences (Prodanov & Naydenov, 2020; Sabitova et al., 2020) and the growth of prices driven by supply deficits (Stroebel & Vavra, 2019). At the macroeconomic level, inflation has also been studied (Anari & Kolari, 2002) as a fundamental factor influencing house prices (Kuang & Liu, 2015; Cohen & Karpavičiūtė, 2017).

The second group of factors includes services related to acquisition, maintenance (Gurmu et al., 2021) and repair (Taggart et al., 2014; Park & Seo, 2024), which also influence house prices. In Bulgaria, newly constructed dwellings are often delivered at the "internal linings and plastering" stage, after which additional expenditure is required to bring them to a habitable standard, including furnishing. A similar situation arises when an existing property is purchased (Passek & Nübel, 2025), as the new owner often undertakes major interior renovations, effectively bringing the property back to a comparable unfinished stage (Aydinli, 2024).

Third, the factors related to energy provision and utility services for housing used by households should be assessed, as they exhibit a sustained trend of increasing volatility under conditions of multiple crises (Ushenko et al., 2023). Homeowners face the burden of increasing energy costs (Shen et al., 2022; Cermáková & Hromada, 2022), utilities (Mazáček & Panoš, 2025), housing rental costs (Doling & Ronald, 2010) and taxes (Iliopoulou et al., 2025). Among these costs, investments to improve the energy efficiency (Zhelyazkova, 2018) of owner-occupied homes should also be considered (Ciot, 2022). A fourth group concerns the impact of the number of new buildings and dwellings constructed, together with the corresponding number of rooms. Design costs and construction materials (Herrera et al., 2020; Zhang et al., 2024), together with the subsequent supply of newly built dwellings (Araya et al., 2024; Pazdzior et al., 2021; Caldera Sánchez & Johansson, 2011) are determinants of house price (Mayer & Somerville, 2000), including when the effects of the COVID-19 pandemic (Yotzov et al., 2020) and the safety measures in the working conditions of construction workers (Ebekozien & Aigbedion, 2021) are taken into account.

The fifth group of factors focuses on households seeking housing, particularly their incomes (Ünalan et al., 2025) and employment. Income (McQuinn & O'Reilly, 2008) and labour market (Hadad et al., 2022), together with employment and unemployment indicators (Irandoust, 2019), constitute an important group of indicators influencing housing demand and have been examined in a number of studies (Girouard et al., 2006). A sixth group concerns credit conditions for the acquisition of residential property. Housing finance conditions and mortgage interest rates are widely recognised as key determinants of housing demand (McQuinn & O'Reilly, 2008; Lin et al., 2022), forming a well-established strand of the empirical literature (Girouard et al., 2006). Finally, a seventh group con-

https://doi.org/10.3390/jrfm19040261

cerns foreign investment in residential property and the role of stock market securities as an alternative vehicle for household wealth accumulation. Home ownership constitutes a significant component of household wealth, and its optimal allocation should take into account investment alternatives, including stock market securities (Zaharieva et al., 2022) and foreign currency-denominated assets, all of which may influence housing prices (Ouhinou et al., 2025).

The grouping of factors influencing housing prices in Bulgaria follows several logical considerations. First, the grouping reflects the nomenclature of indicators published by the NSI, Eurostat and BNB, including residential buildings, housing stock, housing price statistics (NSI, 2026), and interest rates on loans to households (BNB, 2026). Second, it is aligned with the classical four-quadrant model of the real estate market (DiPasquale & Wheaton, 1992), which distinguishes between the market's spatial dimensions—demand and supply—and its financial dimensions—investment, prices, and financing. Third, it takes into account non-systematic local factors specific to the Bulgarian context: (a) the currency board arrangement, which functions as an effective monetary stabilisation mechanism, has contributed to the long-term accumulation of substantial gold and foreign exchange reserves and has enabled commercial banks to offer low mortgage interest rates, generating a clear substitution effect whereby households weigh monthly mortgage payments against monthly rental costs; (b) the significant share of prefabricated panel buildings in Bulgaria's housing stock, in which approximately one quarter of the population resides—properties characterised by a low price base at the beginning of the study period that have subsequently become subject to public and private investment aimed at improving their habitability and investment attractiveness. Fourth, the model accounts for the effects of global crises during the second half of the study period (2020–2024): (a) the COVID-19 pandemic, which directly stimulated demand for larger dwellings and suburban housing meeting home-office standards (Schwartz & Wachter, 2023); (b) the energy crisis of 2021–2022 and the EU decarbonisation agenda, both of which affected residential property markets and utility costs (Brolinson et al., 2026); and (c) the large-scale displacement of Ukrainian refugees to Europe after 2022 (Perry et al., 2026), with a particular impact on countries historically linked to Ukraine, including Poland (Kochaniak et al., 2024) and Bulgaria, where refugee inflows directly affected housing demand. These considerations support the authors' approach of constructing a broad initial set of potential determinants of house prices, which, through econometric testing, analysis, and stepwise selection, yields a final parsimonious model with optimal explanatory power.

Based on the theoretical framework resented above and the identification of groups of factors influencing house prices, the main research hypothesis posits that, regardless of institutional changes and external shocks, the variation in house price growth in Bulgaria is explained by a limited number of predictors. This effect is sustained by the long-term pegging of Bulgaria's national currency to the euro through the currency board and by the household demand for housing, which drives prices to incorporate an *ex ante* appreciation premium due to the prospect of Eurozone accession.

Drawing on the literature review and the discussion of the research gap, we test the following specific research hypotheses regarding the determinants of house prices in Bulgaria:

H1: *Household expenditure constitutes a statistically significant driver of house price dynamics in Bulgaria, with demand-side cost pressures—including costs associated with dwelling maintenance and related services—representing a primary transmission mechanism for residential price appreciation.*

https://doi.org/10.3390/jrfm19040261

H2: *Changes in the rental housing market exert a statistically significant positive effect on growth in the General house price index in Bulgaria, as rising rental costs incentivise ownership demand and capitalise expected returns into residential property valuations.*

H3: *House prices in Bulgaria exhibit significant short-term inertia in price formation, whereby price acceleration persists across consecutive quarters, amplified by the credibility of the currency board arrangement and the ex ante appreciation premium associated with the prospect of Eurozone accession.*

3. Materials and Methods

3.1. European Housing Market Overview

The EU27 Member States are an example of the uniqueness of national characteristics relative to the EU average in terms of household home ownership. On average across the EU27 in 2024, 31.6% of the population lived in rented homes, while 68.4% of the population lived in owner-occupied homes (Eurostat, 2025b). Across the EU27, the gap between the country with the lowest and the country with the highest level of rental housing amounts to 47.1% (See Figure 1).

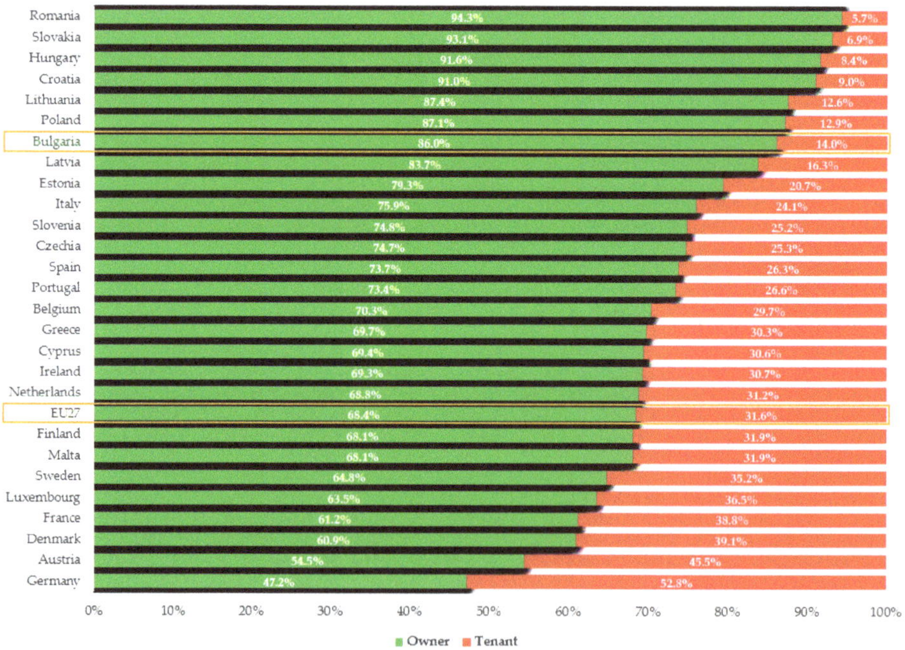

Figure 1. Share of the population living in owner-occupied or rented housing in the EU27 aggregate and individual Member States, 2024, with highlighted data for Bulgaria and EU27. Source: (Eurostat, 2026a), authors' calculations and graphical illustration.

Romania ranks first in terms of home ownership with 94.3%, followed by Slovakia, Hungary, Croatia, Lithuania, Poland, and Bulgaria. In contrast, Germany is the only country where the share of households living in owner-occupied homes is below 50%, compared with 52.8% of households living in rented housing. The data point to the importance of national-level research in the field of housing investment, which may reveal country-specific factors and predictors of HPI growth that are unlikely to be universally applicable across all EU27 countries. The balance between renting and owning a home depends on the relative affordability of the two options, as measured by the price of the home and the cost

https://doi.org/10.3390/jrfm19040261

of renting it. In both cases, the choice may be supported by appropriate financial analysis tools (Nenkov & Hristozov, 2022). According to the latest estimates of the European Parliament, a sustained trend of increasing house prices and rents is observed in the European Union, reaching what is described as a "crisis situation" (European Parliament, 2025). The data indicate an average increase in house prices in the EU27 of 53.44% over the period 2015–2024, with Hungary recording the highest increase in house prices, as measured by the HPI, at 209.86%, followed in the first quartile by Lithuania, Portugal, Czechia, Bulgaria, Estonia, and Poland, which also belong to the group of countries with the highest house price growth rates. At the other end of the scale is Finland, with a HPI increase of only 1.35% over the 10-year period (Eurostat, 2026b). With regard to the residential rents in the EU, average rent growth lags behind house price growth. Using 2010 as the base year, housing rents in the EU had increased by 25% by 2024. The largest increase in housing rents is reported in Estonia (+208%), followed by Lithuania (+177%), Ireland (+108%), and Hungary (+107%), while Greece recorded a 16% decrease in rents (Eurostat, 2025b). The data and graphical evidence suggest substantial cross-country heterogeneity among EU member states in terms of house price dynamics, as measured by the HPI. Among these countries, Bulgaria stands out, particularly in the context of its accession to the Schengen area in early 2025 and to the Eurozone on 1 January 2026 (See Figure 2), as the increase in the house price index in Bulgaria for the period 2015–2024 is 2.2 times higher than the EU average, while its average annual growth rate is 1.82 times higher than that of the EU27 over the same period.

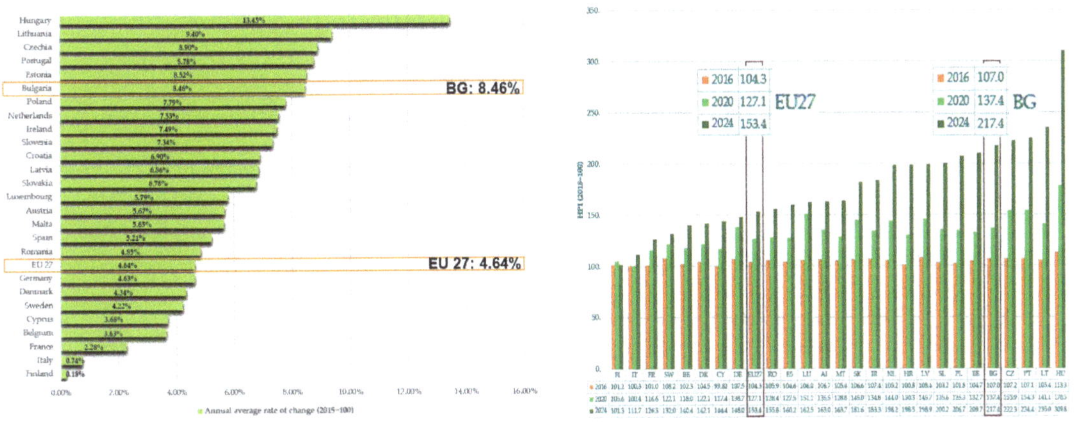

(**a**) (**b**)

Figure 2. EU countries HPI index change (2015 = 100) with highlighted data for Bulgaria and EU27: (**a**) Average annual rate of HPI change per countries and EU27; (**b**) Annual data of HPI per member states and EU27 for 2016, 2020 and 2024. Source: (Eurostat, 2025b), authors' calculations and graphical illustration.

On this basis, it is scientifically relevant to identify the factors driving the GHPI in Bulgaria with a focus on the period 2015–2024 with 2015 as a base year (2015 = 100). The choice of 2015 (resp. 2015Q4) as the base year of the study is determined by the methodology used by the main statistical sources. For Eurostat and the NSI, 2015 is defined as the base year for time series with index indicators related to house prices, which meets the requirements of the European System of Accounts (ESA, 2010) and is consistent with European statistical harmonization (Eurostat, 2014). Accordingly, the data from the BNB registers are consistent with the methodology of these statistical institutions. From

https://doi.org/10.3390/jrfm19040261

an economic perspective, 2015 is also a relatively neutral year, following the prolonged recovery from the 2008–2009 crisis, the collapse of the mortgage bond markets, and the bankruptcy of Lehman Brothers.

The data shown in both figures also correspond to the increase in Bulgaria's GDP per capita which was 2.48 times higher in 2024 than in 2015 (Eurostat, 2025a), and to the increase in GDP at current prices, measured in billion euros, which was 2.37 times higher over the same period. These results were achieved under conditions of macroeconomic equilibrium and sustained compliance with the Maastricht criteria for membership in the Eurozone, with an HICP of 2.6% for 2024.

3.2. Research Data Collection, Grouping and Preselection

For this study, data were collected for 48 candidate variables (See Appendix A.1) selected on the basis of the theoretical literature on housing price determinants in Bulgaria, and covering the construction, renovation, maintenance and utility cost dimensions of the residential property market. From a supply-side perspective, the dataset includes indicators of new dwelling construction, disaggregated by property size, from one-room to six-or-more-room dwellings. On the demand side, the analysis examines financial and economic factors affecting purchasing capacity, including wages, dwelling credits, and mortgage interest rates, as well as the stock market index as an alternative vehicle for household wealth accumulation (Gönül & Omay, 2025). An evaluation of the historical data shows a net increase for 43 of the studied predictors over the period 2015Q4–2025Q3, while 5 predictors show a decrease.

The dependent variable is the General house price index (GHPI), which increased by 2.56 times over the ten-year period, compared with GDP, which increased by 2.75 times, and wages, which increased by 2.86 times. The sub-indices, HPI for existing dwellings (HPIED) and HPI for new dwellings (HPIND), report growth of 2.75 and 2.32 times, respectively. For the studied period, the working-age population of Bulgaria decreased by 7.89%. Among the financial indicators, the most significant change is the decrease in the predictor "Bad and restructured housing loans" by 86.7%, followed by decreases of 58.08% in the BNB interest rate and of 57.92% in the mortgage interest rate. The unemployment rate also decreased by 56.96% and reached 3.3%, the second-lowest level in the EU (Eurostat, 2026c), as of the date of the country's accession to the Eurozone on 1 January 2026.

Econometric modelling of the dataset revealed the following distribution of coefficients of variation across all 48 predictors: 15 predictors with a variation of up to 20% relative to the period average, 16 predictors with variation between 20% and 30%, 12 predictors with variation between 30% and 40%, and the remaining 8 predictors with variation above 40%. The highest coefficient of variation was recorded for the construction of new homes with six or more rooms, reaching 59.13%. The results for selected descriptive statistics indicators and the quarterly dynamics of the factors relative to the GHPI are presented in Appendix A.2. Graphical evidence on the dynamics of the first-differenced data for traditional macroeconomic, financial, demographic and sectoral factors is presented in Appendix A.3.

3.3. Empirical Methodology and Model Specification

3.3.1. Methodology

In the literature, house price modelling represents a methodologically challenging domain, with evidence supporting a wide variety of analytical methods. These methods can be broadly classified into traditional and advanced categories. Traditional methods encompass regression models (Yan, 2024), comparison-based approaches, production cost models, income capitalisation models, and housing investment return models. Advanced methods

https://doi.org/10.3390/jrfm19040261

include artificial neural networks (Mimis et al., 2013), spatial analysis techniques, hedonic pricing models, fuzzy logic methods, and ARIMA-based models (Pagourtzi et al., 2003). The latter group addresses a number of methodological challenges by enabling the joint modelling of historical price dynamics, autocorrelation structure and trend components, yielding models with statistically robust predictive power.

Although many studies employ Vector Error Correction Models and VAR models, in our case the ARIMAX model was methodologically preferred because of the small number of quarterly observations, the focus on a single country, and the research objective of analysing the short-term dynamics of price acceleration. Given the sample of 40 observations, determined by the quarterly frequency of data generated by statistical institutions, the use of a VAR model carries the risk of exhausting the degrees of freedom in constructing the lag structure (Wu, 2025). Similarly, in the case of the VECM, the lack of sufficient observations constitutes an obstacle to the reliable estimation of cointegration vectors (Johansen, 1995). In addition, the VECM models variables in levels and incorporates an error correction mechanism to capture long-run equilibrium relationships, which corresponds to a different research objective than the one pursued in this study. By contrast, through ARIMAX, we focus on price acceleration by transforming the data through second differencing, which directly addresses non-stationarity. Panel models are not applicable in a single-country framework, as they require a comparative cross-country basis.

Drawing on this methodological background, the study employs an ARIMAX model (Kotu & Deshpande, 2019) to examine the dynamics of the General house price index (GHPI) in Bulgaria, using a stepwise variable selection procedure to identify the key determinants and quantify their relative contributions to house price changes. Following that, the methodology consists of five stages, outlined below.

First, the data are tested for stationarity using the Augmented Dickey–Fuller test (Dickey & Fuller, 1981). This test is based on two hypotheses. The null hypothesis (H_0) states that the time series has a unit root, i.e., the series is non-stationary, while the alternative hypothesis (H_1) states that there is no unit root and the series is stationary. To confirm stationarity, the p-value obtained from the ADF test must be below 0.05. To enhance the reliability of the conclusions, the results of the ADF test are further validated using the KPSS test (Kwiatkowski et al., 1992). Unlike the ADF test, the KPSS test evaluates the null hypothesis of stationarity against the alternative hypothesis of a unit root. In this case, to confirm stationarity, the test statistic must be below the critical value at the 5% significance level. The joint application of the two tests, which have opposing null hypotheses provides a more reliable identification of the order of integration, particularly given the limited sample size (n = 40) (Kwiatkowski et al., 1992). The variables are differenced sequentially until the series becomes stationary (Distaso, 2008).

Second, to ensure the correct specification of the model, the dependent variable is tested for seasonality by applying the Kruskal–Wallis test (Kruskal & Wallis, 1952) to compare distributions across quarterly groups. The rationale for employing this test lies in its non-parametric nature—unlike parametric alternatives such as one-way ANOVA, it does not assume a normal distribution of observations, making it particularly appropriate for the small sample size (n = 40) used in this study. The null hypothesis (H_0) states that there are no statistically significant differences between the quarterly groups, indicating the absence of seasonality. The alternative hypothesis (H_1) states that at least one quarterly group differs statistically significantly from the others, indicating the presence of seasonality. The null hypothesis is rejected if the p-value < 0.05, in which case seasonal adjustment or the inclusion of seasonal dummy variables in the model specification is considered.

https://doi.org/10.3390/jrfm19040261

Third, the final model specification was determined through stepwise elimination of variables based on their statistical significance and the diagnostic tests conducted at each stage of the selection procedure.

Fourth, the model fit is assessed, the parameters are estimated, and the model is subjected to financial and economic analysis.

Fifth, diagnostic tests are conducted for autocorrelation in the residuals, normal distribution of residuals, the ARCH effect and robustness.

The primary data processing is performed using IBM SPSS Statistics 27. The ADF test is conducted using the adf.test() function from the tseries package in R 4.4.3, and the KPSS test is performed using the kpss.test() function from the same tseries package in R.

3.3.2. Stationarity and Seasonality Tests

The Augmented Dickey–Fuller test applied to the original dependent variable does not confirm stationarity (Sen, 2008), since the *p*-value > 0.05 ($p = 0.99$), and, therefore, the null hypothesis cannot be rejected. As the first difference also proved non-stationarity (*p*-value = 0.598), second differencing is applied to of the dependent and independent variables. Non-stationarity is also confirmed by the results from the KPSS test (See Appendix A.4). Both tests indicate that the majority of the independent variables become stationary after second differencing. Only 4 of the independent variables are stationary after first differencing (G, NBDC2Rs, HICML, and NFIP), while eight out of 48 variables remain non-stationary after second differencing (HICP, MRM, MRD, MMRD, SMRD, OSRD, FHERHM, and BLSRP) and are therefore excluded from further analysis.

Once stationarity has been achieved, the data are tested for seasonality, using the non-parametric Kruskal–Wallis test. The results ($H = 0.353$; $p = 0.950$) do not indicate statistically significant differences between quarters. As the *p*-value substantially exceeds the 0.05 significance threshold, the null hypothesis is not rejected, suggesting the absence of seasonality in the dependent variable. Therefore, it is not necessary to include a seasonal specification in the ARIMAX model (See Table 1).

Table 1. Test statistics.

Description [a,b]	**GHPI**
Kruskal–Wallis H	0.353
Df	3
Asymp. Sig.	0.950

a. Kruskal–Wallis Test; b. Grouping Variable: Q.

3.3.3. Model Specification

The final model specification is obtained by sequentially excluding the variables initially included in the model and comparing two variants: with and without a constant. The results show that including a constant in the model worsens its characteristics, while the constant coefficient is not statistically significant at a 5% significance level ($\beta = 0.031$, *p*-value = 0.653). Removing the constant improves the model (RMSE, MAPE, BIC and Ljung–Box Q). Finally, an ARIMAX(0,2,1) model is obtained without a constant and with three exogenous variables (OOHE, ARH, and WSMSRD; see Appendix B.1). Formally, the model can be represented as follows (see Formula (1)):

$$\Delta^2 Y_t = \sum_{i=1}^{K} \beta_i \Delta^2 X_{it} + \varepsilon_t + \theta_1 \varepsilon_{t-1}, \quad (1)$$

where

$\Delta^2 Y_t$ denotes the second difference of the dependent variable at time t;

https://doi.org/10.3390/jrfm19040261

$\Delta^2 X_{it}$ is the second difference of the ith independent variable at time t;
β_i is the regression coefficient for the corresponding independent variable;
θ_1 is the first-order MA coefficient;
ε_t is the stochastic error at time t;
ε_{t-1} is the stochastic error from the previous period.

The model specification (see Formula (2)) is as follows:

$$\Delta^2 GHPI_t = \beta_1 \Delta^2 OOHE_{1t} + \beta_2 \Delta^2 ARH_{2t} + \beta_3 \Delta^2 WSMSRD_{3t} + \varepsilon_t + \theta_1 \varepsilon_{t-1} \quad (2)$$

where
Δ^2 denotes the second difference;
GHPI is the General house price index;
OOHE is the Owner-occupiers' housing expenditures;
ARH is the Actual rentals for housing;
WSMSRD is the Water supply and miscellaneous services relating to the dwelling;
θ_1 is the coefficient of the MA(1) component;
β_1, β_2, β_3 are the coefficients of exogenous variables;
ε_t is the stochastic error;
ε_{t-1} is the stochastic error from the previous period.

4. Results

4.1. Model Fit

The model is estimated using second-differenced data, where the ARIMAX(0,2,1) specification includes the following variables: GHPI_D2 as the dependent variable, and OOHE_D2, ARH_D2, and WSMSRD_D2 as independent predictors. Stationary R-squared, RMSE, MAE, and the Ljung–Box Q test are used to assess model fit. The plot of the distribution of the second-differenced values of GHPI over time illustrates that the values vary within a relatively narrow range (approximately from −6.53 to +11.34), with a significant proportion of the observations concentrated around zero (See Figure 3).

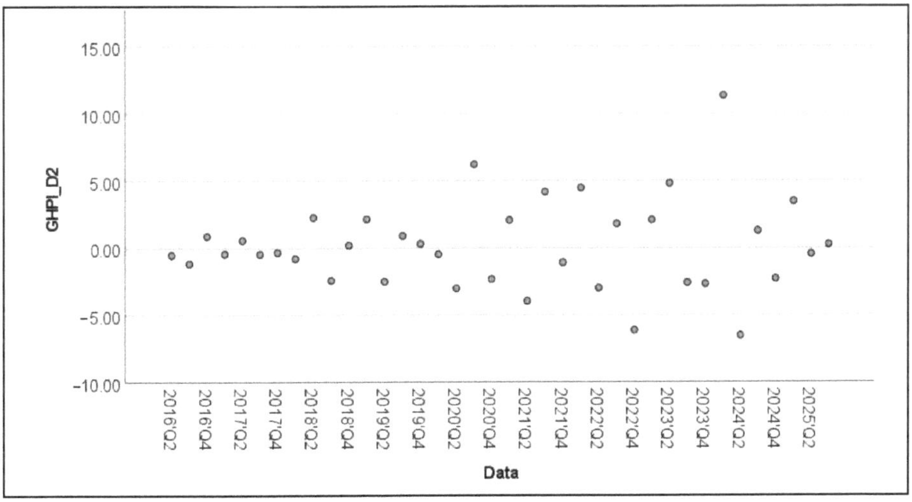

Figure 3. Scatter Plot of GHPI_D2.

At such values, even minimal absolute errors lead to extremely high percentage deviations, which makes MAPE a mathematically inappropriate metric for model evaluation

https://doi.org/10.3390/jrfm19040261

(Hyndman & Koehler, 2006). The stationary R-squared is 0.873, indicating that the model explains 87.3% of the variation in the second differences of the GHPI. In interpretive terms, this means that 87.3% of the variation in the acceleration/deceleration of house price growth is explained by changes in the differenced values of the independent variables (OOHE, ARH and WSMSRD). The remaining 12.7% is attributable to other factors not included in the model.

The mean absolute error (MAE) is 0.902 units, and the root mean square error (RMSE) is 1.252. The ratio MAE/SD = 0.268 indicates that the mean absolute error represents 26.8% of the standard deviation of the stationary series, which may be interpreted as very good relative forecast accuracy. The ratio RMSE/MAE = 1.39 indicates that the errors are relatively evenly distributed, without extreme deviations. The Ljung–Box Q test (See Table 2) confirms the absence of autocorrelation in the residuals ($Q(18) = 11.785$, $p = 0.813$).

Table 2. Model Statistics.

		Model Fit Statistics								Ljung–Box Q(18)			
Model	**Number of Predictors**	**Stationary R-Squared**	**R-Squared**	**RMSE**	**MAPE**	**MAE**	**MaxAPE**	**MaxAE**	**Normalized BIC**	**Statistics**	**DF**	**Sig.**	**Number of Outliers**
GHPI_D2-Model_1	3	0.873	0.873	1.252	94.722	0.902	1017.259	2.825	0.833	11.785	17	0.813	0

4.2. Parameter Estimation

The results reported in the ARIMAX model parameter table show that the coefficients of the exogenous variables and the MA component are positive and statistically significant at the 1% significance level (See Table 3).

Table 3. ARIMAX(0,2,1) Model Parameters.

					Estimate	SE	T	Sig.
GHPI_D2-Model_1	GHPI_D2	No Transformation	MA	Lag 1	0.693	0.149	4.635	0.000 ***
	OOHE_D2	No Transformation	Numerator	Lag 0	0.624	0.070	8.972	0.000 ***
	ARH_D2	No Transformation	Numerator	Lag 0	0.421	0.143	2.937	0.006 **
	WSMSRD_D2	No Transformation	Numerator	Lag 0	0.171	0.058	2.947	0.006 **

*** Significant at the 0.001 level; ** Significant at the 0.01 level.

The coefficient $\beta_1 = 0.624$ ($p < 0.001$) indicates that a one-unit increase in the acceleration of Owner-occupiers' housing expenditures is associated with an increase of approximately 0.624 units in the acceleration of GHPI, and conversely, that a one-unit deceleration is associated with a corresponding deceleration of approximately 0.624 units in GHPI, ceteris paribus. Similarly, $\beta_2 = 0.421$ ($p < 0.01$) and $\beta_3 = 0.171$ ($p < 0.01$) indicate positive and symmetric effects of ARH and WSMSRD respectively on GHPI acceleration, ceteris paribus. The relatively lower unstandardized coefficient of WSMSRD reflects the larger standard error of this variable in the second-differenced data.

The statistically significant first-order Moving Average component ($\theta_1 = 0.693$, $p < 0.001$) confirms the presence of inertia in house price formation, whereby an unexpected price shock in one quarter transmits approximately 69.3% of its effect into the following quarter. Since $|\theta_1| < 1$ the model is reversible and allows for reliable forecasts. To determine the individual contribution of each variable, standardized coefficients were

https://doi.org/10.3390/jrfm19040261

calculated: β_std = 0.79 for OOHE, β_std = 0.26 for ARH, and β_std = 0.26 for WSMSRD. This means that, for an equal change of one standard deviation, OOHE has the strongest effect on house price changes, while the other two factors make similar contributions. Expressed as relative shares of the total standardised effect, OOHE accounts for approximately 60% of the combined influence of the three factors. The descriptive statistics for the dependent and independent variables confirm the robustness of the estimated parameters (See Appendix B.2).

4.3. Financial and Economic Evaluation of the ARIMAX(0,2,1) Results

The financial and economic interpretation of the three factors should reflect the specific characteristics of the Bulgarian housing market, where the net change in the sub-index of existing dwellings is 2.715, while the net change in the sub-index of newly built dwellings is only 2.322 over the ten-year period. This initial observation clearly shows the importance of the costs associated with existing dwellings, given their specific and complex role as pricing factors affecting the general index (GHPI).

The first factor in the ARIMAX(0,2,1) model, Owner-occupiers' housing expenditures, is a synthetic index (2015Q4 = 100) that aggregates various homeowner expenses, including acquisition-related costs such as notary, agency and administrative fees, current expenses such as taxes, and costs related to major repairs and maintenance, together with all other unclassified property-related costs. The key to understanding the significance of this factor lies in the substantial difference in completion standards between newly built and existing homes in Bulgaria. While buyers of existing homes can move in immediately, newly built homes often require additional expenditure to reach an occupancy-ready standard, with such costs amounting to up to 50% of the purchase price. These costs include substantial finishing works and furnishing, which vary depending on the quality of the furniture and electrical equipment. The economic mechanism is demand-pull: *OOHE* covers the full life cycle of homeowner expenditure—from acquisition to ongoing maintenance. The acceleration in these costs directly reflects an increasing willingness to pay in the market and is immediately transmitted to the General house price index. In addition to the acquisition-related costs, including agent fees, notary fees, and local property taxes, this factor also captures all maintenance and ownership costs, which add a cost-push dimension: an increase in the cost of repairs and finishing works raises the full cost of residential use and is capitalised in the market value of residential properties. These costs encompass not only construction materials but also the labour costs associated with bringing residential properties to a habitable and occupancy-ready standard. The contribution of this factor can be expressed as follows: $\text{Contribution}_{OOHE,GHPI} = 0.624 \times \Delta^2 OOHE_t$.

The second factor in the model, Actual rentals for housing, has a lower β-coefficient. Average rent functions as an arbitrage mechanism between the rental and sale segments of the housing market. The relationship follows the logic of the capitalization model (See Formula (3)).

$$P_t = ARHt/(r_t - g_t), \tag{3}$$

where

r_t is the discount rate;

g_t—the expected growth in rents.

The acceleration of rents $\Delta^2 ARHt > 0$ operates simultaneously through two channels: first, rational tenants switch to buying (substitution effect), thereby increasing demand; second, investors revise the profitability of housing assets upwards, which increases prices in the sales market. ARH serves simultaneously as an indicator of housing supply constraints

https://doi.org/10.3390/jrfm19040261

and as a measure of the investment attractiveness of residential property. The contribution of this factor can be expressed as follows: $\text{Contribution}_{ARH,GHPI} = 0.421 \times \Delta^2 ARH$.

The third factor, Water supply and miscellaneous services relating to the dwelling is a synthetic index (based on 2015Q4 = 100), aggregating four components of mandatory infrastructure costs: water supply, refuse collection (Roleders et al., 2024), sewage collection, and other services relating to the dwelling n.e.c. The mechanism of influence is cost-push capitalization: utility tariffs are administratively regulated and increase more smoothly than market prices, which explains the lower coefficient of 0.171. However, their sustained increase is transmitted into residential property prices through two channels: directly, by raising the total cost of occupancy; and indirectly, by generating differentiated price pressures, as households shift demand toward newer, more energy- and infrastructure-efficient dwellings with lower utility costs, thereby driving up their relative prices. In assessing the influence of this factor, consideration is given to the compositional specifics of the underlying sub-indices, notably that waste collection and disposal charges in Bulgaria do not yet reflect the polluter-pays principle, but are instead levied on the basis of the assessed tax value of the property. Since waste collection charges are typically calculated on a base that exceeds the annual property tax by a factor of two or more, a systematic disparity emerges between the charges levied on existing—and often partially depreciated—properties and those levied on newly acquired dwellings. The latter, owing to the mandatory disclosure of mortgage loan values to local tax authorities, are assessed at the full transaction price, resulting in a higher tax and service-charge burden on new dwellings relative to existing housing stock. Administrative regulation delays the price signal, but does not eliminate it. The contribution of this factor can be expressed as follows: $\text{Contribution}_{WSMSRD,GHPI} = 0.171 \times \Delta^2 WSMSRD_t$.

The structural logic of the three-factor model can be interpreted from three analytically distinct perspectives, which together provide a comprehensive account of house price formation in Bulgaria in the context of Eurozone accession (See Formula (4)).

$$\Delta GHPI = f\left(\begin{array}{c}\underbrace{OOHE}_{demand\ pull+cost} + \\ \underbrace{ARH}_{rent/purchase\ arbitration} + \\ \underbrace{WSMSRD}_{infrastructure\ cost/push}\end{array}\right), \quad (4)$$

The *OOHE* predictor captures the total financial effort of homeowner households—from acquisition to maintenance—and is the dominant factor, with the highest coefficient. *ARH* provides the equilibrium arbitrage signal between the two main segments of the housing market. *WSMSRD* captures the mandatory infrastructure component of expenditure, which is capitalized into prices with a longer lag due to its regulatory nature. The MA(1) term = 0.693 captures the inertia of price shocks—unexpected impulses from the previous quarter continue to influence current price acceleration, which is characteristic of housing markets with inherent information lags, transaction costs, and limited liquidity.

Among the three predictors, the OOHE factor captures the tendency of Bulgarian homeowners to invest actively in improving the characteristics of their existing properties. This interpretation is further supported by the observed price differential between new and existing homes, which has shifted in favour of the latter. The inclusion of Actual rentals for housing (ARH) in the model is consistent with the presence of rational economic agents among housing investors, who weigh—at the household budget level—monthly mortgage repayments associated with future homeownership against monthly rental payments for equivalent accommodation. The third factor, WSMSRD, reflects the significance of household utility and maintenance costs, which are incurred by both owners and tenants and depend on both property size and energy efficiency. While the acceleration of house

https://doi.org/10.3390/jrfm19040261

price growth is most strongly transmitted through the OOHE factor for homeowners and through the ARH factor for renters, the third factor WSMSRD exerts a broadly similar effect on both groups of housing market participants in the Bulgarian context.

4.4. Diagnostic Tests

To assess model adequacy, diagnostic tests were conducted for autocorrelation of residuals, normality of distribution, and ARCH effects.

4.4.1. Autocorrelation of Residuals

The Ljung–Box Q test (Q(18) = 11.785, p = 0.813) shows no statistically significant autocorrelation, confirming the independence of the residuals, while the graphical analysis using ACF and PACF of the residuals (See Figure 4) further support the result. Both graphs show that all autocorrelation coefficients for lags 1 to 24 fall within the 95% confidence interval. The absence of significant peaks outside the confidence bounds confirms that the residuals represent white noise, which supports the validity of the statistical conclusions and the reliability of the predictions.

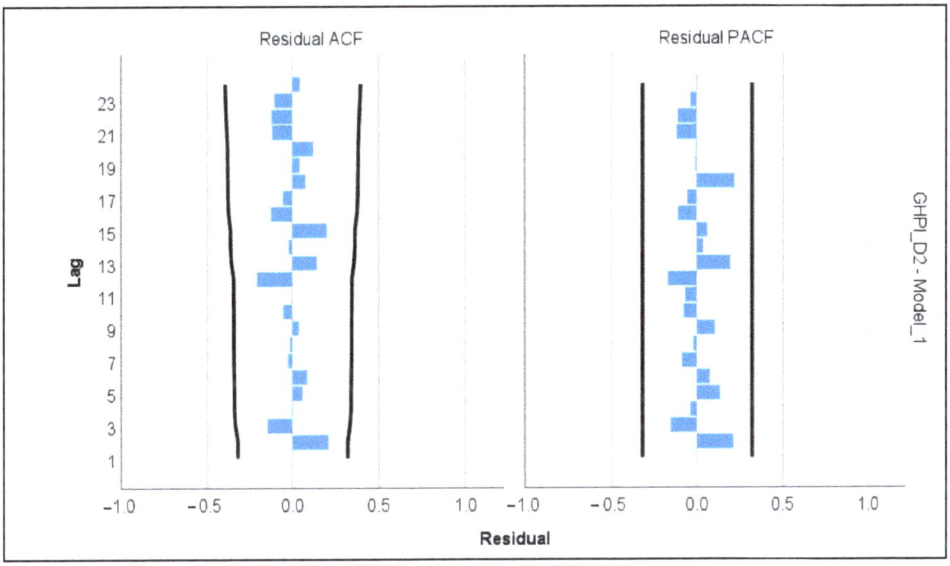

Figure 4. Residual ACF and PACF distribution.

4.4.2. Test for Normal Distribution of Residuals

To assess the normality of the residuals, Shapiro–Wilk and Kolmogorov–Smirnov tests were performed (See Table 4). Both tests showed no statistically significant deviation from the normal distribution. The Shapiro–Wilk test, which is more suitable for samples with $n < 50$, yielded W = 0.983 (p = 0.805), which is well above the critical value of 0.05. A high W value (close to 1) indicates a close correspondence to the normal distribution. The Kolmogorov–Smirnov test also confirms these results (K-S = 0.090, $p \geq 0.200$). The graphical distribution of the residuals further supports the validity of the above conclusions (See Appendix B.3), including the bell-shaped distribution of the residuals.

https://doi.org/10.3390/jrfm19040261

Table 4. Shapiro–Wilk and Kolmogorov–Smirnov test results.

Case Processing Summary

	Cases					
	Valid		Missing		Total	
	N	Percent	N	Percent	N	Percent
Noise residual from GHPI_D2-Model_1	38	95.0%	2	5.0%	40	100.0%

Descriptives

			Statistic	Std. Error
Noise residual from GHPI_D2-Model_1	Mean		0.0018	0.19471
	95% Confidence Interval for Mean	Lower Bound	−0.3927	
		Upper Bound	0.3963	
	5% Trimmed Mean		−0.0057	
	Median		−0.0441	
	Variance		1.4410	
	Std. Deviation		1.20025	
	Minimum		−2.82	
	Maximum		2.70	
	Range		5.52	
	Interquartile Range		1.64	
	Skewness		0.027	0.383
	Kurtosis		0.367	0.750

Tests of Normality

	Kolmogorov–Smirnov [a]			Shapiro–Wilk		
	Statistic	df	Sig.	Statistic	df	Sig.
Noise residual from GHPI_D2-Model_1	0.090	38	0.200 *	0.983	38	0.805

*. This is a lower bound of the true significance.

a. Lilliefors Significance Correction

Coefficients [a,b]

Model		Unstandardized Coefficients		Standardized Coefficients	t	Sig.	95.0% Confidence Interval for B		Correlations			Collinearity Statistics	
		B	Std. Error	Beta			Lower Bound	Upper Bound	Zero-order	Partial	Part	Tolerance	VIF
1	OOHE_D2	0.570	0.061	0.721	9.270	0.000	0.445	0.695	0.778	0.843	0.656	0.828	1.207
	WSMSRD_D2	0.215	0.056	0.331	3.827	0.001	0.101	0.329	0.627	0.543	0.271	0.670	1.493
	ARH_D2	0.347	0.134	0.218	2.591	0.014	0.075	0.619	0.260	0.401	0.183	0.706	1.416

a. Dependent Variable: GHPI_D2

b. Linear Regression through the Origin

4.4.3. ARCH Effect Test

To test for conditional heteroscedasticity (ARCH effects), an ARCH LM test with 12 lags (See Table 5) was conducted, using a linear regression of the squared residuals on their lagged values.

https://doi.org/10.3390/jrfm19040261

Table 5. ARCH effect test results.

Variables Entered/Removed [a]

Model	Variables Entered	Variables Removed	Method
1	NResid_sc_Lag12, NResid_sc_Lag11, NResid_sc_Lag9, NResid_sc_Lag8, NResid_sc_Lag7, NResid_sc_Lag3, NResid_sc_Lag10, NResid_sc_Lag4, NResid_sc_Lag5, NResid_sc_Lag2, NResid_sc_Lag6, NResid_sc_Lag1 [b]	.	Enter

a. Dependent Variable: NResid_sc; b. All requested variables entered.

Model	R	R Square	Adjusted R Square	Std. Error of the Estimate	Change Statistics				
					R Square Change	F Change	df1	df2	Sig. F Change
1	0.567 [c]	0.322	−0.304	2.20574	0.322	0.514	12	13	0.871

c. Predictors: (Constant), NResid_sc_Lag12, NResid_sc_Lag11, NResid_sc_Lag9, NResid_sc_Lag8, NResid_sc_Lag7, NResid_sc_Lag3, NResid_sc_Lag10, NResid_sc_Lag4, NResid_sc_Lag5, NResid_sc_Lag2, NResid_sc_Lag6, NResid_sc_Lag1

ANOVA [a]

Model		Sum of Squares	df	Mean Square	F	Sig.
1	Regression	30.010	12	2.501	0.514	0.871 [c]
	Residual	63.248	13	4.865		
	Total	93.258	25			

Coefficients [a]

Model		Unstandardized Coefficients		Standardized Coefficients	t	Sig.	95.0% Confidence Interval for B	
		B	Std. Error	Beta			Lower Bound	Upper Bound
1	(Constant)	2.302	1.725		1.334	0.205	−1.425	6.029
	NResid_sc_Lag1	−0.026	0.310	−0.023	−0.083	0.935	−0.696	0.645
	NResid_sc_Lag2	−0.244	0.309	−0.215	−0.792	0.443	−0.911	0.423
	NResid_sc_Lag3	−0.207	0.294	−0.183	−0.704	0.494	−0.842	0.428
	NResid_sc_Lag4	−0.307	0.297	−0.273	−1.033	0.321	−0.950	0.335
	NResid_sc_Lag5	−0.122	0.308	−0.108	−0.397	0.698	−0.787	0.543
	NResid_sc_Lag6	0.328	0.308	0.291	1.063	0.307	−0.338	0.994
	NResid_sc_Lag7	−0.238	0.317	−0.206	−0.752	0.465	−0.923	0.446
	NResid_sc_Lag8	−0.010	0.298	−0.009	−0.034	0.973	−0.655	0.634
	NResid_sc_Lag9	−0.041	0.293	−0.036	−0.140	0.891	−0.675	0.593
	NResid_sc_Lag10	0.097	0.294	0.085	0.330	0.747	−0.538	0.732
	NResid_sc_Lag11	−0.094	0.244	−0.105	−0.386	0.706	−0.622	0.434
	NResid_sc_Lag12	−0.127	0.237	−0.143	−0.537	0.600	−0.640	0.385

The regression of the squares of the residuals on their lagged values revealed no statistically significant ARCH effects ($F(12, 13) = 0.514$, $p = 0.871$), further confirming that the variance of the residuals is stable over time.

https://doi.org/10.3390/jrfm19040261

4.5. Robustness Check

To assess the robustness of the estimates, alternative model specifications were used, as presented in Tables 6 and 7. The data in Table 6 show that all five specifications exhibit very similar characteristics. The stationary R-squared varies only slightly (0.873–0.877), and the RMSE is virtually identical across models (in the range 1.248–1.269), with a difference of only 0.021 between the best and worst-performing models. The Ljung–Box test confirms adequate specification for all models (all p-values > 0.25), with the selected ARIMAX(0,2,1) model showing the highest p-value (0.813). By comparison, the ARIMAX(1,2,0) model shows a substantially lower Ljung–Box p-value (0.271), although it has the lowest BIC (0.826). The difference in BIC values between the two models is minimal (ΔBIC = 0.007) and well below the conventional threshold of 2 (Kass & Raftery, 1995). This suggests that the two models receive essentially equivalent support according to the information criterion. The ARIMAX(1,2,2) model has the highest BIC (1.051) and also includes a number of statistically insignificant parameters (see Table 6).

Table 6. Comparative characteristics of alternative ARIMAX specifications.

Model	Stationary R-Squared	RMSE	MAPE	MAE	Normalized BIC	Ljung–Box Q(18) Sig.
ARIMAX(0,2,1)(0,0,0)	0.873	1.252	94.722	0.902	0.833	0.813
ARIMAX(1,2,1)(0,0,0)	0.874	1.263	93.583	0.894	0.945	0.794
ARIMAX(0,2,2)(0,0,0)	0.873	1.267	93.442	0.894	0.952	0.806
ARIMAX(1,2,0)(0,0,0)	0.873	1.248	103.934	0.915	0.826	0.271
ARIMAX(1,2,2)(0,0,0)	0.877	1.269	94.856	0.887	1.051	0.706

Table 7. Estimated coefficients of exogenous variables in alternative ARIMAX specifications.

		ARIMAX (0,2,1)	ARIMAX (1,2,1)	ARIMAX (0,2,2)	ARIMAX (1,2,0)	ARIMAX (1,2,2)
GHPI_D2	AR(1)	-	−0.216 (0.278)		−0.579 *** (0.154)	−0.677 (0.629)
	MA(1)	0.693 *** (0.149)	0.548 * (0.238)	0.738 *** (0.198)		0.071 (0.713)
	MA(2)	-	-	−0.084 (0.195)		0.301 (0.533)
OOHE_D2		0.624 *** (0.070)	0.636 *** (0.071)	0.631 *** (0.071)	0.620 *** (0.062)	0.626 *** (0.071)
ARH_D2		0.421 *** (0.143)	0.406 *** (0.143)	0.413 *** (0.146)	0.357 *** (0.130)	0.386 ** (0.144)
WSMSRD_D2		0.171 *** (0.058)	0.169 *** (0.056)	0.169 *** (0.058)	0.186 *** (0.048)	0.175 *** (0.056)

*** Significant at the 0.001 level; ** Significant at the 0.01 level; * Significant at the 0.05 level.

Table 7 presents the estimated coefficients for all specifications. The main result is that the exogenous variables exhibit a very high degree of stability. The coefficient of OOHE remains within a narrow range from 0.620 to 0.636 and is consistently highly statistically significant ($p < 0.001$) across all tested specifications. The coefficient of ARH ranges from 0.357 to 0.421 and retains its statistical significance ($p < 0.05$) across all specifications. The coefficient of WSMSRD also shows stability, ranging from 0.169 to 0.186, and remains significant at the $p < 0.01$ level in all models.

https://doi.org/10.3390/jrfm19040261

In contrast to the stability of the exogenous variables, the ARIMA components show varying levels of statistical significance. The results indicate that the ARIMAX models (1,2,1), (0,2,2) and (1,2,2) include statistically insignificant parameters, which confirms that ARIMAX(0,2,1) is the simplest specification in which all parameters are statistically significant. Therefore, even when the autoregressive and moving average components vary across specifications, the coefficients of the exogenous variables remain stable both in terms of statistical significance, sign, and magnitude. This confirms the robustness of the main conclusions of the study.

When the robustness check was performed by adding GDP (also at the second difference), the main exogenous factors retained their statistical significance and direction of effect. The lack of statistical significance for GDP confirms that the model successfully isolates sector-specific dependencies from general macroeconomic fluctuations in growth acceleration.

5. Discussion

The ARIMAX model identified the main factors accounting for house price growth in Bulgaria in the decade preceding and immediately following the announcement of Eurozone accession. Following the application of the outlined methodology, the initial set of 48 potential predictors yielded a final ARIMAX(0,2,1) model with the highest explanatory power, comprising three variables significant at $p < 0.01$.

This substantial reduction from 48 to 3 variables suggests that house price dynamics in Bulgaria are driven by a focused set of factors, rather than by a multidimensional set of influences.

The empirical results of this study provide full support for the main research hypothesis and all three specific research hypotheses. Variation in General house price index growth in Bulgaria is indeed explained by a limited number of predictors, confirming that, despite institutional changes and external shocks, the underlying drivers of house price dynamics remain structurally stable and limited in number. Household expenditure and housing maintenance and service costs emerge as the dominant demand-side transmission mechanism, while the rental market reinforces price appreciation through the substitution channel. Critically, the persistence of price formation inertia—combined with the credibility of the currency board arrangement and the *ex ante* appreciation premium embedded in anticipation of Eurozone accession—confirms that house prices in Bulgaria are shaped not only by current economic conditions but also by deeply anchored institutional expectations. Taken together, these findings underscore the explanatory power of a parsimonious, theory-driven model in capturing the determinants of house prices in Bulgaria.

This finding has important implications for both theory and policy.

First, the simplified three-factor model challenges the notion that housing markets in transition countries require complex multidimensional frameworks for adequate explanation. Instead, our results show that even during a period of profound institutional change—including the maintenance of a currency board, the consolidation of EU membership, and eventual Eurozone accession—house price growth responds systematically to a limited number of key variables.

Second, the statistical significance of the final ARIMAX model over the entire sample period 2015–2025 is particularly striking. The dataset covers three distinct phases: pre-convergence (2015–2019), pandemic disruptions (2020–2021) and the period of preparation for Eurozone accession (2022–2025). The fact that the same three factors remain statistically significant across these regime changes suggests structural stability in the determinants of house prices in Bulgaria. This stability may reflect the effect of the currency board mechanism, which pegged the Bulgarian lev to the Deutsche Mark in 1997 and then

https://doi.org/10.3390/jrfm19040261

automatically to the euro. In this way, Bulgaria adapted *ex ante* to the business cycle of the Eurozone countries through the effect of nominal convergence, particularly in the monetary sphere, well before formal membership, in a manner that reflects clear national specificity and differs from the experience of Croatia (Visković & Čipčić, 2025), which joined the Eurozone on 1 January 2023.

Third, the euro adoption in January 2026 provides a natural quasi-experiment to assess whether the identified factors retain their explanatory power under a new currency regime (Marinov, 2017). The last quarters of our sample (Q4 2024–Q3 2025) capture the period immediately before accession, during which expectations of euro adoption strongly influenced both housing demand and credit conditions. Preliminary data from 2025 do not suggest a structural break in the relationship between the three key factors and house price growth, suggesting that the currency change itself may have had a limited independent impact—possibly because markets have already priced in convergence under the currency board arrangement. However, several caveats are worth noting. First, although the stepwise selection procedure is effective in identifying significant predictors, it requires economic justification for the causal relationships identified, beyond the purely mathematical logic of the results. The observed associations between the three predictors and house prices do not exclude the influence of other factors for which no complete data are available for the entire period under study or for which access is partial, highly restricted, or is impossible to obtain them publicly. Second, the quarterly frequency of observations—although standard in macroeconomic housing research—may conceal higher-frequency dynamics, especially during periods of rapid institutional change (Mihaylova-Borisova & Nenkova, 2020). Third, the performance of the model during the Eurozone accession period should be monitored carefully, since structural changes in the available bank lending resources, cross-border capital flows or mortgage market integration may alter the weights of the existing factors or introduce new predictors. This issue is particularly relevant in view of the release by the Bulgarian National Bank of substantial credit resources to commercial banks through the mechanism of the minimum reserve requirement ratio. Specific to the ECB and the BNB is the gap of over 10% in favour of Bulgaria, which releases a significant new credit resource to support housing demand in Bulgaria, *ceteris paribus*.

Looking ahead, the three-factor ARIMAX model offers a practical tool for policymakers and central bankers monitoring housing market stability in Bulgaria's post-accession phase. If the three-factor structure is maintained, it will provide a focused set of indicators for monitoring and designing macroprudential policy. Furthermore, Bulgaria's experience as the 21st and newest member of the Eurozone offers valuable insights for subsequent candidate countries, including those with low exchange rate volatility between their national currencies and the euro. This once again highlights the importance of establishing the consequences and effects of currency integration for the housing market (Visković & Čipčić, 2025), a perspective directly relevant to Bulgaria's post-accession trajectory.

Although the ARIMAX(0,2,1) model effectively captures the short-term dynamics of the Bulgarian housing market and provides reliable one-step-ahead forecasts, its inherent limitation lies in the inability to generate long-term forecasts beyond the assessment horizon. The interpretation of the model results requires careful consideration of the specific properties of the ARIMAX framework, the unique macroeconomic context of Bulgaria as a country operating under a currency board regime for nearly three decades, and the possibility that the significant price appreciation observed in the pre-accession period may be followed by a consolidation phase.

Future research should extend the analysis beyond 2025 to assess the stability of the model in the context of full euro adoption in Bulgaria, including the cessation of price an-

https://doi.org/10.3390/jrfm19040261

nouncements in the former national currency as a regulatory requirement by 8 August 2026. It should also disaggregate national trends across regional markets, and examine potential nonlinear or threshold effects that the ARIMAX model may not capture. Future research could further explore sustainable solutions for housing stock management and civil construction activity (Gabriela et al., 2023) in the context of post-war reconstruction in Ukraine (Sukhomud & Shnaider, 2023). In this regard, international experience in the physical restoration of housing and the recovery of its market value following structural disruptions or catastrophic risk (Ishiwatari et al., 2021) offers valuable insights for informed policy decisions in the pre-reconstruction phase of the ongoing conflict (Ishiwatari et al., 2025).

6. Conclusions

This study provides new evidence on the factors that determine house price dynamics in Bulgaria in the specific context of the transition from a prolonged currency board regime to Eurozone membership. By applying an ARIMAX(0,2,1) model to 40 quarterly observations for the period 2015Q4–2025Q3, the study identifies the key determinants of house price acceleration. The results show that the house price dynamics in Bulgaria is explained by three specific factors: the owner-occupiers' housing expenditures, the actual rentals for housing in Bulgaria and the homeowners' utility expenses. The three predictors are statistically significant at the 1% level, indicating strong and persistent effects. The model explains the variation in house price acceleration with a low mean squared error and high explanatory power. Particularly important is the conclusion that traditional macroeconomic, demographic, financial and sectoral factors do not show a statistically significant relationship with house price dynamics over the ten-year period under study. This result calls for a reconsideration of conventional theoretical approaches to house price formation in the context of transition economies. While the classical literature emphasises the role of interest rates, economic growth, income levels and demographic change, the present study demonstrates that under the specific institutional conditions of Bulgaria, these factors give way to country-specific determinants. The established relationship between house prices and the costs of homeownership, rental payments and utility services reveals an important pricing mechanism, whereby current operating costs exert a stronger influence on house price dynamics than traditional macroeconomic variables. This can be explained by the specifics of the Bulgarian real estate market, where the long-standing currency board has ensured a stable convergent environment, and the process of approval of Bulgaria's membership in the Eurozone has been reflected in the expectations of price convergence with European levels ahead of schedule. The diagnostic analysis confirms model adequacy, indicating the absence of autocorrelation in the residuals and the successful capture of systematic information in the data. The non-parametric correlation analysis further validates the statistically significant monotonic relationships between the regressors and the dependent variable, strengthening confidence in the obtained results. From a methodological point of view, the use of second differencing in the ARIMAX model proves to be an adequate approach to modelling house price acceleration, successfully overcoming the problems of non-stationarity in historical data, influenced by three specific sub-periods: pre-convergence (2015–2019), pandemic disruptions (2020–2021) and the period of preparation for Eurozone accession (2022–2025). The results of the study have important practical applications for the development of policies in the housing sector. The focus on specific national factors shows that measures to regulate the real estate market should account for local specificities, rather than follow general macroeconomic recipes. Regulators should consider policies governing property-related and utility costs, as these directly influence house price dynamics and household affordability. In conclusion, this study contributes to a deeper understanding of house price formation mechanisms in the specific context of a

https://doi.org/10.3390/jrfm19040261

small open economy undergoing currency convergence. It demonstrates the importance of developing empirically grounded models that account for national institutional specificities, rather than uncritically transposing theoretical frameworks developed for advanced economies with fundamentally different institutional characteristics.

Author Contributions: Conceptualization, A.Z., G.Z. and L.S.; methodology, A.Z., G.Z., L.S. and M.O.; software, G.Z.; validation, A.Z., G.Z., L.S. and M.O.; formal analysis, A.Z. and G.Z.; investigation, A.Z., G.Z., L.S. and M.O.; resources, A.Z., G.Z., L.S. and M.O.; data curation, A.Z. and G.Z.; writing—original draft preparation, A.Z. and G.Z.; writing—review and editing, A.Z., G.Z. and L.S.; visualization, A.Z., G.Z. and M.O.; supervision, A.Z., G.Z. and L.S.; project administration, A.Z. and G.Z.; funding acquisition, A.Z. All authors have read and agreed to the published version of the manuscript.

Funding: This research received no external funding.

Institutional Review Board Statement: Not applicable.

Informed Consent Statement: Not applicable.

Data Availability Statement: The data presented in this study are available in Eurostat, NSI, BNB and BSE. These data were derived from the following resources available in the public domains: https://bit.ly/3PFXykR; https://bit.ly/4s7U1cv; https://bit.ly/4m5x748; https://bit.ly/412ATSe (accessed on 31 January 2026).

Conflicts of Interest: The authors declare no conflicts of interest.

Abbreviations

The following abbreviations are used in this manuscript:

ADF	Augmented Dickey–Fuller test
ARCH	Autoregressive Conditional Heteroskedasticity
ARCH LM	Autoregressive Conditional Heteroskedasticity Lagrange Multiplier (test)
ARH	Actual rentals for housing
ARIMA	AutoRegressive Integrated Moving Average
ARIMAX	Autoregressive Integrated Moving Average with Exogenous Variables
BG	Bulgaria
BNB	Bulgarian National Bank
BSE	Bulgarian Stock Exchange
ESA	European System of Accounts
EU27	European Union (27 member states)
Eurostat	Statistical office of the European Union
GDP	Gross Domestic Product
HICP	Harmonised Index of Consumer Prices
GHPI	General house price index
HPIED	House price index for existing dwellings
HPIND	House price index for new dwellings
NSI	National Statistical Institute of Bulgaria
OOHE	Owner-occupiers' housing expenditures
VAR	Vector Autoregression
VECM	Vector Error Correction Model
WSMSRD	Water supply and miscellaneous services relating to the dwelling

Appendix A

Appendix A.1. Independent and Dependent Variables

The initial stage of the study is the selection and grouping of influencing factors for the development of a model analysing the dynamics of the GHPI of Bulgaria (comprising

https://doi.org/10.3390/jrfm19040261

the analytical indices HPIND and HPIED) over the period 2015Q4–2025Q3. Based on 4 main sources—BNB, NSI, Eurostat and BSE—an econometric assessment was carried out, 48 factors were selected, including aggregated and disaggregated, distributed into seven main groups (See Table A1).

Table A1. Selection and grouping of independent and dependent variables.

№	Group	Number of Factors	№	Selected Variables—First Stage	Factor Code	Source
Y.	Dependent variables	3	1	General house price index	GHPI	NSI
			2	House price index for New dwellings	HPIND	NSI
			3	House price index for Existing dwellings	HPIED	NSI
A.	Macro factor	5	1	Gross Domestic Product (thousands of EUR)	GDP	NSI
			2	Export (thousands of EUR)	EXP	NSI
			3	Import (thousands of EUR)	IMP	NSI
			4	Harmonised Index of Consumer Prices	HICP	NSI
			5	GDP per capita	GDPpC	Eurostat
B.	Housing Services	7	6	Owner-occupiers' housing expenditures	OOHE	NSI
			7	Acquisitions of dwellings)	AD	NSI
			8	Other services related to the acquisitions of dwellings	OSRAD	NSI
			9	Ownership of dwellings index	OD	NSI
			10	Major repairs and maintenance index	MRM	NSI
			11	Other services related to ownership of dwellings	OSROD	NSI
			12	Insurance connected with the dwelling	ICD	NSI
C.	Energy and Comunal Services	16	13	Housing, water, electricity, gas and other fuels	HWEGOF	NSI
			14	Actual rentals for housing	ARH	NSI
			15	Maintenance and repair of the dwelling	MRD	NSI
			16	Materials for the maintenance and repair of the dwelling	MMRD	NSI
			17	Services for the maintenance and repair of the dwelling	SMRD	NSI
			18	Water supply and miscellaneous services relating to the dwelling	WSMSRD	NSI
			19	Water supply	WS	NSI
			20	Refuse collection	RC	NSI
			21	Sewage collection	SC	NSI
			22	Other services relating to the dwelling n.e.c.	OSRD	NSI
			23	Electricity, gas and other fuels	EGOF	NSI
			24	Electricity	E	NSI
			25	Gas	G	NSI
			26	Solid fuels	SF	NSI
			27	Heat energy	HE	NSI
			28	Furnishings, household equipment and routine household maintenance	FHERHM	NSI

Table A1. *Cont.*

№	Group	Number of Factors	№	Selected Variables—First Stage	Factor Code	Source
D	Construction	8	29	Newly built residential buildings completed	NBRBC	NSI
			30	Newly built dwelling completed by rooms—total	NBDCRT	NSI
			31	Newly built dwelling completed by rooms—1 room	NBDC1R	NSI
			32	Newly built dwelling completed by rooms—2 rooms	NBDC2Rs	NSI
			33	Newly built dwelling completed by rooms—3 rooms	NBDC3Rs	NSI
			34	Newly built dwelling completed by rooms—4 rooms	NBDC4Rs	NSI
			35	Newly built dwelling completed by rooms—5 rooms	NBDC5Rs	NSI
			36	Newly built dwelling completed by rooms—6+ rooms	NBDC6Rs	NSI
E	Income & Labor market	3	37	Average gross monthly wages and salaries	AGQWS	NSI
			38	Unemployment coefficient	UNEMPL	NSI
			39	Labour Force in '000	LF	NSI
F	Credits	6	40	Dwelling credits	DwCr	BNB
			41	Interest Rate	IRATE	BNB
			42	Bank loans secured by residential property	BLSRP	BNB
			43	Household interest costs on mortgage loans	HICML	BNB
			44	Bad and restructured housing loans	BRHL	BNB
			45	Interest Rate for Mortgage in BGN	IRATEMp	BNB
G	Investment & Wealth	3	46	Net foreign investment in real estate	NFIP	BNB
			47	EUR/USD	ExR	BNB
			48	BSE index SOFIX	Sofix	BSE
Number of factors 1st stage:			48	Number of groups 1st stage:		7

Legend: NSI—National Statistical Institute of Bulgaria; BNB—Bulgarian National Bank, BSE—Bulgarian Stock Exchange; Eurostat—Statistical office of the European Union.

Appendix A.2. Descriptive Statistics

Selected indicators with results from descriptive statistics for the historical data of the 48 descriptors and the three independent variables HPI, HPIND, HPIED in Bulgaria for the period 2015Q4–2025Q3 are presented in the following table (See Table A2).

Table A2. Descriptive statistics of historical data of dependent variables and independent variables from groups A–G.

Factor Code	Data Type	Change t40/t1	AVE	STDEV	CV
GHPI	Index	2.5601	154.95	43.05	27.78%
HPIND	Index	2.3224	147.52	37.00	25.08%
HPIED	Index	2.7154	159.51	47.00	29.47%
GDP	EUR	2.7504	18,308.11	5683.54	31.04%
EXP	EUR	2.7063	10,371.31	3758.78	36.24%
IMP	EUR	2.1661	10,398.46	3248.34	31.24%
HICP	Index	1.4338	115.49	16.05	13.90%

https://doi.org/10.3390/jrfm19040261

Table A2. *Cont.*

Factor Code	Data Type	Change t40/t1	AVE	STDEV	CV
GDPpC	Euro	2.7268	2793.50	934.67	33.46%
OOHE	Index	2.1634	139.65	33.27	23.82%
AD	Index	2.2843	144.32	36.65	25.40%
OSRAD	Index	2.5820	153.47	46.22	30.12%
OD	Index	1.4776	115.09	14.36	12.48%
MRM	Index	1.7211	122.57	24.58	20.06%
OSROD	Index	1.2874	108.90	7.30	6.71%
ICD	Index	0.9893	99.67	2.33	2.33%
HWEGOF	Index	1.6315	122.66	21.57	17.59%
ARH	Index	1.5209	115.32	14.80	12.84%
MRD	Index	1.6091	121.24	22.51	18.57%
MMRD	Index	1.5256	119.51	20.60	17.24%
SMRD	Index	1.8381	125.11	27.45	21.94%
WSMSRD	Index	1.9384	129.22	27.97	21.65%
WS	Index	1.9879	132.87	32.62	24.55%
RC	Index	1.5435	111.97	14.96	13.36%
SC	Index	2.9131	162.41	56.05	34.51%
OSRD	Index	2.0591	134.42	30.54	22.72%
EGOF	Index	1.5847	123.50	21.77	17.62%
E	Index	1.4123	112.80	11.48	10.18%
G	Index	1.5689	137.84	66.51	48.26%
SF	Index	1.9437	146.31	44.41	30.35%
HE	Index	1.8766	137.31	32.95	23.99%
FHERHM	Index	1.2670	108.90	11.49	10.55%
NBRBC	Number	2.2025	935.45	345.63	36.95%
NBDCRT	Number	3.2455	3832.63	1513.38	39.49%
NBDC1R	Number	2.1889	306.25	129.48	42.28%
NBDC2Rs	Number	3.4496	1457.73	578.79	39.71%
NBDC3Rs	Number	3.5357	1295.30	531.94	41.07%
NBDC4Rs	Number	3.1563	430.03	194.75	45.29%
NBDC5Rs	Number	2.6422	184.68	89.87	48.66%
NBDC6Rs	Number	2.5773	158.65	93.80	59.13%
AGQWS	Number	2.8253	171.64	56.09	32.68%
UNEMPL	Index	0.4304	64.30	16.51	25.67%
LF	Number	0.9211	3195.37	142.97	4.47%
DwCr	Mln. Euro	2.8939	14,572.86	5049.09	34.65%
IRATE	Index	0.4192	57.17	16.86	29.49%
BLSRP	Index	3.8291	179.02	78.45	43.82%

https://doi.org/10.3390/jrfm19040261

Table A2. *Cont.*

Factor Code	Data Type	Change t40/t1	AVE	STDEV	CV
HICML	Euro	1.5923	68.30	16.61	24.32%
BRHL	Mln. Euro	0.1330	1040.44	596.75	57.36%
IRATEMp	Percent	0.4218	3.73	1.10	29.46%
NFIP	Index	1.1186	107.03	5.14	4.80%
ExR	USD	1.0746	1.12	0.05	4.84%
Sofix	Number	2.3315	640.90	157.68	24.60%

Source: Calculations of the authors.

Appendix A.3. Historical Dynamics of First-Order Differential Data

After establishing non-stationarity of the historical data, a first-differential data estimate is made for both the dependent and independent variables. Figure A1 presents the relative changes in the values of the indicators for the period 2015Q4–2025Q3 calculated on a chain-wise basis with a number of observations N = 39: (t2 − t1)/t1 (See Figure A1).

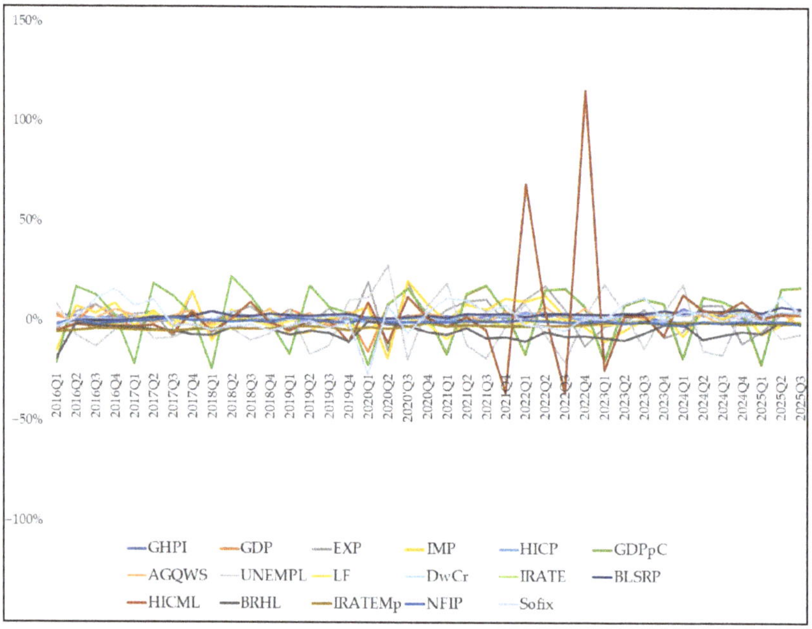

Figure A1. Dynamics of the first differential of the variables of groups A, F, G & E.

Appendix A.4. Stationarity Test Results

DF statistics, p value and stationarity status for the original data, first difference data, and second difference data of the 48 descriptors and the three independent variables HPI, HPIND, HPIED in Bulgaria for the period 2015Q4–2025Q3 are presented in Table A3.

https://doi.org/10.3390/jrfm19040261

Table A3. Stationarity test results for the original data, first difference data, and second difference data for all dependent and independent variables (ADF & KPSS).

Variable	ADF Level	KPSS Level	ADF Diff1	KPSS Diff1	ADF Diff2	KPSS Diff2	Integration Order
GHPI	0.990	0.010	0.598	0.010	0.013	0.100	I(2)
HPIND	0.990	0.010	0.309	0.015	0.010	0.100	I(2)
HPIED	0.990	0.010	0.809	0.010	0.024	0.100	I(2)
GDP	0.955	0.010	0.267	0.042	0.010	0.100	I(2)
EXP	0.793	0.010	0.527	0.100	0.010	0.100	I(2)
IMP	0.556	0.010	0.400	0.100	0.010	0.100	I(2)
HICP	0.489	0.010	0.516	0.100	0.144	0.100	Unclear
GDPpC	0.951	0.010	0.473	0.024	0.010	0.100	I(2)
OOHE	0.990	0.010	0.336	0.010	0.010	0.100	I(2)
AD	0.990	0.010	0.288	0.010	0.010	0.100	I(2)
OSRAD	0.990	0.010	0.206	0.010	0.010	0.100	I(2)
OD	0.990	0.010	0.603	0.017	0.024	0.100	I(2)
MRM	0.763	0.010	0.332	0.026	0.062	0.100	Unclear
OSROD	0.990	0.010	0.963	0.100	0.010	0.100	I(2)
ICD	0.599	0.033	0.106	0.100	0.010	0.100	I(2)
HWEGOF	0.618	0.010	0.315	0.100	0.014	0.100	I(2)
ARH	0.990	0.010	0.716	0.010	0.010	0.100	I(2)
MRD	0.479	0.010	0.458	0.100	0.055	0.100	Unclear
MMRD	0.489	0.010	0.548	0.100	0.084	0.100	Unclear
SMRD	0.884	0.010	0.546	0.010	0.360	0.100	Unclear
WSMSRD	0.990	0.010	0.609	0.016	0.018	0.100	I(2)
WS	0.916	0.010	0.341	0.081	0.010	0.100	I(2)
RC	0.990	0.010	0.836	0.039	0.010	0.100	I(2)
SC	0.990	0.010	0.469	0.047	0.010	0.100	I(2)
OSRD	0.990	0.010	0.632	0.010	0.140	0.100	Unclear
EGOF	0.503	0.010	0.314	0.100	0.010	0.100	I(2)
E	0.990	0.010	0.423	0.023	0.010	0.100	I(2)
G	0.378	0.036	0.046	0.100	0.010	0.100	I(1)
SF	0.272	0.010	0.353	0.100	0.029	0.100	I(2)
HE	0.564	0.010	0.396	0.100	0.010	0.100	I(2)
FHERHM	0.386	0.010	0.564	0.100	0.369	0.100	Unclear
NBRBC	0.912	0.010	0.430	0.100	0.010	0.100	I(2)
NBDCRT	0.648	0.010	0.072	0.100	0.010	0.100	I(2)
NBDC1R	0.418	0.071	0.150	0.100	0.010	0.100	I(2)
NBDC2Rs	0.610	0.010	0.018	0.100	0.010	0.100	I(1)
NBDC3Rs	0.728	0.010	0.108	0.100	0.010	0.100	I(2)
NBDC4Rs	0.620	0.010	0.257	0.100	0.010	0.100	I(2)

https://doi.org/10.3390/jrfm19040261

Table A3. *Cont.*

Variable	ADF Level	KPSS Level	ADF Diff1	KPSS Diff1	ADF Diff2	KPSS Diff2	Integration Order
NBDC5Rs	0.869	0.010	0.093	0.100	0.010	0.100	I(2)
NBDC6Rs	0.575	0.010	0.709	0.100	0.010	0.100	I(2)
AGQWS	0.990	0.010	0.071	0.010	0.010	0.100	I(2)
UNEMPL	0.327	0.010	0.378	0.100	0.010	0.100	I(2)
LF	0.527	0.010	0.296	0.100	0.010	0.100	I(2)
DwCr	0.990	0.010	0.990	0.010	0.037	0.100	I(2)
IRATE	0.010	0.010	0.837	0.010	0.010	0.094	I(2)
BLSRP	0.990	0.010	0.990	0.010	0.925	0.072	Unclear
HICML	0.985	0.018	0.048	0.100	0.010	0.100	I(1)
BRHL	0.985	0.010	0.020	0.011	0.010	0.100	I(2)
IRATEMp	0.010	0.010	0.783	0.010	0.010	0.100	I(2)
NFIP	0.976	0.010	0.018	0.100	0.010	0.100	I(1)
ExR	0.256	0.100	0.081	0.100	0.014	0.100	I(2)
Sofix	0.962	0.022	0.076	0.100	0.031	0.100	I(2)

Note: The ADF test and KPSS test was conducted in R version 4.4.3, using the adf.test() function and the kpss.test() function from the tseries package.

Appendix B

Appendix B.1. First Differencing of Variables with a Statistically Significant Impact on GHPI, Selected in the ARIMAX(0,2,1) Model

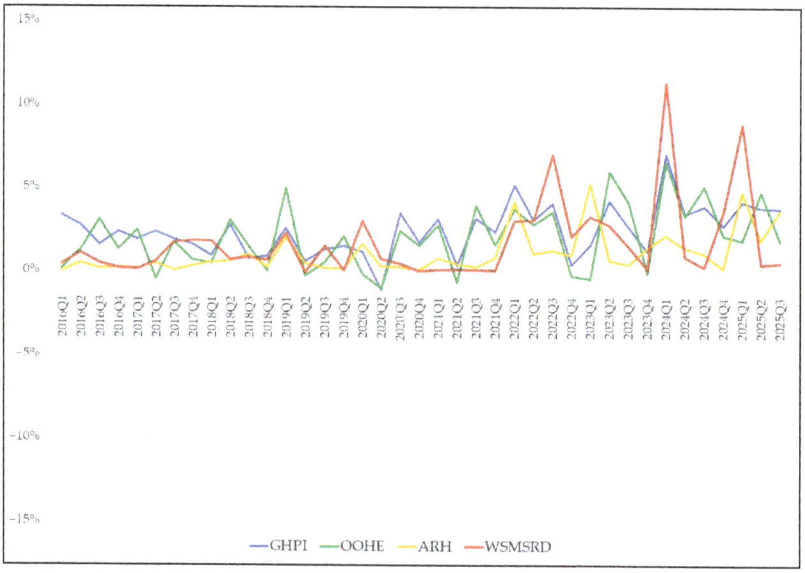

Figure A2. Dynamics of the first differentiated factors in the ARIMAX model (0,2,1): *OOHE, AHE* & *WSMSRD* with a statistically significant impact on GHPI.

Appendix B.2. Descriptive Statistics of Second Deference of the Dependent Variable GHPI_D2 and Independent Variables

Table A4. Descriptive Statistics of GHPI_D2, OOHE_D2, WSMSRD_D2 and ARH_D2.

		GHPI_D2	OOHE_D2	ARH_D2	WSMSRD_D2
N	Valid	38	38	38	38
	Missing	2	2	2	2
Mean		0.157	0.099	0.143	0.017
Std. Error of Mean		0.546	0.691	0.342	0.841
Median		−0.39	−0.39	−0.02	0.00
Mode		−6.53 [a]	−6.89 [a]	−5.52 [a]	−15.61 [a]
Std. Deviation		3.36	4.26	2.11	5.18
Variance		11.31	18.12	4.45	26.88
Skewness		0.853	0.592	0.407	−0.258
Std. Error of Skewness		0.383	0.383	0.383	0.383
Kurtosis		2.35	0.35	2.89	5.51
Std. Error of Kurtosis		0.750	0.750	0.750	0.750
Range		17.87	18.14	11.83	32.48
Minimum		−6.53	−6.89	−5.52	−15.61
Maximum		11.34	11.25	6.31	16.87
Sum		5.98	3.75	5.43	0.63

a. Multiple modes exist. The smallest value is shown.

Appendix B.3. Graphical Evidence from the Test for Normal Distribution of Residuals

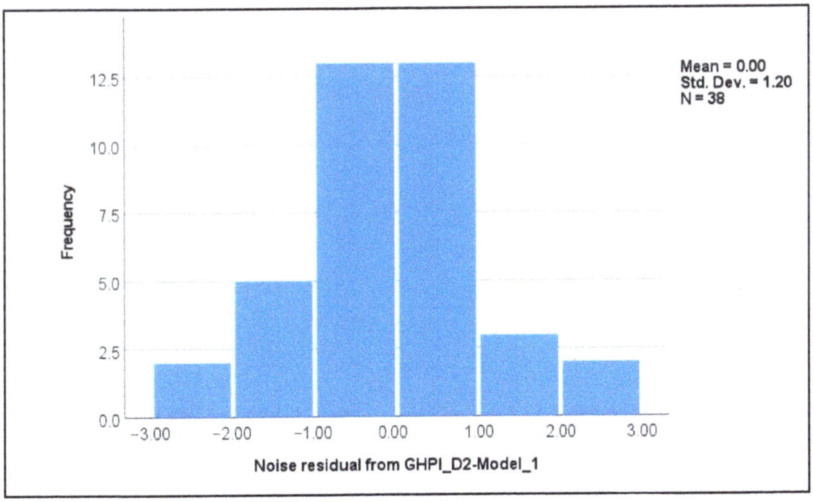

Figure A3. Histogram results.

https://doi.org/10.3390/jrfm19040261

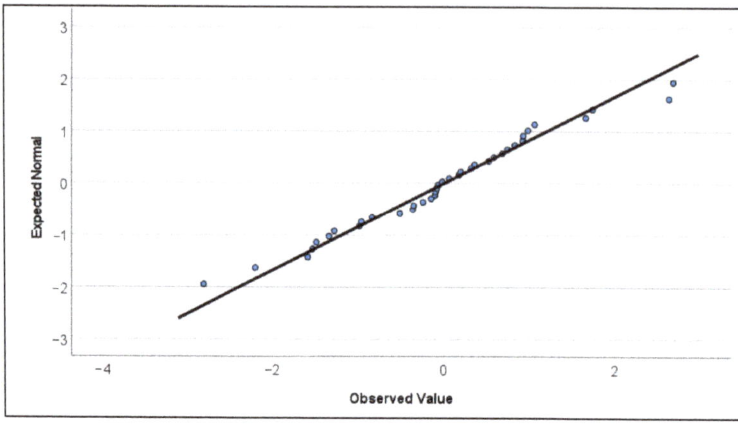

Figure A4. Normal Q-Q Plot of Noise residual from GHPI_D2-Model_1.

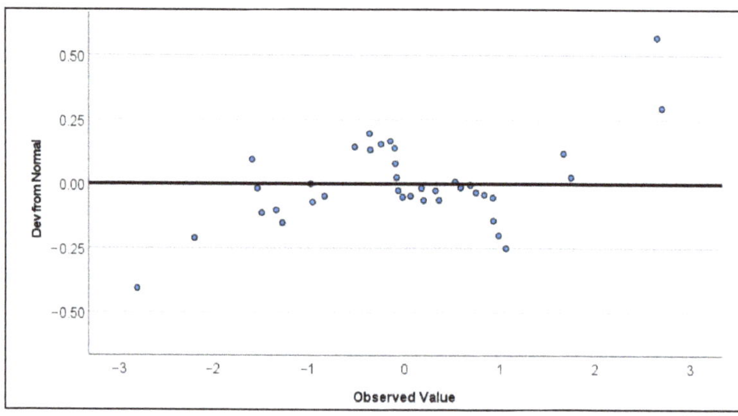

Figure A5. Detrended Normal Q-Q Plot of Noise residual from GHPI_D2-Model_1.

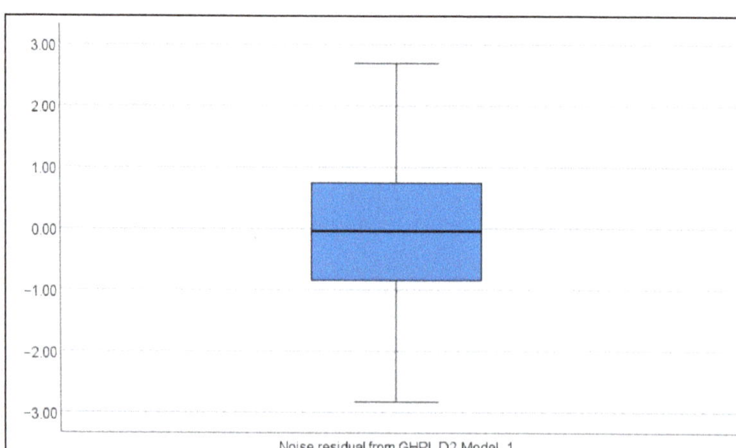

Figure A6. Distribution of Noise residual from GHPI_D2-Model_1.

https://doi.org/10.3390/jrfm19040261

References

Algieri, B. (2013). House price determinants: Fundamentals and underlying factors. *Comparative Economic Studies, 55*, 315–341. [CrossRef]

Anari, A., & Kolari, J. (2002). House prices and inflation. *Real Estate Economics, 30*(1), 67–84. [CrossRef]

Araya, F., Poblete, P., Salazar, L. A., Sánchez, O., Sierra-Varela, L., & Filun, Á. (2024). Exploring the Influence of construction companies characteristics on their response to the COVID-19 pandemic in the Chilean context. *Sustainability, 16*(8), 3417. [CrossRef]

Atanassov, A., Trifonova, S., Saraivanova, J., & Pramatarov, A. (2017). Assessment of the Administrative burdens for businesses in Bulgaria according to the national legislation related to the European Union internal market. *Management: Journal of Contemporary Management Issues, 22*, 21–49.

Aydinli, S. (2024). Impact of unexpected conditions on construction cost forecasting performance: Evidence from Europe. *Construction Management and Economics, 42*(9), 787–801. [CrossRef]

BNB. (2026). *Interest rates on loans—Households and NPISHs.*. Bulgarian National Bank. Available online: https://www.bnb.bg/Statistics/StMonetaryInterestRate/StInterestRate/StIRIROnLoans/StIRIROnLoansHouseholdsAndNPISHs/index.htm (accessed on 31 January 2026).

Brolinson, B., Doerner, W. M., Pollestad, A. J., & Seiler, M. J. (2026). European energy crisis: Did electricity prices shock real estate markets? *Journal of Environmental Economics and Management, 137*, 103283. [CrossRef]

Caldera Sánchez, A., & Johansson, Å. (2011). The price responsiveness of housing supply in OECD countries. *OECD Economics Department Working Papers, 837*, 1–35. [CrossRef]

Cermáková, K., & Hromada, E. (2022). Change in the affordability of owner-occupied housing in the context of rising energy prices. *Energies, 15*(4), 1281. [CrossRef]

Ciarlone, A. (2015). House price cycles in emerging economies. *Studies in Economics and Finance, 32*(1), 17–52. [CrossRef]

Ciot, M.-G. (2022). Implementation perspectives for the European green deal in central and Eastern Europe. *Sustainability, 14*(7), 3947. [CrossRef]

Cohen, V., & Karpavičiūtė, L. (2017). The analysis of the determinants of housing prices. *Independent Journal of Management & Production, 8*(1), 49–63. [CrossRef]

Dandashly, A., & Verdun, A. (2021). Euro adoption policies in the second decade—The remarkable cases of the Baltic States. In *Economic and Monetary Union at Twenty* (pp. 93–109). Routledge. Available online: https://bit.ly/4cxxl17 (accessed on 31 January 2026).

Dickey, D. A., & Fuller, W. A. (1981). Likelihood ratio statistics for autoregressive time series with a unit root. *Econometrica, 49*(4), 1057–1072. [CrossRef]

DiPasquale, D., & Wheaton, W. C. (1992). The markets for real estate assets and space: A conceptual framework. *Real Estate Economics, 20*(2), 181–198. [CrossRef]

Distaso, W. (2008). Testing for unit root processes in random coefficient autoregressive models. *Journal of Econometrics, 142*, 581–609. [CrossRef]

Doling, J., & Ronald, R. (2010). Home ownership and asset-based welfare. *Journal of Housing and the Built Environment, 25*, 165–173. [CrossRef]

Ebekozien, A. A., & Aigbedion, M. (2021). Construction industry post-COVID-19 recovery: Stakeholders perspective on achieving sustainable development goals. *International Journal of Construction Management, 23*(8), 1376–1386. [CrossRef]

Egert, B., & Mihaljek, D. (2007). Determinants of house prices in central and Eastern Europe. *Comparative Economic Studies, 49*(3), 337–489. [CrossRef]

European Commission. (2025). *Convergence report 2025 on Bulgaria* (D.-G. f. Affairs). Publications Office of the European Union. [CrossRef]

European Parliament. (2025). Topics European parliament. In *The housing crisis in Europe: Key facts and EU action (infographics)*. European Parliament. Available online: https://www.housingcoop.eu/resources/knowledge/the-housing-crisis-in-europe-key-facts-and-eu-action (accessed on 1 February 2026).

Eurostat. (2014). *Manual on the changes between ESA 95 and ESA 2010. 2014 edition*. Publications Office of the European Union. [CrossRef]

Eurostat. (2025a). Gross domestic product at market prices. In *National accounts indicator (ESA 2010): Gross domestic product at market prices*. Publications Office of the European Union. [CrossRef]

Eurostat. (2025b). *Housing in Europe—2025 edition*. Interactive Publication. [CrossRef]

Eurostat. (2026a). *Distribution of population by tenure status, type of household and income group*. Publications Office of the European Union. [CrossRef]

Eurostat. (2026b). House price and sales index. In *House price index (2015 = 100)—Annual data*. Publications Office of the European Union. Available online: https://ec.europa.eu/eurostat/databrowser/view/prc_hpi_a/default/table?lang=en (accessed on 31 January 2026).

Eurostat. (2026c). *Unemployment statistics*. Statistics Explained. Available online: https://bit.ly/4avgdXe (accessed on 31 January 2026).

https://doi.org/10.3390/jrfm19040261

Gabriela, C. P., Nijkamp, P., & Kourtit, K. (2023). Regional science knowledge needs for the recovery of the Ukrainian spatial economy: A Q-analysis. *Regional Science Policy & Practice, 15*(1), 75–95. [CrossRef]

Girouard, N., Kennedy, M., Noord, P. v., & André, C. (2006). Recent house price developments: The role of fundamentals. *OECD Economics Department Working Papers, 475*, 1–61. [CrossRef]

Gönül, İ. Ö., & Omay, T. (2025). Dynamic market efficiency assessment in sustainability indices: Rolling fractional integration analysis with multiple estimators. *Borsa Istanbul Review, 25*(6), 1645–1662. [CrossRef]

Gurmu, A. T., Krezel, A., & Ongkowijoyo, C. (2021). Fuzzy-stochastic model to assess defects in low-rise residential buildings. *Journal of Building Engineering, 40*, 102318. [CrossRef]

Haandrikman, K., Costa, R., Malmberg, B., Rogne, A. F., & Sleutjes, B. (2023). Socio-economic segregation in European cities. A comparative study of Brussels, Copenhagen, Amsterdam, Oslo and Stockholm. *Urban Geography, 44*(1), 1–36. [CrossRef]

Hadad, E., Dimitrov, S., & Stoilova-Nikolova, J. (2022). Development of capital pension funds in the Czech Republic and Bulgaria and readiness to implement PEPP. *European Journal of Social Security, 24*(4), 342–360. [CrossRef]

Herrera, R. F., Sánchez, O., Castañeda, K., & Porras, H. (2020). Cost overrun causative factors in road infrastructure Projects: A frequency and importance analysis. *Applied Sciences, 10*(16), 5506. [CrossRef]

Hyndman, R. J., & Koehler, A. B. (2006). Another look at measures of forecast accuracy. *International Journal of Forecasting, 22*(4), 679–688. [CrossRef]

Idirizov, B. (2025). Analysis of the Bulgarian housing price index: Risks, market dynamics, and economic implications. *Economic Studies (Ikonomicheski Izsledvania), 34*(8), 175–195.

Iliopoulou, P., Krassanakis, V., & Kappelos, K. (2025). Modeling the spatial impact of short-term rentals on house prices: The case of Athens, Greece. *Urban Science, 9*(12), 539. [CrossRef]

Irandoust, M. (2019). House prices and unemployment: An empirical analysis of causality. *International Journal of Housing Markets and Analysis, 12*(1), 148–164. [CrossRef]

Ishiwatari, M., Ranghieri, F., Taniguchi, K., & Mimura, S. (2021). Learning from Megadisasters in Japan: Sharing lessons with the world. *Journal of Disaster Research, 16*(6), 942–946. [CrossRef]

Ishiwatari, M., Sakamoto, A., & Nakayama, M. (2025). Expediting recovery: Lessons and challenges from the great East Japan earthquake to war-torn Ukraine. *Sustainability, 17*(3), 1210. [CrossRef]

Johansen, S. (1995). *Likelihood-based inference in cointegrated vector autoregressive models*. Oxford University Press. [CrossRef]

Kass, R. E., & Raftery, A. E. (1995). Bayes factors. *Journal of the American Statistical Association, 90*(430), 773–795. [CrossRef]

Kochaniak, K., Korzeniowska, A., & Pietrzak, M. (2024). Own or public? Later livelihoods of Ukrainian war migrant households in Poland. *International Migration, 62*(5), 53–70. [CrossRef]

Kotu, V., & Deshpande, B. (2019). Chapter 12—Time series forecasting. In O. V. Kotu, & B. Deshpande (Eds.), *Data science* (2nd ed., pp. 395–445). Morgan Kaufmann. [CrossRef]

Kruskal, W. H., & Wallis, W. A. (1952). Use of ranks in one-criterion variance analysis. *Journal of the American statistical Association, 47*(260), 583–621. [CrossRef]

Kuang, W., & Liu, P. (2015). Inflation and house prices: Theory and evidence from 35 major cities in China. *International Real Estate Review, 18*(2), 217–240. [CrossRef]

Kwiatkowski, D., Phillips, P. C., Schmidt, P., & Shin, Y. (1992). Testing the null hypothesis of stationarity against the alternative of a unit root: How sure are we that economic time series have a unit root? *Journal of Econometrics, 54*(1–3), 159–178. [CrossRef]

Li, B., & Zeng, Z. (2010). Fundamentals behind house prices. *Economics Letters, 108*(2), 205–207. [CrossRef]

Lin, Y.-C., Lee, C. L., & Newell, G. (2022). Varying interest rate sensitivity of different property sectors: Cross-country evidence from REITs. *Journal of Property Investment & Finance, 40*(1), 68–98. [CrossRef]

Liu, J., Farahani, H., & Serota, R. A. (2024). Exploring distributions of house prices and house price indices. *Economies, 12*(2), 47. [CrossRef]

Marinković, S., Džunić, M., & Marjanović, I. (2024). Determinants of housing prices: Serbian cities' perspective. *Journal of Housing and the Built Environment, 39*, 1601–1626. [CrossRef]

Marinov, E. (2017). The link between official development assistance and international trade flows—Insights from Economic Theory. *Journal of Financial and Monetary Economics, 4*, 239–247.

Mayer, C. J., & Somerville, C. T. (2000). Residential construction: Using the urban growth model to estimate housing supply. *Journal of Urban Economics, 48*, 85–109. [CrossRef]

Mazáček, D., & Panoš, J. (2025). Key determinants of sales price in the residential developments in Prague. *Journal of European Real Estate Research, 18*(3), 371–400. [CrossRef]

McQuinn, K., & O'Reilly, G. (2008). Assessing the role of income and interest rates in determining house prices. *Economic Modelling, 25*(3), 377–390. [CrossRef]

Mihaylova-Borisova, G., & Nenkova, P. (2020). Expenditure efficiency and macroeconomic performance of balkan countries: DEA approach. In *Conomic and social development, 63rd international scientific conference on economic and social development—Building resilient society* (pp. 439–448). Varazdin Development and Entewpreneurship Agency and University North.
Mimis, A., Rovolis, A., & Stamou, M. (2013). Property valuation with artificial neural network: The case of Athens. *Journal of Property Research*, *30*(2), 128–143. [CrossRef]
Nenkov, D., & Hristozov, Y. (2022). DCF valuation of companies: Exploring the interrelation between revenue and operating expenditures. *Economic Alternatives*, *28*(4), 626–646. [CrossRef]
NSI. (2026). *Housing price statistics*. National Statistical Institute. Available online: https://www.nsi.bg/en/statistical-data/90 (accessed on 31 January 2026).
Ouhinou, M. A., Saoualih, A., Lyaqini, S., Kartobi, S. E., Prodanov, S., & Safaa, L. (2025). Unraveling differences and similarities in sustainable investment through case studies in China, Germany, and the United States: A Multi-algorithm clustering network approach. In *Proceedings of the third ICMDS'24: Machine learning, inverse problems and related fields. ICMDS 2024* (Vol. 1466, pp. 193–202). Springer Nature. [CrossRef]
Pagourtzi, E., Assimakopoulos, V., Hatzichristos, T., & French, N. (2003). Real estate appraisal: A review of valuation methods. *Journal of Property Investment & Finance*, *21*(4), 383–401. [CrossRef]
Park, J., & Seo, D. (2024). Comparative study on housing defect repair cost through linear regression model. *Eng*, *5*(3), 2328–2344. [CrossRef]
Passek, M., & Nübel, K. (2025). Forecasting office construction price indices for cost planning in Germany using regularized VARX models. *Buildings*, *16*(1), 103. [CrossRef]
Pazdzior, A., Sokol, M., & Styk, A. (2021). The impact of the COVID-19 pandemic on the economic and financial situation of the micro and small enterprises from the construction and development industry in Poland. *European Research Studies Journal*, *XXIV*, 751–762. [CrossRef]
Perry, A., Markovska, A., & Smith, C. (2026). Behind the scheme: Challenges faced by professionals addressing safeguarding issues in housing for Ukrainian refugees in the United Kingdom. *Social Sciences*, *15*(2), 89. [CrossRef]
Prodanov, S., & Naydenov, L. (2020). Theoretical, qualitative and quantitative aspects of municipal fiscal autonomy in Bulgaria. *Ikonomicheski Izsledvania*, *29*(2), 126–150.
Reichle, P., Fidrmuc, J., & Reck, F. (2023). The sharing economy and housing markets in selected European cities. *Journal of Housing Economics*, *60*, 101914. [CrossRef]
Roleders, V., Oriekhova, T., Zaharieva, G., Sysoieva, I., Dobizha, V., Pidhaiets, S., & Kucher, L. (2024). Economic justification of recycling in the processing industry. *Cleaner and Responsible Consumption*, *13*, 100195. [CrossRef]
Sabitova, N. M., Shavaleyeva, C. M., Lizunova, E. N., Khairullova, A. I., & Zahariev, A. (2020). Tax Capacity of the Russian Federation Constituent Entities: Problems of Assessment and Unequal Distribution. In L. N. Safiullin, & N. Gabdrakhmanov (Eds.), *Regional economic developments in Russia* (pp. 79–86). Springer. [CrossRef]
Schwartz, A. E., & Wachter, S. M. (2023). COVID-19's impacts on housing markets: Introduction. *Journal of Housing Economics*, *59*, 101911. [CrossRef] [PubMed]
Sen, A. (2008). Behaviour of Dickey–Fuller tests when there is a break under the unit root null hypothesis. *Statistics and Probability Letters*, *78*, 622–628. [CrossRef]
Shen, H., Li, L., Zhu, H., Liu, Y., & Luo, Z. (2022). Exploring a pricing model for urban rental houses from a geographical perspective. *Land*, *11*(4), 4. [CrossRef]
Sivitanides, P. S. (2018). Macroeconomic drivers of London house prices. *Journal of Property Investment & Finance*, *36*(6), 539–551. [CrossRef]
Stroebel, J., & Vavra, J. (2019). House prices, local demand, and retail prices. *Journal of Political Economy*, *127*(3), 1391–1436. [CrossRef]
Sukhomud, G., & Shnaider, V. (2023). Continuity and change: Wartime housing politics in Ukraine. *International Journal of Housing Policy*, *23*(3), 629–652. [CrossRef]
Taggart, M., Koskela, L., & Rooke, J. (2014). The role of the supply chain in the elimination and reduction of construction rework and defects: An action research approach. *Construction Management and Economics*, *32*(7–8), 829–842. [CrossRef]
Ubarevičienė, R., & Aidukaitė, J. (2026). Housing provision: A comparative study of housing availability, accessibility, and adequacy in EU member states. *Journal of International and Comparative Social Policy*, 1–20. [CrossRef]
Ushenko, N., Likhonosova, G., Zahariev, A., Shaulska, L., Kęsy, M., & Hurochkina, V. (2023). Strategies for strengthening business economic security with account to global financial challenges. *Financial and Credit Activity: Problems of Theory and Practice*, *6*(53), 300–317. [CrossRef]
Ünalan, G., Çamalan, Ö., & Yılmaz, H. H. (2025). The impact of increases in housing prices on income inequality: A perspective on sustainable urban development. *Sustainability*, *17*(9), 4024. [CrossRef]
Visković, J., & Čipčić, D. (2025). Effects of eurozone and schengen area accession on real estate prices. *Financial Internet Quarterly*, *21*(4), 84–93. [CrossRef]

https://doi.org/10.3390/jrfm19040261

Wu, Z. (2025). Time series forecasting of texas housing prices: A comparison between the ARIMA and VAR models. *Theoretical and Natural Science*, *80*, 20–27. [CrossRef]
Yan, L. (2024). Predicting house prices with a linear regression model. *Applied and Computational Engineering*, *114*, 107–115. [CrossRef]
Yordanova, Z., & Hristozov, Y. (2025). The evolution of financial analysis: From manual methods to AI and AI agents. *Economics—Innovative and Economics Research Journal*, *13*(3), 2019–2239. [CrossRef]
Yotzov, V., Bobeva, D., Loukanova, P., & Nestorov, N. (2020). Macroeconomic implications of the fight against COVID-19: First estimates, forecasts, and conclusions. *Ikonomicheski Izsledvania*, *29*(3), 3–28.
Zaharieva, G., Tarakchiyan, O., & Zahariev, A. (2022). Market capitalization factors of the Bulgarian pharmaceutical sector in pandemic environment. *Business Management*, *XXXII*(4), 35–51.
Zhang, X., Wang, Y., Xu, S., Yang, E., & Meng, L. (2024). Forecasting total and type-specific non-residential building construction spending: The case study of the United States and lessons learned. *Buildings*, *14*(5), 1317. [CrossRef]
Zhelyazkova, V. (2018). The road to circular economy: What can Europe learn from the experience of Germany and Japan? *Economic Studies Journal*, *6*, 167–177.

https://doi.org/10.3390/jrfm19040261

Journal of
Risk and Financial Management

MDPI

Article

Comparative Analysis of Risks Identified in Scientific Research, Strategic Documents, and Media Publications in Bulgaria

Borislav Borissov [1,*] and Yanko Hristozov [2]

[1] Institute of Economics and Politics, University of National and World Economy, 1700 Sofia, Bulgaria
[2] Department of Finance, University of National and World Economy, 1700 Sofia, Bulgaria; yankohristozov@unwe.bg
* Correspondence: b.borissov@unwe.bg

Abstract

The acceleration of economic, technological, geopolitical and environmental processes has significantly increased the exposure of national economies to interconnected financial and non-financial risks. While global financial risks and corporate risks have been extensively analyzed, significant national risks—such as fiscal sustainability, debt vulnerability, systemic inefficiency and investment uncertainty—are often treated fragmentarily or descriptively within conventional sovereign risk frameworks. This article offers a comparative analytical approach to identifying national financial and non-financial risks by examining the degree of convergence and divergence between risks identified in four different sources: national expert scientific studies, World Economic Forum global risk assessments, strategic development documents of Bulgaria and national media coverage. Using expert data, structured content analysis, a modified media visibility index, and nonparametric statistical tests for linked binary data, the study identifies risks that are consistently recognized across sources and therefore pose an increased threat to financial stability, as well as risks that remain systematically underestimated despite their potential fiscal and macroeconomic consequences. The results show that cross-source comparison significantly improves the detection of national risks and reveals blind spots in fiscal planning, investment, and social policy. This article contributes to the literature on the management of risks with a direct negative financial effect or with an indirect financial impact on the national economy by positioning national risk identification within a governance-oriented, multi-source analytical framework.

Keywords: risk assessment; global risks; national risks; strategic documents; media visibility index

1. Introduction

The aspiration of every self-governing structure is to ensure its future development by achieving its goals with minimal resources. This, however, depends on a number of external and internal factors, some of which are aligned with its efforts for success, while others hinder them. If these factors are already identified and are acting at a given moment, they can be classified as existing problems that the organization must address. If they represent potential adverse events that may occur in the future, they constitute risks that can be avoided or at least whose negative impact on the achievement of organizational goals can be reduced.

Risks arise not only in the development of business structures, public institutions, and other social organizations, but also in the development of entire states. The ability of governing bodies to identify, analyze, and assess these risks in a timely manner determines how effectively they will be able to respond in the future when a risk event occurs. This is why many research institutes around the world are engaged in scientific studies of potential risks—whether facing the world as a whole, individual countries, or specific business sectors.

In order to successfully counteract risks, governing authorities, when drafting their strategic development documents, strive to anticipate the potential risks that could hinder the achievement of their envisaged economic, social, environmental, and other objectives. The media, in turn, seeking to reflect social processes, report on risk events that have already occurred, commenting on the reasons for their emergence and their consequences. Their publications are not scientific in nature and appear post factum, but beyond their purely informational role, they contribute to shaping public attitudes toward combating risks and preventing their recurrence.

This article presents a comparative analysis of the risks identified and analyzed in national and international scientific research with those identified in the analytical sections of the main strategic documents for the development of Bulgaria, as well as with the risks reflected in media publications in 2024 and 2025 in the country. The objective is to determine the extent to which these risks overlap, the areas in which they diverge, and to identify which of them have been underestimated.

What is new in this study is the explicit cross-source comparison of risk identification across expert research, strategic planning documents, and media discourse. By introducing a systematic alignment–misalignment logic, the analysis goes beyond descriptive country risk discussions and enables the identification of financially relevant national risks that are either consistently recognized or structurally underestimated. This approach provides a methodological basis for detecting blind spots in national financial risk governance.

This cross-source comparison can be interpreted through risk governance and risk communication lenses: strategic documents reflect planned policy steering and programmatic feasibility, expert assessments emphasize structural vulnerabilities and longer horizons, while media narratives are shaped by salience, episodic events, and attention dynamics. Therefore, alignment signals institutional coordination, whereas misalignment indicates information asymmetries in national risk communication and risk governance.

2. Materials and Methods

The empirical workflow of the study follows five main steps:

- identification of nationally relevant risks through an expert survey conducted by UNWE;
- extraction of comparable risks from the World Economic Forum's Global Risks Report;
- identification of future-oriented risks articulated in Bulgaria's strategic development documents;
- extraction of risk-related narratives from national media coverage;
- comparative analysis of overlap, divergence, and agreement across sources.

During the period May–June 2025, the Institute of Economics and Policies at the University of National and World Economy (UNWE), within the framework of the Bulgarian Risk Monitor initiative, conducted a study among 82 experts from various organizations on risks specific to Bulgaria's development. The survey was distributed to experts from public administration, academia, the private sector, and non-governmental organizations, selected based on their professional experience in policy analysis, economic research, and risk-related decision-making. As a result of the study, 32 potential risks to the country were identified, whose symptoms of possible future occurrence could already be observed at the time of the survey. The risks were assessed by the experts in terms of their probability

https://doi.org/10.3390/jrfm19030179

of occurrence and impact severity, using a scale from 1 to 5, in accordance with the risk assessment methodology recommended by COSO—the Committee of Sponsoring Organizations (COSO by Deloitte & Touche LLP, 2012) and ENISA—the European Union Agency for Network and Information Security (ENISA, 2006).

This methodology is also described in ISO/IEC ISO/IEC 27001:2022, which establishes guidelines and general principles for initiating, implementing, maintaining and improving information security management in an organization. The objectives outlined provide general guidance on the generally accepted objectives of information security management. ISO/IEC 27001:2022 contains best practices for control objectives and controls in the following areas of information security management (ISO, 2024).

In the document published by COSO in 2012 and prepared by Deloitte & Touche LLP, entitled Risk Assessment in Practice (COSO by Deloitte & Touche LLP, 2012), the risk assessment process is described in detail and includes the following steps:

1. Risk identification.
2. Development of assessment criteria.
3. Risk assessment.
4. Assessment of interactions among risks.
5. Risk prioritization.
6. Risk response.

The questionnaire used in the UNWE study included 32 risks. It was distributed to 100 experts, from whom 82 valid responses were received. These risks were aligned with those identified in the Global Risks Perception Survey 2024–2025 (GRPS), presented in the World Economic Forum (WEF) report published in January 2025, entitled The Global Risks Report. The WEF analyzes global risks across three-time horizons in order to support decision-makers in balancing current crises with long-term priorities. The report discusses 33 risks that may emerge in the short term (two-year horizon) and in the long term (ten-year horizon) (World Economic Forum, 2025).

Based on a content analysis of the strategic documents for the development of Bulgaria in the coming years (SDDB), and, in particular, the Partnership Agreement (European Commission, 2025), the National Recovery and Resilience, and the National Development Programme "Bulgaria 2030" (Council of Ministers, 2025a), references to future risks and problems that the country may face were identified. A total of 17 major risks discussed in the analytical sections of these documents were identified (European Commission, 2025; Council of Ministers, 2025b).

With the assistance of rour artificial intelligence chatbots—namely Gemini 3, BgGPT—Gemma-2-27B-IT-v1.0, DeepSeek V 3.2. and ChatGPT-5—media publications addressing various risks discussed in the public sphere were identified. To address reproducibility, we used a standardized query protocol (fixed date window, Bulgarian-language queries, and identical risk keywords) across four GenAI systems. Candidate media items were consolidated across tools, de-duplicated, and checked for relevance against the risk definition. To mitigate algorithmic bias, cross-model triangulation was applied, and the prompt set and retrieved item list can be archived as a replication supplement.

A Media Visibility Index (MVI) was calculated for individual risks based on the frequency of their mention and the popularity of the respective media. MVI is a metric often applied in public relations, marketing and communications research to quantify how—and to what extent—an organization, individual, topic, issue or event is represented in the media. Calculating MVI has become a popular tool for measuring the frequency of mentions in media content. In their article "Uncovering the Secret Power: How Algorithms Can Influence Content Visibility on Twitter/X", five authors from Italy and the USA investigate the impact of algorithms on content visibility on social media and propose a

https://doi.org/10.3390/jrfm19030179

quantitative approach to measuring it (Galeazzi, 2025). Since the established methodology for calculating the index considers positive, negative and neutral posts, for the purposes of the risk analysis it was modified by excluding positive and neutral posts from the formula. The leading media outlets—BNR, BNT, BTV and Nova TV—received a weight of 2 in the formula, while all other media outlets received a weight of 1. Thus, the formula for calculating the adjusted media visibility index takes the following form:

MVI_adj = 2 × (number of negative publications in BNR/BTV/BNT/Nova TV) + 1 × (number of negative publications in other media)

The Media Visibility Index focuses exclusively on negative publications, as negative framing more directly signals perceived urgency and potential threat, whereas positive or neutral references do not necessarily indicate risk materialization. Higher weights are assigned to leading national media outlets due to their significantly greater audience reach and agenda-setting influence in shaping public risk perception.

The collected information on risks from the UNWE study, the WEF report, the analysis of strategic development documents, and media publications was used to conduct a comparative analysis in order to determine the degree of overlap among them, to identify which risks have been underestimated, and to establish which risks are considered the most significant.

While YES/NO coding enables consistent cross-source comparison of recognition, it does not capture variation in framing intensity or severity across narratives; future work could extend the media and document analysis using sentiment/scoring or topic-model intensity measures to approximate magnitude comparably.

As a robustness check, we computed an unweighted frequency-only index and confirmed that the top-ranked risks remain stable; weighting primarily affects mid-ranked items.

3. Results

The results section presents the comparative structure of risk identification across the four analyzed sources. The analysis highlights both areas of convergence, where risks are consistently identified, and areas of divergence, where certain risks appear only in specific sources. These patterns provide insight into dominant and neglected dimensions of national risk perception. Table 1 presents the results of the study of the risks of the UNWE, of the World Economic Forum (2025), their presence in the country's strategic development documents and in media publications.

Table 1. Risks identified in the UNWE Study, the WEF Report, Strategic Documents for the Development of Bulgaria (SDDB), and the Media.

No.	Name of the Risk	Identified by UNWE	Identified by WEF	Identified by SDDB	Identified by Media
1	Risk of further deterioration of the demographic situation in the country	Yes	Yes	Yes	Yes
2	Risk of deterioration of the education system	Yes	No	Yes	Yes
3	Risk of lack of reform and inefficiency of the healthcare system	Yes	Yes	Yes	Yes
4	Risk of deepening social polarization of society	Yes	Yes	Yes	Yes

https://doi.org/10.3390/jrfm19030179

Table 1. *Cont.*

No.	Name of the Risk	Identified by UNWE	Identified by WEF	Identified by SDDB	Identified by Media
5	Risk of an increase in the share of the population living below the poverty line	Yes	Yes	Yes	Yes
6	Risk of growing distrust in the rule of law	Yes	No	No	Yes
7	Risk of maintaining an unacceptably high level of corruption	Yes	No	No	Yes
8	Risk of loss of national identity	No	No	No	Yes
9	Risk of increasing disinformation and manipulation of public opinion	Yes	Yes	No	No
10	Risk of lagging behind in the pace of economic development	No	Yes	Yes	Yes
11	Risk of labor force shortages for high-tech sectors and R&D	Yes	No	Yes	No
12	Risk of maintaining a high budget deficit and falling into a debt crisis	Yes	Yes	No	Yes
13	Risk of increasing inflation during price conversion	No	No	No	No
14	Risk of widening regional disparities within the country	Yes	No	Yes	No
15	Risk of a breach in the country's energy security	No	Yes	No	Yes
16	Risk of difficulties in the functioning of the pension and social security systems	Yes	No	No	Yes
17	Risk of the emergence of a crisis of statehood	Yes	Yes	Yes	No
18	Risk of deepening internal political tension and social conflicts	Yes	No	No	Yes
19	Risk of changes in the ethnic composition of the Bulgarian nation	No	No	No	Yes
20	Risk of social exclusion and marginalization of part of the population	No	No	No	Yes
21	Risk of negative impact of geopolitical conflicts on Bulgaria	Yes	Yes	No	Yes
22	Risk of loss of state sovereignty and increasing dependence on external factors	No	No	No	Yes
23	Risk of weakening the defense capabilities of the armed forces	Yes	No	No	Yes
24	Risk of increasing dependence on imports of fuels and critical raw materials	No	Yes	Yes	No
25	Risk of Bulgaria's technological lag behind other EU countries	Yes	No	No	No
26	Risk of lagging behind in innovation and digitalization of key state systems	No	No	Yes	Yes
27	Risks related to the introduction of artificial intelligence	Yes	No	Yes	Yes
28	Risks of breaches in information security, increasing cyberattacks and cyber threats	Yes	Yes	Yes	Yes
29	Risks related to climate change	Yes	Yes	Yes	Yes

https://doi.org/10.3390/jrfm19030179

Table 1. *Cont.*

No.	Name of the Risk	Identified by UNWE	Identified by WEF	Identified by SDDB	Identified by Media
30	Risk of deterioration of environmental quality caused by human activity	Yes	Yes	Yes	Yes
31	Risk of inadequate maintenance of infrastructure	High	Yes	Yes	Yes
32	Risk of gender inequality	No	No	Yes	Yes

Source: Authors' research.

The table shows that there is a consensus on the risks to Bulgaria's development in the coming years, identified by the study of the UNWE, SIF, strategic documents and the Bulgarian media—for nine risks, but there are also some differences. The initial risk list was generated through expert-led identification of nationally observable risk symptoms within the Bulgarian Risk Monitor framework. After this expert-driven identification step, labels were harmonized with the WEF GRPS wording where conceptually equivalent, to ensure cross-source comparability while preserving national specificity. For the needs of our analysis, we converted the binary indicators "Yes/No" to "1/0". The transformation of risk identification into binary indicators (Yes/No $\rightarrow$ 1/0) is methodologically required in order to apply Cochran's Q test and McNemar pairwise comparisons, which are designed for paired binary data. This step does not represent an arbitrary simplification but ensures statistical validity and comparability across heterogeneous sources. Figure 1 shows which studies/publications contain the relevant risks and which do not.

3.1. Descriptive Statistics

As can be seen from the following Table 2, out of a total of N = 32 risks analyzed, assessed by four binary indicators (YES/NO), the highest share of coverage was observed for "Media visibility" (78.1%), and the lowest for "Identified by WEF" (46.9%).

Table 2. Number of identified risks in the four studies/publications.

Publication/Source	YES (*n*)	NO (*n*)	YES (%)
Risks identified by UNWE	22	10	68.8
Risks identified by WEF	15	17	46.9
Risks identified by SDDB	17	15	53.1
Risks identified by Media	25	7	78.1

Source: Authors' calculations.

Beyond simple overlap counts, the observed divergences indicate different selection logics across information environments. The SDDB emphasizes risks that can be addressed through planned reforms and EU-programmatic instruments, while expert surveys capture structural vulnerabilities with longer time horizons. Media visibility is driven by event salience and public attention cycles, meaning that episodic shocks can crowd out chronic risks. From a financial risk perspective, divergence implies that relying on a single source can systematically bias fiscal preparedness: strategic plans may underweight fast-emerging threats, while media narratives may underweight slow-onset risks with high cumulative budget impact.

https://doi.org/10.3390/jrfm19030179

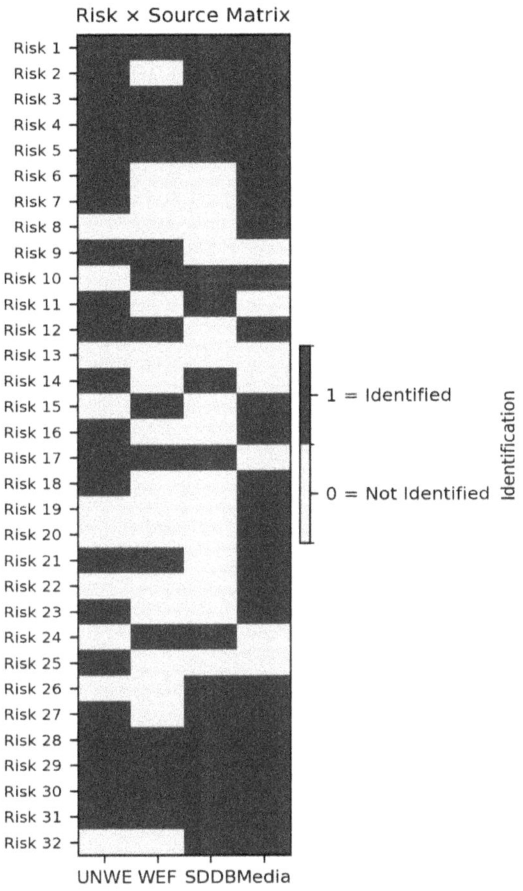

Figure 1. Risk × publication matrix (1 = YES, 0 = NO) showing the structure of risk coverage.

3.2. Differences Between Publications (Cochran's Q Test)

Cochran's Q test (for 4 related proportions) indicates statistically significant differences between publications: Q(3) = 9.30, $p = 0.0256$. This implies that the probability of a risk being covered (YES) is not equal across all sources.

3.3. Post Hoc Pairwise Comparisons (McNemar Tests)

Pairwise McNemar tests (exact p-values) were conducted with Holm correction for multiple comparisons. Table 3 below reports p-values, odds ratios (YES association), and Cohen's κ (agreement). After Holm correction, no pairwise differences remain statistically significant at $\alpha = 0.05$.

Table 3. Multiple comparisons of risks from the UNWE study, in the WEF report, reflected in the SDDB and in the media.

Comparison	p (Exact)	p (Holm)	Significant ($\alpha = 0.05$)	Odds Ratio (YES Association)	K (Cohen)
Risks identified by UNWE vs. risks in the WEF report	0.092285	0.384064	False	2.8	0.206

https://doi.org/10.3390/jrfm19030179

Table 3. *Cont.*

Comparison	p (Exact)	p (Holm)	Significant (α = 0.05)	Odds Ratio (YES Association)	K (Cohen)
Risks identified by UNWE vs. risks identified by SDDB	0.266846	0.800537	False	2.167	0.168
Risks identified by UNWE vs. risks identified by Media	0.581055	1.0	False	0.85	−0.03
Risks identified by WEF vs. risks identified by SDDB	0.753906	1.0	False	5.042	0.377
Risks identified by WEF vs. risks identified by Media	0.021271	0.127625	False	1.231	0.034
Risks identified by SDDB vs. risks identified by Media	0.076813	0.384064	False	0.812	−0.036

Source: Authors' calculations using GenAI.

3.4. Agreement Between Publications (Cohen's Kappa)

Cohen's κ measures agreement beyond chance for binary indicators. Higher values indicate more similar patterns of risk coverage. This is presented in Table 4 and Figure 2. The highest agreement is observed between "Risks in the WEF report" and "Risks reflected in the SDDB" ($\kappa \approx 0.38$), while for some pairs, κ is close to 0 or negative, indicating low agreement.

Table 4. Agreement between publications regarding identified risks.

Publication/Source	Risks in the UNWE Study	Risks in the WEF Report	Risks Identified in the SDDB	Media Visibility of Risks
Risks identified by UNWE	1.0	0.206	0.168	−0.03
Risks identified by WEF	0.206	1.0	0.377	0.034
Risks identified by SDDB	0.168	0.377	1.0	−0.036
Risks identified by Media	−0.03	0.034	−0.036	1.0

Source: Authors' calculations using GenAI.

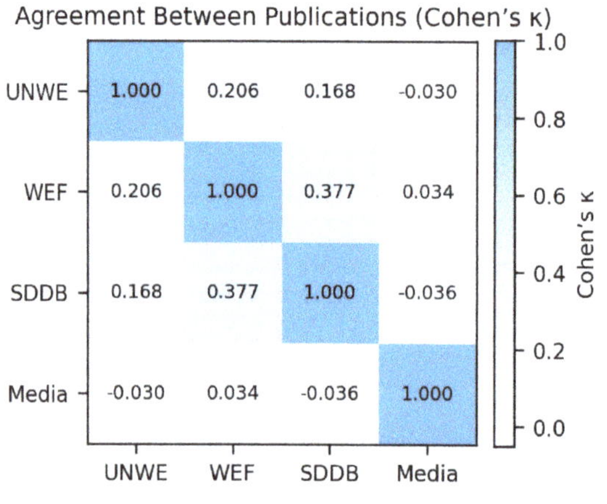

Figure 2. Agreement matrix between publications (Cohen's κ) for YES/NO indicators (higher κ = greater similarity).

The dataset consists of paired binary observations: the same set of risks is checked across multiple publications. Accordingly, Cochran's Q is the appropriate omnibus test, and it shows that overall coverage differs across sources. However, post hoc pairwise Mc-

https://doi.org/10.3390/jrfm19030179

Nemar tests do not yield robust significant differences after multiple-comparison correction, suggesting that differences are distributed across several comparisons and/or the sample size limits power. Agreement analyses (Cohen's κ) indicate low-to-moderate similarity between sources, implying that publications highlight partially overlapping sets of risks. Practically, this means that the sources are not interchangeable, and combining multiple publications improves coverage.

Based on N = 32 risks and 4 sources (YES/NO), the analysis shows that:

- coverage rates vary across sources (YES% ranges from 46.9% to 78.1%);
- overall differences are statistically significant (Cochran's Q(3) = 9.30, $p = 0.0256$);
- no pairwise differences remain significant after Holm correction (McNemar tests);
- agreement between sources is low-to-moderate (κ approximately from −0.04 to 0.38). In practice, using multiple sources increases coverage and reduces the risk of missing publication-specific risk categories.

As noted above, it is natural that there is no complete overlap among the risks identified in scientific studies conducted by different researchers and research institutions, those addressed in the analyses of strategic documents, and those discussed in the media, as they differ in terms of object, subject, scope, and purpose. The comparative analysis of these studies and publications aims to identify which risks are commonly recognized by all sources, in which areas opinions diverge, and which risks have been underestimated.

The risks for which there is full consensus—identified in the scientific studies of UNWE and the WEF, addressed in the SDDB, and reflected in media publications are as follows:

- Risk of further deterioration of the demographic situation in the country;
- Risk of lack of reform and inefficiency of the healthcare system;
- Risk of deepening social polarization of society;
- Risk of an increase in the share of the population living below the poverty line;
- Risk of lagging behind in the pace of economic development;
- Risks of breaches in information security, increasing cyberattacks, and cyber threats;
- Risks related to climate change;
- Risks related to the deterioration of environmental quality caused by human activity;
- Risk of inadequate maintenance of infrastructure.

Of these nine risks, four are assessed as high in the UNWE study, four as medium, and one as low. Among the seventeen risks identified in the three main strategic documents for the development of Bulgaria, six are assessed as high in the UNWE study, seven as medium, and four as low. Seven of the fifteen risks mentioned in the WEF report are included in the list of the ten most significant risks identified in the UNWE study. Of these, five are assessed as medium and three as low. The greatest overlap is observed between the risks identified in the UNWE study and those discussed in Bulgarian media during 2024 and 2025, amounting to 25 risks. For seven of these, the assessments also coincide, as they are classified as high. The remaining risks are assessed as medium or low.

The risks assessed as insignificant in both scientific studies—those of UNWE and the WEF, and not addressed in either the SDDB or the media are the risk of increasing inflation during price conversion and the risk of Bulgaria's technological lag behind other EU countries. While this may be understandable in the context of the WEF's global risk assessment, it is less so with regard to their absence from Bulgaria's strategic development documents.

No explicit references—or only weakly articulated ones—were found in the three strategic documents with regard to certain risks that are widely discussed in the public sphere, such as:

https://doi.org/10.3390/jrfm19030179

- Risks related to cyber threats and breaches of information security, especially in the context of the rapid expansion of artificial intelligence;
- Risk of increased injuries and fatalities on roads as a result of poor road infrastructure;
- Risk of increasing automobile traffic in large cities due to the lack of public parking facilities and inadequate street infrastructure;
- Risk of urban pollution and outbreaks of epidemics resulting from inefficient systems for the collection and treatment of municipal solid waste;
- Risk of the inability to achieve large-scale modernization of agriculture—such as the construction of irrigation infrastructure and the formation of clusters—due to severe land fragmentation and the lack of willingness among agricultural producers to cooperate on the basis of shared interests.

Low or negative "κ" values indicate that risk recognition is not coordinated across institutional domains. In governance terms, this implies information asymmetry, expert-assessed structural risks may not translate into strategic prioritization, and media attention may emphasize episodic shocks over slow-onset vulnerabilities. For financial risk management, weak agreement is consequential because it can delay preventative investment, distort budgeting priorities, and weaken the legitimacy of risk communication. Hence, multi-source triangulation is not only descriptive but governance-relevant.

4. Discussion

In Bulgaria's case, divergence across sources is particularly important because several high-fiscal-pressure risks are slow-onset (demographics, healthcare inefficiency, infrastructure degradation) and may remain underweighted in attention-driven environments. Conversely, episodic events can dominate media narratives and trigger reactive policy cycles. The observed misalignment therefore reflects a real governance challenge: translating expert-identified structural risks into strategic programming and financing decisions before they materialize into budget shocks.

Differences in risk identification across sources reflect their underlying institutional logic. Strategic documents primarily focus on planned priorities and reform targets, and expert assessments emphasize structural and long-term vulnerabilities, while media coverage concentrates on immediate events and public sentiment. These differences help explain why financially relevant risks receive uneven attention across sources.

At the global level, in addition to the WEF reports on global risks facing the world, there are many other studies addressing global or regional risks affecting large regions or groups of countries. For example, Sadat Shuaibu examines the relationship between political and economic risk in four Balkan countries—Greece, Albania, Bulgaria, and Romania (Shuaibu, 2020). Authors from Spain and Lithuania analyze the risks of climate change for Europe, emphasizing the consequences for EU Member States, including political implications (Manuel Echavarren et al., 2019). Four Israeli authors explore perceptions of risk related to natural and anthropogenic disasters across different countries and regions (Bodas et al., 2022).

Other institutions and individual researchers focus their analyses on national risks specific to a given country. For instance, the United Kingdom regularly conducts studies on risk perception, resilience, and preparedness. The most recent survey, conducted between 11 March and 8 April 2025, aimed to understand public perceptions of different types of emergencies and the steps people have taken to prepare for them. The study was funded by the Cabinet Office and the Department for Environment, Food and Rural Affairs (Defra) (UK Cabinet Office, 2025). In this survey, risks are assessed solely in terms of their likelihood of occurrence.

https://doi.org/10.3390/jrfm19030179

Since 2008, the United Kingdom has maintained a National Risk Register, which contains the government's assessment of the most serious risks facing the country (HM Government, 2025). The register includes information on 89 risks, assessed by probability and impact, grouped into the following nine risk themes:

- Terrorism
- Cybersecurity
- State threats
- Geographic and diplomatic risks
- Accidents and systemic failures
- Natural and environmental hazards
- Human, animal, and plant health
- Societal threats
- Conflict and instability

In the United States, the FEMA National Risk Index for Natural Hazards is calculated on the basis of a quantitative assessment of 18 types of natural hazards. The index combines measures of probability, exposure, vulnerability, and resilience, and is calculated at both state and county levels (FEMA, 2025).

Within its annual global business risk surveys, Allianz Global Corporate & Specialty (AGCS) has included studies on Bulgaria since 2020. These analyses, however, focus exclusively on risks that may deteriorate the business environment (Allianz, 2023).

All of this underlines the need to fill the gap created by the lack of dedicated national-level studies focusing on risks to Bulgaria's development—including external, internal, economic, social, environmental, political, and other risks—such as the study conducted by UNWE. This need is further justified by the fact that although Bulgaria's strategic development documents contain analyses describing potential risks, they are developed for relatively long-term horizons, during which significant changes may occur, giving rise to new or different risks. National media do discuss various risks, but primarily in an informative rather than in-depth analytical manner, which does not enable timely policy responses and is not sufficiently representative.

5. Conclusions

For risk management to be effective, Bulgaria must continuously analyze and assess the potential risks to its development. The dynamic international environment, internal political instability, lagging performance in certain sectors, and the increasing frequency of natural disasters require that national-level risk assessments be conducted at least once a year. Based on their results, national strategic documents should be updated annually. Effective organization of risk management at the national level also requires that it be regulated through a dedicated national legal or regulatory framework.

State institutions must recognize that addressing risks should be primarily preventive and that the root cause of most risks lies in the human factor. It is necessary to seek personal accountability from authorized officials in cases where risk situations arise that were not anticipated in annual risk assessments, as well as in cases where previously identified risks are allowed to recur.

The emerging field for future research on national risks should not be limited to their identification and assessment alone, but should be further deepened by examining what measures responsible institutions have taken to prevent identified risks or to mitigate their negative impact, whether such risks recur periodically, and what the actual effects of the measures undertaken have been.

An operational implication of these findings is that Bulgaria should institutionalize a regular national risk prioritization mechanism by maintaining an annual risk register

https://doi.org/10.3390/jrfm19030179

linked to the budget cycle. Major updates of the Strategic Documents for the Development of Bulgaria could include a brief "risk alignment" annex comparing strategic priorities with expert assessments and media-based early signals to make blind spots explicit. Such alignment should be supported by inter-institutional coordination (e.g., the Ministry of Finance and sector ministries), while media/risk-signal monitoring is used as an early-warning complement rather than a substitute for expert evaluation.

From a policy perspective, risks that appear consistently across all sources—such as demographic decline, healthcare system inefficiencies, cybersecurity threats, climate-related risks, and infrastructure degradation—require urgent and coordinated action. At the same time, systematically underestimated risks signal blind spots in fiscal and investment planning. Continuous, multi-source national risk monitoring is therefore essential for effective financial risk management and long-term economic resilience.

Author Contributions: B.B. and Y.H. jointly contributed to the conception, research, and writing of this article. Conceptualization, B.B. and Y.H.; methodology, B.B.; software, B.B. and Y.H.; validation, B.B. and Y.H.; formal analysis, B.B. and Y.H.; investigation, B.B. and Y.H.; resources, B.B. and Y.H.; data curation, B.B. and Y.H.; writing—original draft preparation, B.B. and Y.H.; writing—review and editing, B.B. and Y.H.; visualization, B.B. and Y.H.; supervision, B.B. and Y.H.; project administration, Y.H.; funding acquisition, B.B. and Y.H. All authors have read and agreed to the published version of the manuscript.

Funding: The article was prepared and funded under the Project NID-NI-9-2025 "The Ten Most Important Risks to Bulgaria's Development—Analysis, Assessment, Prevention".

Institutional Review Board Statement: Ethical review and approval were waived due to the use of an anonymous, voluntary questionnaire involving minimal risk and no identifiable personal data. All participants provided informed consent and were adults.

Informed Consent Statement: Informed consent was obtained from all subjects involved in the study.

Data Availability Statement: https://docs.google.com/forms/d/1dVDdEruz262o-Sfa7TlWH-uQNt9DzYPBSkIW2wLiaiI/edit#responses (accessed on 7 December 2025).

Conflicts of Interest: The authors declare no conflicts of interest. The funders had no role in the design of the study; in the collection, analyses, or interpretation of data; in the writing of the manuscript; or in the decision to publish the results.

Abbreviations

UNWE	University of National and World Economy
COSO	Committee of Sponsoring Organizations
ENISA	European Union Agency for Network and Information Security
GRPS	Global Risks Perception Survey
WEF	World Economic Forum
SDDB	Strategic documents for the development of Bulgaria

References

Allianz. (2023, January 17). *Allianz risk barometer 2023*. Allianz Bulgaria. Available online: https://www.allianz.bg/bg_BG/individuals/press-center/press-release/Allianz-Risk-Barometer-2023.html (accessed on 1 December 2025).

Bodas, M., Peleg, K., Stolero, N., & Adini, B. (2022). Risk perception of natural and human-made disasters—A cross-regional comparison. *Frontiers in Public Health, 10*, 825985. [CrossRef] [PubMed]

COSO by Deloitte & Touche LLP. (2012). *Risk assessment in practice*. COSO.

Council of Ministers. (2025a, October 22). *National development programme "Bulgaria 2030"*. Public Consultation Portal. Available online: https://www.strategy.bg/strategicdocuments/View.aspx?lang=bg-BG&Id=1330 (accessed on 1 December 2025).

Council of Ministers. (2025b, October 22). *National recovery and resilience plan*. Council of Ministers of the Republic of Bulgaria. Available online: https://nextgeneration.bg/14 (accessed on 10 December 2025).

https://doi.org/10.3390/jrfm19030179

ENISA. (2006). *Risk management: Implementation principles and inventories for risk management/risk assessment methods and tools*. European Union Agency for Network and Information Security. Available online: https://www.enisa.europa.eu/sites/default/files/publications/D1_Inventory_of_Methods_Risk_Management_Final.pdf (accessed on 12 November 2025).

European Commission. (2025, October 22). *Partnership agreement 2021–2027 approved by the European Commission*. Unified Information Portal of the European Structural and Investment Funds. Available online: https://www.eufunds.bg/bg/node/10509 (accessed on 14 October 2025).

FEMA. (2025, May 7). *National risk index for natural hazards*. Federal Emergency Management Agency. Available online: https://www.fema.gov/flood-maps/products-tools/national-risk-index (accessed on 14 October 2025).

Galeazzi, A. (2025, September 25). *Revealing the secret power: How algorithms can influence content visibility on Twitter/X*. Available online: https://www.semanticscholar.org/paper/Revealing-The-Secret-Power%3A-How-Algorithms-Can-on-Conti-Cristofaro/b9b3cdd7d78549c9339907889b812ba7d767949b (accessed on 25 January 2026). [CrossRef]

HM Government. (2025, January 15). *National risk register*. GOV.UK. Available online: https://assets.publishing.service.gov.uk/media/67b5f85732b2aab18314bbe4/National_Risk_Register_2025.pdf (accessed on 25 September 2025).

ISO. (2024, October 13). *Information security management systems—Requirements* (ISO/IEC 27001:2022). Euro Standard Certification. 3rd Edition. Available online: https://escert.com/standarti/iso-27001/ (accessed on 24 September 2025).

Manuel Echavarren, M., Balžekienė, A., & Telešienė, A. (2019). Multilevel analysis of climate change risk perception in Europe: Natural hazards, political contexts, and mediating individual effects. *Safety Science*, *120*, 813–823. [CrossRef]

Shuaibu, S. (2020). Investigating the nexus between political risk and economic risk: A wavelet coherence analysis for Greece, Albania, Bulgaria, and Romania. *Economic Computation and Economic Cybernetics Studies and Research*, *54*(4), 283–299.

UK Cabinet Office. (2025, July 23). *UK public survey of risk perception, resilience and preparedness 2025: Headline findings*. GOV.UK. Available online: https://www.gov.uk/government/statistics/uk-public-survey-of-risk-perception-resilience-and-preparedness-2025 (accessed on 7 August 2025).

World Economic Forum. (2025). *The global risks report 2025* (20th ed.). World Economic Forum. Available online: https://reports.weforum.org/docs/WEF_Global_Risks_Report_2025.pdf (accessed on 5 February 2025).

https://doi.org/10.3390/jrfm19030179

Journal of
Risk and Financial Management

MDPI

Article

Causality Between the Tax Burden of Direct Taxes and Economic Growth in European Union Countries with Proportional Taxation

Angel Angelov [1,*] and Velichka Nikolova [2]

[1] Department of Finance, University of National and World Economy, 1700 Sofia, Bulgaria
[2] Department of Economics, University of National and World Economy, 1700 Sofia, Bulgaria; vnikolova@unwe.bg
* Correspondence: angelov@unwe.bg

Abstract

The present study examines the relationship between economic growth and the tax burden that is formed as a result of income taxes. The main goal is to verify whether there is a link between these research variables in the long run and if this is confirmed, to analyze the manner in which these processes interact. The research applies a range of econometric techniques, including stationary tests, pairwise Granger causality test, Johansen cointegration test, impulse functions, and variance decompositions in order to investigate causality in the short- and long-term. The study is based on 49 observations and covers four European Union (EU) member states (Bulgaria, Hungary, Romania, and Estonia), which continue to impose a proportional (flat) tax on personal and corporate income. The analysis relies on quarterly data for the period 2013Q1–2025Q1. The results obtained are quite heterogeneous, which can be explained by the significant differences in the tax policy pursued, as well as by a number of other features determining the growth of national economies.

Keywords: direct tax; economic growth; causality; Granger; Johansen

1. Introduction

In the scientific literature, it is a common practice to analyze the relationship between taxation and economic development, including the achievement of economic growth, as a subject of research. A number of authors over the past two centuries have argued that taxes have specific effects on the ability to achieve higher growth, or to attain any growth at all. The topic is extremely relevant today. The analysis often focuses on the reverse effect, in particular—to examine the extent to which economic development and achieved economic growth can contribute to increasing tax efficiency, as well as to providing additional revenue from taxes that is applicable in national legislation. This is of fundamental importance, especially in recent years after the emergence of COVID-19, and above all in the search for mechanisms to increase fiscal sustainability (Cornevin et al., 2024). Undoubtedly, a wide range of research on these topics can be outlined, in both contemporary and earlier studies. Nevertheless, it is important to start from the beginning, to establish whether there is any connection and causality between these processes, and only then can real effects, their strength, and direction of action be identified.

The majority of contemporary research investigates the interaction of taxes and growth in a broader context. These studies usually take into account the total tax burden and analyze its effects on economic growth. The number of articles that emphasize the tax burden of individual components of the tax system is quite limited.

To summarize the above, the present study aims specifically to shift the main focus of interaction. The object of this research is, on the one hand, the tax burden generated by income taxes, and on the other hand, the growth of national economies. The subject of the study is an examination of the relationship and causality between the burden of income taxes and economic growth. The main purpose is to establish whether such a link exists between these individual components, including in the long- and short-term, and if this is confirmed, to be able to trace its direction, strength of impact, and expected effects. The scope of the study includes EU member states that apply proportional income taxation. The key reasons for this choice are related to determining the accuracy of the widespread assumption that proportional income taxation with a lower marginal tax rate can be beneficial, and that it is a tool through which the state can contribute to achieving not only fiscal, but also a number of other macroeconomic goals, such as the growth of its national economy (Cassou & Lansing, 1996; González-Torrabadella & Pijoan-Mas, 2006; Hlavac, 2008; Majcen et al., 2009; Adhikari & Alm, 2013; Vasilev, 2015, etc.). The main hypothesis underlying this study is that the tax burden arising from income taxation can serve as a significant tool to influence the opportunities for stimulating economic growth, but at the same time, the reverse effect is also possible.

The structure of the present study is as follows: Section 2 presents a literature review focused on an examination of the relationship between direct taxes and economic growth; Section 3 provides information on the main countries included in the analysis, the historical aspects of the reform of their income tax systems, and their transition to proportional income taxation; Section 4 introduces the methodological framework of the current research; Section 5 contains the results of the applied methods in assessing the link between the variables under investigation; Section 6 presents a discussion of the results, including the relationship between the findings obtained in the present study and the connections and dependencies established by previous authors; Section 7 is a conclusion.

2. Literature Review

A comprehensive analysis of the theoretical and empirical literature shows that it is difficult to establish a generally accepted opinion on the existence of a relationship between personal and corporate income taxes and the growth of national economies. Previous research on these topics can be distinguished by the following more specific aspects:

- The methodology applied—One group of studies uses a single method of assessment, while other papers conduct tests adopting multiple approaches, sometimes forming different conclusions within the same study. It is worth noting that the majority of the research under consideration evaluates the existence of a linear relationship between income taxes and economic growth, but at the same time, there are studies in which the presence of nonlinearity between the variables is also the subject of analysis. Occasionally, the assessment of the existence of a relationship between taxes and growth is complemented by an examination of the effect of one variable on the other, and conversely.
- The time period covered by the study—Some studies focus only on establishing the relationship in the short-term, in others, the analysis is on the long-term dependence, and in a third group, the evaluation is in both the short- and long-term.
- The territorial scope of the study—Most research covers the examination of the association between variables in the context of a single economy (national), but nevertheless, there are also articles that encompass a group of countries (e.g., Organisation for Economic Co-operation and Development (OECD) countries, European Union (EU), Central and Eastern Europe (CEE), etc.).

- The data frequency—Possible approaches in this regard are the use of annual and quarterly data, where it is common practice to base the analysis on long time series exceeding 40 observations.
- Variables under analysis—Appropriate options from this perspective are, on the one hand, to place emphasis only on income taxes and growth, and on the other hand, to determine the relationship between them in light of a broader scope of analysis, such as considering the entire tax structure, assessing the effects of all direct taxes (not only income taxes), including other non-tax (macroeconomic) components, etc. Another significant feature is that there are differences in the type of factors used, including whether real or nominal variables are considered and whether the indicators are in the form of coefficients or ratios.

In the context of the first specific aspect mentioned above, in particular the methodology used, testing of the relationship between taxes and economic growth is usually carried out through the Søren Johansen (1991) test in the long run. In parallel, the search for causality most often relies on the application of Clive Granger's (1969) test. Helhel and Demir (2012), for example, established, through the Johansen test, a long-term relationship between the tax burden of direct taxes and economic growth in Turkey for the period of 1975–2011. Furthermore, the authors applied the Granger test in order to determine whether there was a causal link between direct taxes and growth. The result of the Granger test did not confirm the existence of such a causal relationship, either between taxes and growth or vice versa. The established long-term dependence of the Turkish economy allows for an additional vector error correction model, combined with impulse response functions and variance decomposition to identify the impact of direct taxes on growth. As a result, the outcomes showed that a possible increase in direct taxes can provoke a decline in GDP in the short-term, followed by a partial recovery, but the effect nevertheless remains negative. Mucuk and Alptekin (2008) carried out an earlier study on this topic, again using the Johansen and Granger test in the context of the Turkish economy. The analyzed period was similar (1975–2006), and they once again confirmed a long-run relationship between direct taxes (% of GDP) and growth. Unlike the study by Helhel and Demir (2012), Mucuk and Alptekin (2008) succeeded in establishing a unidirectional causal link from direct taxes to growth through the Granger test. Moreover, the impact of direct taxes on growth was further examined and the results suggested that direct taxes had a negative influence on the development of the Turkish economy within the research period. Shanmugam and Arunima (2021) also determined, through the Johansen test, a long-run relationship between direct taxes and growth in Puducherry (India) for the period of 2007–2019, but when applying the Granger test, there was, again, no evidence of a causal link between the variables.

Tanchev (2021) also affirmed through the Johansen test that a long-run relationship between personal income tax and economic growth existed in Bulgaria for the period of 1999 Q1–2020 Q1. A characteristic feature of this research is that within the analyzed period, a change occurred in the type of income tax applied to individuals in Bulgaria, as until the end of 2007, the tax was progressive, and from the beginning of 2008 it was proportional. Regardless of the tax reform carried out in the country, a long-term link between PIT and economic growth was confirmed during the two separate sub-periods, and by using VECM it was proven that the impact of the tax on growth in the long run was negative, while in the short run no influence was found, as well as that "a progressive tax is more compatible with economic growth than a proportional tax".

A study by Arikan and Yalcin (2013), based on quarterly data for the period of 2004 Q1–2012 Q1 for the Turkish economy, also found a long-term association between direct taxes and economic growth. In particular, this was valid for personal income tax and real

GDP, but it was not applicable to corporate income tax and real GDP. Similarly to the studies discussed above, there was no evidence of the existence of a causal link from direct taxes to economic growth, but on the other hand, there was a reverse Granger causality—from economic growth to direct taxes. It is worth noting that tests specifically for income taxes showed the reverse causality, specifically, from personal income tax to real GDP, while there was no such relationship in the opposite direction. Kimani (2021), applying the Granger test to Kenya for the period of 1989–2019, also reached a similar result for the causality between income taxes (including both the tax withheld from personal income—pay as you earn (PAYE)—and the tax withheld from corporate income (CIT)) and economic growth.

In the context of analyzing the link between tax structure and economic growth, Stoilova (2023) implemented the Granger causality test for twelve countries from Central and Eastern Europe (Bulgaria, Croatia, Czech Republic, Estonia, Hungary, Latvia, Lithuania, Poland, Romania, Slovakia, and Slovenia) and also found no association between personal income tax (% of GDP) and real economic growth, nor between corporate income tax (% of GDP) and real economic growth. In another study, Stoilova (2024) tested this causality for all EU member states and again the results showed that no similar connection could be established between these two income taxes and the growth of national economies. In both studies, the author developed and presented findings from regression models, which demonstrated that there was a positive (but not strong) correlation between direct and corporate tax revenues, on the one hand, and economic growth, on the other. Tiwari (2012) also found a lack of causality between the tax burden of the two income taxes and growth in the US economy over the period of 1947 Q1–2009 Q3. Unlike most studies that seek causality through the classic Granger test, Tiwari (2012) adopted the approach of Breitung and Candelon (2006), which allowed that study to not only assess the presence of a causal relationship between the variables under study, but also to analyze this effect within the business cycle and, in particular, in the short-term (high frequencies), medium-term (medium frequencies), or long-term (low frequencies) period.

Eren et al. (2018) and Songur and Yüksel (2018) also applied the frequency domain causality test of Breitung and Candelon (2006) to the tax system of the Turkish economy. Eren et al. (2018) established only unidirectional causality from direct taxes to the country's potential for economic development. In contrast, the causality identified by Songur & Yüksel was bidirectional, both in the short- and long-term, and furthermore, a bidirectional causality between GDP and personal income tax revenues was also found. Although part of Songur & Yüksel's analysis also included an examination of the link between corporate income tax and growth, the Breitung and Candelon (2006) test was not applied, as the lack of a long-run association between the variables was previously established through the Johansen test. It is noteworthy that Songur and Yüksel (2018) used a wide range of methods to analyze causality and long-term dependencies. For example, the researchers applied not only the test by Breitung and Candelon (2006) but also the classical Granger test, which demonstrated that GDP influenced direct taxes and personal income tax, and that direct taxes affected economic growth, but at the same time they rejected the causality from direct and corporate income tax to growth, as well as from growth to corporate income tax. Another important point in the study is the use of the test of Toda and Yamamoto (1995), which is an extension of the classical Granger test but also an econometric procedure that allows the robust analysis of causal relationships in non-stationary data (unlike the Granger causality test and the frequency domain causality test by Breitung and Candelon (2006)) and cointegrated series without initial differentiation. The results of both tests are similar, with the difference that the Toda–Yamamoto test confirms a causal link from personal income tax to Turkey's economic growth in the period of 1980–2015. Similar findings also appear in Terzi and Yurtkuran (2016), who use both the Toda–Yamamoto test and the Unrestricted Vector Autoregression (U-VAR) model (Sims, 1980), characterized by the fact that each variable functions as endogenous and depends on its own lags and the lags of the other variable. The authors establish a bidirectional causal relationship between the direct taxes applicable in Turkey and the growth of the national economy, determining that direct taxes negatively affect the prospects for national economic expansion, while growth has a rather positive effect on the revenues generated from direct taxes. A more recent study (Karabacak & Meçik, 2022) of the causality between direct taxes (% of total tax revenues) and GDP per capita as a measure of growth in Turkey, again based on the Toda–Yamamoto test, found no evidence of such a dependency in either direction. A further in-depth study, which also relied on a causality test between income taxes and economic growth using the Toda–Yamamoto model, was created by Saafi et al. (2017). The assessment covered 23 member countries of the Organization for economic cooperation and development, with a focus on the possibility of personal income tax and corporate tax having an impact on macroeconomic processes in the countries, as well as the growth of the economies as a factor that influences the level of revenue collected from the analyzed taxes. The results showed that only 3 out of 22 countries (no data available for Portugal) demonstrated a unidirectional causality established from personal income tax to GDP (Luxembourg, The Netherlands, and Ireland), and in 5 countries there was a unidirectional causality from GDP to personal income tax (Austria, Germany, Ireland, Japan, and the USA). A bidirectional causality between GDP and PIT existed only in Turkey. When testing the relationship between corporate income tax and growth, the analysis identified that only 2 out of 22 countries (Sweden and Switzerland) had a unidirectional causality from CIT to GDP, and 9 countries (Australia, Belgium, Canada, Finland, Germany, Ireland, New Zealand, Spain, and the United Kingdom) had a unidirectional causality from GDP to CIT. Bidirectional causality between corporate tax revenues and growth appeared in only five of the analyzed countries (The Netherlands, Denmark, Finland, Greece, and New Zealand).

Maganya (2020) used the autoregressive distributed lag (ARDL) model to examine the short- and long-run relationships between GDP per capita as a measure of economic growth and a set of variables, including income tax revenue, for the Tanzanian economy. The study period was 1996–2019, and the results showed the existence of a long-term link in which income taxes suppressed growth. Muduli and Manik (2020) reached the same result by applying a panel autoregressive distributed lag (PARDL) model to fourteen Indian states over the period of 1980–2016, testing the long-term effects of state's own direct tax revenue on nominal gross state domestic product and gross state domestic product per capita. It is important to highlight that in the study by Maganya (2020), the results of implementing the Granger test showed that there was no causality between income taxes and economic growth. Using an ARDL model, Nayak et al. (2022) found that there was a long-run relationship between direct taxes and economic growth in India over a period of about 50 years (1970–2021). Unlike the outcomes specific to the Tanzanian economy, the analysis by Nayak et al. (2022) suggested that direct taxes positively affect economic growth in the long run (with ARDL). The results are further supported by an additionally tested multiple regression model, which confirmed the strong positive impact of both personal and corporate income taxes. Once again, the Granger test showed that there was no causality from direct taxes to growth. At a significance level of 10%, it is assumed that there may be a causal relationship from economic growth to direct taxes. In their research, Mashkoor et al. (2010) also applied the ARDL model in order to check whether there was a long-run link between direct taxes (including personal income tax, corporate income tax, property tax, and gift tax) and economic growth in Pakistan during the period of 1973–2008. The analysis verified the existence of such a dependence and confirmed causality from direct taxes (as % of GDP and as a % of total tax revenues) to economic growth.

There are also studies, such as the one by Abdiyeva and Baygonuşova (2016), that have reached divergent conclusions, in particular that no relationship between direct taxes (including personal income tax, corporate income tax, and property tax) and growth emerges in the long run, although the Granger test showed causality. Actually, the results allow researchers to argue that there is such a causal relationship from direct taxes to economic growth. Due to the fact that the Johansen test rejected the existence of cointegration, the authors used a vector autoregression (VAR) model, the results of which suggest that direct taxes have a rather negative effect on the value of GDP, and therefore on growth. Applying the Johansen test to the Romanian economy in the study by Bâzgan (2018) also led to the conclusion that for the period of 2009 Q2–2017 Q2, no long-term relationship can be established between direct taxes (% of GDP) and the growth rate. The subsequently used VAR model shows that the tax structure is decisive, and direct taxes have a considerably weaker effect on growth compared to the effects generated by indirect taxes. Similar findings on the effects of direct and indirect taxes on growth also occurred in Petru-Ovidiu (2015) for the period of 1995–2012 for six Eastern European countries (Bulgaria, Czech Republic, Romania, Hungary, Poland and Slovakia), as well as in Angelov and Nikolova (2021) for the Balkan region (including Bulgaria, Romania, Cyprus, Greece, Croatia, Slovenia, North Macedonia, Turkey, Serbia, Bosnia and Herzegovina, Albania, Kosovo and Montenegro) for the period 2005–2018. Both studies emphasized the significantly more negative effect of direct taxes on growth and more favourable influence characteristic of indirect taxes on growth. Anastassiou and Dritsaki (2005) examined the existence of a relationship between the rate of economic growth and tax revenues in another Balkan country—Greece—for the period of 1965–2002, with the outcomes of the Johansen test indicating that there was a long-run cointegration link between direct taxes and economic growth, although the integration at a later stage of the vector error correction model (VECM) challenged the stability of this long-run relationship. Based on the Granger test, the causality was unidirectional—from direct taxes to the growth rate of the Greek economy. Odum et al. (2018), also using the Granger and Johansen tests (combined with VECM), supported the presence of a long-run direct relationship and causality between direct taxes and growth in Nigeria for the period of 2007–2016, but it is essential to highlight that while a unidirectional causality was observed in Greece, in Nigeria there was a bidirectional association between tax revenues and GDP. Yildiz and Sandalci (2019) further concluded that there was a bidirectional causality between direct taxes (per capita) for 81 provinces in Turkey as a result of applying the Granger's (1969) test and Dumitrescu and Hurlin (2012) test.

Compared to the studies discussed above, which focus on establishing cointegration and linear relationships, the specific scientific literature also includes articles whose object of analysis is the investigation of nonlinear causality between taxes and economic growth. Following this, Karagianni et al. (2012) aimed to determine to what extent the tax burden of certain type of taxes in the United States, such as personal and corporate income taxes, can contribute to achieving a higher GDP per capita in the period of 1948 Q1–2008 Q4. For this purpose, the authors applied two causality tests—the modified Baek and Brock nonlinear causality test proposed by Hiemstra and Jones (1994) and the nonparametric test for Granger non-causality by Diks and Panchenko (2006)—both of which concluded that there was a nonlinear causal relationship between the tax burden of corporate income tax and GDP per capita. Simultaneously, the modified Baek and Brock nonlinear causality test further confirmed such a causality in terms of the tax burden of personal income tax on growth, while the Diks & Panchenko test did not establish this kind of dependency. Within a similar timeframe (1947 Q1–2009 Q3) Tiwari and Mutascu (2014) also managed to prove nonlinear causality from personal income tax to economic growth in the US, and meanwhile, based on classical linear causality tests, they concluded that such causality does not exist, either between personal income tax and growth or between corporate income tax and growth.

3. Data

The current study examines the relationship between economic growth and tax burden through two variables.

The representation of tax burden uses the taxes on the incomes of individuals, households, corporations, and NPIs—group D.51 taxes on income in accordance with the methodology of Eurostat (2013). Income taxes constitute the largest relative share of all direct taxes, and it is entirely reasonable to use them as a basis for analyzing interrelationships with other macroeconomic variables. This paper measures the tax burden (variable TAX) as the ratio of revenue collected from income taxes to GDP.

Due to the fact that the object of the study is to examine the existence of a relationship between the tax burden of direct taxes and economic growth in countries with proportional income taxation in the EU, it is of particular importance to analyze the tax systems in the EU and to outline the countries that apply proportional income taxation. The choice of such a type of taxation, which came into effect in the mid-1990s in most EU member states (positioned in Central and Eastern Europe), is usually justified by the pursuit of simplification of the tax system and increasing administrative efficiency, attempts to reduce the shadow economy and stimulate investment activity, including with a focus on attracting foreign investors, carrying out economic and political reforms, and other relevant aspects.

Estonia is the first EU member state to implement a proportional tax on personal and corporate income. This occurred in 1994, or ten years before the country's accession to the EU. The previously applied progressive tax with a maximum marginal rate of 33% for personal income and 35% for corporate income was replaced with a flat marginal tax rate of 26%. After Estonia's accession to the European Union (in 2004), the marginal income tax rate began to gradually decrease in 2005, reaching 20% by 2015. Since the beginning of 2025, a decision has been made by the legislative body of Estonia to increase the rate for both income taxes to 22% and as of 2026 the marginal tax rate will attain 24%.

Romania, following the example of Estonia, modified the way it taxed the income of individuals and corporations before joining the EU. The country became a member of the EU in 2007, and the changes date back to 2005, when Romania introduced a flat personal and corporate income tax at a rate of 16%. Previously, personal income had been subject to progressive taxation, with a maximum marginal tax rate of 40%, and corporate income had been subject to 25%. Following the reforms of the mid-1900s, corporate tax in Romania remains at 16% to this day, while since 2018, personal income tax has been reduced to 10%.

The third country that still applies proportional taxation today is Bulgaria. Since joining the EU in 2007, the country has applied a flat rate to the income of corporate entities. A year later, in 2008, the tax system adopted proportional personal income tax. The rate for both taxes is 10%. Bulgaria, along with Romania, are the two countries with the lowest marginal tax rate of countries using proportional income tax.

The last among the four EU member states, Hungary, introduced a proportional personal income tax in 2011, seven years after the country became an EU member. The tax rate is 16%, which is a significantly lower tax burden compared to the maximum marginal tax rate in the late 1980s, when it reached 60%. In pursuit of a mechanism to strengthen the competitiveness of the Hungarian tax system (Ministry for National Economy, 2015), in 2016, the personal income tax was reduced to 15%, and since 2017 Hungary has applied the lowest corporate income tax rate in the entire EU—9%. The Hungarian government implemented a flat marginal corporate tax rate until 2010, which declined from 40 to 19% between 1990 and 2010. During the period from mid-2010 to the end of 2012, the corporate tax was progressive. It is worth noting that Hungarian tax legislation also provides for the application of a local business tax of up to 2%, which is determined by local authorities and deducted from corporate income tax, bringing the effective tax burden to around 10.82% (European Commission, 2025).

Therefore, the present research focuses on an analysis of the relationship between income taxes and economic growth in the context of the economies of Romania, Bulgaria, Hungary, and Estonia. All four countries belong to the Eastern Europe region. Most Eastern European countries share the characteristic of a lower fiscal significance of income taxes compared to consumption taxes. For the period since 2013, on an annual basis, income taxes in Estonia have formed between 20 and 25% of the revenue collected in the consolidated budget, and after the recovery from the global economic crisis, a gradual (albeit imperceptible) increase in their relative share has been observed. For the remaining three countries—Bulgaria, Romania, and Hungary—the share of income tax is around, and no more than, 20%. Comparatively, the average value of this indicator for the EU-27 is around 30%, and in some countries, such as Denmark, it exceeds 60–65%. In terms of the ratio of accumulated income tax revenue to GDP, the four analyzed countries rank among the group of member states with the lowest indicator values. In Estonia, income taxes account for approximately 7.7% of GDP (according to the latest available annual data for 2024 it is 9%), in Hungary, this is about 6.5%, in Bulgaria, 5.4% and in Romania, 5.2% (Table 1).

Table 1. Descriptive statistics.

	Bulgaria		Estonia		Hungary		Romania	
	RGDP	TAX	RGDP	TAX	RGDP	TAX	RGDP	TAX
Mean	2331.715	0.056286	5099.163	0.076878	3536.748	0.06649	2770.391	0.053714
Median	2286.302	0.054	5056.159	0.077	3530.617	0.065	2684.227	0.052
Maximum	3248.881	0.109	6022.098	0.114	4282.973	0.083	3947.392	0.081
Minimum	1545.715	0.038	4189.902	0.054	2571.345	0.051	1646.173	0.029
Std. Dev.	419.6829	0.015215	443.7391	0.0121	461.2861	0.006932	594.5673	0.010792
Observations	49	49	49	49	49	49	49	49

Table 1 presents the descriptive statistics of the variables used in this study. The graphs and descriptive statistics presented in this section are based on the use of quarterly unadjusted data (without seasonal or calendar adjustments). The analysis covers the period from the beginning of 2013 (2013 Q1) to the beginning of 2025 (2025 Q1), which includes a total of 49 observations. The reason for choosing this period is that since then, proportional income taxes of individuals and legal entities have been applied in the four selected EU member states.

The study relies on income tax revenue data from Eurostat's (2025c) quarterly non-financial accounts for the general government. It should be noted that the current research uses data that refer to the general government sector. Figure 1 presents the trend in the tax burden by quarter within the period under review.

The available data clearly highlight the aforementioned more significant (increasing) burden that income taxes have in Estonia compared to the other three countries. A possible explanation lies in the income tax reforms launched in recent years, especially with the rise in the marginal tax rates of the main income tax. Another important feature in the presented dynamics of this indicator is the serious fluctuation that has been observed in Bulgaria within the recent two to three budget years, and particularly during the last quarters of each of these years. Romania shows similar trends, but with considerably smaller deviations with respect to the data for Bulgaria.

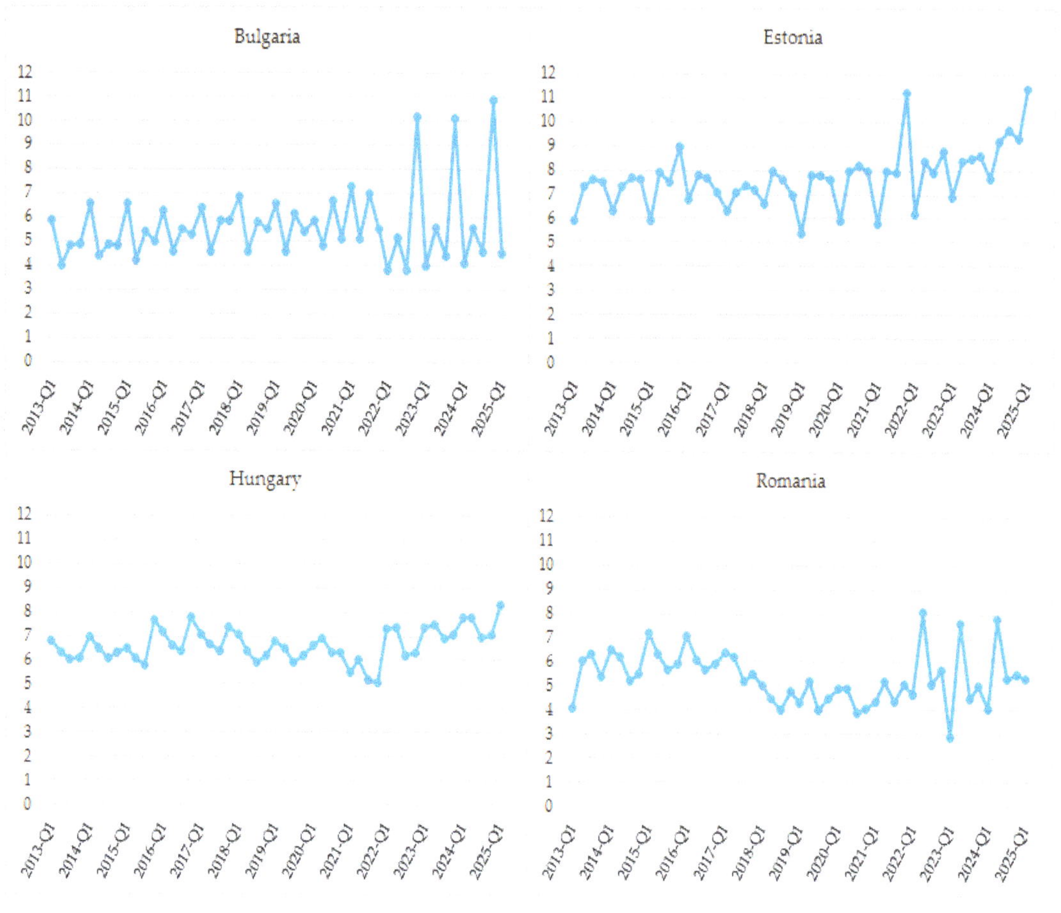

Figure 1. Tax burden of income taxes (%), quarterly data for 2013 Q1 to 2025 Q1.

The analysis uses real gross domestic product per capita (RGDP), which represents economic growth and operates as a second explanatory variable. For the calculation of this indicator, Eurostat data on real GDP and also its data on population in the analyzed countries are applied (Eurostat, 2025a, 2025b). The inclusion of the GDP per capita indicator is persistently observed in econometric research and aims to emphasize the relationship between economic development and tax burden, eliminating the effect of differences in population size and allowing for a more comparable measurement of welfare and productivity across different economies or time periods (Tosun & Abizadeh, 2005; Morley & Abdullah, 2010; Arnold et al., 2011; Karagianni et al., 2012; Causa et al., 2014; Tiwari & Mutascu, 2014; Saafi et al., 2017; Yildiz & Sandalci, 2019; Maganya, 2020; Karabacak & Meçik, 2022; etc.).

Figure 2, below, illustrates the dynamics of the real GDP per capita indicator for the four selected countries.

The data presented in Figure 2 indicate that in three of the countries under consideration there is a sustained increase in real GDP per capita for the period from the first quarter of 2013 to the first quarter of 2025. Estonia is the only country where the indicator shows some variability, including a decline since the beginning of 2021. Nevertheless, it is noteworthy that Estonia is distinguished by the highest value of the assessed indicator.

Estonia also demonstrates inconsistent dynamics between quarters over the years, while in other analyzed countries, and especially in Romania, significant fluctuations occur between the first quarter of each year and the subsequent quarters.

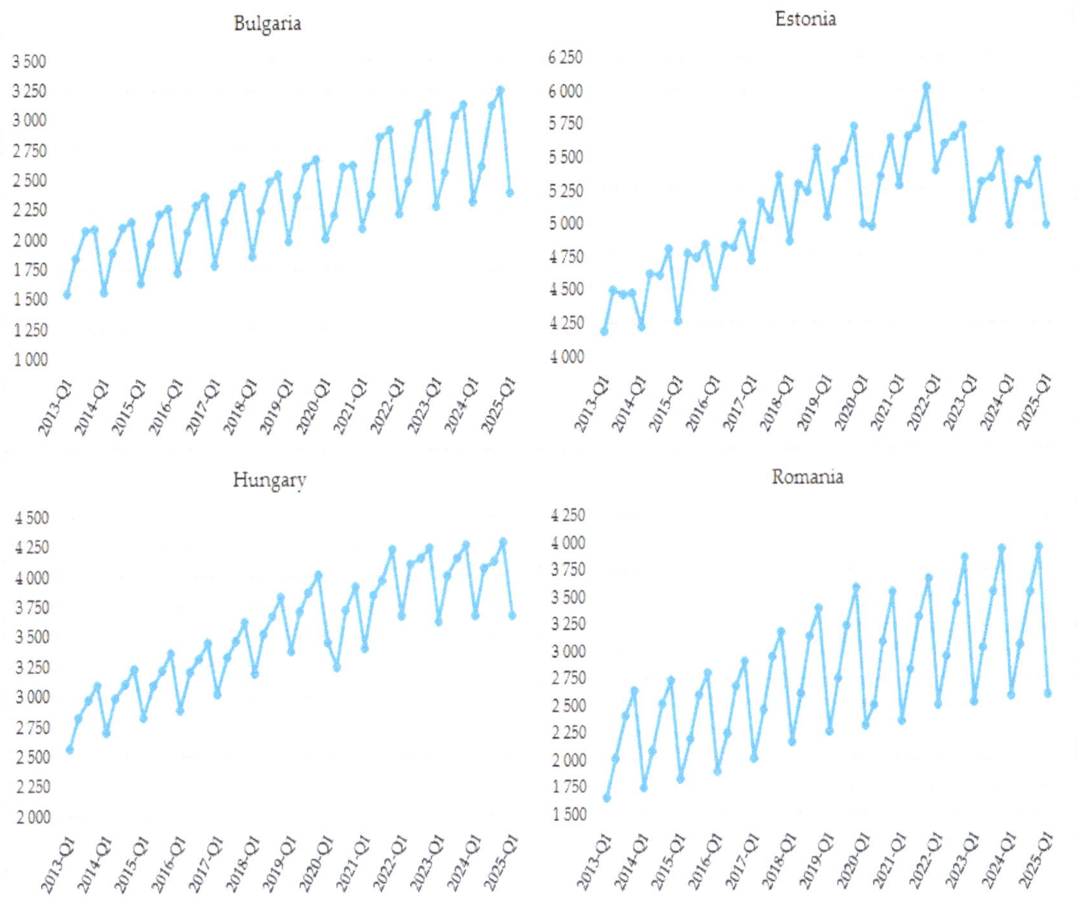

Figure 2. Real GDP per capita (in Euros), quarterly data for 2013Q1 to 2025Q1.

4. Methodology

In order to examine the relationship between economic growth and tax burden, the study consistently applies a set of econometric tests and models widely accepted in the academic literature. In the context of the logical structure of this research, the analysis begins with a seasonal adjustment of the selected variables. This procedure is essential due to the inclusion of quarterly data, which most likely contain seasonal fluctuations, resulting in the inaccurate identification of short-term and long-term relationships. Then, the analysis uses the Census X-13 method. Subsequently, each seasonally adjusted variable is transformed into a logarithm, which aims to improve the precision of the comparative interpretation.

The next step involves conducting stationary tests on the seasonally adjusted and logarithmically transformed variables. The verification is carried out by employing two statistically independent tests, the test of Phillips and Perron (1988) and the Augmented test of Dickey and Fuller (1981), whereas the research implements the information criteria of Akaike and Schwarz separately. The choice of equation specification is consistent with the time dynamics of the variables. The test procedure evaluates the variables subsequently at levels and then at first difference. After conducting stationary tests, if the results indicate that the variables are stationary in first difference and non-stationary in levels, the analysis proceeds with the application of the Johansen test in order to determine whether there is a long-term relationship. Within the framework of the Johansen test, the methodology relies on two statistical procedures—the Trace test (Equation (3)) and Maximum Eigenvalue Test (Equation (6))—and the following hypotheses are defined (Equations (1), (2), (4) and (5)):

Johansen Trace Test

$$\text{Null Hypothesis } (H_0): \text{ There are, at most, } r_0 \text{ cointegrating relations between } LNRGDP_t \text{ and } LNTAX_t, \text{ i.e., } \operatorname{rank}(\Pi) \leq r_0. \quad (1)$$

$$\text{Alternative Hypothesis } (H_1): \text{ There are more than } r_0 \text{ cointegrating relations, i.e., } \operatorname{rank}(\Pi) > r_0. \quad (2)$$

The test statistic is defined as follows:

$$\text{Trace Statistic} = -T \sum_{i=r_0+1}^{n} \ln(1-\hat{\lambda}_i) \quad (3)$$

where T refers to the number of observations, n to the number of variables in Yt (vector of endogenous variables), r_0 to the number of cointegrating relations under null hypothesis H_0, and $\hat{\lambda}_i$ to the estimated i-th eigenvalue of the Π matrix.

For completeness, in the case of a bivariate system (such as between $LNRGDP_t$ and $LNTAX_t$), the cointegration rank can only take values $r_0 = 0$ (no cointegration) or $r_0 = 1$ (one cointegrating vector).

Maximum Eigenvalue Test

$$\text{Null Hypothesis } (H_0): \text{ There are exactly } r_0 \text{ cointegrating relations between } LNRGDP_t \text{ and } LNTAX_t, \text{ i.e., } \operatorname{rank}(\Pi) = r_0. \quad (4)$$

$$\text{Alternative Hypothesis } (H_1): \text{ There is exactly one more cointegrating relation than under } H_0, \text{ i.e., } \operatorname{rank}(\Pi) = r_0 + 1. \quad (5)$$

The test statistic is defined as follows:

$$\text{Max} - \text{Eigen Statistic} = -T \ln(1-\hat{\lambda}_{r0+1}) \quad (6)$$

where T refers to the number of observations, r_0 to the number of cointegrating relations under null hypothesis H_0, and $\hat{\lambda}_{r0+1}$ to the (r_0 + 1)-th largest estimated eigenvalue of the Π matrix.

The Maximum Eigenvalue test examines the null of r_0 cointegrating vectors against the alternative of r_0 + 1, focusing on the largest remaining eigenvalue rather than the sum of all subsequent ones as in the Trace test.

In addition to the analysis, the traditional (classical) Granger causality is applied, which aims to shed light on whether there is a causal relationship between the variables under study, what its direction is, and whether it is possible to make a forecast for the future values of one variable using the temporal dynamics of another (Equations (7) and (8)).

$$LNRGDP_{i,t} = \alpha_{0,i} + \sum_{m=1}^{k} \beta_{i,m} LNRGDP_{i,t-m} + \sum_{r=1}^{z} \gamma_{i,r} LNTAX_{i,t-r} + \varepsilon_{i,t} \quad (7)$$

$$LNTAX_{i,t} = \eta_{0,i} + \sum_{m=1}^{k} \mu_{i,m} LNTAX_{i,t-m} + \sum_{r=1}^{z} \theta_{i,r} LNRGDP_{i,t-r} + \upsilon_{i,t} \quad (8)$$

where α and η refer to intercept terms, i refers to the country (where i = 1, . . ., N); t refers to the time period (where t = 1, . . ., T); r and m refer, respectively, to the lags (where r = 1, . . ., z and m = 1, . . ., k); k and z refer, respectively, to the optimal lag for variables LNRGDP and LNTAX; β refers to the coefficient on lagged growth rates (captures the autoregressive dynamics of economic growth), γ to the coefficient on lagged tax burden (measures the effect of past tax burden on economic growth), μ to the coefficient on lagged tax burden (persistence of tax burden), θ to the coefficient on lagged growth rates (effect of growth on tax burden), and ε and υ are the residual components.

The application of the Granger test involves two hypotheses, as follows (Equations (9)–(12)):

(a) Testing whether tax burden Granger causes economic growth:

$$\text{Null Hypothesis } (H_0): \text{ Tax burden does not Granger cause economic growth} \\ (H_0 : \gamma_{i,1} = \gamma_{i,2} = \cdots = \gamma_{i,Z} = 0) \quad (9)$$

$$\text{Alternative Hypothesis } (H_1): \text{ Tax burden Granger causes economic growth} \\ (H_1 : \exists r \in \{1, \ldots\ldots, z) \text{ such that } \gamma_{i,z} \neq 0) \quad (10)$$

(b) Testing whether economic growth Granger causes tax burden:

$$\text{Null Hypothesis } (H_0): \text{ Economic growth does not Granger cause tax burden} \\ (H_0 : \theta_{i,1} = \theta_{i,2} = \cdots = \theta_{i,Z} = 0) \quad (11)$$

$$\text{Alternative Hypothesis } (H_1): \text{ Economic growth Granger causes tax burden} \\ (H_1 : \exists\, r \in \{1, \ldots\ldots, z)\ such\ that\ \theta_{i,z} \neq 0) \quad (12)$$

Expanding the analytical framework of the study implies the formulation of reliable conclusions from the application of impulse functions and variance decomposition. This is reasonable, considering that it is essential to graphically illustrate how the variables under study respond to shocks in the system and, more specifically, how this affects the temporal dynamics.

From the methodological perspective, the research follows a standard procedure for selecting the optimal number of lags for each of the countries covered by the analysis. The determination of the optimal lag for a specific country is based on the results obtained from the procedure combined with additional considerations in light of the specification of the models, the number of observations, and the reliability of the results. More precisely, the lag order selection criteria (based on a sequential modified Likelihood Ratio test statistic (LR); final prediction error (FPE); Akaike information criterion (AIC); Schwarz information criterion (SC), and Hannan–Quinn information criterion (HQ)) are applied and the lag length identified as optimal by the majority of the criteria is chosen.

5. Results

5.1. Results from Stationarity Tests

The stationarity test of the variables is based on the application of the Augmented test of Dickey and Fuller (1981) and the test of Phillips and Perron (1988). Through the use of two independent tests, the aim is to achieve greater reliability of the analysis. The implementation of stationarity tests follows a sequential procedure, starting with a test at levels and continuing with a test at first differences. Table 2 illustrates the results of testing the LNRGDP and LNTAX variables at levels for all countries included in the analysis.

Table 2. Results from stationarity tests (at levels).

Country	Variable	Prob (Augmented Dickey–Fuller Test) Akaike Info Criterion	Prob (Augmented Dickey–Fuller Test) Schwarz Info Criterion	Prob (Phillips–Perron Test)
Bulgaria	lnrgdp	0.0087	0.1938	0.1104
	lntax	0.2818	0.3697	0.1795
Estonia	lnrgdp	0.9011	0.9011	0.9011
	lntax	0.2323	0.2323	0.1162
Hungary	lnrgdp	0.0781	0.0781	0.0925
	lntax	0.5002	0.5002	0.3856
Romania	lnrgdp	0.4982	0.4982	0.4483
	lntax	0.5233	0.5233	0.3094

The results of the stationarity tests at levels indicate that the variables are not stationary. In general, there is no variable for which, in all the stationarity tests used, the obtained probabilities are less than the 5% significance level. This applies in all cases except for the variable LNRGDP for Bulgaria (based on the Akaike info criterion), but these results are not confirmed in all tests used. In other words, the time series of the variables indicate the presence of unit roots, i.e., there is I(1). As a result, this provides grounds for conducting stationarity tests of the variables at first differences.

Table 3 presents the results of testing the variables LNRGDP and LNTAX at first differences.

Table 3. Results from stationarity tests (at first differences).

Country	Variable	Prob (Augmented Dickey–Fuller Test) Akaike Info Criterion	Prob (Augmented Dickey–Fuller Test) Schwarz Info Criterion	Prob (Phillips–Perron Test)
Bulgaria	Δlnrgdp	0.0066	0.0000	0.0000
	Δlntax	0.0000	0.0000	0.0000
Estonia	Δlnrgdp	0.0000	0.0000	0.0000
	Δlntax	0.0000	0.0000	0.0000
Hungary	Δlnrgdp	0.0000	0.0000	0.0000
	Δlntax	0.0000	0.0000	0.0000
Romania	Δlnrgdp	0.0000	0.0000	0.0000
	Δlntax	0.0000	0.0000	0.0000

The results indicate that there is no variable for which, in all stationarity tests, the obtained probabilities are greater than the 5% significance level. For this reason, the variables included in the study are stationary at first difference.

5.2. Results from Johansen Cointegration Test

After conducting stationarity tests, the results confirm that the variables are non-stationary at levels and, accordingly, stationary at first differences, which provides an adequate reason to proceed to a test for long-run relationships between economic growth and tax burden through the Johansen cointegration test. Table 4 summarizes the results of applying this test for all analyzed countries.

Table 4. Results from Johansen cointegration test.

Hypothesized No. of CE(s)	Trace Statistic	0.05 Critical Value	Prob.	Max-Eigen Statistic	0.05 Critical Value	Prob.
			Bulgaria			
None *	19.96731	12.32090	0.0022	19.88844	11.22480	0.0012
At most 1	0.078874	4.129906	0.8177	0.078874	4.129906	0.8177
			Estonia			
Hypothesized No. of CE(s)	Trace Statistic	0.05 Critical Value	Prob.	Max-Eigen Statistic	0.05 Critical Value	Prob.
None	14.23482	18.39771	0.1736	13.76264	17.14769	0.1456
At most 1	0.472177	3.841466	0.4920	0.472177	3.841466	0.4920
			Hungary			
Hypothesized No. of CE(s)	Trace Statistic	0.05 Critical Value	Prob.	Max-Eigen Statistic	0.05 Critical Value	Prob.
None	16.39372	25.87211	0.4614	11.22167	19.38704	0.4908
At most 1	5.172054	12.51798	0.5719	5.172054	12.51798	0.5719
			Romania			
Hypothesized No. of CE(s)	Trace Statistic	0.05 Critical Value	Prob.	Max-Eigen Statistic	0.05 Critical Value	Prob.
None *	20.62025	18.39771	0.0241	18.80104	17.14769	0.0285
At most 1	1.819212	3.841466	0.1774	1.819212	3.841466	0.1774

* denotes rejection of the null hypothesis at the 0.05 level.

In accordance with the findings from the Johansen test, shown in Table 4, the study demonstrates that for Bulgaria and Romania, there is cointegration between the economic growth and the tax burden, i.e., there is a long-term statistically significant relationship. This is confirmed by the comparison between the values of the trace statistics and the critical value, in a manner similar to that of the Max-Eigen statistics and the critical value, and finally, the estimated p-values, all of which lead to the conclusion that there is one cointegration equation. The results of the Johansen test for Bulgaria and Romania give reason to assert that in the long run, the analyzed variables move together over time, which means that in the long-term, there is a sustainable interdependence. It is therefore reasonable to reject the null hypothesis and accept the alternative, which postulates the existence of a cointegrating relationship. Furthermore, even if it is assumed that serious fluctuations in the dynamics of these variables are possible in the short-term, the outcomes of the cointegration test confirm the understanding that maintaining stability in the long run requires not underestimating the structural features of tax systems and their association with opportunities for development and growth.

In the case of Estonia and Hungary, it is noticeable that the output values for the trace statistics are lower than the critical value, and these conclusions are also valid when comparing Max-Eigen statistics with the critical value. In addition, the p-values are higher than the 5% significance level. This leads to the conclusion that there is no statistically significant long-run relationship between economic growth and the tax burden in Estonia and Hungary. Despite these findings, it is essential to consider the possibility of the existence of a short-term relationship between the analyzed variables.

Outcomes of the current research on the long-run relationship between economic growth and the tax burden of income taxes in the four countries under consideration can also be partially explained by the structure of tax revenues. In the last few years, Romania and Bulgaria have experienced a balance between the burden falling on individuals and corporate entities (with a slightly greater emphasis on the burden on individuals, and even, in 2022, a reverse trend becoming evident), while significant differences in the division of taxpayers are typical for Hungary and Estonia. The Hungarian and Estonian tax systems generate considerably more resources at the expense of individuals (the difference is almost threefold). The reasons for this are mainly due to the lower marginal tax rate for corporate income in Hungary and exemption from tax on retained earnings in Estonia. Such taxation mechanisms aim to stimulate investment activity in the corporate sector, but at the same time do not allow for a direct determination of the relationship between the tax burden and economic growth, especially in the long run.

5.3. Results from Pairwise Granger Causality Tests

Table 5 shows the results of the pairwise Granger causality test. Based on these, it is possible to conclude that there is causality (predictability) between economic growth and the tax burden, which applies only to Bulgaria and Hungary. This is further supported by the acceptance of the alternative hypothesis that there is a Granger causality from economic growth to the tax burden, as evidenced by the computed probability, which is lower than the 5% significance level. These results highlight that past values of economic growth help predict future values of the tax burden. In other words, favourable changes in the economic environment, which lead to strengthened opportunities for the country to achieve high growth rates, can beneficially impact the taxation system and establish prerequisites for implementing an optimal tax structure.

Table 5. Results from pairwise Granger causality tests.

Country	Causal Direction	F-Statistic	Prob.
Bulgaria	ΔLNTAX $\rightarrow$ ΔLNRGDP (H_0: TAX does not Granger Cause RGDP)	0.79087	0.5641
	ΔLNRGDP $\rightarrow$ ΔLNTAX (H_0: RGDP does not Granger Cause TAX)	2.98059	**0.0255**
Estonia	ΔLNTAX $\rightarrow$ ΔLNRGDP (H_0: TAX does not Granger Cause RGDP)	0.72691	0.4895
	ΔLNRGDP $\rightarrow$ ΔLNTAX (H_0: RGDP does not Granger Cause TAX)	0.53165	0.5916
Hungary	ΔLNTAX $\rightarrow$ ΔLNRGDP (H_0: TAX does not Granger Cause RGDP)	0.57322	0.7709
	ΔLNRGDP $\rightarrow$ ΔLNTAX (H_0: RGDP does not Granger Cause TAX)	4.38991	**0.0025**
Romania	ΔLNTAX $\rightarrow$ ΔLNRGDP (H_0: TAX does not Granger Cause RGDP)	1.59654	0.2130
	ΔLNRGDP $\rightarrow$ ΔLNTAX (H_0: RGDP does not Granger Cause TAX)	1.18061	0.2831

The existence of causality from the tax burden to economic growth is rejected for all countries included in the study, and in support of this, the null hypothesis is accepted, stating that past values of the tax burden cannot contribute to predicting future values of economic growth. The obtained probabilities, which are higher than the significance level, support these conclusions. A possible explanation for these causality results in estimating the predictive value of growth may be the sensitivity of the main sources of growth (consumption and investment) to potential changes in income taxation (with the exception of Bulgaria, the other three countries have experienced similar changes, including in the last few years, in the technique of income taxation). It is entirely possible that taxes have effects on both consumption and investment, but over a significantly longer period of time, which would lead to the Granger test demonstrating difficulty in detecting a causal relationship. Another potential contributing factor could be the global instability resulting from the COVID-19 pandemic, as well as the subsequent inflationary shocks caused by the military actions in Ukraine. It is no coincidence that when reviewing the dynamics of the tax burden and growth (in the Data section), significant fluctuations were found over the last few years, which creates additional challenges in the search for clear dependencies and causal relationships between the analyzed processes.

Furthermore, the analysis does not confirm the existence of a bidirectional relationship between the examined variables for any of the countries included in the study. In summary, the results of the pairwise Granger causality test show evidence of a unidirectional causality of economic growth on tax burden, but this is affirmed only for Bulgaria and Hungary.

5.4. Results from Impulse Responses and Variance Decompositions

The subsequent analysis continues with a graphical representation of the impulse functions, combined with a variance decomposition, provided that this is applied to the countries for which a cointegration relationship has been established by the Johansen test (Bulgaria and Romania). The presentation of the impulse functions is preceded by the construction of VECMs for the specified countries with a confirmed cointegrating relationship. The present study gives priority to the graphical representation of the variables' dynamics through impulse functions in order to achieve a better illustration and subsequent analysis of the way in which a given variable responds to a shock in the other variable. To mitigate potential biases from extraordinary macroeconomic disturbances, a dummy variable capturing the crisis period (2020 Q3–2025 Q1) is included in the VECM specification in order to control for unanticipated shocks arising from the joint dynamics of the COVID-19 pandemic, the geopolitical conflict between Russia and Ukraine, and the subsequent inflationary pressure. This adjustment helps isolate the structural effects of crisis-related shocks from the long-run relationship between tax burden and economic growth. Nevertheless, it should be noted that the model does not explicitly account for institutional quality, fiscal governance, or confidence in political institutions, which may still affect both variables and contribute to potential endogeneity.

From a research perspective, it is of interest to trace, on the one hand, how economic growth reacts to a shock in the tax burden and, on the other hand, how the tax burden responds to a shock in economic growth. The impulse functions are constructed based on Cholesky one S.D. innovations, and, more specifically, the shock size is one standard deviation. In the Cholesky decomposition, real economic growth per capita is ordered before the tax burden, assuming that growth does not respond contemporaneously to fiscal changes while taxation may react to current economic developments. This recursive structure ensures an economically consistent orthogonalization of shocks and allows for a causal interpretation of the impulse responses. From a temporal perspective, the impulse functions cover a period of 20 quarters (5 years), which allows for the tracing of both short-term and long-term effects due to one-off shocks in economic growth and tax burden. In addition, when using a longer period of time, it is possible to identify effects that are difficult to detect in the short-term. To assess the statistical reliability of the impulse response functions, a bootstrap procedure with 10,000 replications is applied. Since the distribution of the impulse responses is not analytically known, the bootstrap method provides an empirical approximation by repeatedly resampling the residuals and re-estimating the model. Confidence intervals are constructed using the standard percentile approach, which yields stable and consistent estimates for large samples and in the absence of strong nonlinearities, while avoiding the computational burden associated with bias-corrected or studentized bootstrap variants.

Figure 3 presents the impulse function for the economy of Bulgaria. A tax burden shock of one standard deviation does not lead to a slowdown in the rate of economic growth in the short-term, with the specific characteristic that the effect is statistically significant in the range from the fourth to the ninth quarter. However, as the time horizon increases, this stimulating statistically effect begins to weaken. Based on the results obtained in Figure 3, the analysis leads to the conclusion that, in both the short- and long-term, there is pronounced volatility in the tax burden induced by shocks in economic growth. In the short-term (particularly during the fourth quarter), the tax burden responds negatively to a growth shock, while in the long run, the intensity of this effect decreases; however, wide confidence intervals and a high uncertainty limit firm conclusions.

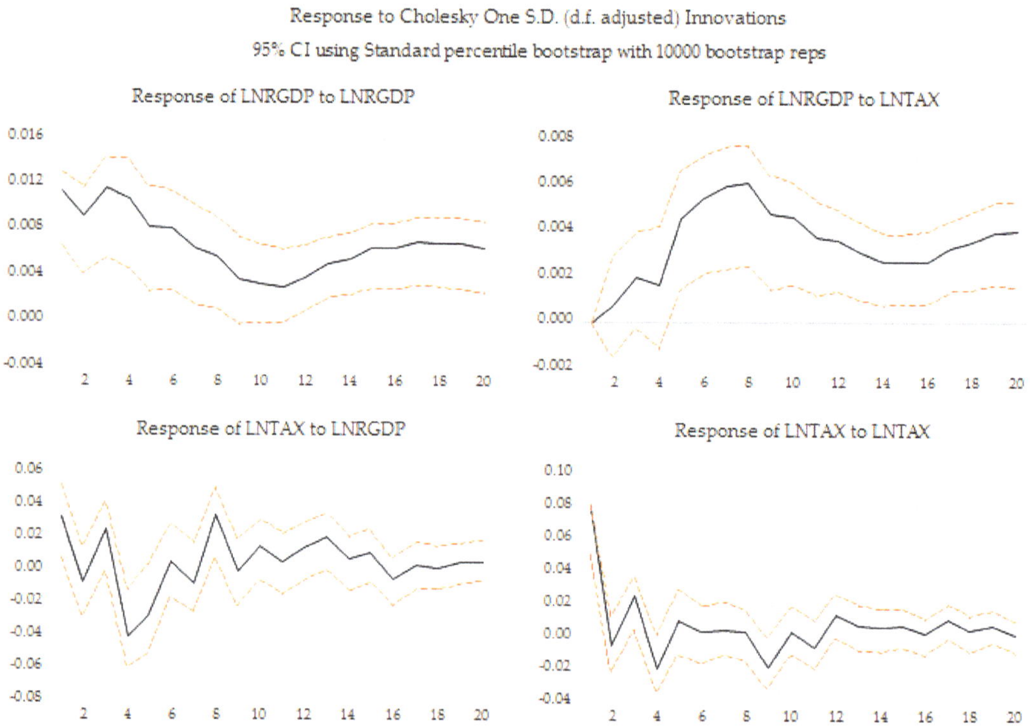

Figure 3. Impulse response of economic growth and tax burden in Bulgaria.

Table 6 outlines the results for Bulgaria from the variance decomposition of economic growth in response to an identified tax burden shock and the variance decomposition of the tax burden after registering an economic growth shock. Assuming a period of 20 quarters, it is possible to trace the effects of variance decomposition, both in the short- and long-term. According to the results of the variance decomposition for Bulgaria, it can be concluded that in the short-term (e.g., the first ten quarters) a significantly larger percentage of the variance in economic growth is due to shocks within the country's economy (approximately 20%), and these findings are not confirmed in the long run, when the variance tends to decrease. This is reasonable, given the possibility of other factors influencing growth, such as determining factors beyond the country's structural components.

The systematized data in Table 6 show that, compared to the short-term, in the long-term, an increasing share of the variance in GDP is explained by shocks in the tax burden. Indicative in this regard is the expanding impact of tax structure, with a comparative increase of nearly 22 p.p. in the significance of tax shocks with regard to economic growth determination. This suggests the strengthening importance of fiscal policy in Bulgaria and its subsequent relationship with effects on the country's economic development.

Table 6. Variance decomposition of economic growth and tax burden in Bulgaria.

Variance Decomposition of ΔLNRGDP				Variance Decomposition of ΔLNTAX			
Period	S. E.	ΔLNRGDP	ΔLNTAX	Period	S. E.	ΔLNRGDP	ΔLNTAX
1	0.011399	100.0000	0.000000	1	0.084959	14.93222	85.06778
2	0.014681	99.74338	0.256616	2	0.085443	15.51095	84.48905
3	0.018874	98.73420	1.265796	3	0.092506	20.63945	79.36055
4	0.021803	98.50613	1.493866	4	0.102843	32.19150	67.80850
5	0.023759	95.07716	4.922838	5	0.107015	36.55259	63.44741
6	0.025691	91.33101	8.668994	6	0.107197	36.66515	63.33485
7	0.027138	87.35994	12.64006	7	0.107578	36.95176	63.04824
8	0.028407	83.76828	16.23172	8	0.112932	42.69784	57.30216
9	0.029036	81.76173	18.23827	9	0.114383	41.62740	58.37260
10	0.029592	79.97759	20.02241	10	0.115389	42.55970	57.44030
11	0.029970	78.93679	21.06321	11	0.115691	42.56979	57.43021
12	0.030428	78.13881	21.86119	12	0.117263	42.78679	57.21321
13	0.030984	77.95309	22.04691	13	0.119248	44.33134	55.66866
14	0.031581	78.05931	21.94069	14	0.119581	44.40085	55.59915
15	0.032328	78.39277	21.60723	15	0.120252	44.69488	55.30512
16	0.033063	78.68933	21.31067	16	0.120390	44.79570	55.20430
17	0.033935	78.82470	21.17530	17	0.120913	44.50591	55.49409
18	0.034804	78.84120	21.15880	18	0.120982	44.46108	55.53892
19	0.035675	78.63640	21.36360	19	0.121279	44.40211	55.59789
20	0.036468	78.35270	21.64730	20	0.121417	44.52233	55.47767

In comparison with the variance in economic growth, the analysis regarding the tax burden is explained to a much greater extent by the impact of shocks on economic growth. While in the short-term (the first four quarters), the variance in the tax burden is to a lesser extent determined by the effects of economic growth shocks, in the long-term, this influence rises, remaining steadily within the range of 36% to just over 44%. The results indicate that in the long-term, the significance of economic growth and its impact on the tax system, or tax revenues, should not be underestimated. In the long run, the share of variance arising from a shock in the tax burden itself gradually decreases, which quite logically enhances the importance of the contribution of other factors that help interpret the variable's value

Figure 4 depicts the results of the impulse function for Romania. There are no positive effects on economic growth as a result of one standard deviation shock in the tax burden, either in the short run or in the long run. Such a conclusion can be drawn with a certain degree of confidence up to the fifth quarter, and after that the data show that the results are characterized by statistical uncertainty. The reaction of the tax burden to a shock in economic growth is characterized by pronounced alternating negative values over time. In the short-term (especially in the third quarter) and in the medium-term (notably in the fifth quarter and from the ninth to twelfth quarters), the findings indicate some reliability, but this does not extend to other periods. Obviously, in years of growth, the expansion of the Romanian economy outpaces the rate at which income tax revenues rise, thus reducing the relative size of the tax burden. To some extent, this stems from proportional taxation, taking into account that it does not impose a greater burden on considerably higher incomes, which usually tend to increase at a faster rate during periods of economic prosperity.

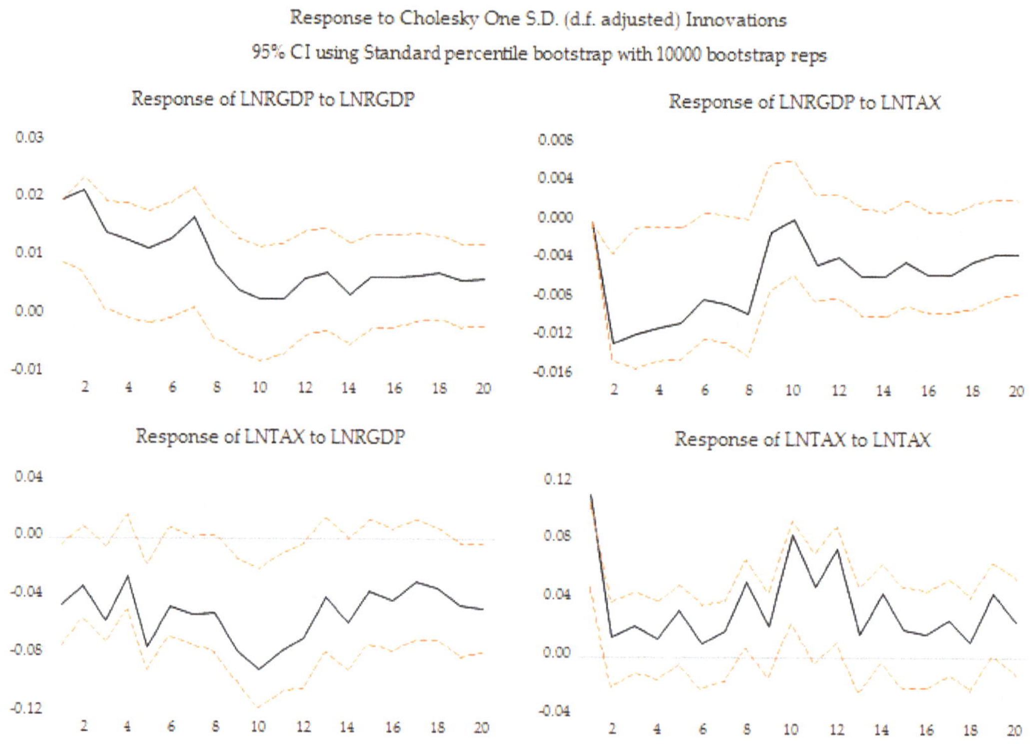

Figure 4. Impulse response of economic growth and tax burden in Romania.

Table 7 shows variance decomposition outcomes for Romania. When examining the variance decomposition of economic growth, it is established that, in both the short and long run, a substantial part of the shocks in growth are due to the growth itself and this effect tends to gradually decrease over time but nevertheless continues to record quite high values. As the period length increases, shocks in the tax burden begin to exert a stronger impact on growth, with approximately 30% of the variance in growth being explained by tax burden shocks by the end of the period. Compared to Bulgaria, in Romania, shocks in the tax burden largely result from economic growth shocks. Specifically, while in Bulgaria, in the long-term, up to approximately 45% of the predictable changes in the tax burden are explained by previous shocks in economic growth, for Romania they reach just over 60%.

Table 7. Variance decomposition of economic growth and tax burden in Romania.

Variance Decomposition of ΔLNRGDP				Variance Decomposition of ΔLNTAX			
Period	**S. E.**	**ΔLNRGDP**	**ΔLNTAX**	**Period**	**S. E.**	**ΔLNRGDP**	**ΔLNTAX**
1	0.020071	100.0000	0.000000	1	0.120021	13.99612	86.00388
2	0.032075	84.57755	15.42245	2	0.125077	19.57805	80.42195
3	0.037084	78.47024	21.52976	3	0.138788	32.29017	67.70983
4	0.040845	74.99165	25.00835	4	0.141829	34.28963	65.71037
5	0.043757	72.44474	27.55526	5	0.163288	46.58906	53.41094
6	0.046459	72.48606	27.51394	6	0.170040	50.40263	49.59737
7	0.050185	73.51885	26.48115	7	0.178733	54.12831	45.87169
8	0.051860	71.75972	28.24028	8	0.192984	53.45119	46.54881
9	0.052072	71.94552	28.05448	9	0.208687	59.18358	40.81642

Table 7. *Cont.*

Variance Decomposition of ΔLNRGDP				Variance Decomposition of ΔLNTAX			
Period	S. E.	ΔLNRGDP	ΔLNTAX	Period	S. E.	ΔLNRGDP	ΔLNTAX
10	0.052151	72.02855	27.97145	10	0.242396	57.71309	42.28691
11	0.052415	71.59315	28.40685	11	0.258834	59.40836	40.59164
12	0.052931	71.66685	28.33315	12	0.277919	57.63045	42.36955
13	0.053769	71.42218	28.57782	13	0.281224	58.30572	41.69428
14	0.054197	70.78853	29.21147	14	0.290288	58.56668	41.43332
15	0.054777	70.81759	29.18241	15	0.293035	58.92559	41.07441
16	0.055461	70.54967	29.45033	16	0.296555	59.58184	40.41816
17	0.056181	70.35443	29.64557	17	0.299062	59.51333	40.48667
18	0.056827	70.50172	29.49828	18	0.301133	59.93984	40.06016
19	0.057266	70.61232	29.38768	19	0.307759	59.59611	40.40389
20	0.057743	70.74651	29.25349	20	0.312367	60.14362	39.85638

In summary, the outcomes from the variance decomposition for both Romania and Bulgaria indicate that the tax burden is significantly more affected by growth shocks. This strengthens the role of the macroeconomic environment and its subsequent relationship with the tax system. In the context of proportional taxation of the incomes of individuals and legal entities, it can be concluded that in the analyzed countries, there is a strong sensitivity of the tax system to economic activity. This further emphasizes the importance of a more in-depth examination of the relationship between the phases of the economic cycle and the state of automatic budget stabilizers.

6. Discussion

One of the key findings of the present study is that the relationship between the tax burden of income taxes and economic growth in the long run is not always evident, but can be established. For two of the countries examined (Romania and Bulgaria), the presence of a similar dependence is demonstrated, which is consistent with the results obtained in the majority of earlier studies (Anastassiou & Dritsaki, 2005; Mucuk & Alptekin, 2008; Mashkoor et al., 2010; Helhel & Demir, 2012; Terzi & Yurtkuran, 2016; Odum et al., 2018; Yildiz & Sandalci, 2019; Maganya, 2020; Shanmugam & Arunima, 2021; Tanchev, 2021). On the other hand, for Hungary and Estonia, the existence of a relevant association in the long run cannot be confirmed, which is also recognized as a conclusion in a significant number of scientific research in the field of taxation and growth of the national economy (Abdiyeva & Baygonuşova, 2016; Eren et al., 2018; Karabacak & Meçik, 2022).

Based on the VECM and the corresponding impulse functions, differences emerge regarding the relationship between shocks and the income tax burden and economic growth in Romania and Bulgaria. In Romania the direction of influence in both cases (from growth to tax burden and from tax burden to growth) is such that growth shocks negatively affect both tax revenue collection and tax burden itself, and the shock in the income tax burden has a restraining (negative) effect on the possibility of achieving a higher level of national economic performance. In Bulgaria, the effect of economic growth on the tax burden of income taxes is quite volatile. Similarly in the case of Romania, in the short run (only in the fourth quarter), the negative effect of growth on the tax burden can be confirmed with statistical certainty. On the other hand, the results of the impulse function show that the low tax burden in Bulgaria has a rather positive effect on the growth opportunities of the national economy in the medium-term, which the analysis does not validate for Romania. Incidentally, the outcomes obtained for the Romanian economy largely coincide with the conclusions reached by Bâzgan (2018). Although both studies demonstrate that—with regard to the impact of tax burden from direct taxes (in case of income taxes) on economic growth—a negative impact is established, characterized by a much lower intensity in the long-term, a significant difference also emerges when examining the influence of the growth of the Romanian economy on the revenue collection from income taxes. The current study outlines a negative trend in this interaction, which applies to both the short- and medium-term, whereas in Bâzgan (2018) the negative shock in subsequent periods is insignificant. These results can, to some extent, be explained by differences in the approach used, as well as the time period of the analysis. It should be noted that the research period in this study covers recent years, which feature a number of social, economic, and health shocks, including the negative impact of COVID-19, the consequences of the war in Ukraine, inflationary shocks, etc. Furthermore, the fiscal policy pursued in Romania over the past few years raises a number of questions about the sustainability of its public finances, not only in the long-term, but also in the short-term. Romania was the only EU member state subject to an ongoing excessive deficit procedure before COVID-19, and this trend persists, with the budget deficit forming a substantially higher share of GDP.

The conclusions drawn regarding the positive impact of the income tax burden on growth in Bulgaria in the medium- and long-term were anticipated to a certain degree. The country has an extremely low tax burden on income, and the changes that occurred at the end of the first decade of the XXI century, including EU accession, aimed to simplify the tax system, reduce the shadow economy, attract foreign investment, and most importantly, contribute to higher economic growth. These findings on the positive impact of income taxes on growth are also observed in the research by Stoilova (2023) for Central and Eastern European countries, as well as in a study by the same author for EU member states (Stoilova, 2024)—including Bulgaria. On the other hand, Tanchev (2021) manages to prove that in Bulgaria, the proportional personal income tax negatively affects economic growth. Nevertheless, this study examines the aggregate burden of all income taxes, not just personal income tax. The corporate income tax in Bulgaria is among the lowest in the entire EU and this can be interpreted as an important fiscal mechanism for stimulating growth, further supporting the difference between our outcomes and those presented by Tanchev (2021). In the context of the four analyzed countries with proportional income taxation, Bulgaria stands out as a country in which personal and corporate income are levied at the same tax rate, with a substantially lower tax rate. Estonia also imposes the same tax rates on corporate and personal income, but its marginal tax rates are twice as high as those in Bulgaria. In Hungary and Romania, there is a difference between the applicable marginal tax rates of the two main income taxes, and this may be among the main reasons for the negative shock of the tax burden on growth in Romania compared to the results in Bulgaria. In addition, the burden of corporate tax is greater (measured by the marginal tax rate).

7. Conclusions

The present study focuses on examining the relationship between, and potential effects of income tax policy and the achievement of economic growth in four Eastern European countries. The choice of these countries is not incidental, as these are currently the only member states of the EU that continue to apply proportional taxation to personal and corporate income. The findings of the research demonstrate that despite the implementation of a similar type of tax policy concerning the taxation of income in the period 2013 Q1–2025 Q1, it is not always possible to establish that the difference in the tax burden of these taxes contributes to generating higher levels of well-being. For Bulgaria and Romania, the analysis identifies a long-term cointegration link between the tax burden and economic growth, whereas Hungary and Estonia do not exhibit such a relationship. The subsequent analysis of the impact of the tax burden on growth in Bulgaria and Romania also leads to variations in the results obtained. While in Bulgaria, the increased shocks in the tax burden have a positive effect on the level of gross domestic product per capita, in Romania, this influence is negative. On the other hand, in Romania, shocks related to the growth of the national economy appear to have negative impact on tax revenue from income taxation, while no distinct effect is defined in Bulgaria, but evidence of an asymmetric response is observed. Such conclusions are frequently associated with growth in the national economy due to economic sectors characterized by reduced (preferential) tax rates, and cases where estimates of the level of the informal economy are significant. Bulgaria and Romania continue to remain among the leading positions in the ranking for the highest level of informal economy in the entire European Union (Schneider & Asllani, 2022).

On the other hand, the Granger test does not find a statistically significant predictive causality from the tax burden to growth in any of the four countries, including Bulgaria and Romania, which means that past values of the tax burden do not contain additional information for predicting growth. These results are not mutually exclusive, as the Granger test examines forecasting, not structural causality, so it is entirely possible to have a long-run relationship and a positive response to shocks without significant predictive power in the tax burden lags. The findings of the Granger test show that it is possible to establish causality when forecasting the tax burden based on economic growth in Bulgaria and Hungary.

Future research on the relationship between income taxes and economic growth can focus on several directions, including tracing the impact of income taxes on specific components of the expenditure structure of GDP (e.g., household consumption spending and investment in strategic sectors for economies), examining the link or dependence between income taxes and the opportunities for achieving environmentally sustainable growth, as well as analyzing the challenges associated with taxing new sources of income (e.g., income from the use of cryptocurrencies) and the subsequent effects of this on consumer behaviour and the conditions for promoting economic development. It is important to consider that the tax policies implemented in the four analyzed countries related to income taxes face future challenges in terms of increasing fiscal instability (especially in Romania and Hungary), harmonization of national and European policies (including the introduction of a higher tax burden in the area of corporate income taxation—this mainly applies to Bulgaria and Hungary), and the growing interest in a fairer model of personal income taxation through implementation of progressive taxation. These challenges should also be the subject of further research, which should include their effects on the examined relationships.

Author Contributions: Conceptualization, A.A. and V.N.; Methodology, A.A. and V.N.; Software, A.A. and V.N.; Validation, A.A. and V.N.; Formal analysis, A.A. and V.N.; Investigation, A.A. and V.N.; Resources, A.A. and V.N.; Data curation, A.A. and V.N.; Writing—original draft, A.A. and V.N.; Visualization, A.A. and V.N. All authors have read and agreed to the published version of the manuscript.

Funding: This work was financially supported by the University of National and World Economy Research Programme (Research Grant No. 13/2024/A).

Institutional Review Board Statement: Not applicable.

Informed Consent Statement: Not applicable.

Data Availability Statement: The raw data supporting the conclusions of this article will be made available by the authors on request.

Conflicts of Interest: The authors declare no conflicts of interest.

Abbreviations

The following abbreviations are used in this manuscript:

AIC	Akaike information criterion
ARDL	Autoregressive distributed lag model
CEE	Central and Eastern Europe
CIT	Corporate income tax
EU	European Union
FPE	Final prediction error
GDP	Gross Domestic Product
HQ	Hannan-Quinn information criterion
LR	Sequential modified Likelihood Ratio test statistic
OECD	Organisation for Economic Co-operation and Development
PAYE	Pay As You Earn
PIT	Personal income tax
SC	Schwarz information criterion
S. D.	Standard deviation
S. E.	Standard error
U-VAR	Unrestricted Vector Autoregression
VAR	Vector Autoregression
VECM	Vector Error Correction Model

References

Abdiyeva, R., & Baygonuşova, D. (2016). Geçiş ekonomilerinde vergi gelirleri ve ekonomik büyüme ilişkisi: Kirgizistan örneği. *Akademik Bakış Uluslararası Hakemli Sosyal Bilimler Dergisi*, (53), 59–71. Available online: https://dergipark.org.tr/tr/pub/abuhsbd/issue/32947/366131 (accessed on 10 September 2025).

Adhikari, B., & Alm, J. (2013, January). Did Latvia's flat tax reform improve growth? In *Proceedings of the annual conference on taxation and minutes of the annual meeting of the national tax association* (Vol. 106, pp. 1–9). National Tax Association.

Anastassiou, T., & Dritsaki, C. (2005). Tax revenues and economic growth: An empirical investigation for Greece using causality analysis. *Journal of Social Sciences*, *1*(2), 99–104. [CrossRef]

Angelov, A., & Nikolova, V. (2021). The impact of tax burden and tax structure on the economic growth of the Balkan region. *Finance, Accounting and Business Analysis (FABA)*, *3*(1), 31–40. Available online: https://faba.bg/index.php/faba/article/view/69 (accessed on 12 September 2025).

Arikan, C., & Yalcin, Y. (2013). Determining the exogeneity of tax components with respect to GDP. *International Journal of Academic Research in Accounting, Finance and Management Sciences*, *3*(3), 242–255. [CrossRef]

Arnold, J. M., Brys, B., Heady, C., Johansson, Å., Schwellnus, C., & Vartia, L. (2011). Tax policy for economic recovery and growth. *The Economic Journal*, *121*(550), F59–F80. [CrossRef]

Bâzgan, R. M. (2018). The impact of direct and indirect taxes on economic growth: An empirical analysis related to Romania. *Proceedings of the International Conference on Business Excellence*, *12*(1), 114–127. [CrossRef]

Breitung, J., & Candelon, B. (2006). Testing for short- and long-run causality: A frequency-domain approach. *Journal of Econometrics*, *132*, 363–378. [CrossRef]

Cassou, S. P., & Lansing, K. (1996). *Growth effects of a flat tax*. (Working Paper 9615). Federal Reserve Bank of Cleveland. Available online: https://www.clevelandfed.org/-/media/project/clevelandfedtenant/clevelandfedsite/publications/working-papers/1996/wp-9615-growth-effects-of-a-flat-tax-pdf.pdf (accessed on 18 September 2025).

Causa, O., Araujo, S., Cavaciuti, A., Ruiz, N., & Smidova, Z. (2014). *Economic growth from the household perspective: GDP and income distribution developments across OECD countries*. (OECD Economics Department Working Papers, No. 1111). OECD Publishing. [CrossRef]

Cornevin, A., Corrales, J. S., & Mojica, J. P. A. (2024). Do tax revenues track economic growth? Comparing panel data estimators. *Economic Modelling*, *140*, 106867. [CrossRef]

Dickey, A. D., & Fuller, W. A. (1981). Likelihood ratio statistics for autoregressive time series with a unit root. *Econometrica*, *49*(4), 1057–1072. [CrossRef]

Diks, C., & Panchenko, V. (2006). A new statistic and practical guidelines for nonparametric Granger causality testing. *Journal of Economic Dynamics & Control*, *30*(9–10), 1647–1669. [CrossRef]

Dumitrescu, E.-I., & Hurlin, C. (2012). Testing for Granger non-causality in heterogeneous panels. *Economic Modelling*, *29*(4), 1450–1460. [CrossRef]

Eren, M. V., Ergin, A., & Aydın, H. İ. (2018). Türkiye'de vergi gelirleri ile ekonomik kalkinma arasindaki ilişki: Frekans alani nedensellik analizi. *Doğuş Üniversitesi Dergisi*, *19*(1), 1–18. Available online: https://dergipark.org.tr/tr/download/article-file/2152122 (accessed on 22 September 2025). [CrossRef]

European Commission. (2025). *Data on taxation trends. Statutory tax rates.* Available online: https://ec.europa.eu/taxation_customs/document/download/6e2a5960-f13c-4aef-b115-60e3ba232966_en?filename=statutory_rates_2022.xlsx (accessed on 27 August 2025).

Eurostat. (2013). *European system of accounts: ESA 2010.* Publications Office. [CrossRef]

Eurostat. (2025a). *Gross domestic product (GDP) and main components (output, expenditure and income).* Available online: https://ec.europa.eu/eurostat/databrowser/view/namq_10_gdp/default/table?lang=en (accessed on 3 September 2025).

Eurostat. (2025b). *Population on 1 January by age and sex.* Available online: https://ec.europa.eu/eurostat/databrowser/view/demo_pjan/default/table?lang=en (accessed on 2 September 2025).

Eurostat. (2025c). *Quarterly non-financial accounts for general government.* Available online: https://ec.europa.eu/eurostat/databrowser/view/gov_10q_ggnfa/default/table?lang=en (accessed on 12 September 2025).

González-Torrabadella, M., & Pijoan-Mas, J. (2006). Flat tax reforms: A general equilibrium evaluation for Spain. *Investigaciones Económicas*, *30*(2), 317–351. Available online: https://www.fundacionsepi.es/investigacion/revistas/paperArchive/May2006/v30i2a5.pdf (accessed on 16 September 2025).

Granger, C. W. J. (1969). Investigating causal relations by econometric models and cross-spectral methods. *Econometrica*, *37*(3), 424–438. [CrossRef]

Helhel, Y., & Demir, Y. (2012, May 31–June 1). *The relationship between tax revenue and economic growth in Turkey: The Period of 1975–2011.* 3rd International Symposium on Sustainable Development, Sarajevo, Bosnia and Herzegovina. Available online: https://omeka.ibu.edu.ba/items/show/2341 (accessed on 10 September 2025).

Hiemstra, C., & Jones, J. D. (1994). Testing for linear and nonlinear granger causality in the stock price-volume relation. *Journal of Finance, American Finance Association*, *49*(5), 1639–1664. [CrossRef]

Hlavac, M. (2008). *Fundamental tax reform: The growth and utility effects of a revenue-neutral flat tax.* MPRA paper No. 24241. Available online: https://mpra.ub.uni-muenchen.de/24241/1/MPRA_paper_24241.pdf (accessed on 18 September 2025).

Johansen, S. (1991). Estimation and hypothesis testing of cointegration vectors in gaussian vector autoregressive models. *Econometrica*, *59*(6), 1551–1580. [CrossRef]

Karabacak, M., & Meçik, M. (2022). Analysing the tax structure of turkish economy: A time-varying causality analysis. *Sosyoekonomi*, *30*(51), 149–164. [CrossRef]

Karagianni, S., Pempetzoglou, M., & Saraidaris, A. (2012). Tax burden distribution and GDP growth: Non-linear causality considerations in the USA. *International Review of Economics & Finance*, *21*(1), 186–194. [CrossRef]

Kimani, F. K. (2021). *The causal effect between tax revenue and economic growth in Kenya* [MOI UNIVERSITY]. Available online: https://ikesra.kra.go.ke/server/api/core/bitstreams/a7aabd7f-45da-48e6-961c-e0c3768bfcea/content (accessed on 5 September 2025).

Maganya, M. H. (2020). Tax revenue and economic growth in developing country: An autoregressive distribution lags approach. *Central European Economic Journal*, *7*(54), 205–217. [CrossRef]

Majcen, B., Verbič, M., Bayar, A., & Čok, M. (2009). The income tax reform in Slovenia: Should the flat tax have prevailed? *Eastern European Economics*, *47*(5), 5–24. [CrossRef]

Mashkoor, M., Yahya, S., & Ali, A. (2010). Tax revenue and economic growth: An empirical analysis for Pakistan. *World Applied Sciences Journal*, *10*(11), 1283–1289. Available online: http://www.idosi.org/wasj/wasj10%2811%2910/3.pdf (accessed on 12 September 2025).

Ministry for National Economy. (2015). *Major changes expected to increase tax competitiveness in Hungary.* Available online: https://2015-2019.kormany.hu/download/1/61/a0000/Hungarian%20Outlook_Major%20changes%20expected%20to%20increase%20tax%20competitiveness%20in%20Hungary.pdf (accessed on 2 September 2025).

Morley, B., & Abdullah, S. (2010). *Environmental taxes and economic growth: Evidence from panel causality tests' bath economics research working papers, no. 4/10.* Department of Economics, University of Bath. Available online: https://purehost.bath.ac.uk/ws/portalfiles/portal/301474/0410.pdf (accessed on 15 September 2025).

Mucuk, M., & Alptekin, V. (2008). Türkiye'de vergi ve ekonomik büyüme ilişkisi: VAR analizi (1975–2006). *Maliye Dergisi*, (155), 159–174. Available online: https://ms.hmb.gov.tr/uploads/2019/09/10.Mehmet.MUCUK_Volkan.ALPTEKIN.pdf (accessed on 12 September 2025).

Muduli, D. K., & Manik, N. (2020). Tax structure and economic growth in general category states in India: A panel auto regressive distributed lag approach. *Theoretical and Applied Economics*, 2(623), 225–240. Available online: https://store.ectap.ro/articole/1464.pdf (accessed on 10 September 2025).

Nayak, P. P., Palai, P., Khatei, L., & Mallick, R. K. (2022). Tax revenue and economic growth nexus in India: An ARDL bounds testing approach. *Orissa Journal of Commerce*, *43*(3), 118–131. [CrossRef]

Odum, A. N., Odum, C. G., & Egbunike, F. C. (2018). Effect of direct income tax on gross domestic product: Evidence from the Nigeria fiscal policy framework. *Indonesian Journal of Applied Business and Economic Research*, *1*(1), 59–66. Available online: https://www.researchgate.net/publication/328207120_Effect_of_Direct_Income_Tax_on_Gross_Domestic_Product_Evidence_from_the_Nigeria_Fiscal_Policy_Framework (accessed on 11 September 2025).

Petru-Ovidiu, M. (2015). Tax composition and economic growth. A panel-model approach for Eastern Europe. *Annals of the "Constantin Brâncuşi" University of Târgu Jiu, Economy Series*, *1*, 89–101. Available online: https://www.utgjiu.ro/revista/ec/pdf/2015-01.Volumul%202/14_Mura.pdf (accessed on 12 September 2025).

Phillips, P. C. B., & Perron, P. (1988). Testing for a unit root in time series regression. *Biometrika*, *72*(2), 335–346. [CrossRef]

Saafi, S., Mohamen, M. B. H., & Farhat, A. (2017). Untangling the causal relationship between tax burden distribution and economic growth in 23 OECD countries: Fresh evidence from linear and non-linear Granger causality. *The European Journal of Comparative Economics*, *14*(2), 265–301. [CrossRef]

Schneider, F., & Asllani, A. (2022). *Taxation of the informal economy in the EU. Policy department for economic, scientific and quality of life policies directorate-general for internal policies. Study requested by the FISC committee.* Available online: https://www.europarl.europa.eu/RegData/etudes/STUD/2022/734007/IPOL_STU(2022)734007_EN.pdf (accessed on 22 September 2025).

Shanmugam, V. P., & Arunima, P. (2021). Impact of direct and indirect tax revenue on economic growth of puducherry. *Dogo Rangsang Research Journal UGC Care Group I Journal*, *11*(2), 92–101. Available online: https://papers.ssrn.com/sol3/papers.cfm?abstract_id=3797439 (accessed on 10 September 2025).

Sims, C. A. (1980). Macroeconomics and reality. *Econometrica*, *48*(1), 1–48. [CrossRef]

Songur, M., & Yüksel, C. (2018). Vergi yapisi ile ekonomik büyüme arasindaki nedensellik ilişkisi: Türkiye örneği. *Finans Politik Ve Ekonomik Yorumlar*, (643), 47–70. Available online: https://dergipark.org.tr/en/pub/fpeyd/issue/47979/607023 (accessed on 11 September 2025).

Stoilova, D. (2023). The impact of tax structure on economic growth: New empirical evidence from central and eastern Europe. *Journal of Tax Reform*, *9*(2), 181–196. [CrossRef]

Stoilova, D. (2024). Tax structure and economic growth: New empirical evidence from the European Union. *Journal of Tax Reform*, *10*(2), 240–257. [CrossRef]

Tanchev, S. (2021). Long-run equilibrium between personal income tax and economic growth in Bulgaria. *Journal of Tax Reform*, *7*(1), 55–67. [CrossRef]

Terzi, H., & Yurtkuran, S. (2016). Türkiye'de dolayli/dolaysiz vergi gelirleri ve Gsyh ilişkisi. *Maliye Dergisi*, *171*, 19–33. Available online: https://ms.hmb.gov.tr/uploads/2019/09/171-02.pdf (accessed on 5 September 2025).

Tiwari, A. K. (2012). Tax burden and GDP: Evidence from frequency domain approach for the USA. *Economics Bulletin*, *32*(1), 147–159. Available online: http://www.accessecon.com/Pubs/EB/2012/Volume32/EB-12-V32-I1-P15.pdf (accessed on 7 September 2025).

Tiwari, A. K., & Mutascu, M. (2014). A revisit on the tax burden distribution and GDP growth: Fresh evidence using a consistent nonparametric test for causality for the USA. *Empirical Economics*, *46*(3), 961–972. [CrossRef]

Toda, H. Y., & Yamamoto, T. (1995). Statistical inference in vector autoregression with possibly integrated processes. *Journal of Econometrics*, *66*, 225–250. [CrossRef]

Tosun, M. S., & Abizadeh, S. (2005). Economic growth and tax components: An analysis of tax changes in OECD. *Applied Economics*, *37*(19), 2251–2263. [CrossRef]

Vasilev, A. (2015). The welfare effect of flat income tax reform: The case of Bulgaria. *Eastern European Economics*, *53*(3), 205–220. [CrossRef]

Yildiz, F., & Sandalci, U. (2019). Vergi yapisi ve ekonomik büyüme arasindaki nedensellik ilişkisi: Türkiye'de iller düzeyinde ampirik bir analiz (2004–2014). *Vergi Dünyası*, *38*(452), 20–34. Available online: https://www.researchgate.net/publication/332143460 (accessed on 11 September 2025).

Journal of
Risk and Financial Management

MDPI

Article

Specific Features of the Application of IFRS 17—Valuation of Insurance Contracts and Profit and Loss Management

Radostin Vazov [1,2,*] and Zhelyo Hristozov [1,*]

[1] Faculty of Economics and Business Administration, Sofia University St. Kliment Ohridski, 125 Tsarigradsko Shose Blvd., Block 3, 1113 Sofia, Bulgaria
[2] Department of Intellectual Property, University of National and World Economy, Str. "8-mi Dekemvri" 19, 1000 Sofia, Bulgaria
* Correspondence: vazov.rado@gmail.com (R.V.); jelio_hristozov@abv.bg (Z.H.); Tel.: +359-886838464 (R.V.)

Abstract

The scope of this topic stems from the change in insurance companies and the subsequent transition to IFRS 17. The new code came into force on 1 January 2023. Therefore, the purpose of this article is to compare the two standards in terms of methodology and process logic. To highlight the new aspects of the new standard and to present the author's view that IFRS 17 provides more opportunities for timely action and intervention by company management in the processes and improvement of results compared to IFRS 4. To examine how the application of the standard has affected the strategy for recognising, measuring, and reporting liabilities under insurance contracts, as well as financial results in the insurance sector in China. The study uses a mixed approach, combining a comparison of IFRS 4 and IFRS 17 with examples illustrating actual practice in the sector to examine differences in accounting treatment. It cites examples from European and Asian traders to assess how things will develop in practice. Contribution: This study adds new evidence on the impact of IFRS 17 on value and profit management. Our study found that the new standard introduces a single model for measuring insurance contracts, which significantly increases transparency and comparability in financial statements. Furthermore, one of its most important findings is that, with the equalisation of the margin on contractual services and the recognition of profits over the entire term of insurance contracts, the balance sheets for all years will show more consistent reports of profits and losses. It also calls for attention to the challenges insurers met in developing cash flow discounting methods or putting the general measurement model into effect. Overall, the report found that search engine IFRS 17 has made comparability and transparency better while making suggestions to industry stakeholders about what problems came out when they were discovered afterwards.

Keywords: general measurement model; variable fee approach; premium allocation approach; risk management; contractual service margin

1. Introduction

The adoption of International Financial Reporting Standard 17 (2017) introduced substantial changes to the financial reporting of insurance contracts, replacing the previous standard that had been in use since 2004. This transition reflects a move toward a more consistent and transparent framework for recognising and measuring insurance liabilities. Unlike the previous standard, International Financial Reporting standards (IFRS) 4 (2004), which allowed a variety of accounting practices and offered limited comparability between companies and jurisdictions, IFRS 17 introduces a consistent framework for the recognition, measurement, and presentation of insurance contracts. This has made the standard particularly relevant in the post-financial crisis context, where transparency and comparability in financial disclosures have become essential to restoring investor confidence and ensuring effective risk management. The topic is particularly urgent as insurance companies around the world are currently undergoing or have recently completed the transition to IFRS 17, which became effective on 1 January 2023. However, the process of adopting and applying the new standard has uncovered a range of conceptual, technical, and operational challenges, particularly in the areas of contract valuation and profit and loss (P&L) management.

The application of IFRS 17 introduces profound changes to the way insurance contracts are valued and how profit and loss are recognised and managed. A comparative analysis of recent academic and industry studies reveals several key insights and trends. According to Palmborg et al. (2020), the introduction of IFRS 17 significantly enhances the transparency of insurers' financial statements by replacing the previous fragmented valuation approaches with a unified, forward-looking model. Their study emphasises that while the new standard improves comparability and provides better insight into the financial position of insurance companies, it also increases volatility in profit recognition due to the more dynamic revaluation of insurance liabilities. This change is especially pronounced in long-term insurance contracts, where the impact of discount rate changes and assumption updates is substantial. Hamza et al. (2024) analysed the anticipated impacts of IFRS 17 adoption on the solvency and profitability of insurance firms listed on the Amman Stock Exchange within a regional framework. Their findings indicate that the adoption of IFRS 17 is expected to reduce short-term profitability for many insurers due to the deferral of revenue recognition through the contractual service margin (CSM). At the same time, the standard enhances the alignment of revenue with the actual provision of services. Their study suggests that while initial adoption costs may be high, the long-term effect on solvency ratios is likely to be positive due to improved liability measurement and more robust risk management practices.

Effendie and Hayyin (2024) propose a stochastic state space model for estimating claim reserves under IFRS 17, highlighting the complexity of the standard's requirement for continuous assumption updates. Their empirical application demonstrates that traditional deterministic models used under IFRS 4 are inadequate under IFRS 17, as the new framework necessitates stochastic modelling techniques to reflect the uncertainty and variability of insurance liabilities more accurately. Their results underscore the importance of actuarial sophistication in adapting to the new standard. From a life insurance perspective, Yousuf et al. (2021) conducted a detailed study on the CSM, which plays a crucial role in spreading profits over the lifetime of insurance contracts. They argue that the CSM is one of the most complex components of IFRS 17 but also one of the most important in achieving consistency in profit recognition. The paper outlines how the CSM reduces short-term earnings volatility while improving the matching of revenue with insurance service delivery.

However, the authors also highlight that frequent recalibration of assumptions and the risk adjustment process may lead to operational burdens for insurers. Lindner et al. (2024) explored the practical implications of IFRS 17 on the Hungarian insurance sector, revealing that most insurers faced significant challenges during the transition, particularly in system upgrades, actuarial model adjustments, and workforce training. The study notes that although implementation costs were substantial, the long-term benefits of better financial control, strategic planning, and investor communication outweigh the initial burdens. Notably, more than 70% of surveyed insurers reported changes in liability valuations exceeding 15% compared to their IFRS 4 figures, illustrating the material impact of the standard on financial reporting.

Overall, the research findings across different countries and contexts confirm that IFRS 17 leads to a paradigm shift in insurance accounting. The standard improves financial reporting quality, enhances investor confidence, and promotes consistency across markets. However, it also introduces greater complexity in valuation methods and operational requirements. The combined evidence from the analysed sources demonstrates that the successful implementation of IFRS 17 requires not only technical compliance but also strategic adaptation and long-term investment in actuarial and IT capabilities. This article was to provide a comprehensive analysis of the specific features of IFRS 17 application, with an emphasis on how the new standard changes the approach to insurance contract valuation and P&L management.

International Financial Reporting Standard 17 (IFRS 17) seeks to rectify the issues that stem from the lack of consistency, as well as the lack of comparability, that were present when working with the previous IFRS 4 Standard. IFRS 17 seeks to improve comparability of reporting in the insurance industry and improve transparency and financial reporting of insurers. Unlike IFRS 4, which permitted differing national practices, IFRS 17 mandates the use of current estimates of future cash flows, the use of explicit risk margin, and the CSM (Contractual Service Margin), which serves to defer unearned profit. This marks a change from the implicit conservatism of the methodology to a more market-consistent out-of-pocket liability measurement. This is also the first time IFRS 17 permits and also requires, at every reporting period, that insurance liabilities should be brought up to date (re-valued) based on current expectations of usage in every financial period, and it moves to include a CSM, as well as non-financial risk and explicit margins, which were new to the methodology.

The execution of IFRS 17 has been linked with IFRS 9 (Financial Instruments) together to be able to provide insurers with a unified financial report. Insurers were allowed to postpone IFRS 9's adoption until IFRS 17 came into effect, and that signifies the importance of balancing the accounting of assets and liabilities. The classification and measurement of financial assets in IFRS 9 has a great impact on the profit volatility in IFRS 17. Several insurers opted for accounting policies (e.g., measuring assets at fair value through profit or loss) to lessen the discrepancies caused by the mismatch between the asset returns and the updated valuation of the insurance liabilities. The adoption of IFRS 9 simultaneously with IFRS 17 is to ensure that there is a report with respect to the gains or losses advanced by the investment portfolios that the insurers have alongside the measurement with IFRS 17 of the insurance liabilities, and thus, the financial reporting is more consistent.

The expected consequence of IFRS 17 on the insurance industry has received academic attention. Some of this literature even predates the implementation of new accounting standards and suggests that IFRS 17 will improve the quality and transparency of the financial statements of the insurers, even if these earnings will be more volatile due to the assumptions and frequent remeasurements. Thus, Palmborg et al. (2020) were hoping that the IFRS 17 unified valuation model would improve comparability of the insurers; however, the model would be more profitable than the benchmark. It was expected that the insurance revenue would be recognised over the CSM, and given that profits were expected to be lower in the earlier periods compared to IFRS 4, this ultimately was a more profitable model (Hamza et al., 2024). It has also been noted that the CSM would have a smoothing effect on earnings (Yousuf et al., 2021; Yanik & Bas, 2017). Some of the conflicts were in relation to the assumed contracts, and as identified in the literature, the CSM would bring about challenges for the insurers (Effendie & Hayyin, 2024; Basu & Grace, 2022).

There is empirical evidence from early adopters that supports the theory. In Ter Hoeven et al.'s (2024) analysis of the first-year reports of European Insurers with the new IFRS 17, greater financial statement transparency and consistency were reported; granular additions by some insurers contributed additional sophistication to the reporting. Lindner et al. (2024) for Hungary and several other study countries describe implementation challenges such as the need for new actuarial and substantial IT systems, and, long-term, the gains from better risk management and liability valuations. In practice, the above challenges describe the transition period after regulators first implemented IFRS 17, in that most insurers reported larger insurance liabilities and lower ending equity, reflecting the new conservative valuations and the introduction of the Contracted Service Margin (CSM). In summary, the effort, skill, and knowledge of most practitioners with actuarial and financial reporting are required to meet the long-term gains in financial reporting, transparency, and confidence associated with IFRS 17.

Accordingly, the present study aims to provide a comprehensive analysis of IFRS 17's specific application features, with an emphasis on how the new standard changes the approach to insurance contract valuation and P&L management. Furthermore, this research clearly defines its objectives and originality by addressing gaps in prior literature and demonstrating how IFRS 17 impacts financial reporting beyond existing findings.

2. Materials and Methods

The methodology of this study is based on a theoretical-analytical approach, involving a systematic review and interpretation of IFRS 17 (International Accounting Standards Board, 2017) in the context of the valuation of insurance contracts and their impact on profit and loss management. The research includes an in-depth analysis of the conceptual framework and structure of the standard as introduced by the International Accounting Standards Board and compares it with previous guidelines under IFRS 4 (International Accounting Standards Board, 2004). A central focus of the study lies in the evaluation of the three core models outlined by IFRS 17: the General Measurement Model (GMM), the Premium Allocation Approach (PAA), and the Variable Fee Approach (VFA). The analysis highlights their specific features, differences, and respective areas of application, emphasising essential elements such as the estimation of future cash flows, risk adjustment, and the determination and release of the Compatibility Support Module (CSM).

To provide a comprehensive view, the study integrates regulatory perspectives and national adaptations, including the Law of the Republic of Bulgaria "On Accounting" (2016) and Ordinance No. 53 of the Financial Supervision Commission (2016), which define the requirements for financial reporting among insurers and relate closely to IFRS implementation within transforming economies. In addition, the paper examines the insights from leading consulting firms and their interpretations of IFRS 17's impact on financial reporting, including those from KPMG (2024), PricewaterhouseCoopers Limited (2017), Grant Thornton (2022), and IFRS 17 (2025). These sources offer practical recommendations and lessons learnt from early adoption phases, especially relevant for insurers operating in or transitioning through economic reforms.

To calculate insurance obligations, profitability, and residual coverage under IFRS 17, the research used the following calculations. The relative difference in the residual coverage liability between the General Measurement Model and the Premium Allocation Approach is calculated using Formula (1):

$$(LRC_{GM} - LRC_{PAA}) / LRC_{GM} \leq \Delta\%, \qquad (1)$$

where Δ%—relative difference in the residual coverage liability calculated by the two approaches; LRCGM—residual coverage liability calculated by the general model; LRCPAA—residual coverage liability calculated using the PAA.

In cases where conversion is applicable, the POR is calculated according to the following Formula (2):

$$\text{POR} = (365 - \text{Elapsed Time}) \times \text{Contribution Amount.} \quad (2)$$

CSM is calculated using the following Formula (3):

$$\text{CSM at time (t)} = \text{CSM at beginning of period} + \text{Profit recognised in period-Loss recognised in period-interest accrued on the margin of the contractual service.} \quad (3)$$

This formula is fundamental in determining the present value of future cash flows, calculating the risk adjustment, and tracking the CSM, which are essential components of applying IFRS 17 to insurance contracts. In turn, the last component in the above formula, namely the interest accrued on the CSM, is determined by the following Formula (4):

$$\text{Interest accrued on CSM} = \text{Margin on contract service} \times \text{Discount rate.} \quad (4)$$

Profit or loss recognition for an insurance contract under IFRS 17 is made using the following Formula (5):

$$\text{Profit or loss recognised for the period} = \text{Recognised income from insurance contracts-Recognised expenses related to insurance contracts,} \quad (5)$$

where Formula (6) and (7):

$$\text{Recognised on revenue for insurance contracts} = \text{Recognised cash flows from performance-Change in CSM during the period,} \quad (6)$$

$$\text{Recognised expenses related to insurance contracts} = \text{Recognised acquisition costs for the period} + \text{Other recognised costs for the period.} \quad (7)$$

Result on insurance services (net) from general insurance business = I − II + III.

The financial result is obtained by comparing the income from an activity with the expenditure from that activity. The financial result is therefore derived from the current income and expenditure transactions, or Formula (8):

$$\text{Financial result} = \text{Income} - \text{Expenditure,} \quad (8)$$

The restated result for tax purposes is Formula (9):

$$\text{Restated result} = \text{Financial result} - \text{Revenue not recognised for tax purposes} + \text{Expenses not recognised for tax purposes.} \quad (9)$$

In addition, a specialised software environment was applied for audit of IFRS 17 calculations. Microsoft Excel 365 with the Solver and Power Query extensions (USA) was used, including a dedicated actuarial platform Moody's RiskIntegrity™ (USA) for IFRS 17 to ensure consistency with regulatory reporting standards. This multi-software approach provided reproducibility, traceability of each computational step, and compliance with the audit requirements of insurance reporting under IFRS 17.

3. Results

The transition from IFRS 4 (2004) to IFRS 17 (2017) addressed many previous issues, including eliminating diversity in accounting and presentation of insurers' financial statements across jurisdictions, standardising insurance contract treatment and liability valuation, updating original evaluations of long-duration contracts that were not previously updated, and incorporating discounting and time value of money. The main goal of IFRS 17 is to enhance transparency, comparability, and reliability of insurers' financial statements worldwide, providing a better understanding of insurance contracts and their risks. Unlike IFRS 4, a transitional standard allowing departures from IFRS principles, IFRS 17 applies a consistent and structured approach that is more detailed and rigorous.

IFRS 17 introduces a new approach to recognising revenue and expenses for insurance contracts based on market value and future cash flows, requiring insurers to allocate income and expenses over the contract life according to risks and duration, with revenue recognised progressively, proportional to risk coverage. It requires a detailed profit split, ensuring revenues and costs are allocated over the contract life, not only at signing. Profit sharing is proportional throughout the contract stages; when the contract ends, or a claim occurs, expenses and income are fully recognised for that period. IFRS 17 requires insurers to allocate income and expenses over the coverage period, recognising insurance revenue in line with the provision of services. This approach spreads profit recognition throughout the contract term rather than at inception, ensuring that by the end of the contract or when a claim occurs, the corresponding income and expenses are fully recognised for that period. To evaluate the suitability of the Premium Allocation Approach (PAA) as a substitute for the General Measurement Model (GMM), the comparative disparity in the residual coverage obligation between the two methodologies was computed using formula (1). When the percentage difference $\Delta\%$ remained within materiality requirements (e.g., 5%), the simplified PAA might be appropriately used for short-term insurance contracts. This result suggests that if the disparity is below a defined threshold, the PAA serves as a valid proxy for the GMM—a point evidenced by the fact that roughly 90% of non-life insurance liabilities were valued using the PAA in practice.

The standard demands a more detailed and updated assessment of insurance liabilities, considering expected costs, profits, and risks. Insurers must distinguish between different insurance contract types to avoid mixing risks and to improve reporting accuracy. Contracts are segmented by nature and terms, such as short-term vs. long-term, different risk levels, numbers of insured risks (e.g., explosion, fire), and contracts with variable cash flows like life insurance with variable premiums or pay-outs. Liabilities are valued based on current market data using current cash flows, expected costs, and profits, with forecasting of future premiums, claims, expenses, and other elements. Claims reserves must be updated regularly, depending on changes in future cash flow expectations. To facilitate a clearer understanding of the key differences between the measurement models under IFRS 17, Table 1 below provides a concise comparison of the GMM, the PAA, and the VFA. These models differ in terms of complexity, applicability, and data requirements, and each is suitable for specific types of insurance contracts depending on their structure, duration, and risk profile.

International Financial Reporting Standard 17 provides three models for measuring insurance liabilities, depending on the type of contract. The General Measurement Model is the basic approach used when there is no significant difference between premiums and liabilities. It values contracts based on the present value of future cash flows, which includes expected insurance payments, premiums adjusted for probability, risk adjustments for uncertainty, and expected costs such as administrative expenses and profits or losses. The Premium Allocation Approach is a simplified method applied to short-term, non-complex contracts, such as property, car, or health insurance. Under this model, premiums are allocated proportionally over the coverage period without the need for complex cash flow calculations. It is suitable for contracts with a duration of up to one year and predictable cash flows, allowing insurers to avoid unnecessary complexity. Revenue is recognised as earned premiums minus expected payments and the costs of risk coverage. The Variable Fee Approach is intended for long-term contracts that include an investment component, where policyholders participate in the insurer's investment results, such as in life insurance. This model measures liabilities by estimating future premiums and costs, taking into account investment management expenses and claims. It incorporates changes in the value of investment assets that affect the insurer's liabilities and requires a market-based valuation of the investment-related components.

Table 1. Summary comparison of GMM, PAA, and VFA under IFRS 17.

Feature	GMM (General Model)	PAA (Premium Allocation)	VFA (Variable Fee Approach)
Use Case	Default model for all contracts	Short-term, simple contracts	Contracts with investment components
Complexity	High	Low	Very high
Cash Flow Estimation	Required	Not required (if immaterial difference)	Required, including variable investment returns
CSM Treatment	Required and released over time	Optional/simplified	Adjusted for changes in underlying asset values
Risk Adjustment	Yes	Simplified	Yes
Best for	Life insurance, long-duration contracts	Property, health, auto	Unit-linked life, annuities with policyholder sharing

Source: created by the authors using data from Aina et al. (2018), Alcántara and Vogel (2021), Ter Hoeven et al. (2024).

Valuation under the new standard is a central requirement and involves measuring insurance liabilities and assets over the life of the contract based on expected future cash flows, including premiums, costs, payments, and risk factors. The standard requires that all rights and obligations be re-measured using unbiased and current assumptions at each reporting period under the General Measurement Model. However, the Premium Allocation Approach may be applied if the coverage period is one year or less, the Residual Coverage Liability under this approach is not materially different from that under the General Measurement Model (taking into account variability in expected performance cash flows and embedded derivatives), and there are no onerous groups of insurance contracts at the time of initial recognition.

Differences in Residual Coverage Liability between GMM and PAA models depend on coverage length, initial CSM, stability of costs, contract characteristics (e.g., single premium vs. annual premium), and catastrophic event impact. IFRS 17 does not provide specific guidance on materiality thresholds for comparing the two models, so judgement is required. The standard also requires the determination of "reasonably expected" future scenarios affecting residual coverage liability valuation during the pre-claim period, allowing companies to apply judgement based on contract characteristics and circumstances. Once the materiality thresholds for the difference and the range of scenarios for the specific characteristics are defined (e.g., a threshold for the difference in the residual coverage liability calculated either way not to exceed a certain percentage or the coverage period of the insurance contracts not to be more than a certain period), the acceptability of the PAA for a specific group should be assessed. For this purpose, the company's actuaries may use judgement to determine whether the differences in estimates between the two approaches differ materially.

In some cases, actuaries may perform a qualitative assessment for certain groups of insurance contracts where it is sufficient, such as groups with aggregate valuation significantly below the materiality threshold, groups similar to those with formal assessments, or renewed groups with unchanged characteristics. Eligibility can be determined using quantitative, qualitative, or combined assessments. IFRS 17 requires that when using the PAA, the residual coverage liability is netted against acquisition costs unless the insurer elects to expense these costs, provided the coverage period is one year or less. The Liability for Remaining Coverage under PAA is measured at initial recognition as premiums received, less acquisition cash flows (unless expensed), adjusted for write-offs of acquisition-related assets or liabilities. At each reporting period, the liability is updated by adding premiums received, adjusting for acquisition cash flows and amortisation (unless expensed), adjusting funding components, and deducting insurance income for services rendered and any investment components paid or transferred to claims liability (Lee & Jagga, 2024).

Figure 1 illustratively presents the Premium Outstanding Reserve (POR) and premium income as per IFRS 17.

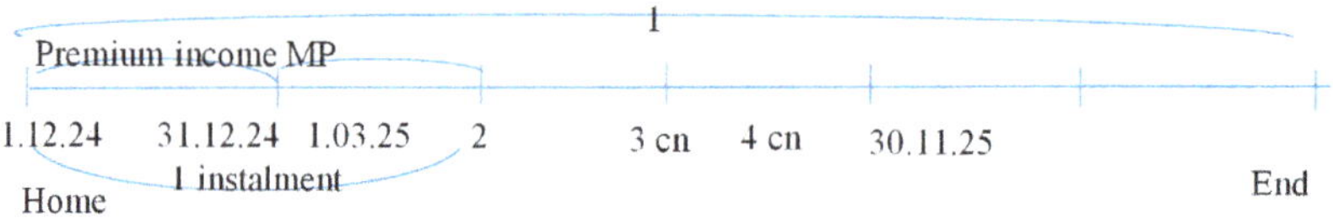

Figure 1. POR and premium income as per IFRS 17. Source: created by the authors.

To compute the POR for deferred payment contracts, Formula (2) was used. As of 31 December 2024, after 31 days and a daily payment of BGN 3.29, the POR amounted to BGN 1099.96. As of 31.12.2024, the residual coverage liability was determined as the difference between the premium paid and the unexpired portion of the coverage period. Premium income under IFRS 17 was the premium relating to the elapsed portion of the contract. Under IFRS 17, premium income was equivalent to the earned premium under IFRS 4. Under IFRS 4, once an insurance contract was entered into, the entire premium was recognised as a written premium. At inception, the whole amount was considered a carry-forward premium reserve. The earned premium corresponded to the expired portion of the contract: on the first day, 1/365th of the premium was earned; on the second day, 2/365ths were earned, and so on. Under IFRS 4, the earned premium was calculated as the written premium plus the change in the premium reserve (ΔUPR). In IFRS 4, the entire premium was recorded upfront as written premium and then released as earned premium proportionally over the coverage term (through the reduction in the UPR). IFRS 17 achieves a comparable allocation of revenue over the contract's life, but through its unified service-based model rather than the previous UPR method.

Under IFRS 4, if an insurance contract concluded in a previous year was terminated early, and the premium was reversed, the reversal was recognised as an expense in the profit and loss statement. This treatment did not affect the earned premium, because the premium had already been recognised in full as written in the prior year. In contrast, if a contract concluded in the current year was terminated early under IFRS 4, the premium reversal was still treated as an expense, but it could affect the current period's premium income, since the contract was still within its earning period. IFRS 17 significantly changed this approach. Rather than relying on the UPR method, it introduced a model that recognises insurance revenue in line with the provision of insurance services over time. This shift aimed to better reflect the economics of the contract and enhance consistency in profit recognition and valuation of insurance liabilities. IFRS 17 also removes the inconsistency in premium cancellation treatment that existed under IFRS 4. In the old approach, cancelling a policy mid-term could distort premium income depending on whether the premium had been fully earned or not. The IFRS 17 model, by recognising revenue strictly as services are provided, handles policy terminations uniformly and transparently, thereby improving consistency in profit recognition and liability valuation.

The Out-of-Pocket amount also included the insurer's future costs required to fulfil the insurance coverage obligations. These costs encompassed expenses related to policy administration, claims handling, and other administrative activities. In contrast to the insurance liability measured under the General Measurement Model (GMM), the Residual Coverage Liability (RCL) also incorporates an estimate of future gains or losses arising from the insurance contract. These estimates could vary in line with changes in the expected risk profile and the premiums anticipated to be received under the contract. At the end of each reporting period, which generally coincided with the end of the coverage period, a portion of the residual cover liability was recognised as income. This recognition reflected the portion of coverage that had already been provided. Premium income was recognised at the earlier of the following: the date of first maturity, the policy start date, or, in the case of a group of onerous contracts, the date when the group became onerous. Recognition continued up to the next due date for premium payment.

In the absence of a contractual due date, the first payment by the policyholder shall be deemed to be due when received (Figure 2).

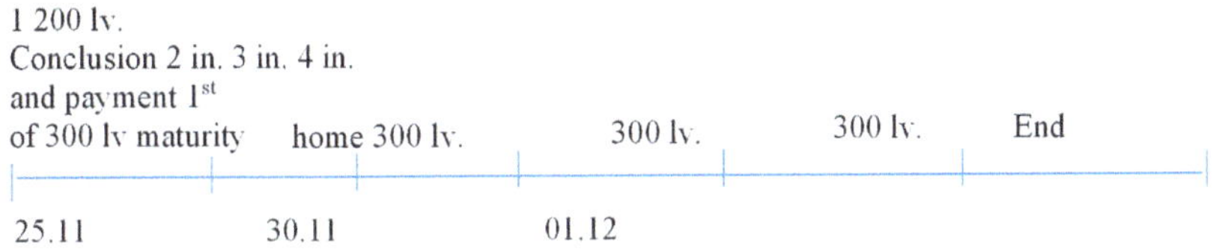

Figure 2. Recognition of insurance premiums under IFRS 17: Instalment-based approach. Source: created by the authors.

The premium was paid on 25.11 when the insurance was taken out. Despite being paid, the insurance company did not report anything until the first due date of 30.11, as if it had not taken out an insurance policy. The money sits in a checking account. On the 30.11. the 300 BGN of the policy will be transferred from the checking account, and it becomes a POR because the contract has not expired yet. With each passing day after 01.12 (the start of the policy), the measurement of performance (MP) will decrease, and the premium income will increase. On 01.12. the premium income is 0. Only at the end of the day, it will be 1/91 of GBP 300 = BGN 3.29 (because the premium of the policy, which is BGN 1200, is paid in four equal instalments, and the first instalment is BGN 300, and the period to which it applies is 3 months or 91 days).

If the premium is paid in one lump sum, then under IFRS 17, the entire premium will be recognised; otherwise, if the payment is deferred, it is recognised in parts. In the same example, if the premium is paid in a lump sum of GBP 1200, at the end of 01.12 authors would have 1/365 of GBP 1200 or GBP 3.29. If there are claims or other events that affect the valuation of the liability, the value of the other comprehensive income may be adjusted if it is determined that the insurer will need to provide larger payments than expected. Let us consider a scenario where authors have an unpaid premium at the end of the reporting period (Figure 3).

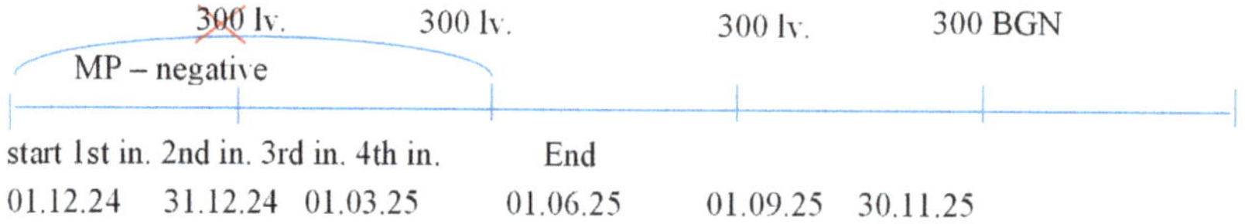

Figure 3. Accounting treatment of unpaid but earned premiums. Source: created by the authors.

If at the end of the accounting period an unpaid premium is present, but it has already been earned (i.e., has matured), a negative P&L will result. The P&L is equal to negative income. In Example 1 above, where a premium of GBP 300 was paid on 01.12 and the residual cover liability was also GBP 300 on the same date, GBP 3.33 is recognised daily as premium income, resulting in a total premium income of GBP 300 over the coverage period. The MP decreases accordingly. If the premium has not been paid, as of 01.12, the POR remains at 0 BGN, while BGN 3.33 continues to be recognised daily, leading to a negative POR. Once the premium is paid, this deficit is offset, and the POR becomes positive.

If the insurance company uses deferred acquisition costs, then the POR will be reduced by them. If you recognise acquisition costs at inception, they are marked "-", i.e., a loss. Then by recognising a premium, it offsets those losses, and because of business continuity, this is covered. IFRS 17 introduces the concept of CSM, which is a key element in the valuation of insurance contracts. CSM is the difference between the value of the future cash flows received under the insurance contract and the value of the liabilities associated with it. The CSM changes over the contract period based on new data and forecasts. When the contract margin is determined, it shall be reflected in the insurer's accounts as part of the status of liabilities and assets. At the start of the contract, the margin will be equal to the difference between the premium receipts and the payout value. If it is determined that future cash flows will result in a profit, the margin will be positive and will be reported in future financial results. If, at a later stage, it is determined that future cash flows will not cover expenses, the margin may become negative and a loss recognised in the corresponding period.

In practice, certain adjustments to the CSM serve to neutralise changes in the expected future cash flows related to the residual coverage liability. When these adjustments fully compensate for the changes in cash flows, the total carrying amount of the residual coverage liability remains unchanged. However, if the changes in the margin associated with the insurance service do not entirely offset the variations in those expected cash flows, the insurer must recognise the resulting difference as income or expense in accordance with the principles outlined in paragraph 41 of IFRS 17. The CSM at the reporting date was revised using Formula (3), which incorporates profit recognition, losses, and interest accrual. An initial CSM of BGN 1000 rose by BGN 150 in recognised profit and dropped by BGN 2.55 owing to interest, culminating in a closing balance of BGN 1147.45. The interest accumulated on the CSM was calculated using Formula (4), using an annual discount rate of 3%, proportionately adjusted for the 31-day reporting period.

The study offers a detailed and contextualised analysis of IFRS 17 by incorporating both regulatory frameworks and practical interpretations. It refers specifically to the Law of the Republic of Bulgaria "On Accounting" (2016) and Ordinance No. 53 of the Financial Supervision Commission (2016), which set out national financial reporting requirements for insurers. These documents are essential in understanding how IFRS, particularly IFRS 17, are applied in countries with transforming economies, such as Bulgaria. They provide the local regulatory foundation necessary to align domestic practices with international accounting standards, thereby facilitating the standard's implementation at the national level.

In parallel, the study draws on reports and practical insights from major consulting firms such as KPMG (2024), PricewaterhouseCoopers Limited (2017), Grant Thornton (2022), and IFRS 17 (2025), which have been actively involved in guiding insurance companies through the IFRS 17 transition. These sources contribute practical guidance on challenges encountered during the early stages of adoption. They highlight the need for robust IT infrastructure, the complexity of modelling future cash flows, and the importance of cross-functional training and governance. The integration of these perspectives into the study allows for a balanced evaluation of IFRS 17—not only as a theoretical accounting framework but also as a real-world regulatory and operational challenge for insurers navigating economic and institutional change.

Cash flow discounting under IFRS 17 is a key element of the valuation of insurance liabilities and premiums, as well as the calculation of financial performance for insurance companies. It is important for the accurate representation of future costs and revenues expected to be paid or received at different points in time. Expected cash flows should be discounted to the present with a curve appropriate to the insurance company. The basis for the discounting requirement is the time value of money principle, i.e., money to be received or paid in the future has a different value compared to money currently available. Life insurers make long-term commitments, often in the order of 20 years or more. These long-term liabilities generate cash flows that will be incurred far into the future and must be valued with reference to their present value equivalent to avoid overstating costs and liabilities and to ensure that reported insurance contract liabilities and premium income are consistent with the actual value that the insurance company must provide or receive.

Unlike the Ordinance of the Financial Supervision Commission (2016) No. 53 "On Requirements to Financial Reporting of Insurers, Reinsurers and Health Insurance Companies" and IFRS 4, where reserves were not discounted, reserves are discounted under IFRS 17. The insurance company adjusts estimates of future cash flows to reflect the time value of money and the financial risks associated with those cash flows to the extent that those financial risks are not included in the cash flow estimates. Discount rates applied to estimates of future cash flows: reflect the time value of money, cash flow characteristics, and liquidity characteristics of insurance contracts; are consistent with observable current market prices (if any) of financial instruments with cash flows whose characteristics are consistent with those of insurance contracts in terms of, for example, timing, currency, and liquidity.

The future cash flows of the insurance contract (premiums, costs, benefits) must be discounted to present value using an appropriate interest rate. This process is important because money to be received or paid in the future has a lower value now. Insurers can use different approaches to determine an appropriate interest rate, based on market interest rates or specific risk assessment models. To discount future cash flows under IFRS 17, the current market risk-free interest rate may be used, which may vary depending on currency and market conditions. An interest rate that reflects the risk-free rate is used to discount future cash flows and is generally based on interest rates on long-term government securities or other instruments that are considered to be risk-free and stable and have an insignificant risk of default. It represents the return an investor would expect to receive from a risk-free investment.

Under IFRS 17, insurers must recognise all gains and losses on insurance contracts throughout the contract's life, leading to earlier and more transparent recognition compared to IFRS 4. Unlike IFRS 4, which allowed more flexibility, IFRS 17 requires profits to be recognised progressively as the insurer provides coverage, reflecting the performance of the contract over time. Changes in future cash flow estimates, such as updated forecasts of premiums, costs, or risks, require regular review and adjustment of recognised gains and losses. This process can be complex, but it ensures a more accurate reflection of the insurer's financial position. Adjustments may arise from shifts in market conditions, claims experience, regulations, or economic factors. For example, if increased natural catastrophe losses are anticipated, insurers must revise estimates and recognise additional losses promptly. Under IFRS 17, profits or losses initially recognised are adjusted based on updated expectations, unlike IFRS 4, where adjustments were made at contract completion. This ongoing valuation reflects a dynamic assessment of future cash flows and risks.

IFRS 17 provides insurers with new risk management options and greater flexibility by allowing more accurate reflection of insurance contract risks through regular adjustments and updates to forecasts. Naturally, difficulties may arise in the calculation and forecasting of future cash flows and in forecasting models, resulting in additional costs and effort on the part of the insurer's actuaries. IFRS 17 requires the recognition of both the gain on a contract when it is entered into and the recognition of a loss if it is expected to result in a loss in the future. This is a novelty compared to older standards such as IFRS 4, which allowed for no loss recognition at earlier stages.

Under IFRS 17, if the difference between the premium income and the expected cost of the contract is negative (i.e., a loss is expected), that loss must be recognised immediately. Thus, if an insurer sells a product with too low a premium that does not cover expected claims and management expenses, it should recognise the loss immediately rather than defer it to future periods. Recognising losses immediately can be challenging because insurers may doubt the accuracy of their estimates at the outset of the contract. In the case of onerous contracts, the insurance company should recognise a loss up to the amount of the net outflow for the group of onerous contracts, with the result that the carrying amount of the liability for the group is equal to the cash flows for performance, and the margin of the contracted service to the group is zero. Once an entity has recognised a loss on an onerous group of insurance contracts, it is required to allocate subsequent changes in the expected cash flows related to the fulfilment of the residual coverage liability in a structured manner. Specifically, any systematic changes in future cash flows must first be allocated between the loss component of the residual coverage liability and the portion of that liability that excludes the loss component. These changes are allocated exclusively to the loss component until it is fully reduced to zero.

In addition, if there is a reduction in future service-related cash flows, for example, due to updated estimates regarding future fulfilment cash flows or adjustments to the risk margin for non-financial risk, that reduction also affects the measurement of the group. Furthermore, any subsequent increase in the entity's share of the fair value of the underlying items must also be taken into account, as it may contribute to reducing the burden of the previously recognised loss. IFRS 17 is based on forecasts of future cash flows, which means that insurers must be as realistic as possible in their forecasts. If reasonable forecasts are made and there is sufficient evidence to indicate that the contract will be loss-making, this will be reflected in due course. At the same time, the standard allows insurers to review their contract forecasts, which means that they can update and adjust their loss estimates as circumstances change. For example, if they begin to receive better payout results, they may adjust the losses originally recognised.

For insurance contracts that may turn out to be loss-making in the long term (for example, because of high claims payouts or increased administrative expenses), the pressures that IFRS 17 places on loss recognition at inception may have financial consequences at the outset of the contract, when the results of the insurance business are not yet clear. Insurers will typically want to monitor the contract over time and assess whether they will face a loss rather than recognising one immediately. This can affect their public image and lead to poor revenue and loss of recognition in the early stages of the contract when there is still uncertainty about financial performance. While it may be awkward to recognise losses at the outset, the IFRS 17 approach can be seen as a way of providing long-term stability and transparency in insurers' accounts, ensuring that financial results are clearer for investors and other stakeholders. If insurers choose not to recognise losses immediately and to defer their recognition, this could create distortions in financial performance and create risks to the financial health of the company in the future. The underlying principle of recognising losses on a line of business from the outset underlines the importance of careful and accurate risk management by insurance companies on the one hand and the quality of forecasts in the insurance sector on the other.

IFRS 17 requires insurers to recognise losses on onerous groups of contracts at an early stage. This represents a significant shift from the approach under IFRS 4, where loss recognition could be delayed. Although this requirement may reduce reported profits in the short term, it ensures a more accurate reflection of risks and the insurer's true financial position. By addressing potential losses upfront, IFRS 17 enhances the transparency and reliability of financial reporting, increasing the level of trust from investors, regulators, and other stakeholders. This approach strengthens financial discipline and supports the long-term sustainability of the insurance sector.

Unlike IFRS 4, which allowed more flexibility and less consistency in recognising losses, IFRS 17 introduces a more robust and principle-based framework. This improves the comparability of financial statements across insurers and jurisdictions. The key differences between IFRS 4 and IFRS 17 in terms of loss recognition are presented in Table 2.

Table 2. Differences between IFRS 4 and IFRS 17 for loss recognition.

	IFRS 4	IFRS 17
Recognition of losses	Losses are recognised only when it is determined that the contract costs exceed the premiums collected. Losses may be recognised at a later stage when the contract is found to be unprofitable	Losses are recognised immediately on initial recognition of the contract if future cash flows result in a negative margin
Estimation of losses	The estimate is more general and may not include detailed projections of future cash flows. The loss assessment can be made under certain conditions	It requires detailed forecasting of future cash flows, which are discounted and estimated against the value of the contractual obligations. Losses are recognised immediately if the cash flows show a negative margin
Recognition of losses over the term of the contract	Losses may be recognised at different stages of the contract, depending on the forecasts and analyses	Losses are recognized immediately upon contract recognition and may be adjusted if changes in estimates result in a change in the value of the liability

Source: created by the authors.

In summary, IFRS 17 introduces stricter and more precise requirements for the recognition of losses on insurance contracts than IFRS 4, requiring losses to be recognised immediately on initial recognition of the contract if future cash flows result in a negative margin. IFRS 4 provides more flexibility and allows deferral of loss recognition if losses are not immediately identified. Authors will look at the technical result under IFRS 17 for a life insurance company and a general insurance company, respectively.

Insurance revenue from insurance contracts includes income recognised under the premium allocation approach (PAA) and the general model for both direct insurance and active reinsurance. This income covers expected cash flows such as estimated claims, acquisition and administrative costs, release of risk adjustments, and the release of the CSM. Additionally, investment adjustments and other insurance income are included. Costs of insurance services also depend on the measurement approach used (PAA, general model, or variable remuneration approach) and include gross claims incurred, claims settlement expenses, changes in liabilities for claims and risk adjustments, acquisition and administrative costs, losses on onerous contracts, and other expenses related to insurance contracts. The gross result from insurance services is calculated as insurance revenue minus the costs of insurance services. For pre-purchased reinsurance contracts, insurance costs include ceded premiums, changes in liabilities related to residual cover and reinsurer default risk, expected cash flows ceded, and acquisition and administrative costs ceded. Insurance proceeds from reinsurance contracts include damages recovered, settlement costs ceded, changes in liabilities related to claims and risk adjustments, and other related expenses. The net result on insurance services from life business is the sum of insurance revenue minus insurance service costs plus the net result from pre-purchased reinsurance contracts.

IFRS 17 is significantly more complex than IFRS 4, creating numerous challenges for insurers and accountants that extend beyond technical and methodological issues to include broader concerns related to operational efficiency and financial sustainability. Although the primary objective of the standard is to enhance transparency and comparability in financial reporting, its implementation requires careful planning, substantial effort, and considerable resources. One of the central difficulties lies in the valuation process. IFRS 17 mandates the use of sophisticated models to estimate the value of insurance contracts and future cash flows. These models involve a wide range of variables and are sensitive to unpredictable events, making accurate forecasting particularly challenging. As a result, insurers face significant costs related to the development, testing, and maintenance of these models.

In addition, the financial impact of transitioning to IFRS 17 has been considerable. The adoption of new valuation and revenue recognition principles has led to substantial adjustments in financial statements, particularly affecting insurance reserves and capital structures. In some cases, companies have been compelled to inject additional capital or revise their dividend distribution policies to maintain regulatory compliance and investor confidence. Another major challenge is the need for staff training. The implementation of IFRS 17 requires an in-depth understanding of new accounting concepts and processes, demanding extensive education and upskilling across multiple departments, including finance, actuarial, and IT. This cross-functional effort often leads to short-term declines in operational efficiency as teams adapt to new systems and workflows. Furthermore, the transition has been complicated by a lack of clear and consistent guidance from regulators and international standard-setting bodies. The absence of uniform interpretation has resulted in discrepancies in application across jurisdictions, making global adoption more difficult and potentially undermining the comparability that the standard is intended to promote.

These challenges become particularly evident when examining the concrete financial implications of IFRS 17 on individual insurance contracts. As of 31 December 2024, for example, a policy with a coverage duration of 31 days recorded premium income under IFRS 17 amounting to BGN 102.20. This amount reflects the portion of the contract considered earned, based on the POR method. The unearned balance of the first premium instalment, calculated as the POR, was BGN 197.80. Meanwhile, the CSM, which represents the unearned profit from the contract, initially stood at BGN 1000. It increased by BGN 150 due to profit recognition and decreased by BGN 2.55 from interest accrual, calculated using a 3% annual discount rate as outlined in Formula (4). Consequently, the closing CSM at the end of the reporting period amounted to BGN 1147.45.

Recognised insurance revenue was determined as BGN 152.55, calculated as the difference between the cash inflows from performance obligations and the change in CSM (Formula (6)). At the same time, operating and acquisition expenses linked to the insurance contract totalled BGN 80 (Formula (7)). Thus, the net profit for the period, derived under the IFRS 17 methodology in accordance with Formula (5), was BGN 72.55. Taking into account all recognised cash flows, the technical result amounted to BGN 200 (Formula (8)). For tax purposes, adjustments were made: BGN 20 of unrecognised income was deducted, while BGN 30 of non-deductible expenses were added, yielding a final taxable profit of BGN 210 (Formula (9)).

This applied example illustrates the practical implementation of IFRS 17, including the assessment of the residual coverage liability, the effect of discounting on the CSM, and the structured approach to revenue and profit recognition. It also highlights the technical outcome calculation and tax considerations within the context of life insurance contracts. These detailed computations reflect the complex interplay between actuarial and accounting assumptions, underscoring both the benefits and challenges of adopting the IFRS 17 framework.

4. Discussion

The implementation of IFRS 17 is a landmark change in insurance accounting, fundamentally affecting the valuation of insurance contracts and the management of profit and loss. Gatzert and Heidinger (2019) provide an empirical analysis of market reactions to the first IFRS 17 financial disclosures within the European insurance industry. They identify increased market sensitivity to assumptions like discount rates and risk adjustments, leading to volatility in reported profits. This aligns closely with the results, which reveal that IFRS 17's requirement for ongoing liability revaluation causes profit and loss volatility, demanding robust actuarial and accounting coordination. This study extends their findings by emphasising the need for insurers to develop sophisticated internal processes to manage this volatility and communicate it effectively to stakeholders, preventing misinterpretation of short-term earnings fluctuations. Wüthrich and Merz (2013) approach IFRS 17 from an actuarial modelling perspective, stressing that valuation must incorporate timing and uncertainty of future cash flows along with solvency considerations. Their theoretical framework supports the findings that the IFRS 17 valuation model is dynamic and requires continuous updates, especially concerning the CSM. This study found that this dynamic valuation significantly affects profit recognition patterns, confirming Wüthrich and Merz's (2013) assertion about the necessity of actuarial precision and frequent revaluation to reflect economic realities.

Yanik and Bas (2017) and Puławska and Strzelczyk (2025) evaluate IFRS 17 insurance contract standards, emphasising the CSM as a key mechanism for smoothing profit recognition over the contract lifecycle. These results corroborate their view that the CSM reduces earnings volatility and better reflects the insurer's service provision. Ter Hoeven et al. (2024) analyse the first year of IFRS 17 application in European insurers' financial statements, noting increased transparency and comparability but also increased complexity and reporting burdens. Findings mirror these conclusions, particularly regarding the operational and governance implications of IFRS 17's detailed disclosure requirements. It was also added that while transparency improves market confidence, the increased workload necessitates insurers' investments in systems and cross-functional coordination, confirming the transitional challenges reported by Ter Hoeven et al. (2024).

Alonso-García et al. (2024) explore taxation and policyholder behaviour in the context of guaranteed minimum accumulation benefits, a specific contractual feature affected by IFRS 17's measurement rules. Their study highlights that tax considerations and policyholder responses can materially influence contract valuation and profit patterns. While research is broader, focusing on overall valuation and profit/loss management, Alonso-García et al.'s (2024) work provides important insights into how contractual features and external factors such as taxation may further complicate IFRS 17 applications, underlining the importance of considering jurisdiction-specific elements alongside standard requirements. Esqueda et al. (2019) analyse the effect of government contracts on corporate valuation, providing a valuation framework that includes the impact of external contractual obligations. Although their focus is not exclusively on insurance contracts, their findings about the sensitivity of valuation to contract terms and market expectations relate closely to IFRS 17's approach of valuing insurance liabilities based on updated estimates of future cash flows. This study supports their general conclusion that contract characteristics and external conditions must be carefully modelled to achieve accurate valuation and profit measurement, reinforcing the complexity inherent in IFRS 17's implementation.

In addition to the academic and empirical perspectives, the study also incorporates national regulatory frameworks and professional interpretations of IFRS 17. It takes into account the Law of the Republic of Bulgaria "On Accounting" (2016) and Ordinance No. 53 of the Financial Supervision Commission (2016), both of which play a crucial role in shaping the financial reporting requirements for insurers within transforming economies. These documents provide the legal infrastructure necessary to harmonise local practices with international standards and facilitate the effective adoption of IFRS 17. Furthermore, the paper draws on practical insights from leading consulting firms, such as KPMG (2024), PricewaterhouseCoopers Limited (2017), Grant Thornton (2022), and IFRS 17 (2025), who have documented early implementation challenges and offered strategic guidance. These contributions are especially relevant for insurers operating in dynamic regulatory environments, as they reflect on IT system adaptation, actuarial modelling requirements, and corporate governance improvements necessitated by IFRS 17.

The examination of IFRS 17 implementation issues, seen through the lens of regional adaptation, aligns with the findings of Fegri (2023), who investigated the Nordic insurance industry. They emphasise that even mature markets have challenges with data granularity, modelling complexity, and resource limitations, all of which were also noted in the firms examined in the present research. These problems are more pronounced in nations implementing accounting changes, where regulatory misalignment and training deficiencies intensify transitional risks.

The implementation of present value discounting and insurance revenue recognition based on coverage performance aligns with the guidance provided by the European Insurance and Occupational Pensions Authority (2025) regarding risk-free interest rate structures, as well as the dynamic measurement principles established by the International Accounting Standards Board (2017). These reliable sources substantiate the conclusion that precise discount rate selection and scenario-based forecasting are crucial for the equitable value of insurance obligations. National adaptations, shown by Ordinance No. 53 from the Bulgarian Financial Supervision Commission (2016), provide a pertinent parallel, illustrating the integration of IFRS 17 criteria into regulatory frameworks within transitioning economies. This aligns with research findings on the need to incorporate IFRS 17 into both accounting systems and country regulatory frameworks and legal structures.

In addition to the technical ramifications of IFRS 17, the present study highlights the wider socioeconomic and demographic framework within which insurers operate. The increasing proportion of senior individuals, the need for long-term care, and the evolution of housing types for older persons significantly impact the design of insurance products and liability projections. Research conducted by Bao et al. (2022), Nowossadeck et al. (2023) and Ayoubi-Mahani et al. (2023) underscores the increasing need for health-related coverage, mobility-adjusted services, and finance for social care, trends that must be included in actuarial assumptions and anticipated cash flow modelling.

Similarly, the research conducted by Arrigoitia and West (2020), Kazak (2023) and Grazuleviciute-Vileniske et al. (2020) indicates that the ageing demographic is progressively pursuing alternate housing and co-living arrangements, often co-financed or underpinned by insurance-backed goods. These results underscore the need to integrate variable contract terms, life-cycle forecasting, and customer behaviour modelling into IFRS 17 valuation frameworks, a facet largely explored in present research via scenario-based discounting and profitability forecasts. This study indicates that IFRS 17 is not only a technical accounting change but also a framework requiring the integration of demographic, behavioural, and regulatory knowledge. The use of its valuation concepts for ageing-related insurance products, including long-term care, annuities, and reverse mortgages, necessitates an interdisciplinary approach that harmonises accounting precision with social and economic developments. This study's results corroborate the established theoretical and industrial literature about the technological advantages and difficulties of IFRS 17. They further build upon previous research by illustrating the interplay between actuarial value, profit recognition, and regulatory compliance with wider environmental factors, such as ageing populations, housing changes, and national regulatory limitations. These variables must be considered for IFRS 17 to operate properly across various countries and kinds of insurers.

Andersson and Svensson (2023) examined the influence of several stakeholder groups on the formulation of IFRS 17. They demonstrated how lobbying influence from preparers and industry associations altered the final design of the standard. This aligns with the findings about the many compromises inherent in IFRS 17, reinforcing the notion that its final design is predicated on both theoretical coherence and institutional negotiation. Their study substantiates the idea that effective implementation requires an understanding of both the technical and political dimensions of standard-setting. Gavaza (2024) developed a risk adjustment model for life insurance contracts in Zimbabwe, concentrating on the risk of policy lapse. His findings demonstrate the need for national actuarial modelling to align with the global norms of IFRS 17 while integrating market-specific characteristics. This supports the assertion that effective adoption of IFRS 17 necessitates actuarial solutions customised for each market, particularly in emerging or evolving markets characterised by significant lapse volatility.

Teplanova (2023) analysed the financial and socio-economic consequences of IFRS 17 adoption, emphasising its impact on the comparability of financial statements and strategic reporting. Her views correspond with the results about the improved transparency and cross-border comparability enabled by IFRS 17, particularly in long-term contracts. She also discusses the social and economic ramifications of reporting obligations and internal restructuring. This study corroborates the findings by examining the operational and resource challenges encountered during deployment. Basu and Grace (2022) questioned the intricacy of IFRS 17, asserting that insurance accounting is "too difficult" due to its abstract nature and significant reliance on actuarial inputs. This work unequivocally confirms the observations on the difficulty insurers have in comprehending the standard and the associated expenses incurred. It contributes to the ongoing discussion about how accessible IFRS

17 is for individuals outside the actuarial and financial reporting professions, particularly regarding its use and auditing.

Winkler and Kansal (2025) provide a practical approach for managing IFRS 17, including optimum strategies for implementation, change management, and model selection. Their findings corroborate the assertion that strategic cross-functional teamwork is essential to overcome initial challenges. Insurance firms that invested in system enhancements and training at the outset saw smoother transitions and more reliable disclosures.

Alharasis et al. (2024) evaluated the quality of financial statements before and after the implementation of IFRS 7 in the Iraqi banking sector. Their focus on an alternative standard makes their technique for assessing pre- and post-implementation comparability and transparency pertinent to the study's IFRS 17 evaluation methodology. Their findings underscore the need for conducting long-term impact studies, a recommendation the authors of the present research also proposed for future research. Song and Trimble (2022) analysed the difficulties and global disparities in the execution of IFRS. Their analysis of structural, cultural, and economic barriers is evident in the findings about the variable implementation and interpretation of IFRS 17 across nations. They argue that total comparability is limited by national contexts, a conclusion that aligns with the observations about regulatory fragmentation and the need for jurisdiction-specific adjustments. Sayegh (2018) investigated the potential uses of blockchain technology in the insurance industry, including claims processing and premium management. While not directly related to IFRS 17, it pertains to the broader technological transformation within the industry. Present research supports their claim that the integration of advanced IT solutions, such as blockchain or AI, is essential for meeting the data and modelling demands of IFRS 17.

The analysis demonstrates that the adoption of IFRS 17 significantly reshapes insurance accounting by improving the fidelity of contract valuation and aligning profit recognition with service delivery. These changes bring both enhanced clarity for stakeholders and new challenges for insurers' internal processes. Understanding the relationships between results and those of other researchers deepens insight into IFRS 17's implications and underscores the need for continued practical and academic exploration.

5. Conclusions

The introduction of IFRS 17 represents a significant change in the accounting practice of insurance companies, aiming at a higher degree of transparency, comparability, and reliability of financial statements. The standard introduces a consistent and comprehensive framework for the valuation of insurance contracts and the management of profits and losses, while placing significant demands on insurance companies in terms of technical infrastructure, data processing, staff qualifications, and the management of the risks associated with forecast data.

IFRS 17 requires significant changes to the methodology for estimating cash flows and requires insurers to update their forecasts regularly, increasing the challenges in its practical application. Despite the difficulties associated with implementing the standard, including the financial and resource investment, it brings long-term benefits, particularly in terms of increased confidence from investors, regulators, and other stakeholders. Successful implementation of IFRS 17 requires strategic planning and careful management of the adaptation processes to the new accounting standards. Insurance companies should actively use this period to evaluate and improve their internal processes and systems, which would contribute not only to compliance with the standards but also to the overall efficiency and sustainability of their business.

The introduction and implementation of IFRS 17 for the first time was a major challenge for insurance companies due to various technical, operational, and financial issues.

The transition to this standard required significant efforts to implement new processes and technologies, while there were also numerous risks associated with the estimation of future cash flows and reserves. Such companies as KPMG, PwC, Grant Thornton, and Forvis Mazars encountered a number of difficulties that revealed the need for significant upgrades in actuarial modelling techniques, modifications to IT systems, and stronger cross-functional collaboration across departments. These challenges often included complex requirements for modelling future cash flows, higher levels of disclosure in financial reporting, and elevated initial implementation costs.

Despite the burden, many early adopters reported improvements in investor communication, enhanced financial discipline, and greater internal financial control. These outcomes indicate that, although demanding, the implementation of IFRS 17 can contribute to long-term operational resilience and strategic clarity within insurance organisations. Future research should concentrate on longitudinal evaluations of post-implementation effects across various regulatory contexts, emphasising financial performance, solvency dynamics, and actuarial modelling methodologies under IFRS 17.

The recommendations and suggestions from the findings are multifaceted. More work and money from insurance firms into IFRS 17's actuarial and technical operational facets of training, incorporation, and inter-departmental work. There will need to be more guidance, and possibly transitional assistance, from Regulators and standard setters to smaller Insurers and Insurers from Developing Regions, to help ensure standard setting is not inequitable. There are clear benefits from IFRS 17's socio-economic impact and transparency. There are economic benefits from increased market discipline, stakeholder trust, and protection of policyholders. There are also economic costs that need to be considered, policy cost considerations, the following costs on policyholders, and the overall impact on market competition, and on the costs to Insurers. There is resource potential to be studied regarding Insurers' economic behaviour that will come from IFRS 17, the associated risks, long-term Insurers' economic, and potential resource complementary flows, here with the Market Stability and Financial Regulatory Capital interdependencies.

Author Contributions: Conceptualization, R.V.; formal analysis, Z.H. All authors have read and agreed to the published version of the manuscript.

Funding: This research received no external funding.

Institutional Review Board Statement: Not applicable.

Informed Consent Statement: Not applicable.

Data Availability Statement: The original contributions presented in this study are included in the article. Further inquiries can be directed to the corresponding authors.

Conflicts of Interest: The authors declare no conflict of interest.

References

Aina, F., Agbesanwa, A., Jolayemi, T., Owoyemi, J., Ibirongbe, A., & Akinola, Y. (2018). Aging under socio-demographic transition: Perceived social relation and support among elders presenting at a geriatric clinic, South West Nigeria. *The International Annals of Medicine*, *2*(10). Available online: https://scispace.com/papers/aging-under-socio-demographic-transition-perceived-social-31atmuy9uz (accessed on 7 October 2025). [CrossRef]

Alcántara, A., & Vogel, C. (2021). Rising housing costs and income poverty among the elderly in Germany. *Housing Studies*, *38*(7), 1220–1238. [CrossRef]

Alharasis, E. E., Marei, A., Almakhadmeh, A. A. R., Abdullah, S., & Lutfi, A. (2024). An evaluation of financial statement quality in pre-versus post-IFRS-7 implementation: The case of Iraqi banking industry. *Discover Sustainability*, *5*(1), 277. [CrossRef]

Alonso-García, J., Sherris, M., Thirurajah, S., & Ziveyi, J. (2024). Taxation and policyholder behavior: The case of guaranteed minimum accumulation benefits. *ASTIN Bulletin: The Journal of the IAA*, *54*, 185–212. [CrossRef]

Andersson, O., & Svensson, O. (2023). *Intressenters inflytande vid nya redovisningsstandarder: En studie om intressentgruppers inflytande vid utformningen av IFRS 17*. University of Gothenburg. Available online: https://hdl.handle.net/2077/79146 (accessed on 7 October 2025).

Arrigoitia, M., & West, K. (2020). Interdependence, commitment, learning and love: The case of the United Kingdom's first older women's co-housing community. *Ageing and Society*, *41*(7), 1673–1696. [CrossRef]

Ayoubi-Mahani, S., Eghbali-Babadi, M., Farajzadegan, Z., Keshvari, M., & Farokhzadian, J. (2023). Active aging needs from the perspectives of older adults and geriatric experts: A qualitative study. *Frontiers in Public Health*, *11*, 1121761. [CrossRef]

Bao, J., Zhou, L., Liu, G., Tang, J., Lu, X., Cheng, C., Jin, Y., & Bai, J. (2022). Current state of care for the elderly in China in the context of an aging population. *Bioscience Trends*, *16*(2), 107–118. [CrossRef]

Basu, S., & Grace, M. F. (2022). Insurance: In or out of the "too difficult" box? *Accounting and Business Research*, *52*(5), 510–535. [CrossRef]

Effendie, A. R., & Hayyin, R. A. (2024). Measurement claim reserving insurance contract in accordance with IFRS 17 using stochastic state space model. *ITM Web of Conferences*, *58*, 04005. [CrossRef]

Esqueda, O. A., Ngo, T., & Susnjara, J. (2019). The effect of government contracts on corporate valuation. *Journal of Banking and Finance*, *106*, 305–322. [CrossRef]

European Insurance and Occupational Pensions Authority. (2025). *Risk-free interest rate term structures*. Available online: https://www.eiopa.europa.eu/tools-and-data/risk-free-interest-rate-term-structures_en (accessed on 7 October 2025).

Fegri, K. L. (2023). *IFRS 17: Challenges, opportunities and the road ahead for Nordic insurers*. Available online: https://www.ey.com/en_se/insights/financial-services/ifrs-17-challenges-and-opportunities (accessed on 7 October 2025).

Financial Supervision Commission. (2016). *Ordinance No. 53 on the requirements to the reporting, valuation of assets and liabilities and establishment of technical provisions of insurers, reinsurers and the Guarantee Fund*. Available online: https://www. abz.bg/public/uploads/files/ordinance_53_en.pdf (accessed on 7 October 2025).

Gatzert, N., & Heidinger, D. (2019). An empirical analysis of market reactions to the first solvency and financial condition reports in the European insurance industry. *Journal of Risk and Insurance*, *87*(2), 407–436. [CrossRef]

Gavaza, L. (2024). *An IFRS 17 risk adjustment model for policy lapse risk in Zimbabwean life insurance*. University of Zimbabwe. [CrossRef]

Grant Thornton. (2022). *IFRS 17: The final stretch*. Available online: https://www.grantthornton.co.uk/insights/ifrs-17-the-final-stretch/ (accessed on 7 October 2025).

Grazuleviciute-Vileniske, I., Seduikyte, L., Teixeira-Gomes, A., Mendes, A., Borodinecs, A., & Buzinskaite, D. (2020). Aging, living environment, and sustainability: What should be taken into account? *Sustainability*, *12*(5), 1853. [CrossRef]

Hamza, M., Obeid, A., Haddad, H., Binsaddig, R., & Hisham, A. H. (2024). The expected impact of applying the insurance contracts standard (IFRS 17) in the solvency and profitability of insurance companies listed on the Amman stock exchange. *Journal of Ecohumanism*, *3*(7), 4839–4849. [CrossRef]

IFRS 17. (2025). Available online: https://www.ifrs.org/content/dam/ifrs/publications/pdf-standards/english/2022/issued/part-a/ifrs-17-insurance-contracts.pdf?bypass=on (accessed on 7 October 2025).

International Accounting Standards Board. (2004). *International financial reporting standard 4 insurance contracts*. Available online: https://www.ifrs.org/issued-standards/list-of-standards/ifrs-4-insurance-contracts/ (accessed on 7 October 2025).

International Accounting Standards Board. (2017). *International financial reporting standard 17 insurance contracts*. Available online: https://www.ifrs.org/issued-standards/list-of-standards/ifrs-17-insurance-contracts/#about (accessed on 7 October 2025).

Kazak, J. (2023). Intergenerational social housing for older adults: Findings from a Central European city. *Habitat International*, *142*, 102966. [CrossRef]

KPMG. (2024). *Insurers' first annual reporting under IFRS 17 and IFRS 9*. Available online: https://assets.kpmg.com/content/dam/kpmgsites/xx/pdf/ifrg/2024/isg-real-time-ifrs-17-first-annual-reporting-talkbook.pdf.coredownload.pdf (accessed on 7 October 2025).

Law of the Republic of Bulgaria "On Accounting". (2016). Available online: https://lex.bg/bg/laws/ldoc/2136697598 (accessed on 7 October 2025).

Lee, T., & Jagga, A. (2024). Sufficient mathematical conditions for identical estimation of the liability for remaining coverage under the general measurement model and premium allocation approach. *British Actuarial Journal*, *29*, e17. [CrossRef]

Lindner, Z., Dénes, B., Kosztik, G., Merész, G., & Sándorné, M. S. (2024). Main impacts of the Introduction of IFRS 17 on the Hungarian insurance sector. *Financial and Economic Review*, *23*(3), 71–98. [CrossRef]

Nowossadeck, S., Gordo, L., & Alcántara, A. (2023). Mobility restriction and barrier-reduced housing among people aged 65 or older in Germany: Do those who need it live in barrier-reduced residences? *Frontiers in Public Health*, *11*, 2023. [CrossRef]

Palmborg, L., Lindholm, M., & Lindskog, F. (2020). Financial position and performance in IFRS 17. *Scandinavian Actuarial Journal*, *2021*(3), 171–197. [CrossRef]

PricewaterhouseCoopers Limited. (2017). *IFRS 17: Insurance contracts*. PwC Nigeria. Available online: https://www.pwc.com/ng/en/assets/pdf/ifrs-17-newsletter.pdf (accessed on 7 October 2025).

Puławska, K., & Strzelczyk, W. (2025). IFRS 17 implementation: Market participants' perspective. *Central European Management Journal*, *33*(3), 455–477. [CrossRef]

Sayegh, K. (2018). *Blockchain application in insurance and reinsurance*. Skema Business School. Available online: https://www.researchgate.net/profile/Katia-Sayegh/publication/327987901_Blockchain_Application_in_Insurance_and_Reinsurance/links/5c38675d299bf12be3be7459/Blockchain-Application-in-Insurance-and-Reinsurance.pdf (accessed on 7 October 2025).

Song, X., & Trimble, M. (2022). The historical and current status of global IFRS adoption: Obstacles and opportunities for researchers. *The International Journal of Accounting*, *57*(2), 2250001. [CrossRef]

Teplanova, P. (2023). Analysis of the impact of applying the new international standard IFRS 17–Insurance contracts on the financial statements of insurance companies. In T. Kliestik, & E. Nica (Eds.), *Globalization and its socio-economic consequences* (pp. 435–446). Peter Lang. [CrossRef]

Ter Hoeven, R., Borelli, A., & van Vlijmen, P. (2024). First year's application of IFRS 17 in the financial statements of European insurance companies. *Monthly Journal for Accountancy and Business Economics*, *98*(6), 403–422. [CrossRef]

Winkler, M., & Kansal, S. K. (2025). *Navigating IFRS 17: A practical guide to accounting and actuarial implementation*. VVW Karlsruhe. Available online: https://www.researchgate.net/publication/389076382_Navigating_IFRS_17_A_Practical_Guide_to_Accounting_Actuarial_Implementation (accessed on 7 October 2025).

Wüthrich, M., & Merz, M. (2013). *Financial modeling, actuarial valuation and solvency in insurance*. Springer. [CrossRef]

Yanik, S., & Bas, E. (2017). Evaluation of ifrs 17 insurance contracts standards for insurance companies. *Pressacademia*, *6*(1), 48–50. [CrossRef]

Yousuf, W., Stansfield, J., Malde, K., Mirin, N., Walton, R., Thorpe, B., Thorpe, J., Iftode, C., Tan, L., Dyble, R., Pelsser, A., Ghosh, A., Qin, W., Berry, T., & Er, C. (2021). The IFRS 17 contractual service margin: A life insurance perspective. *British Actuarial Journal*, *26*, e2. [CrossRef]

Journal of
Risk and Financial Management

MDPI

Article

The Chinese Government Auditing and Green Finance: The Mediating Role of Fiscal Execution Efficiency

Jifang Chen *, Aidi Ahmi and Zakiyah Sharif

Tunku Puteri Intan Safinaz School of Accountancy, Universiti Utara Malaysia, Sintok 06010, Kedah, Malaysia; aidi@uum.edu.my (A.A.); zaez2205@uum.edu.my (Z.S.)
* Correspondence: chenjifang123@163.com

Abstract

Amidst the dual constraints of insufficient resource supply and an imperfect institutional environment hindering the development of green finance in China, the Chinese government has actively advanced reforms to its government audit system to enhance fiscal execution efficiency. This study utilizes panel data covering 30 provinces in China from 2010 to 2021 and employs Hausman regression to assess the impact of Chinese government auditing on green finance. Furthermore, it empirically examines the mediating effects of fiscal revenue and expenditure execution efficiency on the relationship between the two. The empirical results indicate that Chinese government auditing has a significant impact on enhancing the development level of green finance. However, fiscal expenditure execution efficiency exhibits a significant full mediating effect. Correspondingly, the role of fiscal revenue execution efficiency is limited, exhibiting only a partial mediating effect. These findings highlight the institutional advantages of Chinese government auditing in promoting the development of green finance by improving fiscal execution efficiency. This study integrates government auditing, green finance, and fiscal execution efficiency into a unified analytical framework, enriching the theoretical system of green finance driving mechanisms. The research results also provide policy support for local governments in China to enhance their auditing models and strengthen fiscal execution capabilities, thereby improving the overall effectiveness of green finance development.

Keywords: green finance; Chinese government audit; fiscal revenue execution efficiency; fiscal expenditure execution efficiency

1. Introduction

Green finance refers to financial activities that utilize financial instruments, such as credit, bonds, investments, and insurance, to direct financial funds towards energy conservation, emission reduction, environmental protection, and the development of green industries, aiming to promote the harmonious development of the economy and the ecological environment (World Bank, 2018; OECD, 2020). Therefore, green finance is considered a key policy tool for alleviating environmental constraints and promoting high-quality economic development. In recent years, as the world's largest developing country and a major carbon emitter, despite the continuous advancement of China's green finance system, its overall development level remains low, resulting in inefficient allocation of green financial resources and negative impacts on society and the environment. On the supply side, an insufficient supply of green finance has led to a lack of adequate green funding in some regions, allowing high-pollution and high-energy-consuming industries to continue occupying a large proportion of the market (Lv et al., 2021). This prevents fiscal resources from effectively flowing to truly ecologically beneficial financial projects. In terms of the institutional environment, inadequate information disclosure and imperfect incentive mechanisms in green finance make it difficult for investors to assess the risks and returns of green investments accurately (R. Wang et al., 2025), resulting in insufficient public confidence in green finance and hindering widespread social participation and green consumption.

In recent years, against the backdrop of multiple obstacles to the development of green finance, the Chinese government has continued to promote reforms in government auditing and fiscal budget performance management. As a crucial component of public finance operations and government governance systems, government auditing plays a governance role in fiscal execution, promoting the improvement and development of green finance (Bo et al., 2020; Cao et al., 2022). Specifically, Audit institutions at all levels regularly conduct audits of budget execution, fiscal final accounts, and special funds, systematically revealing and rectifying problems in fiscal execution efficiency. Improved fiscal execution efficiency enables the government to invest budgetary funds in green finance projects more promptly (H. Liu et al., 2024). Furthermore, the government actively and continuously promotes the environmental resource auditing system. This auditing system focuses on reviewing the compliance and efficiency of fiscal funds for ecological protection, pollution control, and green industries, providing resource supply and institutional guarantees for the development of green finance (Fu et al., 2023; L. Sun et al., 2025).

However, there remains a lack of reliable empirical evidence demonstrating whether government audits can overcome the challenges of insufficient resource supply and imperfect institutional environments in green finance development by enhancing fiscal execution efficiency to reduce delays, idleness, and wastage of funds. Particularly within China's institutional context, the intrinsic logical relationship among government audits, fiscal execution efficiency, and green finance has yet to be fully elucidated. Existing research predominantly emphasizes the pivotal role of green finance in promoting harmonious economic and environmental development in China (Ma & Xi, 2025; Y. Sun et al., 2024; C. Wang et al., 2023). Few studies have empirically demonstrated the influence of government audits on the development of green finance. This absence of robust empirical evidence makes it difficult to accurately assess the governance role of government audit in enhancing fiscal execution efficiency. Consequently, governments may encounter policy implementation challenges when allocating resources for green finance, thereby undermining the effectiveness of green finance development.

Based on panel data from 30 provinces in China from 2010 to 2021, this study further explores the impact of Chinese government auditing on green finance and examines whether fiscal execution efficiency plays a mediating role. This study makes a positive contribution by focusing on the core issue of whether government auditing can effectively promote green finance development by improving fiscal execution efficiency. Theoretically, this study incorporates government auditing and fiscal execution efficiency into a unified analytical framework, enriching the theoretical explanation of green finance development. Practically, by providing reliable empirical evidence, this study offers practical guidance and reference for government auditing and fiscal execution policies in promoting green finance development. This helps optimize China's government auditing system and fiscal governance framework, and is particularly relevant for similar developing countries.

2. Literature Review and Hypotheses

Public governance theory emphasizes the core role of institutional constraints and accountability mechanisms in government governance. Furthermore, it stresses the cyclical

https://doi.org/10.3390/jrfm19010017

governance process of policy formulation, implementation, and feedback (Rhodes, 1996). Based on this theory, fiscal efficiency is a crucial link connecting government policy and the feedback loop of green finance development (Alqooti, 2020). By constraining and monitoring the execution of fiscal budgets and the use of public funds, government auditing effectively reduces waste and inefficient allocation of fiscal resources. Against the backdrop of numerous obstacles to the development of green finance in China, government auditing significantly improves fiscal efficiency by revealing and reducing delays in fiscal payments and resource waste. This helps green finance overcome the challenges of insufficient resource supply and a weak institutional environment, ultimately promoting the sustainable development of green financial instruments such as green credit and green bonds.

2.1. Green Finance and Government Auditing

Due to varying government policies worldwide, most countries' government audits currently lack a focus on green environmental governance. Consequently, international research on the relationship between government audits and green finance is relatively scarce. However, several studies (Bostan et al., 2021; Goolsarran, 2007; Gulmammadov, 2025; Sułkowski & Dobrowolski, 2021; van Leeuwen, 2004) agree that government audits play a positive role in environmental protection, resource conservation, climate change mitigation, and sustainable development. In recent years, with the Chinese government's establishment of an environmental resource auditing system, the academic community has increasingly focused on whether this system has a governance role in promoting green finance development. Some studies (R. Huang & Zou, 2025; X. Li et al., 2023; L. Sun et al., 2025; W. Wang et al., 2023) argue that by strengthening oversight of environmental responsibility fulfillment, green project implementation, and the use of pollution control funds, government auditing can effectively improve the green investment environment and reduce policy uncertainty for green projects.

Particularly in resource and environmental auditing, Sitompul et al. (2023) and You and Wang (2025) point out that government auditing is considered a crucial system for improving the quality of environmental governance; its audit results can encourage companies to raise their environmental awareness, thereby increasing their likelihood of obtaining green loans, green bonds, and other green financial instruments. F. Chen et al. (2025) and Hou et al. (2024) found that the public disclosure of government audit results can reduce information asymmetry in the green finance market, enhance the reliability of financial institutions' environmental information judgments, and encourage them to expand credit investment and capital allocation for green industries and projects.

This study acknowledges the previous role of the Chinese government's auditing in resource and environmental matters, arguing that government auditing strengthens environmental governance responsibility by revealing and correcting the misuse of public funds. This can rectify resource allocation distortions, thereby creating a favorable institutional environment for the development of green finance. Furthermore, the public disclosure of audit information enhances the transparency of green projects, strengthens investor confidence in green industries, and expands and strengthens financing channels. Thus, government auditing plays a comprehensive role in the green finance system, acting as a constraint, incentive, and credit enhancement mechanism. This study proposes the following hypotheses:

H1. *Chinese government audits have a positive impact on the development of green finance.*

2.2. Fiscal Execution Efficiency and Government Auditing

Despite the differences in government auditing systems across countries, international research generally agrees that government auditing plays a significant role in enhancing

https://doi.org/10.3390/jrfm19010017

fiscal efficiency, particularly in countries that implement budget performance management, fiscal transparency, and accountable government systems (OECD, 2025). Some international studies (Bednarek & Ciak, 2022; Blume & Voigt, 2011; Bostan et al., 2021; Šalienė et al., 2024) have empirically demonstrated that audit oversight of budget execution and public project expenditures helps reduce fiscal waste, lower the risk of corruption, and improve the accuracy of budget allocation. Several studies (Cordery & Hay, 2019; Otia & Bracci, 2022; Volodina & Grossi, 2025) argue that if auditing synergizes with budget performance systems, fiscal transparency reforms, and electronic budgeting systems, it can significantly enhance fiscal efficiency and the creation of public value.

With the deepening reforms of China's government auditing and fiscal policies, Chinese studies generally agree that government auditing plays a crucial external supervisory role in improving the efficiency of fiscal fund utilization and standardizing budget execution (Cao et al., 2022; J. Liu, 2017). Some studies (F. Chen et al., 2023; Z. Chen & Hu, 2025; Fang et al., 2024; D. Zhang et al., 2022) empirically demonstrate that local governments with stronger and broader audit capabilities tend to exhibit higher efficiency in the allocation and execution of fiscal funds. Furthermore, some Chinese studies suggest that government auditing influences fiscal execution efficiency through three mechanisms: regulatory constraint (Lu et al., 2025), information enhancement (Fang et al., 2024; OECD, 2025; H. Wang et al., 2024), and rectification and promotion (J. Chen & Aidi, 2025; Fang et al., 2025). Other studies (Assakaf et al., 2018; F. Chen et al., 2023, 2025) also point out that the impact of government auditing on fiscal execution efficiency exhibits significant heterogeneity across regions, fiscal structures, and institutional environments for auditing.

This study argues that Chinese government auditing, as a crucial external oversight force for national fiscal operations, effectively improves overall fiscal efficiency by uncovering irregularities in fiscal revenue and expenditure. Regarding the efficiency of fiscal revenue execution, the timeliness, completeness, and accuracy of fiscal revenue are legally ensured through audit monitoring and rectification mechanisms, which contribute to the improved predictability and stability of budgetary revenue (W. Li et al., 2019; J. Liu & Lin, 2012). Regarding the efficiency of fiscal expenditure execution, government auditing, through accountability and penalty mechanisms, regulates budgetary expenditure, promotes performance management of funds, and curbs waste, thereby significantly enhancing expenditure efficiency (J. Liu, 2015; Yali, 2023). Therefore, the following hypotheses are proposed:

H2. *Chinese government audits have a positive impact on fiscal execution efficiency.*

H2a. *Chinese government audits have a positive impact on fiscal revenue execution efficiency.*

H2b. *Chinese government audits have a positive impact on fiscal expenditure execution efficiency.*

2.3. *The Mediating Effect of Fiscal Execution Efficiency on Government Auditing in Promoting Green Finance*

While international and Chinese studies have confirmed the positive role of government auditing in promoting green finance and fiscal efficiency, the relationship among these three factors remains largely unexplored. In the context of green development, Chinese government audits enhance revenue execution efficiency by strengthening oversight of fiscal revenue collection, thus contributing to a robust and transparent fiscal foundation (Guo et al., 2024). This empowers the government to provide long-term support for green finance service projects (Xia, 2024). Furthermore, higher fiscal revenue execution efficiency reduces financial risk, enabling financial institutions to more accurately assess the potential

https://doi.org/10.3390/jrfm19010017

benefits of green finance, thereby increasing the availability of green credit and green financial products (W. Wang et al., 2023).

Regarding fiscal expenditure, government auditing, through accountability mechanisms, performance audits, and rectification, has effectively corrected the problems of delayed, wasteful, and inefficient fiscal spending. This will encourage the government to allocate its limited fiscal resources more rationally to areas related to green development (You & Wang, 2025). Furthermore, improved efficiency in fiscal expenditure execution not only enhances the credibility of green finance but also increases the transparency and certainty of green investment, thereby alleviating information asymmetry for financial institutions in green credit and investment decisions, and further boosting public expectations and confidence in green finance investment (L. Sun et al., 2025). Therefore, this study argues that these three factors form a transmission chain of "audit constraints—improved fiscal administration efficiency—enhanced green financial services." The efficiency of fiscal revenue and expenditure execution can play a significant mediating role in the process by which government auditing influences the development of green finance.

H3. *Fiscal execution efficiency has the effect of mediating between the Chinese government audit and Green finance.*

H3a. *Fiscal revenue execution efficiency has the effect of mediating between the Chinese government audit and Green finance.*

H3b. *Fiscal expenditure execution efficiency has the effect of mediating between the Chinese government audit and Green finance.*

3. Materials and Methods

3.1. Research Variables and Data Sources

Dependent variable: The dependent variable in this study is green finance (GF), and the Entropy Method is used for weighted calculation. The entropy method is an objective weighting method based on the dispersion of indicators. The greater the dispersion of an indicator across regions, the more information it provides, and the greater its weight in the comprehensive evaluation. Therefore, the entropy method can effectively avoid subjective weighting and fully reflect the differences and information contributions of indicators. Referring to H. K. Liu and He (2021), S. Zhang and Ren (2024), Xie and Zhou (2023), and Mao and Wang (2024), this study selects seven green finance indices as primary indicators (Table 1).

Table 1. Indicator system for GF.

Primary Indicator	Measurement Method
Green Credit	Total Credit for Environmental Protection Projects in the Province/Total Credit in the Province
Green Investment	The proportion of environmental pollution control investment in GDP
Green Insurance	Environmental Pollution Liability Insurance Revenue/Total Premium Revenue
Green Bonds	Total Green Bond Issuance/Total Bond Issuance
Green Support	Fiscal Environmental Protection Expenditure/General Budget Expenditure
Green Funds	Total Market Value of Green Funds/Total Market Value of All Funds
Green Equity	Pollution Discharge Rights Trading/Total Equity Market Transactions

All indicator data were standardised according to entropy requirements to eliminate differences in measurement units, thereby ensuring comparability across provincial levels.

https://doi.org/10.3390/jrfm19010017

Data sources: Various authoritative statistical yearbooks of China, including the Statistical Yearbook of Science and Technology in China, Statistical Yearbook of Energy in China, Financial Yearbook of China, Statistical Yearbook of Agriculture in China, Statistical Yearbook of Industry in China, and Statistical Yearbook of the Tertiary Industry in China.

Independent variable: The dependent variable in this study is Chinese government auditing (CGA). Following the research methodology of J. Chen and Aidi (2025), based on the principle of variance contribution rate weighting, employ weighted principal component analysis (WPCA) to calculate this variable. Specifically, the three indicators of Chinese government auditing (Table 2) are weighted according to the ratio of each principal component's eigenvalue to the total eigenvalue. The principal component scores are then weighted and summed to construct a composite index. Since the larger the eigenvalue of the principal component, the greater the variance contribution rate, and the more variance explained to the original variable, this method has high objectivity and reliability. Data are sourced from the annual China Auditing Yearbook.

Table 2. Indicator system for CGA.

Indicator	KMO	MVTEST	Eigenvalue	Comp1	Comp2	Comp3
Natural logarithm of the rectification of the amount in question	0.5424	Adjusted LR chi2(3) = 128.69 Prob > chi2 = 0.0000	1.63947	0.6258	−0.3996	0.6699
The natural logarithm of the number of audit opinions adopted	0.5363		0.873497	0.6579	−0.1909	−0.7285
The number of people held accountable and punished after being transferred by the audit	0.6856		0.487034	0.4190	0.8966	0.1434
Overall WPCA	0.5546					

As shown in Table 2 above, the overall KMO value for the audit (WPCA) is 0.5546, which exceeds 0.5, indicating that the data are suitable for principal component analysis. Although the structure is not robust enough, it can still be used for dimensionality reduction. Kaiser (1974) and Hutcheson and Sofroniou (1999) both noted that a KMO value greater than 0.5 and less than 0.6 still meets the minimum requirements for principal component analysis. At the same time, the diagonality test of the covariance matrix (MVTEST) is significant ($p < 0.001$), indicating a significant correlation between the indicators. Therefore, the data is generally suitable for weighted principal component analysis (WPCA).

Mediating and Control Variables: drawing on studies by Jin and Zou (2005) and Wen et al. (2025), this study utilizes the ratio of the settlement amount to the budget amount of fiscal revenue and expenditure for each Chinese province to measure the efficiency of fiscal revenue (RE) and expenditure (EE). Data for these two mediating variables are sourced from the China Fiscal Yearbook for each year. Additionally, referring to studies by Fang et al. (2024) and Zhu et al. (2021), this study uses the ratio of each Chinese province's foreign trade volume to GDP to measure the degree of openness to the outside world (OP). The industrialization level (IL) is the ratio of industrial added value to GDP, used to measure the degree of industrialization in each province. Performance level (PV) is the ratio of each province's total enterprise revenue to GDP. Data for these three control variables are all sourced from the China Statistical Yearbook for each year.

3.2. Scope of the Study and Descriptive Statistical Analysis

This study uses panel data from 30 provinces in China from 2010 to 2021 as its research scope. Descriptive statistical analysis (Table 3) shows that the standard deviations

https://doi.org/10.3390/jrfm19010017

for green finance (GF) and government audit (CGA) are 0.1211 and 0.7593, respectively, indicating significant unevenness in the development of green finance and government audit capabilities among Chinese provinces. Regarding fiscal execution efficiency, the mean execution rates of fiscal revenue (RE) and expenditure (EE) are 103.36 and 92.92, respectively, indicating that most provinces can meet or even exceed their annual budget revenue targets. Furthermore, the minimum and maximum values of openness to the outside world (OP) and industrialization level (IL) indicate significant differences in openness and industrialization levels among provinces. The standard deviation for performance level (RV) is 0.0317, showing a moderate degree of difference in provincial enterprise performance and economic vitality.

Table 3. Descriptive Statistical Analysis.

Variables	Measure	Count	Min	Max	Mean	Std
GF	The entropy method combines seven indicators of green finance.	360	0.0835	0.6093	0.3159	0.1211
CGA	The WPCA method merges three government audit indicators.	360	−1.5804	7.7746	0	0.7593
RE	The ratio of the fiscal revenue settlement amount to the budget amount in various provinces of China	360	73.8	131.3	103.3628	6.5008
EE	The ratio of the fiscal expenditure settlement amount to the budget amount in various provinces of China	360	78.1	99	92.915	4.3716
OP	The ratio of foreign trade volume to GDP of Chinese provinces	360	0.0076	1.4638	0.2773	0.2945
IL	The ratio of industrial added value to GDP	360	0.1007	0.4976	0.3052	0.0732
RV	The ratio of each province's total enterprise revenue to GDP	360	0.0584	0.2452	0.1140	0.0317

Notably, Table 3 shows that the minimum value of the composite index CGA is negative, and the mean is close to zero. This characteristic stems from the weighted average analysis (WPCA) method of CGA. Specifically, its numerical results reflect the degree of deviation of each observation from the sample average level, rather than the absolute value (I. Jolliffe, 2011). Therefore, a negative value only indicates that the overall level of the region is lower than the sample average level, and does not imply a negative economic meaning. Additionally, the zero mean indicates that the composite measure is centered at the sample mean, resulting from the standardization procedure (I. T. Jolliffe & Cadima, 2016). This characteristic is consistent with the statistical properties of constructing composite indices using principal component analysis and aligns with standard practices in existing empirical studies.

3.3. Research Model

This study uses provincial panel data from China from 2010 to 2021 as its research object and employs Stata 17.0 for data analysis. Based on the hypotheses proposed in the previous section and following the three steps of testing the classic mediation effect proposed by Baron and Kenny (1986), this study first verifies the direct impact of government auditing on green finance (Model 1), then verifies the effect of government auditing on the fiscal revenue (expenditure) execution efficiency (Models 2 and 3), and finally verifies the mediating role of revenue (expenditure) (Models 4 and 5). To mitigate the bias of omitted

https://doi.org/10.3390/jrfm19010017

variables in the model and ensure that the research conclusions accurately reflect the effects of government auditing and fiscal execution efficiency, thereby enhancing the reliability of the recommendations, this study draws on the research of Heckman et al. (1999). It selects openness to the outside world (OP), industrialization level (IL), and performance level (PV) as control variables for the model. As indicated in Figure 1, the research framework of this study is as follows:

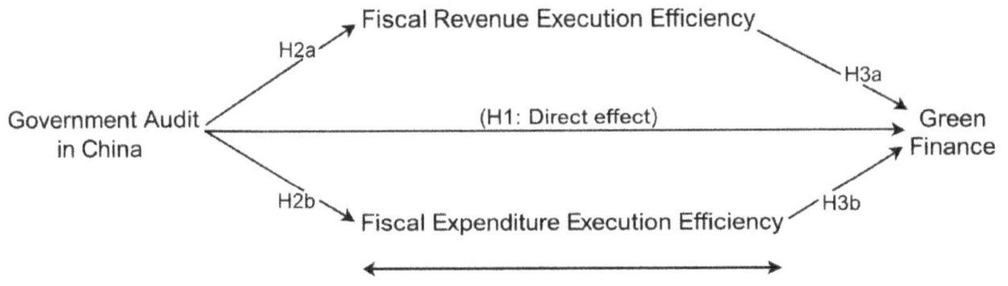

Figure 1. Conceptual mediation framework. Note: Fiscal revenue execution efficiency and fiscal expenditure execution efficiency are treated as parallel mediators.

The model is based on Hypothesis 1:

$$GFi,t = \beta 0 + \beta 1CGAi,t + \beta 2OPi,t + \beta 3ILi,t + \beta 4RVi,t + \alpha i + \lambda t + \varepsilon i,t \quad (1)$$

Based on Hypotheses 2 (2a, 2b), the following model was designed:

$$REi,t = \beta 0 + \beta 1CGAi,t + \beta 2OPi,t + \beta 3ILi,t + \beta 4RVi,t + \alpha i + \lambda t + \varepsilon i,t \quad (2)$$

$$EEi,t = \beta 0 + \beta 1CGAi,t + \beta 2OPi,t + \beta 3ILi,t + \beta 4RVi,t + \alpha i + \lambda t + \varepsilon i,t \quad (3)$$

Based on Hypotheses 3 (3a, 3b), the following model was designed:

$$GFi,t = \beta 0 + \beta 1CGAi,t + \beta 2REi,t + \beta 3OPi,t + \beta 4ILi,t + \beta 5RVi,t + \alpha i + \lambda t + \varepsilon i,t \quad (4)$$

$$GFi,t = \beta 0 + \beta 1CGAi,t + \beta 2EEi,t + \beta 3OPi,t + \beta 4ILi,t + \beta 5RVi,t + \alpha i + \lambda t + \varepsilon i,t \quad (5)$$

The data contains provinces (i) and periods (t). Individual, regional, and time effects are controlled by dummy variables (αi, βi, and λt), and the error term is represented by ε.

4. Results Analysis

4.1. Data Quality Testing

Before conducting the Hausman test, this study performed a series of data quality checks on the sample data, including Pearson correlation coefficient analysis, a multicollinearity test (VIF), a heteroscedasticity test, and an autocorrelation test. The correlation coefficient and VIF tests help identify potentially high correlations between variables, avoiding the instability of coefficient estimates and standard error inflation caused by multicollinearity. Heteroscedasticity and autocorrelation tests are used to determine whether the error term violates classical regression assumptions, thus avoiding statistical inference distortion. Through these data quality diagnoses, this study ensured the reliability and robustness of the Hausman test and panel regression results.

4.1.1. Pearson Coefficient and VIF Test

This study performed the Pearson coefficient and VIF tests (Table 4). Clearly, the correlations among the variables were low, with the absolute values of the Pearson coefficients not exceeding 0.52, and far below the commonly used threshold of 0.70 for assessing the

https://doi.org/10.3390/jrfm19010017

risk of multicollinearity. This suggests that there is no significant linear correlation among the main explanatory variables in this study. The variance inflation factor (VIF) test results indicate that the VIF values for each variable range from 1.07 to 1.85, which is far below the empirically used threshold of 5, suggesting very weak correlations among the variables. This further confirms that the model is not subject to multicollinearity.

Table 4. Pearson correlation analysis and VIF test.

Variables	GF	CGA	RE	EE	OP	IF	RV	VIF
GF	1							
CGA	0.2445	1.0000						1.85
RE	−0.2002	−0.1417	1.0000					1.49
EE	0.0300	0.1162	−0.2378	1.0000				1.33
OP	0.3999	−0.0644	−0.0327	−0.0767	1.0000			1.20
IL	0.1569	−0.1777	0.0426	0.0583	−0.0152	1.0000		1.07
RV	0.0047	−0.3546	−0.0170	0.1630	0.5159	−0.0355	1.0000	1.07

4.1.2. Heteroscedasticity and Autocorrelation Test

The Wooldridge (2010) test results in this study (Table 5) showed that the model had significant first-order autocorrelation (F = 35.794, $p < 0.001$). This study further performed first-order differencing on the core variables, and the autocorrelation test results were no longer significant after differencing (F = 0.023, $p = 0.882$), indicating that serial correlation had been effectively eliminated. Furthermore, the Breusch–Pagan test results in this study showed that the heteroscedasticity test results of the original model were not significant ($p = 0.081$), and the test results after logarithmic transformation of the variables were also not significant ($p = 0.205$). This indicates that the model does not have significant heteroscedasticity issues.

Table 5. Heteroscedasticity and Autocorrelation Test.

Breusch–Pagan Test		**Wooldridge Test**	
Raw Data	After Logarithmic Transformation	Raw Data	After taking the first-order difference in the variable
chi2(1) = 3.04 Prob > chi2 = 0.0813	chi2(1) = 1.61 Prob > chi2 = 0.2046	F(1, 22) = 35.794 Prob > F = 0.0000	F(1, 12) = 0.023 Prob > F = 0.8815

4.2. Hausman Test Results

From the results of the F-statistic and Prob > F (Table 6), except for Model 2, the F-values of the other models are all higher than 10. However, the Prob > F values for all models are significantly lower than 0.01, indicating that the overall regression of each model is significant and the explanatory variables have a certain explanatory power for the dependent variable. The R values range from 0.0584 to 0.5210, indicating that there are differences in the explanatory power of different models. Among them, the model containing the mediating variable performs better, and its explanatory power is significantly improved. In addition, the chi2 (4) test of all models is significant (Prob > chi2 < 0.05), which further verifies the robustness of the overall model estimation.

The empirical results of Model 1 (Table 3) show that government auditing (CGA) has a significant positive effect on the development of green finance (GF). This result is consistent with Hypothesis 1 and also indicates that government auditing improves the transparency and reliability of green finance projects by regulating fiscal execution and supervising the use of local funds. Furthermore, the results of Models 2 and 3 show that

https://doi.org/10.3390/jrfm19010017

CGA has a significant negative effect on the efficiency of fiscal revenue execution (RE) and a significant positive impact on the efficiency of fiscal expenditure execution (EE). Finally, the RE and EE variables in Models 4 and 5 are both highly significant. However, in Model 4, the variable CGA is highly significant, but its coefficient (0.0094) is smaller than that in Model 1 (0.0126). According to the mediation criterion of Baron and Kenny (1986), the results suggest that RE partially mediates the relationship between CGA and GF. In Model 5, the variable CGA becomes insignificant, suggesting that EE plays a complete mediating role in the relationship between CGA and GF.

Table 6. Hausman Test Results.

Variable	Model 1	Model 2	Model 3	Model 4	Model 5
CGA	0.0126 *** (0.0033)	−1.8056 ** (0.6774)	1.4958 *** (0.3437)	0.0094 ** (0.0031)	0.0054 (0.0029)
RE	-	-	-	−0.0017 *** (0.0003)	-
EE	-	-	-	-	0.0048 *** (0.0005)
OP	−0.1822 *** (0.0193)	9.2234 * (3.9659)	−12.3827 *** (2.0120)	−0.1659 *** (0.0182)	−0.1226 *** (0.0180)
IL	0.0894 * (0.0411)	0.3485 (3.4491)	−0.2424 (4.2865)	0.0900 * (0.0384)	0.0906 * (0.0357)
RV	−0.5193 *** (0.1275)	−2.3340 (5.1929)	0.7795 (3.2886)	−0.5234 *** (0.1190)	−0.5230 *** (0.1105)
N	360	360	360	360	360
F-statistic	34.35	3.77	16.91	38.76	52.64
Prob > F	0.0000	0.0054	0.0000	0.0000	0.0000
R	0.3599	0.0584	0.2178	0.4447	0.5210
chi2(4)	36.52	12.67	99.34	49.93	25.93
Prob > chi2	0.0000	0.0130	0.0000	0.0000	0.0001

Note: $p < 0.001$: '***', $p < 0.01$: '**', $p < 0.05$: '*', which show that the regression coefficient is significant at the levels of 1%, 5%, and 10%. The brackets show the standard error.

4.3. Endogeneity Testing

Following the methodologies of studies Wooldridge (2010) and Cameron and Trivedi (2005), and employing the Durbin-Wu-Hausman (DWH) method, this study uses lagged terms of independent variables as instrumental variables to test for endogeneity issues in all models. This study combines the first-stage F-test criterion proposed by Stock and Yogo (2002) with the R^2 test criterion proposed by Shea (1997) to identify problems associated with weak instrumental variables.

This study evaluated the endogeneity of independent variables and the effectiveness of instrumental variables in five models (Table 7). The F-values and p-values of the Durbin-Wu-Hausman (DWH) test showed that no significant endogeneity issues existed in the independent variables of any of the five models (all p-values were greater than 0.05). Furthermore, the test results (Table 7) showed that the first-stage F-values for Models 1, 2, and 3 were 18.3367, 18.3367, and 12.701, respectively, all significantly higher than the commonly used weak instrument judgment threshold of 10, indicating that these three models did not have significant endogeneity issues. Meanwhile, the Shea partial R^2 for CGA and EE were 0.5505 and 0.7458, respectively, indicating that the corresponding instrumental variables had strong explanatory power. In contrast, the Shea partial R^2 for RE in Model 4 was only 0.0556, suggesting a certain risk of weak instrumentality for this instrumental variable, but the overall impact was manageable.

https://doi.org/10.3390/jrfm19010017

Table 7. Endogeneity Testing.

Test or Variable	Model 1	Model 2	Model 3	Model 4	Model 5
DWH Test (endogeneity)					
F	0.2182	1.1578	0.8441	0.0041	0.1607
p	0.6450	0.2936	0.3682	0.9959	0.8525
First-stage regression summary statistics					
Adjusted R^2	0.5539	0.5539	0.2942	-	-
F	18.3367	18.3367	12.701	-	-
Prob > F	0.0000	0.0000	0.0000	-	-
				Shea's partial R-sq.	Shea's partial R-sq.
CGA				0.5505	0.3803
RE				0.0556	-
EE				-	0.7458

4.4. Placebo Test

Following the methods proposed by Hagemann (2019) and Lei and Sudijono (2024), this study randomly generated a set of placebo variables independent of the main explanatory variables. It incorporated them into the Hausman panel regression models, which include both fixed and random effects, to replace the core independent variables in the regression analysis. In this study (Table 8), none of the placebo variables in any model showed significance ($p > 0.05$), indicating that the results of all previous Hausman tests in this study were not spurious regression results, ruling out the possibility of model misspecification or other random factors leading to spurious relationships. Thus supporting the robustness of the previous model results.

Table 8. Placebo Test.

Variable	Model 1	Model 2	Model 3	Model 4	Model 5
Placebo	−0.0121 (0.0070)	−0.1287 (1.4172)	−0.8084 (0.7340)	−0.0124 (0.0064)	−0.0081 (0.0059)
RE	-	-	-	−0.0019 *** (0.0003)	-
EE	-	-	-	-	0.0050 *** (0.0005)
OP	−0.1953 *** (0.0195)	10.9434 ** (3.9706)	−13.8794 *** (2.0565)	−0.1742 *** (0.0183)	−0.1255 *** (0.0181)
IL	0.0629 (0.0420)	2.9892 (3.5537)	−2.9950 (4.4301)	0.0686 (0.0387)	0.0779 * (0.0357)
RV	−0.5205 *** (0.1305)	−3.1961 (5.5826)	0.9846 (3.7677)	−0.5266 *** (0.1203)	−0.5254 *** (0.1109)
N	360	360	360	360	360
F-statistic	29.88	5.94	11.65	36.90	52.04
Prob > F	0.0000	0.003 **	0.0000	0.0000	0.0000
R	0.3297	0.1309	0.1610	0.4326	0.5181
chi2(4)	38.13	9.10	22.62	51.57	26.31
Prob > chi2	0.0000	0.0059	0.0002	0.0000	0.0001

Note: $p < 0.001$: '***', $p < 0.01$: '**', $p < 0.05$: '*', which show that the regression coefficient is significant at the levels of 1%, 5%, and 10%. The brackets show the coefficient values. The brackets show the standard error.

5. Discussion

The results of Model 1 support Hypothesis 1, namely that Chinese government auditing has a positive impact on the level of green finance. The findings are similar to those of studies by L. Sun et al. (2025) and L.-Q. Huang et al. (2024). Therefore, this study provides further empirical evidence that government auditing promotes the development of green finance. This result suggests that government auditing, as an external oversight mechanism, helps mitigate information asymmetry in the green finance market, the public disclosure of audit results increases the transparency of government departments and project implementing units, thereby enhancing investors' ability to identify risks in green credit, green bonds, and green investments, and enabling financial institutions and investors to more accurately assess the risks and expected returns of green projects, thereby enhancing the service quality of green finance.

Furthermore, the results of Model 2 show that government auditing hurts the efficiency of fiscal revenue execution, which is inconsistent with Hypothesis 2 and also indicates that government auditing does not play a positive role in promoting revenue execution. This may stem from the highly institutionalized and mandatory nature of the fiscal revenue collection mechanism, with limited autonomy for local governments in the tax collection process. Relying solely on auditing is unlikely to improve revenue execution efficiency directly (Amyulianthy, 2022). Furthermore, auditing intervention may increase administrative burdens in the short term, leading to a certain degree of decline in revenue execution efficiency. Conversely, Model 3 shows that government auditing significantly improves the efficiency of fiscal expenditure execution, supporting Hypothesis 3. This is because fiscal expenditure processes have greater discretionary power, such as project approval, budget allocation, fund disbursement, and performance evaluation (Afonso et al., 2024). Auditing can directly intervene in these key stages, correcting irregular, delayed, and inefficient expenditure behaviors, thereby significantly improving the efficiency of fiscal fund utilization.

The results of Models 4 and 5 indicate that the efficiency of fiscal revenue execution plays a partial mediating role in the mechanism by which audits influence green finance, while the efficiency of fiscal expenditure execution plays a full mediating role. This means that the role of auditing in promoting green finance is mainly achieved by improving the standardization, transparency, and performance of fiscal expenditures (Allen et al., 2013). On the one hand, although government auditing can provide a more stable funding base for green finance by strengthening revenue, this channel is not the only way auditing influences green finance. Its role in promoting green finance still partially depends on other institutional factors (Campiglio, 2016), such as budget management systems, the degree of coordination in financial supervision, and the effectiveness of implementing green industry policies.

The efficiency of fiscal expenditure execution exhibits a complete mediating effect, indicating that the primary mechanism by which government auditing promotes green finance development lies in improving the efficiency of fiscal expenditure. By standardizing budget execution, strengthening performance supervision, and reducing irregular expenses and waste of funds, auditing enables fiscal resources to be more effectively directed towards green industries, energy conservation and emission reduction projects, and environmental infrastructure construction (Montes et al., 2019). This not only improves the efficiency of public fund utilization but also effectively reduces information asymmetry and risk expectations for investors in green project financing (W. Li et al., 2023), thereby significantly enhancing the expected benefits of green finance, such as green credit and green investment.

6. Conclusions

Based on panel data from 30 provinces in China from 2010 to 2021, this study finds that government auditing has a significant positive impact on the development of green finance in China. While the efficiency of fiscal revenue execution has a partial mediating effect on this relationship, the efficiency of fiscal expenditure execution has a full mediating effect.

https://doi.org/10.3390/jrfm19010017

This implies that although the impact of fiscal revenue execution efficiency is relatively limited, it can still provide beneficial resource guarantees and support for the development of green finance. However, to fully leverage the role of government auditing in promoting green finance, it should focus on improving the efficiency of fiscal expenditure execution by standardizing and optimizing fiscal expenditure processes to achieve efficient and transparent use of funds.

Implications: Theoretically, this study enriches the theoretical perspectives on government auditing, fiscal execution efficiency, and green finance research. The findings reveal the promoting role and mechanism of government auditing in green finance, clarifying the fully mediating role of fiscal expenditure execution efficiency, and expanding the existing theoretical framework on how government auditing influences green finance development through fiscal efficiency. Secondly, this study distinguishes the different roles of fiscal revenue and fiscal expenditure execution efficiency in the relationship between auditing and green finance. This reflects the explanation of institutional implementation differences and governance efficiency by public governance theory, providing a more refined reference for subsequent research on green finance. This finding helps to understand the economic effects of government governance on green finance under different fiscal backgrounds, expanding new perspectives and policy implications for green finance research.

In practice, this study underscores the pivotal role of government auditing in promoting green finance development, particularly by facilitating efficient resource allocation and risk management through enhanced effectiveness in fiscal expenditure execution. To further leverage the function of auditing, policymakers should focus on improving fiscal expenditure management mechanisms, optimizing budget approval, fund disbursement, and performance evaluation processes, as well as enhancing the transparency and standardization of public funds. Furthermore, the public disclosure of audit results should be strengthened to reduce information asymmetry in the green finance market and improve the ability of financial institutions and investors to assess the risks and returns of green projects, thereby promoting the sound development of green finance.

Limitations and Suggestions for Future Research: This study acknowledges certain limitations. First, this study is primarily based on provincial-level macroeconomic data, which may not fully reflect the heterogeneity among local governments at different levels. Second, the variables selected in this study only cover a portion of the indicators related to government auditing, green finance, and fiscal execution efficiency, which may not comprehensively characterize the proper relationship among the three. Therefore, future research could consider incorporating data from more administrative levels, as well as variables of more dimensions and types, to more precisely identify the interaction mechanisms among the three at different levels and time periods, thereby gaining a more comprehensive understanding of the role of Chinese government auditing and fiscal execution efficiency in promoting the development of green finance.

Author Contributions: Conceptualization, J.C.; methodology, J.C.; software, J.C.; validation, J.C.; resources, J.C.; writing—original draft preparation, J.C.; writing—review and editing, A.A.; supervision, Z.S. All authors have read and agreed to the published version of the manuscript.

Funding: No financial assistance was provided to the authors of this article to complete the research, authorship, and/or publishing of this article.

Institutional Review Board Statement: Not applicable.

Informed Consent Statement: Not applicable.

Data Availability Statement: Data supporting the findings of this study are available from the corresponding author upon reasonable request.

Conflicts of Interest: The authors declare no conflicts of interest.

References

Afonso, A., Jalles, J. T., & Venâncio, A. (2024). A tale of government spending efficiency and trust in the state. *Public Choice*, *200*(1), 89–118. [CrossRef]

Allen, R., Hemming, R., & Potter, B. H. (2013). Introduction: The meaning, content and objectives of public financial management. In *The international handbook of public financial management* (pp. 1–12). Springer. [CrossRef]

Alqooti, A. A. (2020). Public governance in the public sector: Literature review. *EuroMid Journal of Business and Tech-Innovation*, 14–25. [CrossRef]

Amyulianthy, R. (2022). *The effect of audit results, performance measurement system, and good governance on local government performance*. Universiti Teknologi MARA (UiTM).

Assakaf, E. A., Samsudin, R. S., & Othman, Z. (2018). Public sector auditing and corruption: A literature. *Asian Journal of Finance & Accounting*, *10*, 226–241. [CrossRef]

Baron, R. M., & Kenny, D. A. (1986). The moderator–mediator variable distinction in social psychological research: Conceptual, strategic, and statistical considerations. *Journal of Personality and Social Psychology*, *51*(6), 1173. [CrossRef] [PubMed]

Bednarek, P., & Ciak, J. (2022). Performance audit effectiveness indicators: Evidence from Poland. *Journal of Public Governance*, *61*(3), 43–56. [CrossRef]

Blume, L., & Voigt, S. (2011). Does organizational design of supreme audit institutions matter? A cross-country assessment. *European Journal of Political Economy*, *27*(2), 215–229. [CrossRef]

Bo, S., Wu, Y., & Zhong, L. (2020). Flattening of government hierarchies and misuse of public funds: Evidence from audit programs in China. *Journal of Economic Behavior & Organization*, *179*, 141–151. [CrossRef]

Bostan, I., Tudose, M. B., Clipa, R. I., Chersan, I. C., & Clipa, F. (2021). Supreme audit institutions and sustainability of public finance. Links and evidence along the economic cycles. *Sustainability*, *13*(17), 9757. [CrossRef]

Cameron, A. C., & Trivedi, P. K. (2005). *Microeconometrics: Methods and applications*. Cambridge University Press.

Campiglio, E. (2016). Beyond carbon pricing: The role of banking and monetary policy in financing the transition to a low-carbon economy. *Ecological Economics*, *121*, 220–230. [CrossRef]

Cao, H., Li, M., Lu, Y., & Xu, Y. (2022). The impact of strengthening government auditing supervision on fiscal sustainability: Evidence from China's auditing vertical management reform. *Finance Research Letters*, *47*, 102825. [CrossRef]

Chen, F., Dong, B., Zhang, M., & Chen, Q. (2025). Government environmental auditing and synergistic governance outcomes: Evidence from Chinese cities. *Sustainability*, *17*(19), 8962. [CrossRef]

Chen, F., Guo, Q., & Jiang, B. (2023). Government audit supervision and fiscal sustainability: Evidence from interprovincial China. *SSRN*, 4474309. [CrossRef]

Chen, J., & Aidi, A. (2025). Chinese government auditing and economic growth: The mediating effect of corruption. *Veredas Do Direito*, *22*(2), e3124. [CrossRef]

Chen, Z., & Hu, M. (2025). Does national auditing improve local fiscal transparency? Evidence from China. *International Studies of Economics*, *20*(2), 153–161. [CrossRef]

Cordery, C. J., & Hay, D. (2019). Supreme audit institutions and public value: Demonstrating relevance. *Financial Accountability & Management*, *35*(2), 128–142. [CrossRef]

Fang, C. J., Ahmi, A., & Sharif, Z. (2024). Government auditing, government transparency, and corruption: Empirical evidence from provincial levels in China. *South Eastern European Journal of Public Health*, *2024*, 1780–1796. [CrossRef]

Fang, C. J., Ahmi, A., & Sharif, Z. (2025). Fiscal decentralization and corruption: The moderating role of economic responsibility audit in China. *International Journal of Innovative Research and Scientific Studies*, *8*(1), 854–863. [CrossRef]

Fu, C., Lu, L., & Pirabi, M. (2023). Advancing green finance: A review of sustainable development. *Digital Economy and Sustainable Development*, *1*(1), 20. [CrossRef]

Goolsarran, S. A. (2007). The evolving role of supreme audit institutions. *The Journal of Government Financial Management*, *56*(3), 28.

Gulmammadov, V. (2025). Involvement of supreme audit institutions in climate performance assessment: International and local experiences, realities and challenges. *International Journal of Government Auditing*, *52*(1), 66–72.

Guo, Y., Wang, J., Wang, H., & Zhang, F. (2024). The impact of big data tax collection and management on inefficient investment of enterprises—A quasi-natural experiment based on the golden tax project III. *International Review of Economics & Finance*, *92*, 678–689. [CrossRef]

Hagemann, A. (2019). Placebo inference on treatment effects when the number of clusters is small. *Journal of Econometrics*, *213*(1), 190–209. [CrossRef]

Heckman, J. J., LaLonde, R. J., & Smith, J. A. (1999). The economics and econometrics of active labor market programs. In *Handbook of labor economics* (Vol. 3, pp. 1865–2097). Elsevier. [CrossRef]

Hou, H., Wang, Y., & Zhang, M. (2024). Impact of environmental information disclosure on green finance development: Empirical evidence from China: H. Hou et al. *Environment, Development and Sustainability, 26*(8), 20279–20309. [CrossRef]

Huang, L.-Q., Li, Y. J., & Xu, H. (2024). Government environmental audit and corporate green governance. *Journal of University of Electronic Science and Technology of China (Social Sciences Edition), 26*(4), 98–112.

Huang, R., & Zou, X. (2025). Accountability audits of natural resources and industrial green total factor productivity: Evidence from China. *Humanities and Social Sciences Communications, 12*(1), 1–17. [CrossRef]

Hutcheson, G. D., & Sofroniou, N. (1999). *The multivariate social scientist: Introductory statistics using generalized linear models.* Sage Publications.

Jin, J., & Zou, H.-f. (2005). Fiscal decentralization, revenue and expenditure assignments, and growth in China. *Journal of Asian Economics, 16*(6), 1047–1064. [CrossRef]

Jolliffe, I. (2011). Principal component analysis. In *International encyclopedia of statistical science* (pp. 1094–1096). Springer.

Jolliffe, I. T., & Cadima, J. (2016). Principal component analysis: A review and recent developments. *Philosophical transactions of the royal society A: Mathematical, Physical and Engineering Sciences, 374*(2065), 20150202. [CrossRef]

Kaiser, H. F. (1974). An index of factorial simplicity. *Psychometrika, 39*(1), 31–36. [CrossRef]

Lei, L., & Sudijono, T. (2024). Inference for synthetic controls via refined placebo tests. *arXiv*, arXiv:2401.07152. [CrossRef]

Li, W., Pittman, J. A., & Wang, Z.-T. (2019). The determinants and consequences of tax audits: Some evidence from China. *The Journal of the American Taxation Association, 41*(1), 91–122. [CrossRef]

Li, W., Xia, L., & Zhang, Q. (2023). Fiscal-audit separation and government disclosure quality. *Journal of Accounting and Public Policy, 42*(4), 107100. [CrossRef]

Li, X., Tang, J., Feng, C., & Chen, Y. (2023). Can government environmental auditing help to improve environmental quality? Evidence from China. *International Journal of Environmental Research and Public Health, 20*(4), 2770. [CrossRef] [PubMed]

Liu, H., Jafri, M. A. H., Zhu, P., & Hafeez, M. (2024). Fiscal policy-green growth nexus: Does financial efficiency matter in top carbon emitter economies? *Environment, Development & Sustainability, 26*(8). [CrossRef]

Liu, H. K., & He, C. (2021). Mechanisms and Validation of green finance in promoting high-quality urban economic development: Empirical evidence from 272 prefecture-level cities in China. *Investment Research, 40*, 37–52.

Liu, J. (2015). *Study on the auditing theory of socialism with Chinese characteristics.* John Wiley & Sons.

Liu, J. (2017). *Study on the auditing system of socialism with Chinese characteristics.* John Wiley & Sons.

Liu, J., & Lin, B. (2012). Government auditing and corruption control: Evidence from China's provincial panel data. *China Journal of Accounting Research, 5*(2), 163–186. [CrossRef]

Lu, F., Ren, Q., Sun, J., & Wang, H. (2025). Natural disasters and local governments' fiscal misconduct: Evidence from five earthquakes in China. *Policy Studies Journal.* [CrossRef]

Lv, C., Bian, B., Lee, C.-C., & He, Z. (2021). Regional gap and the trend of green finance development in China. *Energy Economics, 102*, 105476. [CrossRef]

Ma, R., & Xi, C. (2025). Can green financial policies promote green urbanization? Evidence from China. *Frontiers in Sustainable Cities, 7*, 1637944. [CrossRef]

Mao, X., & Wang, R. (2024). Green finance and new productivity: Promotion or repression?—A perspective based on technological innovation and environmental concern. *Journal of Shanghai University of Finance and Economics, 26*(5), 31–45. [CrossRef]

Montes, G. C., Bastos, J. C. A., & de Oliveira, A. J. (2019). Fiscal transparency, government effectiveness and government spending efficiency: Some international evidence based on panel data approach. *Economic Modelling, 79*, 211–225. [CrossRef]

OECD. (2020). *Developing sustainable finance definitions and taxonomies: Green finance and investment.* OECD Publishing. [CrossRef]

OECD. (2025). *Quality budget institutions: Developments in OECD countries.* OECD Publishing.

Otia, J. E., & Bracci, E. (2022). Digital transformation and the public sector auditing: The SAI's perspective. *Financial Accountability & Management, 38*(2), 252–280. [CrossRef]

Rhodes, R. A. W. (1996). The new governance: Governing without government. *Political Studies, 44*(4), 652–667. [CrossRef]

Shea, J. (1997). Instrument relevance in multivariate linear models: A simple measure. *Review of Economics and Statistics, 79*(2), 348–352. [CrossRef]

Sitompul, R., Sanusi, Z. M., Alsayegh, M. F., Erum, N., Kazemian, S., & Hitam, M. (2023). Enhancing green investment efficiency through audit quality. *European Proceedings of Social and Behavioural Sciences, 131*, 1260–1269. [CrossRef]

Stock, J. H., & Yogo, M. (2002). *Testing for weak instruments in linear IV regression.* National Bureau of Economic Research.

Sułkowski, Ł., & Dobrowolski, Z. (2021). The role of supreme audit institutions in energy accountability in EU countries. *Energy Policy, 156*, 112413. [CrossRef]

Sun, L., Luo, K., Zhou, C., & Yan, J. (2025). Can the government environmental audits improve corporate green investment? Evidence from China. *International Review of Economics & Finance, 97*, 103782. [CrossRef]

Sun, Y., Zhong, H., Wang, Y., Pan, Y., & Tang, D. (2024). The effect of green finance on the transformation and upgrading of manufacturing industries in the Yangtze River economic belt of China. *Frontiers in Environmental Science, 12*, 1473621. [CrossRef]

https://doi.org/10.3390/jrfm19010017

Šalienė, A., Tamulevičienė, D., & Tvaronavičienė, M. (2024). Focus of performance audit recommendations on the approach of public value creation: The case of the National Audit Office of Lithuania. *Journal of International Studies*, *17*(4), 1–28. [CrossRef]

van Leeuwen, S. (2004). Auditing international environmental agreements: The role of supreme audit institutions. *Environmentalist*, *24*(2), 93–99. [CrossRef]

Volodina, T., & Grossi, G. (2025). Digital transformation in public sector auditing: Between hope and fear. *Public Management Review*, *27*(5), 1444–1468. [CrossRef]

Wang, C., Qiao, G., Ahmad, M., & Ahmed, Z. (2023). The role of the government in green finance, foreign direct investment, technological innovation, and industrial structure upgrading: Evidence from China. *Sustainability*, *15*(19), 14069. [CrossRef]

Wang, H., Tang, Z., Zhang, Z., & Deng, W. (2024). Can government environmental auditing and fiscal transparency promote the green development of heavy-polluting firms? *Environmental Research Letters*, *19*(7), 074054. [CrossRef]

Wang, R., Duan, Y., & Li, D. (2025). Beyond scale to efficiency: A dual-perspective framework for green finance in China. *Discover Sustainability*, *6*(1), 483. [CrossRef]

Wang, W., Wang, Z., & Mei, Y. (2023). Have government environmental auditing contributed to the green transformation of Chinese cities? *Heliyon*, *9*(12), e22709. [CrossRef]

Wen, M., Guo, X., & Luo, X. (2025). Do government audits reduce budgetary non-compliance?—An empirical analysis of budget execution audits in central government departments in China. *Chinese Studies*, *14*(2), 71–90. [CrossRef]

Wooldridge, J. M. (2010). *Econometric analysis of cross section and panel data*. MIT Press.

World Bank. (2018). Introduction to green finance. Available online: https://documents1.worldbank.org/curated/en/405891487108066678/pdf/112831-WP-PUBLIC-Introduction-to-Green-Finance.pdf?utm_source=chatgpt.com(accessed on 20 November 2025).

Xia, Z. (2024). The impact of smart audit on green finance: Evidence from China. *Advances in Economics and Management Research*, *12*(1), 744. [CrossRef]

Xie, F., & Zhou, M. (2023). A study on the impact of green finance on the digital economy and green development. *Chongqing Social Sciences*, *7*, 35–50. [CrossRef]

Yali, L. (2023). Performance audit: The development conditions in China. *Финансы: Теория и Практика*, *27*(4), 80–92. [CrossRef]

You, C., & Wang, J. (2025). State audit digitization and green technology innovation in state-owned enterprises. *SAGE Open*, *15*(2), 21582440251335996. [CrossRef]

Zhang, D., Shen, X., & Peng, C. (2022). National audit, media attention, and efficiency of local fiscal expenditure: A spatial econometric analysis based on provincial panel data in China. *Sustainability*, *15*(1), 532. [CrossRef]

Zhang, S., & Ren, C. (2024). The impact of green finance on high-quality agricultural development—an examination based on threshold and mediation effect models. *Cutting-Edge Engineering Management Technology*, *4*, 72–78. Available online: https://link.cnki.net/urlid/34.1013.N.20241128.0949.008 (accessed on 20 November 2025).

Zhu, W., Zhu, Y., Lin, H., & Yu, Y. (2021). Technology progress bias, industrial structure adjustment, and regional industrial economic growth motivation—Research on regional industrial transformation and upgrading based on the effect of learning by doing. *Technological Forecasting and Social Change*, *170*, 120928. [CrossRef]

https://doi.org/10.3390/jrfm19010017

Journal of
Risk and Financial Management

MDPI

Article

Analysis of the Financial Markets in the Bulgarian Agricultural Sector

Lyubomir Lyubenov [1,2] and Byulent Idirizov [3,4,*]

[1] Department Economics and International Relations, Faculty Business and Management, University of Ruse "Angel Kanchev", 8 Studentska Str., 7004 Ruse, Bulgaria; llyubenov@uni-ruse.bg or llyubenov@ts.uni-vt.bg
[2] Department of Economic Theory and International Economic Relations, Faculty of Economics, University of Veliko Tarnovo "St. Cyril and St. Methodius", Sveta Gora, 2 Teodosiy Tarnovski Str., 5003 Veliko Tarnovo, Bulgaria
[3] Department of Mathematics, Faculty of Natural Sciences and Education, University of Ruse "Angel Kanchev", 8 Studentska Str., 7004 Ruse, Bulgaria
[4] Department of Information Modeling, Institute of Mathematics and Informatics, Bulgarian Academy of Sciences, Acad. G. Bonchev Str., Bl. 8, 1113 Sofia, Bulgaria
* Correspondence: bidirizov@uni-ruse.bg or bidirizov@math.bas.bg

Abstract

The purpose of this study is to examine the interrelationships between public and corporate finance, gross value added (GVA), and the output of the agricultural sector in Bulgaria. The value of crop production shows a strong correlation with all financial indicators of the agricultural sector in Bulgaria—public, corporate, and total—as well as with corporate finance in the national economy. The value of the final output of the agricultural sector in Bulgaria also exhibits a strong correlation with national corporate finance, the corporate finance of the agricultural sector, and this sector's total financial resources, both public and private. The regression analysis demonstrates that public funding plays a leading role in mobilising private capital in the agricultural sector. A strong dependency is observed between state support, corporate lending, and total financial resources, confirming that public funds promote trust and stimulate investment activity. Crop production is identified as the structural driver of productivity and gross value added (GVA) of the agricultural sector in Bulgaria. However, excessive public subsidies may reduce its efficiency. Private loans—particularly agricultural credits—are emerging as a key mechanism for transforming the potential of the agricultural sector into actual growth. The regression models indicate the possibility that 1 billion BGN in loans lead to the creation of more than 2 billion BGN worth of crop production output, and more than 6 billion BGN in terms of final products. These findings justify that the sustainable development of the agricultural sector in Bulgaria is based on a balanced interaction between public financing and active private investment.

Keywords: public finance; corporate finance; gross value added; production; statistics

1. Introduction

The strategic importance of the agricultural sector for the social, environmental, and food security of every country motivates the research of the influence of financial markets on the performance of the agricultural sector. The agricultural sector in Bulgaria contributes approximately 5% to the gross domestic product (GDP) of Bulgaria and provides permanent employment of about 7% of the workforce in the national economy (Ministry of Agriculture, 2024). However, when considering its interrelationships with numerous other sectors, the significance of the agricultural sector determines the structure of the national economy. The increase in the competitiveness of the agricultural sector necessitates its modernisation and innovation, which in turn require both public and corporate financing. The important role of the agricultural sector in the social and economic development of each country motivates this research, which examines the influence of finance on the results achieved by the agricultural sector, such as gross value added (GVA), the value of total output, and other related indicators.

The financial markets of the agricultural sector play an important role in ensuring its stable and accelerated development. They influence the production of agricultural goods and contribute to both food and social security. These markets also affect the development of a range of other related markets—land, labour, machinery, feed, seeds, fertilisers, pesticides, etc. Overcoming a number of challenges such as climate change, the weaker position of farmers within the agri-food value chain, dealing with pandemics—COVID-19, avian flu, swine flu, etc. (Zaharieva et al., 2022)—and declining soil fertility, requires both public and corporate financing of the agricultural sector.

The prosperity of Bulgarian agriculture—through digitalisation, scientific research, consultancy and other services (Bezgin et al., 2022), the green economy, and the implementation of new production and distribution technologies—depends heavily on the availability of finance. The access to financial resources is limited by poorer infrastructure in rural areas, underdeveloped communications, weaker integration of the agricultural sector with suppliers and consumers, and the disadvantaged position of farms in terms of market access, information assurance, availability of human resources, and material security. Therefore, public funding plays a particularly significant role for the agricultural sector in Bulgaria.

The financial markets in the agricultural sector are characterised by higher risk and lower profitability compared to non-agricultural financial markets. Institutions in the financial sector, other than banks, that would support Bulgarian agriculture are underdeveloped (Lyubenov & Lyubenova, 2023). This further constrains the farms' access to finance. The opportunities for issuing secure financial instruments, including those to be used as collateral for agricultural financing, are limited. Thus, crediting remains the dominant source of funding for agricultural farms.

Financial credit is vital for agricultural farms as it provides access to capital that they do not possess, while at the same time offering a cheaper source of financing than their own equity. It enables farms not only to acquire seeds, fertilisers, and crop protection products, but also to access land, labour, and other factor and product markets essential for sustainable development and overcoming the shortages of their own financing. Depending on the effective use of production factors and access to them, credit affects the productivity of agricultural farms (Bento & Restuccia, 2017; Yang et al., 2018). The efficiency of agricultural credits also depends on the agricultural land market (Britos et al., 2022; Aragón et al., 2024; Bento & Restuccia, 2017).

The shortage of credits negatively affects the productivity of agricultural farms and the overall development of the agricultural sector (Cianian et al., 2011a). The access to credits depends on production capacity (Njogu et al., 2018); it is easier for larger farms to obtain credits and, consequently, to achieve better performance. The productivity of the agricultural sector which is relatively lower compared to non-agricultural sectors imposes stricter requirements on agricultural credits (Barry & Robison, 2001). It should also be noted that agricultural lending is characterised by greater complexity, higher risk, and greater uncertainty of information (Cianian et al., 2011a). Therefore, the limited access to finance in the agricultural sector calls for a proactive government policy in the field of public finance (Mishra & Lence, 2005; Onyiriuba et al., 2020; Pokrivčák & Tóth, 2022), which is ensured by the Common Agricultural Policy (CAP) within the European Union.

The subsidies that are not related to production have an impact similar to that of long-term credits, whereas production-related subsidies primarily act as short-term credits (Cianian et al., 2011b). The subsidies under both pillars of the EU CAP influence the access of agricultural farms to long- and short-term credits. Subsidies function as a form of credit guarantee, reducing the risk for banks when lending to agricultural producers and thereby increasing the willingness of the banks to provide credits to the agricultural sector. However, the expansion of the EU CAP subsidies to agricultural producers can have a limiting effect on the agricultural credits provided by the banks (Myyra, 2013). It should also be noted that access to public funding—such as subsidies and project financing—under the EU CAP often requires farms to make greater use of bank credits.

The agricultural sector represents a priority area for the banks as it attracts financing that amounts to approximately 3 billion BGN per year at the end of the analysed period (Appendix A.1, Table A1). The largest banks provide working capital based on expected direct payments from the State Fund "Agriculture" (SFA) which are used as the main form of collateral. The Bulgarian Development Bank (BDB) and the SFA offer targeted financial instruments with lower interest rates and guarantee schemes aimed at modernisation and support for small farms (SFA website, accessed on 10 March 2025). The main difficulties arise from the banks' requirements for additional guarantees beyond subsidies, which are difficult to meet for smaller farms. Climate change and fluctuations in agricultural commodity prices in recent years make the forecasting of farm revenues challenging for banks. Complex application procedures for EU funds and the risk of sanctions related to agricultural subsidies further undermine the banks' confidence in agricultural farms.

Digital finance and the digitalisation of agriculture contribute significantly to agricultural production (Cao & Wang, 2024). Digital finance encourages the transformation of agriculture, the organisation of agricultural producers, and the socialisation of agricultural services by optimising the structure of inputs for agricultural production and improving the efficiency of agricultural capital (Wu et al., 2025). Through processes of gradual supplementation and inventory optimisation, digital finance promotes capital immersion and enhances total factor productivity in agriculture. Atashov et al. (2024), using evidence from ten countries worldwide with different levels of economic development, identified a relationship between the dynamics of agricultural production and state financing, and also determined its optimal proportion relative to private financing.

Baylan (2025) examined the impact of the financialization of agriculture on agricultural production using annual data from 1994 to 2023 for Türkiye and identified three key findings. Firstly, the financialization of agriculture has a significant impact on agricultural production in Türkiye. Secondly, the time series used in the empirical model are cointegrated, indicating the existence of a stable long-term relationship between the variables. Thirdly, the elasticity of agricultural production with respect to the financialization of agriculture is relatively high. This implies that an increase in the financialization by 1% leads to an increase in agricultural production of more than 1%. Overall, the empirical findings emphasise that the financialization of agriculture is an exceptionally important factor for the agricultural sector in Türkiye.

According to Patwary et al. (2023), the bank credits for agriculture, pesticide consumption, and the use of arable land exhibit a long-term relationship with agricultural production. Xu and Wang (2023) find that digital inclusive finance through the internet and other technologies can improve the level of agricultural production by encouraging mechanisation and increasing the farmers' willingness to engage in insurance schemes. The relationships identified across different countries represent relatively rare bibliographic evidence

https://doi.org/10.3390/jrfm19020100

regarding the links between financing in the agricultural sector and agricultural production. These findings are indirectly related to the present study, which also addresses other dimensions of agricultural finance in Bulgaria. Nevertheless, collectively they enrich the available bibliography and support the formulation of new agricultural sector policies, including financial, production-related, and other policy measures.

Research on the domestic financial markets of the Bulgarian agricultural sector has mainly focused on determining their size, structure, and development trends (Lyubenov & Lyubenova, 2017, 2023), while other research examines the dynamics of credits provided by commercial banks and their relationship with the gross value added of the agricultural sector after Bulgaria jointed the EU. The interrelations between state and corporate finance in the Bulgarian agricultural sector, as well as the relationship between total finance (state and corporate), gross value added, and agricultural output, have not yet been sufficiently explored. The verification of these relationships constitutes the purpose of the present study—a statistical analysis of the interrelations between state and corporate finance, gross value added, and the output of Bulgaria's agricultural sector.

The academic literature indicates a clear gap and a limited number of studies examining the impact of state and corporate financing of the agricultural sector in Bulgaria and in other countries on the results achieved by the sector, including gross value added, the value of crop production, and total agricultural output. In particular, there is a lack of time series analyses covering comparatively long periods of 20 years or more. While a substantial body of research addresses the effectiveness and efficiency of production factors in agriculture, including financial factors, there remains a notable absence of comprehensive studies focusing specifically on the financing of the agricultural sector and its production performance. These research gaps in the field of state and corporate agricultural finance render the present study timely and relevant, and consistent with both scientific and practical interests, not only for the agricultural sector itself, but also for numerous related sectors, while also highlighting its current contribution.

The existing literature devoted to the financing of the agricultural sector and its production and value added is relatively limited in the international context and even more so in the Bulgarian context, which enhances the significance of the present research. The study outlines directions for future research on state and credit policies in Bulgaria and in other countries that may contribute to ensuring food, environmental, and social security, as well as improving the competitiveness of agricultural farms. It provides valuable theoretical evidence and practical implications for policymakers and stakeholders regarding the enhancement of agricultural production through financing. Furthermore, the research provides guidance for the development of modern agriculture that can ensure the security of agricultural raw materials and food production and support its digital, financial, and other transformations.

2. Materials and Methods

Research dedicated to the analysed problem is relatively limited, while its importance for the accelerated and sustainable development of the Bulgarian agricultural sector is significant. Therefore, shedding light on this issue will contribute to improving the progress of the agricultural sector. The need for this study arises from the topicality of the subject and the development prospects of the national agricultural sector. The research employs statistical data obtained from the Ministry of Agriculture of the Republic of Bulgaria, the Bulgarian National Bank, as well as other sources and the authors' own calculations. The information from these various sources was subjected to a critical analysis concerning the dynamics of the studied financial markets over the period 2000–2023 to establish a solid foundation for the statistical analysis of the interrelations between them. The study

https://doi.org/10.3390/jrfm19020100

is based on a comprehensive combination of methods for analysis, synthesis, grouping, specification, and primarily, on mathematical and statistical methods.

It is evident that following Bulgaria's accession to the European Union in 2007, public financing of Bulgarian agriculture increased substantially, and this was accompanied by a parallel increase in corporate financing (Appendix A.1, Tables A1 and A2). At the same time, the area of cultivated land in the national agricultural sector began to expand, as did the price and rent of agricultural land. Income derived from agricultural activities also increased. Processes of consolidation of Bulgarian agricultural farms accelerated, along with the restructuring of the national agricultural sector (Ministry of Agriculture, 2024). These processes have influenced the gross value added generated by the Bulgarian agriculture sectors, as well as the volume of total output and crop production, which motivates the scientific novelty and analytical framework of the present study examining the impact of finances in the Bulgarian agricultural sector on these outcomes.

Financing of the agricultural sector, both public and corporate, is shaped by international, European Union, and national policies, such as tariffs, fees, etc. The European Union provides substantial public financing for the agricultural sectors of its member states. However, this financing depends on conflicting interests and changes in agricultural policy of different countries, and is also influenced by endogenous and exogenous factors, including BREXIT, the COVID-19 pandemic, military conflicts, etc. Internal factors affecting the development of Bulgarian agriculture, such as natural conditions (relief, climate, and water resources), demographic and social factors (quantity and quality of the labour force), technical and economic factors (mechanisation, automation, and use of chemicals), and organisational factors (structure and size of agricultural farms) also influence the volume and structure of agricultural financing. Endogenous and exogenous factors jointly exert a complex influence on agricultural financing and on its final outcomes, including gross value added and agricultural production.

The complexity and ambiguity of the outcomes associated with public and private financing of the agricultural sector necessitate, at an initial stage, the application of more conventional and conservative methods for regression modelling and for forecasting correlations and relationships between the studied variables (public and private financing, gross value added, agricultural production, etc.) within the research framework. These methods make it possible to assess the current state of financing in the Bulgarian agricultural sector in relation to the value added created and the output produced. Subsequently, in accordance with the results obtained, the analysis may be extended and deepened through the application of additional and more advanced methods, models, and analytical approaches. The findings of the present study will also outline directions for future research on the financing of the Bulgarian agricultural sector and of agricultural sectors in other countries.

The stationarity properties of the selected series were examined using the Augmented Dickey–Fuller (ADF) and Kwiatkowski–Phillips–Schmidt–Shin (KPSS) tests. The results indicate that all series, with the exception of the recovery plan variable, exhibit non-stationarity, as the ADF test fails to reject the null hypothesis of a unit root, while the KPSS test rejects the null hypothesis of stationarity. The recovery plan series, in contrast, satisfies the stationarity condition in levels. Rather than applying transformations such as differencing, the present analysis proceeds with the original series within a dynamic regression framework. The baseline regression model was evaluated using the Durbin–Watson test to detect autocorrelation and subsequently expanded to include lagged dependent variables. This dynamic specification effectively captures temporal dependencies and addresses potential persistence in the data, ensuring that the estimated relationships remain reliable. By integrating the original series into a model that accounts for both current and past val-

https://doi.org/10.3390/jrfm19020100

ues of the dependent variable, the analysis preserves the integrity of the empirical findings and provides a robust foundation for the subsequent correlation and regression analyses.

The next stage of the analysis involves correlation analysis and the construction of a correlation matrix to assess the degree of interdependence among the examined variables, including public and corporate finance indicators. This problem was solved by establishing the so-called correlation coefficients. The Pearson–Bravais correlation coefficient was employed, as the analysis was conducted independently.

The statistical significance of the correlation coefficients was evaluated using Student's t-test, under the assumptions of normality and independence. Two hypotheses were tested: the null hypothesis (H_0), which posits no statistically significant relationship between the variables, and the alternative hypothesis (H_2), which assumes the presence of a statistically significant relationship. The significance level was set at $\alpha = 0.05$, and a two-tailed test was applied.

For a sample size of $n = 24$, the degrees of freedom are $n - 2 = 22$, yielding a critical value of $t_T \approx 1.71714$. The null hypothesis is rejected when the empirical statistic exceeds the critical value $\left(t_{emp} > t_T\right)$, indicating statistical significance.

The results show that the null hypothesis was rejected in all cases, as the empirical t-statistics exceeded the critical value. Accordingly, the correlation coefficients are statistically significant, confirming the existence of stable and robust linear relationships among the analysed variables.

The presence of statistically significant correlations provides a justified basis for constructing a simple linear regression model (Pearson, 1895). The simple linear regression model is expressed as follows:

$$Y_I = p_1 \times x_i + p_2, \tag{1}$$

where p_1 and p_2 represent the regression coefficients.

For better visualisation, the names of the studied indicators are denoted by variables from X1 to X7, described in Appendix A.3, Table A9. The highest-rated single-factor linear regression models are presented in Tables A10–A12. In some of these models, certain variables are treated as independent, while in others the same variables are treated as dependent, in order to compensate for the inability of correlation analysis to capture causal relationships. Credits in the national economy, represented by variable X2, credits to farms, represented by variable X3, and total agricultural sector finance, including public and private components, represented by variable X4, are specified as dependent variables, while public agricultural sector finance, represented by variable X1, is specified as an independent variable in Table A10. In another set of regression models, variables X2 and X3 are specified as independent variables, while the value of crop production, represented by variable X6, and the value of total output, represented by variable X7, are specified as dependent variables, as shown in Table A12.

Within the framework of the analysis, the Durbin–Watson test was applied to verify the presence of autocorrelation in the baseline regression model (Gujarati & Porter, 2009; Durbin & Watson, 1950). Due to the presence of only one independent variable, the test for multicollinearity is not applicable in this case. The model was subsequently expanded through the inclusion of lagged variables. In this way, a dynamic regression model was constructed, wherein the dependent variable y_t depends not only on the current values of the explanatory variables X_t, but also on its own lagged values $y_{t-1}, y_{t-2}, \ldots, y_{t-n}$.

The research framework and methods applied in the study are subject to a number of limitations that should be carefully considered when assessing the reliability of the results and the adequacy of the models. The correlation methods employed are limited in their ability to identify and confirm causal relationships, as they primarily capture statistical associations rather than underlying mechanisms. In addition, the regression models used

https://doi.org/10.3390/jrfm19020100

may not fully account for structural changes in the agricultural sector, which may affect the stability and explanatory power of the estimated relationships over time.

Another limitation arises from potential data constraints, including differences in data coverage, methodology, and reliability across the analysed period. In particular, discrepancies in statistical reporting before and after Bulgaria's accession to the European Union may influence the comparability of the data and the consistency of the results. The availability and quality of long-term time series data may also restrict the precision of the estimates and the scope of the analysis.

Furthermore, the models do not explicitly incorporate all relevant external factors, such as climate variability, policy shocks, market volatility, or technological change, which may have a significant impact on agricultural production and financial flows. The exclusion of certain qualitative and institutional factors, including governance quality and administrative capacity, may also limit the explanatory depth of the analysis.

These limitations indicate the need for further and more comprehensive research, employing additional data, alternative modelling approaches, and more advanced econometric techniques. Future studies could extend the analysis by incorporating dynamic models, structural breaks, and comparative cross-country perspectives in order to enhance the robustness of the findings and provide a more complete understanding of the relationship between financing and performance in the agricultural sector.

3. Results and Interpretation

The Common Agricultural Policy (CAP) of the European Union has had a substantial impact on the development of the financial markets of the agricultural sector in Bulgaria. Therefore, the periodisation and analysis correspond to the stages of the CAP and the pre-accession SAPARD Programme. The latter was implemented during the pre-accession period (2000–2006), before Bulgaria joined the EU. The period 2007–2013 marked the beginning of the application of the legislative, financial, and administrative instruments of the CAP in Bulgaria, with the gradual increase in direct payments starting at 25% of level EU-15, which was reached only by 2016, i.e., during the 2014–2020 programming period. The start of the current programming period (2021–2027) was marked by the COVID-19 crisis, because of which 2021 and 2022 were declared transitional years, and the financial framework was corrected for the 2023–2027 period.

During the 2000–2006 period, banks provided limited financing to the agricultural sector in Bulgaria, as it was considered much riskier and less profitable than the industrial and service sectors. The market for agricultural land, which serves as collateral for credits, was underdeveloped, so warehouse receipts for grain deposits were used instead, providing only 0.12 billion BGN during the period (Ministry of Agriculture, 2024). The agricultural sector accounted for a small share of total crediting—ranging from 1.6% to 2.4% by the end of the period—but the total amount of farm credits increased more than 4.2 times (Appendix A.1, Table A2).

In 2001, payments under the SAPARD Programme began, with Bulgaria providing national co-financing equal to 25% of the total public support. Farms financed their projects mainly through bank credits. During the 2000–2006 period, SAPARD provided 0.524 billion BGN, with an additional 0.371 billion BGN disbursed during the 2007–2010 period, totalling 0.895 billion BGN.

In the same period, public financing of the agricultural sector in Bulgaria was administered by the State Fund "Agriculture" (SFA) under the Ministry of Agriculture. The SFA provided targeted credits and subsidies to farms—short-term financing prevailed at the beginning of the period, shifting towards long-term by its end. A significant share of subsidies was allocated to tobacco production, which still accounted for about 2/3

https://doi.org/10.3390/jrfm19020100

(0.22 billion BGN) of total subsidies at the end of the period, while credits made up just over 1/3 (0.342 billion BGN) of total state financing in 2006. In the same year, total public support—including state aid, SAPARD, and other programmes—reached 0.48 billion BGN (Appendix A.1, Table A1), while farm credits amounted to 0.53 billion BGN (Appendix A.1, Table A2), marking the first occasion in which private financing exceeded public support.

The 2007–2013 period marked the beginning of solid CAP-based financing for the agricultural sector in Bulgaria. The first pillar of financial support took the form of direct payments and market measures, and the second pillar of financing was implemented through the Rural Development Programme. The fisheries and aquaculture sectors were supported through European agricultural and fisheries funds. National financing continued in the form of state aid and transitional national support, remaining at similar levels to those of the previous period.

Most public funds (more than 80% in the second half of the period) came from direct payments and Rural Development Programme support, which together exceeded 2.2 billion BGN by the end of the period. Total public financial resources during the 2007–2013 period increased more than 6.7 times compared to the previous period (Appendix A.1, Table A1).

Farm credits in 2007 amounted to 0.86 billion BGN (Appendix A.1, Table A2), comparable to the total public financing that year—0.88 billion BGN (Appendix A.1, Table A1). Credits continued to grow steadily, reaching 1.5 billion BGN by the end of the period. Nevertheless, they lagged behind public financing, which increased 1.8 times in the second year of the period and exceeded 2.7 billion BGN in its final year. Direct payments accounted for around 1/2 of all public transfers throughout the 2007–2013 period, significantly transforming agricultural financing, which had not previously relied on such extensive subsidisation. Direct payments functioned as substantial working capital support, reducing the farms' need for additional short-term credits.

During the 2014–2020 period, the nature and structure of public funding in the agricultural sector in Bulgaria remained similar to those of the previous period. In 2015, under Rural Development Programme 2014–2020, approximately 1.45 billion BGN from the previous Rural Development Programme 2007–2013 was absorbed, increasing the total public financial resources for the year to 3.6 billion BGN. Over the period, total public funding increased 1.3 times compared to the 2007–2013 period (Appendix A.1, Table A1). Farm credits continued to grow steadily—from 1.6 billion BGN at the beginning to 2.4 billion BGN at the end of the period. In the second half of the period, farm credits equalled and then exceeded total public financing for the agricultural sector in Bulgaria—a trend that continued through 2023. This indicates that public financial resources were insufficient to fully support farm development.

In the current period 2021–2027, the structure of public funding remains largely similar to the one of the previous cycle. Public funding levels for the transitional years 2021 and 2022 are comparable to those of the 2014–2020 period, but 2022 and 2023 show a substantial increase in state aid (Appendix A.1, Table A1). In 2023, additional financing was provided to the agricultural sector in Bulgaria through the National Recovery and Resilience Plan (NRRP)—a new source that was not available in previous periods. Public financing during the first three years of the current period suggests that total amounts will likely exceed those of the 2014–2020 period.

For the upcoming 2028–2034 period, public financing will depend significantly on the EU's financial state, policy changes, climate dynamics, and ongoing military conflicts in Europe. Corporate financing in the agricultural sector already exceeds public funding during the first three years of the 2021–2027 period.

https://doi.org/10.3390/jrfm19020100

Appendix A.2, Table A4 presents the correlations between the public finances of the agricultural sector, the corporate finances of agricultural farms, and the total financial resources (public and corporate) of the agricultural sector and corporate credits within the national economy of Bulgaria. The values of their correlation coefficients indicate strong and predominantly very strong correlations between them, meaning that they change together. Based on these strong positive correlations between the gross value added of the agricultural sector, the value of crop production, and the value of total agricultural output (Appendix A.2, Table A5) it may be assumed that a very strong correlation is present between these variables, which should be further substantiated or rejected.

Furthermore, the analysis of the values in Table A4 indicates that the total amount of public financial resources allocated to support the agricultural sector in Bulgaria, including the funds from the Rural Development Programme—as an essential component of public financing (Table A1)—are in a very strong correlation with the total financial resources (public and corporate) of the agricultural sector (r = 0.97). A strong to very strong relationship is also observed with agricultural credits to farms (r = 0.85) and credits in the national economy of Bulgaria (r = 0.87). These interdependencies suggest that public financing is related to corporate financing and to national credit flows, thus forming a complex system of interconnected capital sources for the agricultural sector in Bulgaria, which should be logically justified.

A strong correlation can be observed (Table A6) between corporate agricultural credits and the gross value added, as well as with the value of crop and final agricultural production. It is particularly noteworthy that the value of crop production exhibits a strong correlation with all financial indicators of the agricultural sector—public, corporate, and total—as well as with the corporate finances of the national economy of Bulgaria, meaning that they change together. The value of total agricultural production also demonstrates a strong correlation with national corporate finances, with the corporate finances of the agricultural sector, and with the total (public and corporate) finances of the sector. A moderate correlation is identified between the agricultural gross value added and the corporate and total finances of the agricultural sector, and a weaker correlation with the public finances of the agricultural sector. The latter correlate moderately with the value of final agricultural production. These relationships should be verified and confirmed.

At the same time, Table A6 reveals that total financial resources (public and corporate) are strongly and very strongly correlated with the value of crop production (r = 0.83) and with the value of total agricultural output (r = 0.73). Strong relationships are also evident between corporate agricultural loans and the production indicators of the agricultural sector (r = 0.77–0.88). These results suggest that not only public financing, but also total financing (public and corporate), exerts a significant influence on the production performance of the agricultural sector, stimulating both crop production and overall agricultural output. Therefore, it may be assumed that, when acting jointly, public and private financing generate a so-called leverage effect.

The modernisation of agricultural farms through the Rural Development Programme requires co-financing by farms in order to gain access to public funding. Banks offer specialised credit products in which future public payments serve as collateral for the provision of working capital financing to agricultural farms. Automation, digitalisation, irrigation, and green technologies necessitate the use not only of public financing, which is insufficient on its own, but also of private financing. Bank credits, as an element of corporate financing, and agricultural subsidies, as a component of public financing, both compete with and complement each other. Effective resource management in agricultural farms requires the use of low-interest loans and guarantees provided by European and national institutions, which improve access not only to public but also to private financing,

https://doi.org/10.3390/jrfm19020100

including through their combination, thereby explaining their high degree of interdependence.

Gross value added exhibits a particularly strong dependence on crop production, which represents the leading sub-sector of Bulgarian agriculture, as it accounts for the largest share of total output. As a result, the value of gross value added is highly sensitive to the performance of crop production. Crop production receives the largest share of subsidies, which do not alter market prices but increase the overall nominal volume of its output at base prices. The strong correlation observed is attributable to the fact that a decrease or increase in crop production output, or in international prices of cereals and oilseed crops, leads, respectively, to a decrease or increase in the gross value added of the agricultural sector in Bulgaria. The strong correlations between gross value added and the value of final output, as well as that of crop production, which holds a dominant share within it, can be explained by the key economic and structural factors outlined below.

Gross value added is calculated as the difference between the value of final output and intermediate consumption, including expenditure on seeds, fertilisers, fuels, etc. Since output constitutes the principal component of this relationship, any change in its volume or price is directly reflected in gross value added. The export of cereals and oilseed raw materials, characterised by relatively low intermediate consumption costs in relation to their final prices, causes gross value added to move almost in parallel with their market prices. The prices of these export commodities largely determine the value of crop production. Increases in yields or in global prices lead to growth in gross value added, following the trend of total output. Investments in improved machinery and higher-quality seeds simultaneously increase the value of crop production and added value, as they enhance efficiency per unit of expenditure.

The analysis of direct payments and the Rural Development Programme, which together represent the principal components of public financing, reveals a clear divergence in the reliability and magnitude of the observed correlations. The Rural Development Programme exhibits consistently strong and robust correlations with both corporate and public financial resources, whereas the correlations associated with direct payments are weak, unstable, and generally unreliable. Direct payments display only a moderate correlation with public and total financial resources and a weak correlation with corporate financing, indicating that these relationships cannot be interpreted with confidence. While direct payments tend to substitute short-term corporate financing of agricultural farms, the implementation of Rural Development Programme projects typically requires a combination of substantial public financing and longer-term credit instruments. Furthermore, Rural Development Programme resources show moderate and more dependable correlations with the value of crop production, and total agricultural output. In contrast, the correlations between direct payments and these key economic indicators are weakly negative and statistically questionable, suggesting that direct payments do not exert a positive or reliable economic effect on sectoral performance, with the exception of public financial resources (Table A7).

In contrast, as explicitly required for Appendix A.2, Table A5, not all correlation coefficients withstand Student's *t*-test. Because the underlying data series differ in length, the theoretical *t*-value for direct payments is 1.75305 and for the Rural Development Programme it is 1.720743. While the correlation between direct payments and public financial resources approaches significance, the remaining correlations associated with direct payments do not pass the test. Conversely, most correlations linked to the Rural Development Programme exceed the critical *t*-value and are therefore statistically validated, except for correlation between Rural Development Programme measures and gross value

https://doi.org/10.3390/jrfm19020100

added. These exceptions are noted directly under Appendix A.2, Table A5 for clarity and transparency.

From a practical perspective, the results confirm the existence of strong and statistically verified relationships—except for the explicitly identified non-significant cases in Appendix A.2, Table A5 between direct payments and credits in the national economy, agricultural credits to farms, total financial resources, gross value added of the agricultural sector, value of crop production at producer prices excluding product-related subsidies and, value of total agricultural output at prices including product-related subsidies, and also between the Rural Development Programme and Gross value added of the agricultural sector.

In financial mathematics, such behaviour is characterised as a regime-switching economy, in which transitions between different states are associated with particular economic or financial developments, yet these shifts are treated as stochastic events occurring at random moments in time (Georgiev, 2019). Overall, the accepted alternative hypothesis (H_1) in most of the cases highlights the coherent and substantive linkages within the financial and production dimensions of the agricultural sector in Bulgaria. This requires an analysis of the economic, structural, and other interrelationships between these factors in order to confirm or reject the correlations and Student's t-test results (Table A8).

The direct payments have restructured national crop production towards the use of large areas for cereal crops, driven primarily by the subsidies received per unit of area. The production of most of these crops, such as barley and wheat, involves a lower risk of drought, allows the achievement of high and stable yields, and requires relatively low labour input, particularly under highly mechanised production technologies. This has led to a shift away from more intensive, higher value-added subsectors such as livestock farming, fruit growing, and vegetable production, which are characterised by substantially higher labour costs and greater technological risk. Investment in energy-intensive machinery for crop production, including combine harvesters and tractors, increased after Bulgaria's accession to the European Union, while investment in equipment for animal husbandry, fruit cultivation, and vegetable production declined (Agricultural Report, from 2010 to 2020). This development explains the low correlation between direct payments and gross value added, as well as other indicators presented in Table A8.

All models presented in Table A12 express the causal nature of the positive impact of national and agricultural sector financing, represented by the independent variables X2, X1, and X3, on gross value added and on the value of total agricultural output, including crop production, represented by the dependent variables X5, X6, and X7. The models in Table A11 demonstrate a positive impact of the value of crop production, represented by the independent variable X6, on the gross value added of the agricultural sector and on the value of final agricultural output, represented by the dependent variables X5 and X7. The model X5 = f(X7) from Table A11 outlines the negative impact of subsidies embodied in the value of final agricultural output, represented by the independent variable X7, on the gross value added of the agricultural sector, represented by the dependent variable X5. The regression models complement and compensate for the limitations of correlation analysis in relation to uncertain causal relationships.

The regression analysis clearly demonstrates a pronounced interrelationship between public financing and private financial resources in the agricultural sector. The estimated equations $X2 = 19.87 + 10.72 \times X1$ and $X3 = 0.7466 + 0.07899 \times X1$ indicate that each increase of 1 billion BGN in government support results (Table A13), respectively, in an increase of 10.72 billion BGN in the total volume of credit, and an increase of 79 million BGN in agricultural credits.

The model X2 = f(X1) from Table A10 demonstrates a strong multiplier effect of public agricultural finance on credit activity. The sector is among the key drivers of bank crediting through large-scale investment programmes and state subsidies. It provides substantial public funding amounting to almost 3 billion BGN in 2023, thereby encouraging farms to seek reciprocal and increased bank crediting for both short-term and long-term co-financing. The agricultural sector is among the most intensive users of financial resources due to weakened liquidity resulting from seasonality and long-term investments in machinery and land. In addition to product and financial markets, the agricultural sector also shapes labour and land markets, as well as markets for means of production such as animal feed, fertilisers, water, veterinary medicines and plant protection products, genetics, machinery and equipment, and services, all of which are significant consumers of credit within the national economy of Bulgaria.

The finances of the agricultural sector in Bulgaria affect not only added value and the value of agricultural output, but also many other non-agricultural sectors. The introduction of digital, green, and other new technologies, the intensification of climate change, and the growing requirements for more sustainable and environmentally friendly agricultural practices increase the need for both public and private financing of the agricultural sector. The agrochemical industry, machinery manufacturing, construction, processing and food industries, wholesale and retail trade, and other related sectors are integrated with and dependent on agriculture, just as agriculture is dependent on them. Accordingly, in response to changes within the agricultural sector, these industries also require financing for investment and modernization. For this reason, public and private agricultural sector finance exerts a multi-layered impact on credit activity throughout the national economy of Bulgaria.

The strongest dependency is observed in the model $X4 = 1.747 + 0.07899 \times X1$, where $R^2 = 0.9335$, indicating an almost perfect linear relationship (Table A11). Within this context, public financial resources perform the role of a systemic financial generator, which not only determines the scale of the resource base but also stimulates private capital through the mechanisms of trust and risk reduction.

The second group of models delineates the structural dependence of agricultural productivity on crop production. The equation $X5 = 0.4418 + 1.697 \times X6$ demonstrates that every additional 1 billion BGN of crop production generates an increase of 1.697 billion BGN in gross value added, while $X7 = 0.8724 + 3.833 \times X6$ reveals an even stronger effect on total agricultural output. These results, combined with $R^2 = 0.9164$, emphasise that crop production constitutes a structural determinant of the overall productivity of the agricultural sector in Bulgaria. At the same time, the negative coefficient in $X5 = 0.4862 - 0.07977 \times X7$ may be interpreted as an indicator of a dampening effect, whereby excessive subsidies from direct payments (Table A12) reduce the efficiency of transforming production value into real added value. The results concerning the impact of private loans on agricultural production are of particular significance. The models $X6 = 0.06291 + 2.117 \times X2$ and $X6 = 1.674 + 2.659 \times X3$ show that 1 billion BGN in loans leads to the generation of more than 2 billion BGN in crop production. Moreover, the equations for total agricultural output—the models $X7 = 0.05311 + 5.759 \times X2$ and $X7 = 1.335 + 6.321 \times X3$—indicate an effect in the range of 5.8 to 6.3 billion BGN, with R^2 values of approximately 0.60–0.64 (Table A12). These findings reveal an exceptionally high financial multiplicative effect of credit financing, where the coefficients p_2 should be regarded as financial multipliers. Public transfers act as a stabilising foundation for the mobilisation of capital. However, it is private credit—particularly agricultural credits—that transforms potential into tangible growth in production and value added, establishing itself as a key driver of the sustainable development of the agricultural sector in Bulgaria.

https://doi.org/10.3390/jrfm19020100

The study makes it possible to synthesise the following important findings: (1) the nature and magnitude of the distinctly positive influence of national and agricultural sector financing on gross value added and on the value of total output, including output from crop production, have been identified; (2) the positive nature and strength of the influence of the value of crop production on the gross value added of the agricultural sector and on the value of its final output have been established; (3) the existence of strong collaboration between public agricultural finance and credit in the national economy, and the credit extended to agricultural and non-agricultural farms, has been delineated; (4) indications have been identified of a negative impact of direct payments, as a principal component of public agricultural finance, on the gross value added of the agricultural sector.

Strong positive autocorrelation is evident in the baseline specifications, as indicated by Durbin–Watson (DW) statistics substantially below unity. Following the inclusion of one to three lags of the dependent variable, the DW statistic consistently converges towards its theoretical value of approximately 2, indicating that residual autocorrelation has been largely eliminated and the assumption of error independence satisfied. The Durbin–Watson test results are presented in Table A13.

Across the 15 estimated models, the static specifications exhibit clear evidence of positive autocorrelation, with initial Durbin–Watson statistics ranging from 0.51 to 1.22. Following the introduction of lagged variables, DW values consistently converge towards the theoretical benchmark of 2, typically falling between approximately 1.93 and 2.38. In these cases, residual autocorrelation is effectively eliminated. The inclusion of lagged terms leads to a systematic and substantial improvement in the stability of the error structure and the adequacy of the estimated models.

These findings confirm that dynamic specifications provide a more appropriate representation of temporal dependencies, yielding statistically valid parameter estimates and more reliable inference. Accordingly, models augmented with lagged terms constitute a superior econometric framework for analysing the relationships among the examined variables. One lag corresponds to a one-year period.

The key conclusions derived from the Durbin–Watson test are:

1. In the static models, positive autocorrelation was identified, which is characteristic of time-series data exhibiting high inertia.
2. Upon the implementation of a second lag, the DW values stabilise around 2.0, confirming the complete absence of autocorrelation.
3. The dynamic (lagged) models are statistically valid, economically stable, and suitable for forecasting purposes.
4. The elimination of autocorrelation confirms that the regression estimates are efficient and reliable, and that the system of interrelations between public and private financial flows remains stable over time.

4. Discussion

Average annual financing (public and corporate, billion BGN/year) has also increased consistently over the periods: (0.38 + 0.3 = 0.68) for 2000–2006; (1.92 + 1.16 = 3.08) for 2007–2013; (2.41 + 2 = 4.41) for 2014–2020; and (2.6 + 2.71 = 5.31) for 2021–2023. In 2025, the public finances of the agricultural sector in Bulgaria reached a record amount of over 4.4 billion BGN, while in the previous year they were 3.84 billion BGN (State Fund "Agriculture", 2025). Corporate finances in the agricultural sector in Bulgaria as of 30 September 2025 were 3.153 billion BGN, and for 2024 they were 3.1 billion BGN (Bulgarian National Bank, 2025). Chronologically, public and corporate financing of the Bulgarian agricultural sector follow a common trend, with the corporate one overtaking the public one at the end of the

https://doi.org/10.3390/jrfm19020100

studied period, and then the public one, and so on, complementing each other through the so-called leverage effect.

Historically, overall public and corporate financing have grown steadily during the analysed periods of the EU CAP: 4.7 billion BGN for the pre-accession period 2000–2006; 21.6 billion BGN for 2007–2013; 30.9 billion BGN for 2014–2020. Looking ahead, we can forecast a value of approximately 37 billion BGN for 2021–2027, based on the first three years of the period. The above-mentioned current data show that this forecast is adequate, i.e., no significant changes in the trend of public and corporate finances of the agricultural sector in Bulgaria are expected by the end of the current period. The sustainable trend of growth of public finances over the past quarter of a century will most likely be broken in the period 2028–2034.

The perspective for the Common Agricultural Policy (CAP) of the EU envisions a draft budget of approximately 300 billion EUR for the 2028–2034 period, representing a significant reduction compared to the current 386 billion EUR budget for 2021–2027. Expectations are that the majority (80%) of these funds will remain allocated to direct payments and farmer support (European Commission, 2025). The previous two-pillar structure is being transformed into "one policy, one set of measures," intended to eliminate overlaps and constraints between the pillars. Consolidating various budgetary instruments into national plans aims to optimise their use and incentivize governments to implement reforms.

For Bulgaria, this 20–25% reduction in financial support for 2028–2034 is unacceptable, as it is expected to decrease the competitiveness and sustainability of its agricultural sector, as indicated by the conducted regression analysis. The unstable, complex, and sometimes contradictory financial framework of the EU CAP negatively affects the sustainable development and vitality of the European agricultural sector. Specifically for Bulgaria, there is a need to equalise farmer subsidies with other EU member states and provide additional funding for irrigation, which currently covers less than 1% of arable land, compared to more than 20% 40 years ago. It is also crucial that the future CAP financing for Bulgaria includes support for agricultural product processing and investment in irrigation infrastructure beyond farm boundaries.

The investments in the irrigation infrastructure financed through public and corporate sources are expected to have a positive effect on stabilising and increasing yields in crop production and, consequently, on the value of its output, particularly in the context of climate change towards increasing aridity. The Bulgarian crop production is highly dependent on climatic conditions, given the very small share of irrigated arable land. The financial effects associated with the modernisation and expansion of irrigation infrastructure are likely to be substantial, as the crop production sector makes a dominant contribution to the value of total output in the Bulgarian agricultural sector. Investments in irrigation infrastructure require significant capital outlays, which are recouped only over a relatively long period of time. The constructed regression model will therefore remain adequate to a certain extent only as long as there are no substantial changes in the conditions under which it was developed.

The "Single National Plan" approach may result in a more complex structure and decision-making process due to the unstable political environment in Bulgaria, leading to uncertainty among farmers, and potential bankruptcies. Potential reductions in public funding for the agricultural sector in Bulgaria under the CAP during 2028–2034 are expected to negatively impact its development. The correlation analysis indicates that decreasing public financing will adversely affect corporate financing (especially via the Rural Development Programme, PRSR) and national credit flows. Crop production value is also projected to decline due to its strong correlation with public funding in Bulgaria's agricultural sector, while final production value shows moderate correlation with these funds.

https://doi.org/10.3390/jrfm19020100

Reductions in public financing as a share of total sector financing are likely to reduce overall production outcomes.

The conducted regression analysis also allows for estimating the strength of these relationships, thereby predicting the consequences of a 20–25% reduction in public financing. Given the linear nature of equation X2, in which any increase in state support raises agricultural credits even when accounting for the model's limitations, a reduction in public financing would lead to a corresponding decrease in these credits. Consequently, the role of public funds as a systemic "financial generator," which not only defines the resource base but also stimulates private capital by lowering risk and enhancing confidence, will diminish. At the same time, X5 shows that excessive public financing, such as area-based direct payments, can reduce the efficiency of transforming agricultural output into real added value.

The establishment of area-based direct payments during the initial period of implementation of the Common Agricultural Policy (CAP) of the European Union in Bulgaria accelerated processes of restructuring and concentration in the agricultural sector towards monocultural farming dominated by cereal and oilseed crops, at the expense of subsectors with higher value added, such as livestock farming, fruit growing, and vegetable production. Direct payments contributed to the formation of very large farms specialising in cereal production. Their weaker impact on gross value added, together with the imbalances arising from their large share in public finances, suggests a lower level of economic efficiency. This necessitates a reconsideration of national policy in the field of area-based direct payments and their approval of reorientation towards investments and the modernisation of irrigation, processing, and other types of infrastructure.

In the long term, a gradual reduction in public financing for area-based direct payments should be approved, with the released financial resources redirected towards the so-called second pillar, including the Rural Development Programme and related instruments, in order to finance investments and innovations across all subsectors of Bulgarian agriculture, regardless of farm size, while providing opportunities for agricultural activities with higher value added. Such an approach to the allocation of public financing would significantly support a more balanced development of the agricultural sector in Bulgaria as a whole. As a result, Bulgarian agricultural producers would have greater capacity to respond to market requirements by leveraging their competitive advantages, supported by adequate public and private financing.

The stabilising and mobilising role of public financing for corporate finances in Bulgarian farms, given its transformative potential for real production growth, makes it a key driver of sustainable development in the Bulgarian agricultural sector. Equations X6 (Appendix A.3, Table A12) indicate that 1 billion BGN in agricultural credits is possible to generate over 2 billion BGN in crop production, while equations for final production X7 indicate a likely effect of approximately 6 billion BGN (Appendix A.3, Table A12). These empirical results demonstrate that public financing stabilises and mobilises corporate financing in the agricultural sector in Bulgaria, and any reduction will proportionally decrease corporate financing for Bulgarian agricultural and non-agricultural farms, as suggested by the model X2 = f(X1).

The regression model presented above, together with its justification in the preceding section, reveals the structurally determining role of Bulgarian agriculture for the national economy, as well as the strong influence of public agricultural finance not only on the agricultural sector itself but also on many non-agricultural sectors that depend on its development. Unlike non-agricultural sectors, agriculture is the only sector with a positive balance, and is therefore the principal "donor" to the external trade account of Bulgaria, possessing comparative advantages on international markets. A reduction in public and

https://doi.org/10.3390/jrfm19020100

other forms of financing for the agricultural sector would diminish Bulgaria's export potential and increase the dependence on imported agricultural products, which could lead to the formation of agflation. This would also reduce the competitiveness of Bulgarian farms compared with farms benefiting from higher and more stable subsidies, and would slow the overall economic growth of Bulgaria.

The financing of Bulgarian agriculture is shaped by a wide range of diverse and often contradictory internal and external factors, which makes it reasonable to assume that their interactions are not purely linear in nature, as implied by the constructed regression models. This constitutes one of the principal limitations of the study, while at the same time laying the foundations and prerequisites for subsequent research in this field and outlining its future directions. In addition, correlation analysis approximates and identifies linear relationships between the examined variables. Nevertheless, the substantiation of the interrelationships between the examined variables confirms their existence, while the regression models also reveal the causal relationships between them.

Other limitations of the study should be taken into account, such as the greater dispersion of statistical data about agriculture caused by the stochastic influence of natural, political, and other factors, leading to greater deviations of the independent, respectively, dependent variables. Structural changes in the sectors of Bulgarian agriculture, which may affect the effectiveness of its finances, have not been taken into account. If a significant proportion of the large grain producers reorient themselves towards livestock, fruit, and vegetable production in order to diversify market risk, direct payments will play the role of a kind of restructuring mechanism towards mixed specialisation and reallocation of resources to sectors with higher added value.

5. Conclusions

The conducted study allows for the following conclusions regarding the financial markets of the agricultural sector in Bulgaria:

1. The solid investments in better equipment, seeds, and preparations in Bulgarian crop production in recent decades have simultaneously increased the value of its production and the added value, as they have improved the efficiency of unit cost. The correlation and regression analyses demonstrate the positive impact of the value of crop production on the GVA of the agricultural sector and the value of its final output.
2. Crop production is a leading sector of Bulgarian agriculture, accounting for about 3/4 of the value of its production, which is why it is structurally decisive for the productivity and GVA of the agricultural sector in Bulgaria. Correlation and regression analyses confirm that solid investments in it through public and private finances have a positive impact on the GVA and the value of total production and that of crop production.
3. Public and private agrifinance has a multi-layered impact on credit in the national economy, as agriculture is linked to many non-agricultural sectors (agrochemistry, mechanical engineering, construction, processing and food industry, wholesale and retail trade, etc.), which, in accordance with the changes in it, need financing in order to successfully adapt to them.
4. Correlation and regression analysis reveal a strong collaboration between public agrifinance and credits in the national economy and credits to agricultural and non-agricultural farms. Since public financing cannot satisfy the needs of agricultural and related non-agricultural farms, private financing is also used, and in their interaction, they realise the so-called leverage effect.
5. The correlation and regression analysis jointly outline a negative impact of direct payments on the value of final agricultural production on the GVA of the agricultural sector in Bulgaria in its current structure with predominant products with low added

https://doi.org/10.3390/jrfm19020100

value—cereals and oilseeds. Direct payments should also be reoriented towards production with higher added value—fruits, vegetables, etc.

6. In the long term, public and private agrifinance, and national finances, should be reoriented towards investments and innovations in subsectors of Bulgarian agriculture that have comparative competitive advantages in international markets, as well as in infrastructure (irrigation, digitalization, automation, etc.) and agricultural activities with higher added value.
7. The obtained theoretical and empirical results and synthesised insights in this study reveal its innovative nature with regard to the relations and models for public and private finances, GVA, value of total production, and crop production of Bulgarian agriculture, which together with the proposed solutions to the research problem also form the contribution of the authors.

Author Contributions: Conceptualization, L.L. and B.I.; Methodology, L.L.; Validation, L.L.; Formal analysis, L.L. and B.I.; Investigation, L.L. and B.I.; Resources, L.L.; Data curation, L.L.; Writing—original draft, L.L. and B.I.; Writing—review & editing, L.L. and B.I.; Visualization, L.L. and B.I.; Supervision, L.L. and B.I.; Project administration, L.L.; Funding acquisition, L.L. All authors have read and agreed to the published version of the manuscript.

Funding: This research was supported by the "Scientific Research" Fund of Ruse University "Angel Kanchev".

Institutional Review Board Statement: Not applicable.

Informed Consent Statement: Not applicable.

Data Availability Statement: The data used in this study is contained within the article appendices. Further inquiries can be directed to the corresponding author.

Acknowledgments: The authors would like to thank the reviewers for their constructive comments which has contributed to improving the quality of the paper.

Conflicts of Interest: The authors declare no conflicts of interest. The funders had no role in the design of the study; in the collection, analyses, or interpretation of data; in the writing of the manuscript; or in the decision to publish the results.

Appendix A

Appendix A.1. Public and Corporate Finance, Gross Value Added, and Output of the Agricultural Sector in Bulgaria

Table A1. Public financial resources allocated for the support of the agricultural sector in Bulgaria (Sources: Ministry of Agriculture, 2024; author's own calculations).

Year	Direct Payments	Market Measures	Transitional National Aid	State Aid	Rural Development Programme and Strategic Plan Under the Common Agricultural Policy	SAPARD Programme 2001–2009	Fisheries and Aquaculture	National Recovery and Resilience Plan	Public Financial Resources for the Agricultural Sector (Total)
	Billions of BGN	Billions of BGN	Billions of BGN	Billions of BGN	Billions of BGN	Billions of BGN	Billions of BGN	Billions of BGN	Billions of BGN
2000				0.2644	0.0130				0.2774
2001				0.2516	0.0060	0.0020			0.2596
2002				0.2662	0.0050	0.0270			0.2982
2003				0.3426	0.0050	0.0700			0.4176
2004				0.2735	0.0040	0.1350			0.4125
2005				0.3505	0.0040	0.1730			0.5275
2006				0.3420	0.0147	0.1170			0.4737
2007	0.4307	0.0022		0.3639		0.0900			0.8868
2008	0.8191	0.0631		0.3873	0.2004	0.1270	0.0030		1.5999
2009	0.8091	0.0717		0.3041	0.2774	0.1390	0.0070		1.6083

Table A1. *Cont.*

Year	Direct Payments	Market Measures	Transitional National Aid	State Aid	Rural Development Programme and Strategic Plan Under the Common Agricultural Policy	SAPARD Programme 2001–2009	Fisheries and Aquaculture	National Recovery and Resilience Plan	Public Financial Resources for the Agricultural Sector (Total)
	Billions of BGN	Billions of BGN	Billions of BGN	Billions of BGN	Billions of BGN	Billions of BGN	Billions of BGN	Billions of BGN	Billions of BGN
2010	0.9886	0.0529	0.1957	0.1311	0.7219	0.0035	0.0080		2.1017
2011	0.9351	0.0741	0.1876	0.1371	0.7405	0.0112	0.0173		2.1029
2012	1.0349	0.1164	0.1844	0.1304	0.9265		0.0297		2.4223
2013	1.2854	0.1043	0.1799	0.1459	0.9666		0.0246		2.7067
2014	1.3505	0.0851	0.2164	0.1919	0.3879		0.0221		2.2539
2015	1.5988	0.1478	0.1604	0.1993	1.4811		0.0501		3.6375
2016	1.2836	0.1141	0.1715	0.2130	0.3648		0.0141		2.1611
2017	1.1867	0.1049	0.1599	0.2510	0.4879		0.0109		2.2013
2018	0.8983	0.1251	0.1499	0.2700	0.5829		0.0163		2.0425
2019	0.8704	0.0944	0.1395	0.2781	0.8443		0.0327		2.2594
2020	0.9310	0.0922	0.1281	0.3495	0.8152		0.0271		2.3431
2021	0.8721	0.0915	0.1252	0.3833	0.7078		0.0266		2.2065
2022	0.8583	0.1369	0.1223	0.9811	0.6845		0.0228		2.8059
2023	0.7369	0.1278	0.1229	0.7445	0.7075		0.0225	0.3156	2.7777

Table A2. Corporate finance within the national economy, within the agricultural sector in Bulgaria, and in aggregate (Source: Bulgarian National Bank, 2025; author's own calculations).

Year	Credits in the National Economy	Share of Agricultural Credits	Agricultural Credits to Farms	Total Financial Resources
	Billions of BGN	%	Billions of BGN	Billions of BGN
2000	7.894	1.58%	0.1250	0.4024
2001	9.357	1.76%	0.1650	0.4246
2002	10.784	1.55%	0.1676	0.4658
2003	13.013	2.02%	0.2634	0.6810
2004	19.736	1.91%	0.3762	0.7887
2005	18.029	2.47%	0.4460	0.9735
2006	22.299	2.38%	0.5310	1.0047
2007	36.635	2.34%	0.8580	1.7448
2008	48.348	2.22%	1.0710	2.6709
2009	50.08	2.09%	1.0450	2.6533
2010	50.692	2.09%	1.0590	3.1607
2011	52.334	2.35%	1.2310	3.3339
2012	53.808	2.59%	1.3960	3.8183
2013	53.822	2.73%	1.4680	4.1747
2014	49.487	3.14%	1.5530	3.8069
2015	48.756	3.59%	1.7480	5.3855
2016	49.176	3.75%	1.8420	4.0031
2017	50.828	4.00%	2.0330	4.2343
2018	54.739	3.94%	2.1590	4.2015
2019	58.827	3.90%	2.2920	4.5514
2020	65.873	3.63%	2.3930	4.7361
2021	71.553	3.36%	2.4060	4.6125
2022	80.675	3.49%	2.8140	5.6199
2023	90.667	3.20%	2.9030	5.6807

https://doi.org/10.3390/jrfm19020100

Table A3. Values of the production of the agricultural sector in Bulgaria for the period 2000–2023 (Ministry of Agriculture, 2024).

Year	Gross Value Added of the Agricultural Sector	Value of Crop Production at Producer Prices Excluding Product-Related Subsidies	Value of Total Agricultural Output at Prices Including Product-Related Subsidies
	Billions of BGN	Billions of BGN	Billions of BGN
2000	3.30	2.76	6.87
2001	3.53	3.19	7.57
2002	3.49	3.43	7.11
2003	3.49	3.39	6.36
2004	3.46	3.68	6.77
2005	3.40	3.38	6.56
2006	3.26	3.57	6.79
2007	2.95	3.15	6.48
2008	4.28	4.83	8.78
2009	3.09	3.91	7.45
2010	3.17	4.24	7.47
2011	3.71	5.10	8.52
2012	3.74	5.31	8.65
2013	3.78	5.29	8.60
2014	3.82	5.40	8.41
2015	3.60	5.06	7.89
2016	3.87	5.12	7.83
2017	4.15	5.48	8.24
2018	3.72	5.64	8.18
2019	3.90	5.76	8.23
2020	4.20	5.21	7.87
2021	6.04	8.13	10.82
2022	6.25	9.80	12.90
2023	4.66	7.14	10.55

Appendix A.2. Correlation Analysis of the Finances of Bulgaria's Agricultural Sector

Table A4. Correlation between public financial support for Bulgaria's agricultural sector, corporate financial resources of farms, and total financial resources in the agricultural sector in Bulgaria.

	Public Financial Resources for the Agricultural Sector	Credits in the National Economy	Agricultural Credits to Farms	Total Financial Resources
Public financial resources for the agricultural sector	1.00			
Credits in the national Economy	0.87	1.00		
Agricultural credits to farms	0.85	0.94	1.00	
Total financial resources	0.97	0.94	0.96	1.00

https://doi.org/10.3390/jrfm19020100

Table A5. Correlation between the gross value added of the agricultural sector, the value of crop production at producer prices, and the value of total agricultural output at prices including product-specific subsidies.

	Gross Value Added of the Agricultural Sector	Value of Crop Production at Producer Prices Excluding Product-Related Subsidies	Value of Total Agricultural Output at Prices Including Product-Related Subsidies
Gross value added of the agricultural sector	1.00		
Value of crop production at producer prices excluding product-related subsidies	0.91	1.00	
Value of total agricultural output at prices including product-related subsidies	0.92	0.96	1.00

Table A6. Correlation between public, corporate, and total financial support for the agricultural sector in Bulgaria, and its gross value added and the value of crop and total agricultural production.

	Gross Value Added of the Agricultural Sector	Value of Crop Production at Producer Prices Excluding Product-Related Subsidies	Value of Total Agricultural Output at Prices Including Product-Related Subsidies
Public financial resources for the agricultural sector	0.47	0.73	0.64
Credits in the national Economy	0.66	0.86	0.80
Agricultural credits to farms	0.70	0.88	0.77
Total financial resources	0.60	0.83	0.73

Table A7. Correlation of direct payments and the Rural Development Programme with public and corporate financial resources, gross value added, and the value of crop and total agricultural output in Bulgaria's agricultural sector.

	Direct Payments	Rural Development Programme
Public financial resources for the agricultural sector	0.68	0.92
Credits in the national economy	−0.20	0.72
Agricultural credits to farms	0.01	0.70
Total financial resources	0.38	0.85
Gross value added of the agricultural sector	−0.09	0.31
Value of crop production at producer prices excluding product-related subsidies	−0.01	0.57
Value of total agricultural output at prices including product-related subsidies	−0.09	0.47

https://doi.org/10.3390/jrfm19020100

Table A8. Values of the empirical characteristics of Student's *t*-test between direct payments and the Rural Development Programme and public and corporate financial resources, gross value added, and the value of crop and total agricultural output in Bulgaria's agricultural sector.

	Direct Payments (t_T = 1.75305)	Rural Development Programme (t_T = 1.720743)
Public financial resources for the agricultural sector	3.58	10.95
Credits in the national economy	−0.80	4.76
Agricultural credits to farms	0.04	4.50
Total financial resources	1.58	7.44
Gross value added of the agricultural sector	−0.35	1.50
Value of crop production at producer prices excluding product-related subsidies	−0.04	3.17
Value of total agricultural output at prices including product-related subsidies	−0.37	2.46

Appendix A.3. Regression Analysis of the Finances of Bulgaria's Agricultural Sector

Table A9. Studied economic indicators of the agricultural sector in Bulgaria used in the linear single-factor regression models, represented by the variables (X1, X2, …, X7).

Examined Indicator	Variable Description (Billions of BGN)	Variable Code
Public finance for the agricultural sector in Bulgaria	Public financial resources for the agricultural sector	X1
Corporate finance at the national level	Credits in the national economy	X2
Corporate finance of agricultural farms	Agricultural credit to farms	X3
Combined public and corporate finance of the agricultural sector	Total financial resources—public and farm-level	X4
Gross value added	Gross value added of the agricultural sector	X5
Value of crop production	Value of crop production at producer prices excluding product-related subsidies	X6
Value of final agricultural output	Value of total agricultural output at prices including product-related subsidies	X7

Table A10. Results of the best-performing linear single-factor regression models for the national corporate finances, and for the corporate and overall finances of the agricultural sector.

$Y = p_1X + p_2$	p_1	p_2	SSE	R^2	Adjusted R^2	RMSE
X2 = f(X1)	19.870000	10.720000	2939.000000	0.753700	0.742500	11.560000
X3 = f(X1)	0.746600	0.078990	4.951000	0.719600	0.706800	0.474400
X4 = f(X1)	1.747000	0.078990	4.951000	0.933500	0.930500	0.474400

Table A11. Results of the best-performing linear single-factor regression models for the agricultural sector's gross value added, and for the value of crop production and total agricultural output.

$Y = p_1X + p_2$	p_1	p_2	SSE	R^2	Adjusted R^2	RMSE
X5 = f(X6)	0.441800	1.697000	2.474000	0.834300	0.826800	0.335400
X5 = f(X7)	0.486200	−0.079770	2.400000	0.839300	0.832000	0.330300
X7 = f(X6)	0.872400	3.833000	4.433000	0.916400	0.912600	0.448900

https://doi.org/10.3390/jrfm19020100

Table A12. Results of the best-performing single-factor linear regression models for the agricultural sector's gross value added and the value of crop production and total agricultural output.

$Y = p_1X + p_2$	p_1	p_2	SSE	R^2	Adjusted R^2	RMSE
X5 = f(X1)	0.383900	3.216000	11.580000	0.224900	0.189600	0.725500
X6 = f(X1)	1.224000	2.836000	29.710000	0.534700	0.513500	1.162000
X7 = f(X1)	0.981600	6.453000	31.070000	0.414100	0.387400	1.188000
X5 = f(X2)	0.023320	2.832000	8.449000	0.434400	0.408600	0.619700
X6 = f(X2)	0.062910	2.117000	16.610000	0.739800	0.728000	0.869000
X7 = f(X2)	0.053110	5.759000	19.360000	0.634800	0.618200	0.938200
X5 = f(X3)	0.645800	2.998000	7.574000	0.492900	0.469900	0.586800
X6 = f(X3)	1.674000	2.659000	14.370000	0.775000	0.764800	0.808100
X7 = f(X3)	1.335000	6.321000	21.560000	0.593500	0.575100	0.989800

Table A13. Results of the Durbin–Watson test.

№	Regression Model	DW (Without Lags)	DW (1 Lag)	DW (2 Lags)	DW (3 Lags)
01	$\widehat{X2} = 19.8700 \times X1 + 10.7200$	0.9636	2.5190	2.0174	2.0572
02	$\widehat{X3} = 0.74660 \times X1 + 0.07899$	0.7812	2.4857	1.9205	2.0542
03	$\widehat{X4} = 1.74700 \times X1 + 0.07899$	0.7064	2.4857	1.9205	2.0542
04	$\widehat{X5} = 0.44180 \times X6 + 1.69700$	0.7116	1.9109	2.3849	2.0120
05	$\widehat{X5} = 0.48620 \times X7 - 0.07977$	0.7839	1.8262	1.9975	1.9384
06	$\widehat{X7} = 0.87240 \times X6 + 3.83300$	0.5094	1.8391	1.8938	2.0701
07	$\widehat{X5} = 0.38390 \times X1 + 3.21600$	0.5164	2.7997	1.9704	2.0808
08	$\widehat{X6} = 1.22400 \times X1 + 2.83600$	0.8899	2.6581	1.9583	2.0477
09	$\widehat{X7} = 0.98160 \times X1 + 6.45300$	0.7169	2.7853	1.9669	2.0811
10	$\widehat{X5} = 0.02332 \times X2 + 2.83200$	0.5865	1.1066	1.8160	2.0160
11	$\widehat{X6} = 0.06291 \times X2 + 2.11700$	1.1581	0.9839	1.8544	1.9699
12	$\widehat{X7} = 0.05311 \times X2 + 5.75900$	0.9209	0.9552	1.7304	1.9317
13	$\widehat{X5} = 0.64580 \times X3 + 2.99800$	0.6666	2.2485	2.0494	2.0854
14	$\widehat{X6} = 1.67400 \times X3 + 2.65900$	1.2238	2.2301	1.9036	2.1901
15	$\widehat{X7} = 1.33500 \times X3 + 6.32100$	0.7242	2.2831	2.0564	2.0587

References

Aragón, F., Restuccia, D., & Rud, J. (2024). Assessing misallocation in agriculture: Plots versus farms. *Food Policy, 128*, 102678. [CrossRef]

Atashov, B., Valiyeva, S., & Gafarov, N. (2024). Government spending in the agricultural sector: Optimal ratio with lending and the impact on the agricultural production. *Problems and Perspectives in Management, 22*(3), 67–79. [CrossRef]

Barry, P., & Robison, L. (2001). Agricultural finance: Credit, credit constraints and consequences. In B. Gardner, & G. Rausser (Eds.), *Handbook of agricultural economics* (Vol. 1A, pp. 513–571). Elsevier.

Baylan, M. (2025). The impact of agricultural financialization on agricultural output: The case of Türkiye. *Turkish Journal of Agricultural and Natural Sciences, 12*(3), 802–811. [CrossRef]

Bento, P., & Restuccia, D. (2017). Misallocation, establishment size, and productivity. *American Economic Journal: Macroeconomics, 9*(3), 267–303. [CrossRef]

Bezgin, K., Zahariev, A., Shaulska, L., Doronina, O., Tsiklashvili, N., & Wasilewska, N. (2022). Coevolution of education and business: Adaptive interaction. *International Journal of Global Environmental Issues, 21*(2/3/4), 259–275. [CrossRef]

Britos, B., Hernandez, M., Robles, M., & Trupkin, D. (2022). Land market distortions and aggregate agricultural productivity: Evidence from Guatemala. *Journal of Development Economics, 155*, 102787. [CrossRef]

Bulgarian National Bank. (2025, August 6). *Deposits and credits quarterly data*. Available online: http://www.bnb.bg/Statistics/StMonetaryInterestRate/StDepositsAndCredits/StDCCredits/StDCQuarterlyData/ (accessed on 15 January 2026).

Cao, L., & Wang, G. (2024). Impact of digital finance on agricultural output: From the perspective of digital development of agriculture. *Finance Research Letters, 66*, 105698. [CrossRef]

Cianian, P., Falkowski, J., Kancs, D., & Pokrivčák, J. (2011a, September 29). *Productivity and credit constraints: Farm-level evidence from propensity score matching* (Working Paper No. 3). Factor Markets.

Cianian, P., Pokrivčák, J., & Snegenyova, K. (2011b, September 29). *Do agricultural subsidies crowd out or stimulate rural credit institutions? The case of CAP payments* (Working Paper No. 3). Factor Markets.

https://doi.org/10.3390/jrfm19020100

Durbin, J., & Watson, G. S. (1950). Testing for serial correlation in least squares regression I. *Biometrika, 37*(3–4), 409–428. [CrossRef]
European Commission. (2025). *Multiannual financial framework of the EU for the period 2028–2034*. European Commission.
Georgiev, S. G. (2019). Numerical and analytical computation of the implied volatility from option price measurements under regime-switching. *AIP Conference Proceedings, 2172*, 070007. [CrossRef]
Gujarati, D. N., & Porter, D. C. (2009). *Basic econometrics* (5th ed.). McGraw–Hill Education.
Lyubenov, L., & Lyubenova, A. (2017). Long-term financial markets in agribusiness. *Journal of Mountain Agriculture on the Balkans, 20*(3), 397–409.
Lyubenov, L., & Lyubenova, A. (2023). Bulgaria's financial markets in agribusiness—Size, structure and development trends. *Economic Archive*, (2), 48–61. [CrossRef]
Ministry of Agriculture. (2024). *Agricultural reports (2001–2024). Аграрен доклад*. Ministry of Agriculture.
Mishra, A. K., & Lence, S. H. (2005). Risk management by farmers, agribusinesses, and lenders. *Agricultural Finance Review, 65*(2), 131–148. [CrossRef]
Myyra, S. (2013). Agricultural credit in the EU. In J. Swinnen, & L. Knops (Eds.), *Land, labor and capital markets in European agriculture: Diversity under common policy* (Chapter 22, pp. 260–271). Centre for European Policy Studies (CEPS).
Njogu, G., Olweny, T., & Njeru, A. (2018). Relationship between farm production capacity and agricultural credit access from commercial banks. *International Journal of Economics and Finance, 3*(1), 159–174.
Onyiriuba, L., Okoro, E. U. O., & Ibe, G. I. (2020). Strategic government policies on agricultural financing in African emerging markets. *Agricultural Finance Review, 80*(4), 563–588. [CrossRef]
Patwary, M. S. H., Islam, M. S., & Mosharrafa, R. A. (2023). Effect of bank credit on agricultural gross domestic product. *Agricultural and Resource Economics, 9*(1), 188–204. [CrossRef]
Pearson, K. (1895). Notes on regression and inheritance in the case of two parents. *Proceedings of the Royal Society of London, 58*, 240–242. [CrossRef]
Pokrivčák, J., & Tóth, M. (2022). Financing gap of Agro-food firms and the role of policies. *Agris Online Papers in Economics and Informatics, 14*(3), 85–96. [CrossRef]
State Fund "Agriculture". (2025, March 10). Available online: www.dfz.bg (accessed on 15 January 2026).
Wu, Y., Wu, B., Liu, X., & Zhang, S. (2025). Digital finance and agricultural total factor productivity—From the perspective of capital deepening and factor structure. *Finance Research Letters, 74*, 106449. [CrossRef]
Xu, S., & Wang, J. (2023). The impact of digital financial inclusion on the level of agricultural output. *Sustainability, 15*(5), 4138. [CrossRef]
Yang, M., Yang, F., & Sun, C. (2018). Factor market distortion correction, resource reallocation and potential productivity gains: An empirical study on China's heavy industry sector. *Energy Economics, 69*, 270–279. [CrossRef]
Zaharieva, G., Tarakchiyan, O., & Zahariev, A. (2022). Market capitalisation factors of the Bulgarian pharmaceutical sector in a pandemic environment. *Business Management, XXXII*(4), 35–51.

https://doi.org/10.3390/jrfm19020100

Journal of
Risk and Financial Management

MDPI

Article

A Panel Study on the Determinants of Profitability of Bulgarian Commercial Banks

Petar Ilkov Peshev

Economics Department, Faculty of General Economics, University of National and World Economy, 1700 Sofia, Bulgaria; p.peshev@unwe.bg

Abstract

This study examines the determinants of profitability for 21 Bulgarian commercial banks over the period from the first quarter of 2007 to the first quarter of 2025, using financial statement data. Bank profitability is measured by return on assets (ROA) and return on equity (ROE) and modeled within a panel autoregressive distributed lag (PMG-ARDL) framework. The empirical specification combines bank-specific and macroeconomic variables, allowing for the identification of both long-run equilibrium relationships and short-run bank-level dynamics. The long-term results indicate that the net interest margin (NIM), net fee and commission margin (NFM), government bond yields, the growth of the gross domestic product (GDP), and the loan-to-deposit ratio (LDR) positively affect profitability. On the other hand, higher unemployment, rising housing prices, increased loan loss impairments, and the ratio of cash holdings to total assets reduce profitability. The findings provide policy-relevant insights for bank management, regulators, and macroprudential authorities regarding efficiency, income diversification, and credit risk management. The findings facilitate a more comprehensive assessment of banking sector resilience and provide a foundation for the development and refinement of macroprudential and supervisory policy measures.

Keywords: bank profitability; panel data analysis; macroeconomic determinants; return on assets; return on equity; PMG-ARDL

1. Introduction

The profitability of commercial banks in Bulgaria is one of the most important factors for financial system stability and efficiency in a country highly dependent on bank financing. The profitability of commercial banks in Bulgaria depends on both microeconomic and macroeconomic factors. Understanding the degree of influence that commercial banks' profitability has from various influencing factors is of great importance. In addition to being the dominant sector of the financial system of the country, commercial banks are the main sources of financing of firms and households. As such, they contribute to the country's economic stability and growth. Following the 2008–2009 financial crisis, the banks in Bulgaria have been subject to a prolonged period of low interest rates. The banks have also had to comply with more stringent national and EU regulations as well as the effects of the COVID-19 pandemic, the post-2022 high-inflation environment, the monetary tightening after the high-inflation period, and the continued transition to the Eurozone. The 2012 Government debt crisis in selected EU countries and the 2014 default of Corporate Commercial Bank additionally challenged the banking system stability.

Following its peak in 2007, the profitability of Bulgarian commercial banks began to decline, reaching a trough in 2012 and partially recovering in the years that followed. Profitability remains a central issue for both policymakers and banking managers and owners. Bank profits are the main source of capital accumulation and improve the capacity to lend. Banks' profitability represents the capacity of banks to generate income and their ability to absorb shocks, maintain lending activity, and contribute to economic growth. While the sector has demonstrated resilience and strong capital adequacy and liquidity, profitability has fluctuated substantially due to various microeconomic and macroeconomic factors. These dynamics justify the need for a comprehensive evaluation of the main factors affecting the profitability of Bulgarian commercial banks in the short term and in the long run.

This paper contributes to the empirical literature by analyzing the profitability of 21 Bulgarian commercial banks over the period from the first quarter of 2007 to the first quarter of 2025, using quarterly, publicly available bank-level and macroeconomic data. The study employs a pooled mean group autoregressive distributed lag (PMG-ARDL) panel framework following Pesaran et al. (1999), which is well suited to the data structure and allows for the simultaneous estimation of heterogeneous short-run dynamics and homogeneous long-run equilibrium relationships between profitability measures and a set of bank-specific and macroeconomic determinants.

This study offers additional contributions to a well-developed body of literature on bank profitability by offering results for the underdeveloped area of the Central and Eastern European (CEE) countries, specifically Bulgaria, in several ways. First, most of the studies rely on annual data and static panel econometric techniques. Most studies do not capture the long-term adjustment toward equilibrium and assume homogeneity across banks. Second, available research typically covers shorter time periods and does not cover multiple structural breaks, such as the Global Financial Crisis of 2007–2009, followed by the massive quantitative easing (QE), the COVID-19 pandemic, and the recent high-inflation period and monetary tightening. Third, while there exists a significant body of literature concerning the CEE region or Bulgaria, it is rare for studies to be limited solely to these regions. Fourth, none of the studies provide a microeconomic analysis of the panel constituents and their individual dynamic coefficients. Fifth, the combination of microeconomic and macroeconomic variables in the study was not applied to Bulgarian banks, either as part of a broader study or as a study focused on Bulgaria. These gaps are addressed in this article by applying the PMG-ARDL framework of Pesaran et al. (1999). The methodology is applied to quarterly microeconomic data for Bulgarian commercial banks over the period from the first quarter of 2007 to the first quarter of 2025. This study will contribute to the current debates regarding financial stability, monetary policy transmission mechanisms, and sustainable banking practices. By identifying the primary factors driving profitability in the short and long term, this study will provide valuable insight for regulators, bank management, and policymakers seeking to promote a more stable and competitive banking industry in Bulgaria.

Several aspects impose limitations on the research. The sample of 21 banks is largely representative of the banking system, but still it excludes banks with missing data for the whole period analyzed. M&A activity in the sector also omits data for acquired banks prior to their acquisition or merger. The panel of banks comprises heterogeneous banks and bank branches, owned by domestic or international entities. Changes in accounting and reporting requirements necessitate the discretionary adjustments to previously reported data to conform to the new classification categories. The results should be considered with caution due to the 2026 euro adoption in Bulgaria, which could alter the relationship

https://doi.org/10.3390/jrfm19020156

between profitability and its determinants in the future. Finally, the study focuses on quantitative analysis and ignores qualitative investigation methods.

Despite these limitations, the study offers a robust and comprehensive empirical framework that can be amplified in the future by adding more variables, expanding the period, and introducing new constituents to the panel, including on a regional or EU-wide basis.

The object of the paper is the profitability of Bulgarian commercial banks. The subject of the study is the determinants of profitability of Bulgarian commercial banks, including microeconomic factors such as capital adequacy, liquidity, asset quality, and operational efficiency as well as macroeconomic factors such as GDP growth, unemployment, housing prices, and government bond yields. The goal of the study is to identify and evaluate the key determinants of profitability for Bulgarian commercial banks, approximated by the (ROA) and (ROE), during the period between the first quarter of 2007 and the first quarter of 2025. The main thesis of this paper is that the profitability of Bulgarian commercial banks is determined by a mix of bank-specific financial indicators and macroeconomic factors, with long-term equilibrium relationships existing between them.

The remainder of the paper is structured as follows. Section 2 reviews the theoretical and empirical literature on bank profitability determinants. The literature review focuses almost exclusively on emerging markets. Section 3 reveals the data and methodology of the study. Section 4 provides the empirical results and a brief analysis and discussion. Section 5 concludes with key findings and policy implications for the Bulgarian banking sector.

2. Literature Review

Bank profitability factors are scrutinized in the empirical literature, and the CEE region lately attracts the interest of researchers. Three general groups of factors can be outlined: bank-specific (microeconomic), macroeconomic, and institutional factors.

Bank-specific factors directly influence profitability, revealing managerial efficiency, risk management, and operational performance. The cost-to-income ratio (CIR) negatively affects ROA, ROE, and the net interest margin (NIM) in numerous studies (see B. P. Athanasoglou et al., 2006; Căpraru & Ihnatov, 2014; Onofrei et al., 2018; Niu, 2024; Dietrich & Wanzenried, 2011; García-Herrero et al., 2009; Mirzaei et al., 2013; Endri et al., 2025). Analyzing a panel of 143 commercial banks from Romania, Hungary, Poland, Czech Republic, and Bulgaria from 2004 to 2011, Căpraru and Ihnatov (2014) found that ROA, ROE, and NIM (as dependent variables) are negatively associated with CIR. Niu (2024) analyzes 9027 banks using quarterly data over the period between 2001 and 2016 and finds similar negative association. The results of Dumicic and Rizdak (2013) also support the negative effect of CIR on profitability in their GMM panel study on the main determinants of the net interest margin of CEE banks during the 1999–2010 period. Onofrei et al. (2018) also identify the presence of such a negative link in Bulgaria, Czech Republic, Hungary, Lithuania, Latvia, Poland, and Romania between 2003 and 2012. Dietrich and Wanzenried (2011) analyze the profitability of 372 commercial banks in Switzerland over the period from 1999 to 2009 using a panel GMM evaluation technique. García-Herrero et al. (2009) analyze the Chinese banks for the period 1997–2004, using a GMM panel econometric approach. Mirzaei et al. (2013) analyze 1929 banks in 40 emerging and advanced economies over the 1999–2008 period using fixed effect (FE) and random effect (RE) panel estimation methodologies. In a recent study, Endri et al. (2025) analyze Indonesian banks using quarterly data for the period 2018 to 2022, applying FE panel modeling. B. P. Athanasoglou et al. (2006) use FE and RE panel least squares methodology in researching bank profitability between 1998 and 2002 in Albania, Bosnia and Herzegovina, Bulgaria, FYROM, Romania, and Serbia-Montenegro. Lending of Bulgarian commercial banks is subject to a panel investigation

https://doi.org/10.3390/jrfm19020156

in the works of Peshev and Stamenova (2025), and profitability measures are among the determinants. However, panel studies analyzing profitability in Bulgaria are scarce.

In a similar way, loan-loss provisions and non-performing loans are negatively associated with profitability, indicating that poor asset quality reduces returns (see Căpraru & Ihnatov, 2014; Dumicic & Rizdak, 2013; B. P. Athanasoglou et al., 2006; Djalilov & Piesse, 2016; Horobet et al., 2021; Dietrich & Wanzenried, 2011). In early European transition countries, during the 2000–2013 period, the loan-loss provision ratio exhibits a positive link with ROA, revealed by the panel GMM study of Djalilov and Piesse (2016). Horobet et al. (2021) analyze bank profitability in the CEE region, using a GMM methodology. B. P. Athanasoglou et al. (2006) use FE and RE panel least squares methodology in researching bank profitability between 1998 and 2002 in Albania, Bosnia and Herzegovina, Bulgaria, FYROM, Romania, and Serbia-Montenegro.

The capital-to-assets ratio (CAR) exhibits a positive relationship with both ROA and ROE (Căpraru & Ihnatov, 2014; Djalilov & Piesse, 2016; García-Herrero et al., 2009; Claeys & Vander Vennet, 2008; and Zajñac & Paczos, 2025; Endri et al., 2025), implying that better-capitalized banks tend to be more profitable. From another perspective, Horobet et al. (2021), Niu (2024), and Dietrich and Wanzenried (2011) find a negative relationship, suggesting that higher CAR may signal lower risk-taking or constrained lending, harming profitability. Zajñac and Paczos (2025) analyze a panel of 1033 banks in 11 CEE EU states using 2006–2020 data.

The bank size matters, but it has mixed effects on profitability in the covered studies. The natural logarithm of total assets is negatively linked to profitability, indicating diseconomies of scale (Căpraru & Ihnatov, 2014; Djalilov & Piesse, 2016; Mirzaei et al., 2013; Dietrich & Wanzenried, 2011). On the contrary, larger institutions benefit from diversification and economies to scale (B. P. Athanasoglou et al., 2006; García-Herrero et al., 2009; Zajñac & Paczos, 2025). The natural logarithm of assets leads to higher ROA but reduces ROE in the work of Niu (2024).

Liquidity measures, such as the liquid assets-to-total assets, exert negative relationships with profitability, according to Niu (2024) and Zajñac and Paczos (2025). The coefficient on the loan-to-deposit ratio (LDR) is positive with respect to ROA in the study of Endri et al. (2025).

Macroeconomic factors considerably influence bank profitability. In the studies analyzed and logically justifiable, the GDP growth has a positive effect on bank profitability (Albertazzi & Gambacorta, 2009; Căpraru & Ihnatov, 2014; Zajñac & Paczos, 2025; Dietrich & Wanzenried, 2011; Onofrei et al., 2018; Niu, 2024) because of the pro-cyclical nature of banking. Karkowska and Pawłowska (2017) do not find significant association between the GDP growth rate and the dependent profitability measures. Claeys and Vander Vennet (2008) report a negative relationship between economic growth and net interest margin (NIM), suggesting that higher economic growth may be associated with lower interest margins.

Inflation has mixed effects on profitability according to the reviewed studies. It has a positive effect in the works of Căpraru and Ihnatov (2014), B. P. Athanasoglou et al. (2006), García-Herrero et al. (2009), and Zajñac and Paczos (2025). On the contrary, Horobet et al. (2021) identify inflation as a negative factor for bank profitability. Moderate inflation is possibly healthy for the banking sector, but perhaps excessive inflation can erode bank profit margins and destabilize the bank.

The state of the labor market is indicative of the bank performance. The credit risk and non-performing loans increase with a higher unemployment rate, leading to lower profitability. The unemployment rate deteriorates the profitability of banks in the works of Horobet et al. (2021) and Niu (2024).

https://doi.org/10.3390/jrfm19020156

The stock market volatility is positively associated with ROE and in the study of Albertazzi and Gambacorta (2009) but demonstrates a negative association in their model with the profit before tax variable. This illustrates that broader macro-financial variables can affect banks through multiple transmission channels, from credit risk to investment returns.

Together with bank-specific and macroeconomic determinants and institutional and structural factors, such as regulatory and regime changes, the ownership structure further shapes the profitability of banks.

Empirical evidence from Claeys and Vander Vennet (2008), B. P. Athanasoglou et al. (2006), and García-Herrero et al. (2009) indicates a positive relationship between market share and bank profitability, consistent with the view that larger banks achieve efficiency gains through economies of scale and enhanced pricing power. In the study of Borisov (2017), mergers and acquisitions (M&A) led to increased efficiency and higher profitability for Bulgarian banks. Djalilov and Piesse (2016) identify a positive effect of the concentration measure (HHI) on ROA. In the studies of Claeys and Vander Vennet (2008) and Horobet et al. (2021), the concentration ratio exhibits a negative link with the NIM variable.

García-Herrero et al. (2009) find that state-owned banks in China are less profitable than privately owned institutions, perhaps due to inefficiency and policy-driven lending. In the study of Dietrich and Wanzenried (2011), state-owned (co-owned) banks have a positive effect on bank profitability. Foreign ownership has positive effect on profitability in the work of Mirzaei et al. (2013), probably due to better know-how and access to financial support by the acquiring company. Evidence from Karkowska and Pawłowska (2017) suggests that foreign bank ownership does not exert a statistically significant effect on the dependent variable.

Other institutional factors, such as ERM II and euro adoption, affect bank profitability. Zajñac and Paczos (2025) analyze a panel of 1033 banks in 11 CEE EU states using 2006–2020 data. Euro adoption and ERM entry improve ROA and ROE according to the panel regression comprising only those two variables (Zajñac & Paczos, 2025). In the models with a broader set of bank-specific and macroeconomic variables, the euro adoption even plays a negative role for ROA and ROE (ibid.).

Dumicic and Rizdak (2013) identify a negative link between the 3-month money market rate and NIM. Niu (2024) suggests the presence of a negative link between the term spread and profitability. Interest spreads support the bank profitability in the paper of Mirzaei et al. (2013).

The literature review performed in the current section demonstrates that bank profitability is determined by a complex set of microeconomic, macroeconomic, and institutional factors. Sometimes, even in the same study, the same set of factors play different role in profitability, e.g., small vs. large banks, transition countries vs. old Western EU countries, etc. Also, it is not uncommon for different panel econometric techniques applied on the same data to produce contradictory results, as in the study of Djalilov and Piesse (2016).

3. Data and Methodology

This study followed a structured multi-stage empirical procedure designed to identify and evaluate the determinants of profitability of Bulgarian commercial banks using dynamic panel econometric techniques. The methodological framework integrated data preparation, statistical diagnostics, model selection, and dynamic panel estimation, enabling the identification of both long-run equilibrium relationships and short-run adjustment dynamics.

First, a balanced panel dataset was constructed comprising quarterly observations for 21 Bulgarian commercial banks over the period from the first quarter of 2007 to the first quarter of 2025. Profitability was measured using return on assets (ROA) and return on

https://doi.org/10.3390/jrfm19020156

equity (ROE), while the explanatory variables included bank-specific financial indicators and macroeconomic variables reflecting operational efficiency, income structure, liquidity, credit risk, and macroeconomic conditions. The variables were introduced as ratios, rates, and natural logarithms, consistent with standard empirical practice in macro-financial panel studies.

Second, preliminary statistical analysis was performed to examine the distributional properties and relationships among variables. This stage included descriptive statistics, normality tests, and correlation analysis to identify potential outliers, heterogeneity, and multicollinearity. These diagnostics provided essential insights into the statistical characteristics of the dataset and guide the selection of appropriate econometric techniques.

Third, panel unit root tests were conducted to determine the order of integration of each variable and to avoid spurious regression results. Macroeconomic and financial variables are frequently characterized by non-stationary stochastic properties.

Fourth, diagnostic tests were performed to examine cross-sectional dependence and to determine the appropriate panel estimation framework. In addition, model selection between the mean group (MG) and pooled mean group (PMG) estimators was conducted using the Hausman specification test.

Fifth, the core empirical estimation was conducted using the pooled mean group autoregressive distributed lag (PMG-ARDL) approach of Pesaran et al. (1999). This methodology allowed for heterogeneous short-run dynamics across banks while imposing homogeneity on long-run relationships, making it particularly suitable for macro-financial data. The presence of cointegration was further verified using the Kao (1999) residual-based cointegration test, confirming the existence of stable long-run equilibrium relationships between profitability and its determinants.

Finally, the empirical results were interpreted in two complementary dimensions. The long-run equations identified the structural determinants of bank profitability, while the short-run error-correction models captured adjustment dynamics and the speed at which profitability returned to equilibrium following shocks. In addition, the PMG framework allowed for estimation of individual bank-level short-run coefficients, providing insights into heterogeneity across banks in terms of profitability adjustment and sensitivity to financial and macroeconomic conditions.

Overall, this methodological procedure ensured robust empirical identification of profitability determinants by combining rigorous statistical diagnostics with a dynamic panel econometric framework capable of capturing both equilibrium relationships and transitional dynamics. The results of these procedures are presented and analyzed in the following chapter.

The panel comprised quarterly data for 10 variables (two of which were the dependent variables) of 21 Bulgarian commercial banks over the period between the first quarter of 2007 and the first quarter of 2025, producing 1533 observations.

Table 1 provides information about data constituents. The source of microeconomic data was the publicly available financial statements section of the web site of Bulgarian National Bank. Most of the macroeconomic variables were fetched from the website of National Statistical Institute.

The bank selection process was based on data availability for the analyzed period. Selected 21 banks had data for the whole analyzed period, and the sample represented the population well in terms of share of profit, equity, loans, liabilities, and assets in comparison to the whole banking system. The panel omitted banks with incomplete data for the whole period to avoid biases arising from unbalanced panels. The panel constituents possessed heterogeneous features since some banks varied by ownership, business model, asset and operation size, and whether they are a bank or bank branch, established by the

https://doi.org/10.3390/jrfm19020156

mother company in Bulgaria for a specific reason. As of the end of the period, banks owned or controlled by Bulgarian entities or individuals are International Asset Bank; CHPB Texim, Central Cooperative Bank; Tokuda bank; TB Investbank; Municipal Bank; First Investment Bank; Bulgarian American Credit Bank, Bulgarian Development Bank. Banks with Bulgarian ownership hold around 20% of the assets as of the end of the period. Banks with foreign ownership own around 80%, of which bank branches account for approximately 1.6% of the bank assets. The four largest banks operating in Bulgaria (United Bulgarian Bank, Unicredit Bulbank, DSK bank, and Eurobank Bulgaria) are owned and controlled by foreign financial groups and control roughly 70% of bank assets.

Table 1. Panel constituents (list of banks).

Bank ID	Bank Name
120	TB Investbank
130	Municipal Bank
145	ING Bank N.V.-Sofia branch
150	First Investment Bank
160	Bulgarian-American Credit Bank
200	United Bulgarian Bank
230	Procredit Bank (Bulgaria)
240	Commercial Bank D
250	City Bank Europe-Bulgaria Branch
260	Tokuda Bank
300	DSK Bank
310	TBI Bank (Former NLB Bank West-East)
350	TE-DZHE Zirat Bank-Sofia branch
440	BNP Paribas S.A.—Sofia branch
470	International Asset Bank
545	CHPB Texim
561	Allianz Bulgaria Commercial Bank
620	Bulgarian Development Bank (former Nastarchitelna Bank)
660	Unicredit Bulbank
790	Central Cooperative Bank
920	Eurobank Bulgaria (Bulgarian Postbank)

Source: Bulgaria National Bank.

Table 2 provides the list of bank-specific and macroeconomic indicators. The literature review to a large degree supported the data selection process. The study encompassed variables commonly used in banking and economic analysis. Profitability of individual banks was measured by ROA and ROE for the twelve trailing months (TTM). Specifically, profit for the most recent twelve-month period (four quarters) was divided by the average total assets and average equity, respectively. The CIR variable accounted for operational efficiency, with lower values indicating better cost efficiency. It was calculated as the ratio of operating expenses to net banking income. The net interest margin (NIM) was calculated as the ratio of net interest income to interest-earning assets. The net fee and commission (NFM) was calculated as the ratio between net fees and commission income to interest-earning assets. NIM and NFM were the main sources of net banking income for Bulgarian banks, which operate under a traditional business model. The yield on 10-Year Government Bonds (GYIELD) was the benchmark for long-term interest rates and anchors to some extent lending and deposit interest rates, which are important for the macroeconomy. The natural logarithm of the house price index (HPR) tracks house price dynamics. The unemployment rate (UR) accounts for labor market health and for the capacity utilization in the economy. The dynamics of the LDR can be interpreted as an indicator of banks' risk-taking appetite and liquidity preferences. The LDR indicator

https://doi.org/10.3390/jrfm19020156

was calculated as the ratio of total loans granted to total deposits received, reflecting the extent to which deposits were used to finance lending activities. The economic growth was represented by the natural logarithm of seasonally adjusted quarterly real GDP figures (GDP). The cash-to-assets ratio (CASHR) is indicative of the liquidity position and for the risk aversion of the bank. The CASHR variable was calculated as the ratio of cash and cash equivalents to total assets, measuring the share of highly liquid funds available to the bank relative to its total asset base. The loan-loss-to-loans ratio (LLR) measures credit risk and asset quality. The LLR variable was calculated as the ratio of loan loss provisions to total gross loans, measuring the extent of expected credit losses relative to the bank's total lending portfolio. The mix of selected variables provided a comprehensive view of financial stability, profitability, and macroeconomic conditions and was in line with literature review and logical inference.

Table 2. Variables.

Variables	Description
ROE	Return on equity
ROA	Return on assets
CIR	Cost-to-income ratio
NIM	Net-interest-margin ratio
NFM	Net-fee and commission income ratio
GYIELD	Yield till maturity on 10-year government bonds
HPR	Natural logarithm of the house price index
UR	The unemployment rate
LDR	Loan-to-deposit ratio
GDP	Natural logarithm of the seasonally adjusted quarterly real GDP
CASHR	Cash-to-assets ratio
LLR	Loan-loss-to-loans ratio

It is standard practice in empirical research on banking system indicators to combine variables expressed in natural logarithms—such as bank size (measured by total assets), gross domestic product (GDP), monetary aggregates, and other monetary values—with variables expressed as ratios and interest rates (Albertazzi & Gambacorta, 2009; B. P. Athanasoglou et al., 2006; P. P. Athanasoglou et al., 2008; Căpraru & Ihnatov, 2014; García-Herrero et al., 2009; Koetter & Poghosyan, 2010; Killins, 2000; Sufian & Chong, 2008; Peshev & Stamenova, 2025). This approach reflected the distinct statistical properties and economic interpretation of scale variables, which were appropriately modeled in logarithmic form, and proportional or rate-based indicators, which retained their natural interpretation when expressed as percentages or ratios.

Accordingly, this study employed a semi-logarithmic specification in which the dependent variable was expressed as a ratio, while the explanatory variables consisted of a combination of financial and macroeconomic indicators introduced as rates, ratios, and natural logarithms. In this framework, the estimated coefficients on logarithmic explanatory variables had a semi-elasticity interpretation: a 1% increase in GDP or in the house price index led to a change in the dependent variable—such as return on assets (ROA) or return on equity (ROE)—equal to one-hundredth of the corresponding coefficient, expressed in percentage points (pp). By contrast, for explanatory variables expressed as ratios or rates, a one percentage point increase (i.e., an absolute increase of 0.01) resulted in a change in the dependent variable equal to the estimated coefficient multiplied by 0.01 pp. This specification facilitated a consistent and economically meaningful interpretation of coefficients across variables measured in different functional forms.

https://doi.org/10.3390/jrfm19020156

Usually, financial and macroeconomic variables exhibited time-varying statistical properties, such as the mean, median, and variance. Varying statistical features signaled that variables were non-stationary at levels and had unit roots. The data of the study were tested for the presence of unit roots. The panel unit root tests applied in the study included Levin, Lin, and Chu (LLC), ADF-Fisher, Im–Pesaran–Shin (IPS) of Im et al. (2003), cross-sectionally augmented IPS (CIPS) test of Pesaran (2007), and PP-Fisher tests. The results of the unit root tests, along with the correlation analysis and descriptive statistics, are presented in the following section.

The PMG-ARDL approach of Pesaran et al. (1999) deals well with a combination of I(0) and I(1) variables. This method is well suited for panel data with variables integrated of different orders, as long as none are I(2).

$$\Delta y_{it} = \phi_i * \left(y_{i,t-1} - \beta' * x_{i,t-1}\right) + \sum_{j=1}^{p-1} \lambda_{ij} * \Delta y_{i,t-j} + \sum_{j=0}^{q-1} \delta'_{ij} * \Delta x_{i,t-j} + \mu_i + \epsilon_{it} \quad (1)$$

where

- Δy_{it} is the change in the dependent variable (ROA or ROE) for the i-th cross-sectional unit (bank) over a period-t;
- Δx_{it} is vector of the changes in the explanatory variables for the i-th cross-sectional unit (bank) over a period-t;
- ϕ_i is error correction term coefficient for the i-th cross-sectional unit (bank);
- β is common long-run coefficients (assumed homogeneous across groups);
- λ_{ij} is short-run coefficients for the i-th cross-sectional unit (bank)'s dependent variable with j-lags;
- δ_{ij} is short-run coefficients for the i-th cross-sectional unit (bank)'s explanatory variable with j-lags;
- μ_i is group-specific fixed effects, the intercept term for each cross-sectional unit (bank)-I;
- ϵ_{it} is the error term for the i-th cross-sectional unit (bank) over a period-t.

The cointegration equation exhibits the long-run equation and is introduced in Equation (2).

$$y_{it} = \beta' x_{it} + \eta_{it} \quad (2)$$

where

- y_{it} is the dependent variable (ROA or ROE) for the i-th cross-sectional unit (bank) over a period-t;
- x_{it} is vector of explanatory variables for the i-th cross-sectional unit (bank) over a period-t;
- η_{it} is the stationary process (the long-run error).

The error-correction term (ECT) employed in the PMG–ARDL short-run equation (Equation (1)) and revealed in Equation (3) is the lagged cointegration residual of Equation (2).

$$ECT_{i,t-1} = \eta_{i,t-1} = y_{i,t-1} - \beta' * x_{i,t-1} \quad (3)$$

Equation (1) specifies the formal representation of the PMG estimator. The model assumes homogeneity of long-run coefficients across all groups (cross-sections); at the same time, it allows for heterogeneity across short-run coefficients (see Pesaran et al., 1999).

4. Results and Discussion

The current section presents the empirical results of the study. It systematizes the results of the descriptive and statistical analysis of the variables performed, including unit root tests and correlation tests. The section then details the long-run equilibrium relationships and the short-run ones for ROA and ROE models using the PMG-ARDL approach. This section also details the analysis of the short-term error-correction models for each individual bank.

Tables 3 and 4 present the descriptive statistics based on an individual sample of 1533 for each variable. The profitability results, measured through ROA and ROE, signal high heterogeneity in the results despite being positive on average (see Figures A1 and A2). High standard deviations and kurtosis, particularly for ROE, are perhaps caused by dividend payouts, the impact of financial crises, credit impairments, and economic fluctuations.

Table 3. Descriptive stat (individual sample).

	ROA	ROE	CIR	NIM	NFM	GYIELD	HPR
Mean	0.01	0.17	0.70	0.01	0.00	0.03	4.84
Median	0.01	0.09	0.61	0.01	0.00	0.03	4.78
Maximum	0.10	11.77	28.16	0.08	0.03	0.08	5.47
Minimum	−0.08	−11.86	−18.96	−0.06	−0.08	0.00	4.56
Std. Dev.	0.02	0.67	1.14	0.01	0.00	0.02	0.25
Skewness	0.08	1.24	8.22	2.72	−9.45	0.22	0.84
Kurtosis	10.59	158.40	315.54	18.26	271.94	2.19	2.77
Jarque-Bera	3532	147,943	6,256,468	16,763	4,642,931	55	184
Probability	0.00	0.00	0.00	0.00	0.00	0.00	0.00
Sum	15	244	1078	15	6	49	7417
Sum Sq. Dev.	0.35	662	1996	0.13	0.02	0.67	92.97
Observations	1470	1470	1533	1533	1533	1533	1533

Table 4. Descriptive stat (continuation).

	UR	LDR	GDP	CASHR	LLR
Mean	0.07	0.79	10.27	0.18	0.01
Median	0.06	0.79	10.25	0.15	0.01
Maximum	0.14	3.72	10.49	0.88	0.33
Minimum	0.04	0.09	10.10	0.01	−0.16
Std. Dev.	0.03	0.29	0.11	0.13	0.02
Skewness	0.61	2.94	0.50	2.33	5.07
Kurtosis	1.98	26.31	1.97	10.15	71.77
Jarque-Bera	162	36,928	131	4659	295,961
Probability	0.00	0.00	0.00	0.00	0.00
Sum	112	1215	15,751	271	16
Sum Sq. Dev.	1.41	125.11	18.35	25.36	0.82
Observations	1533	1533	1533	1533	1470

The CIR variable displays substantial variability and irregularity, with a maximum of 28.16 and a minimum of −18.96, having high skewness of 8.22 and kurtosis above 310, indicating severe non-normality and large heterogeneity across banks' operational efficiency.

The net interest margin (NIM) reports a 1% on average per quarter and keeps the margin relatively stable. The kurtosis and skewness statistics, however, indicate that few large banks achieve high margins in specific periods.

The net fee-to-operating-income ratio (NFM) shows considerable heterogeneity across banks. The variable's high skewness and kurtosis suggest that few banks register high net fee and commission margin, whereas most generate more modest income from this source.

The government bond yield (GYIELD) averages about 3.2%. The skewness and kurtosis capture the transition from high yields in the post-crisis years to low yields during the ECB's unconventional monetary easing period and the post-2022 increases.

The natural logarithm of the house price index (HPR) shows moderate variation and a slight right-skewed distribution.

Table 4 presents summarized descriptive statistics for the rest of the variables from the dataset. The unemployment rate (UR) variable has an average value of 7.3% and shows moderate variation around the mean, signaling the common cyclical behavior of the Bulgarian labor market over the sample period.

The LDR exerts a considerable deviation from the central tendency, with values spanning between 0.09 and 3.72, and displays considerable positive skewness of 2.94.

The ratio of loan loss provisions to total loans (LLR) is low on average, but outliers probably reflect high credit risk periods during downturns.

The natural logarithm of the real seasonally adjusted quarterly GDP maintains low volatility, as it is the natural logarithm of a trending seasonally adjusted macroeconomic variable.

The Jarque–Bera test statistics and corresponding p-values lead to the rejection of the null hypothesis of normality for all variables, indicating the presence of non-normal distributions and potential outliers.

The panel unit root tests applied in the study include LLC, ADF-Fisher, IPS, CIPS test of Pesaran (2007), and PP-Fisher tests. The results are reported in Table 5. The LLC test assumes a common unit root process, while the ADF-Fisher and PP-Fisher tests allow for heterogeneity. All tests' results are valid at the 1% level of significance. Using both IPS and CIPS strengthens the empirical strategy by demonstrating that the stationarity results are robust to both independence and cross-dependence assumptions, thereby supporting the validity of the subsequent PMG-ARDL estimation. The panel unit root tests are performed on a balanced panel covering 21 cross-sections and 1 470 observations from the first quarter of 2007 until the first quarter of 2025. The results from the unit root tests in Table 5 reveal the distinction between level-stationary and first-difference stationary variables. Most of the variables are level stationary. The following variables are non-stationary at levels but integrated of one, I(1): HPR, GDP, CASHR, and LDR. The mix of I(0) and I(1) will lead to spurious results if a proper panel econometric technique is not selected. The PMG-ARDL approach of Pesaran et al. (1999) deals well with a combination of I(0) and I(1) variables. This method is well suited for panel data with variables integrated of different orders as long as none are I(2). The PMG-ARDL approach allows for short-run heterogeneity across units while imposing long-run homogeneity. The long-run association, represented by the cointegration equations, is the same for all banks, while short-run dynamics vary among individual banks.

The PMG-ARDL approach is also preferred for a mix of I(0) and I(1) data in panels with moderate cross-sections and long-time series (Roodman, 2009; Pesaran et al., 1999).

The correlation matrix in Table 6 shows ROA and ROE do not experience strong positive or negative correlation with other variables. The macroeconomic variables exert strong negative or positive correlations with each other, especially HPR, UR, and GDP, suggesting potential presence of multicollinearity among some of the variables (see Table 7).

https://doi.org/10.3390/jrfm19020156

Table 5. Unit root tests.

Variable	Level-Stationary	First Differences Stationary
ROE	I(0) ***	
ROA	I(0) ***	
LDR		I(1) ***
CIR	I(0) ***	
NFM	I(0) ***	
NIM	I(0) ***	
CASHR		I(1) ***
LLR	I(0) ***	
GDP		I(1) ***
GYIELD	I(0) ***	
HPR		I(1) ***
UR	I(0) ***	

Note that *** denotes significance at the 1% level.

Table 6. Correlation matrix.

	ROA	ROE	CIR	NIM	NFM	GYIELD
ROA	1					
p-value	-----					
ROE	0.180	1				
p-value	0	-----				
CIR	−0.141	−0.019	1			
p-value	0.000	0.471	-----			
NIM	0.349	0.020	−0.0744	1		
p-value	0	0.4449	0.0043	-----		
NFM	0.14	0.04	−0.01	0.35	1.00	
p-value	0	0.1066	0.7455	0	-----	
GYIELD	0.13	0.02	−0.05	0.09	−0.08	1.00
p-value	0	0.5447	0.0555	0.0004	0.0012	-----
HPR	0.28	0.07	−0.07	0.05	0.00	−0.12
p-value	0	0.006	0.0062	0.0415	0.85	0
UR	−0.28	−0.06	0.05	−0.06	−0.03	0.37
p-value	0	0.0211	0.0561	0.0336	0.2412	0
LDR	0.13	−0.10	−0.06	0.05	−0.30	0.37
p-value	0	0.0002	0.0214	0.0773	0	0
GDP	0.11	0.04	−0.04	−0.01	0.03	−0.51
p-value	0.0001	0.1535	0.1619	0.7263	0.2841	0
CASHR	−0.02	0.13	0.04	−0.01	0.29	−0.45
p-value	0.4884	0	0.1344	0.666	0	0
LLR	−0.21	−0.09	−0.02	0.20	0.13	0.05
p-value	0	0.0005	0.4204	0	0	0.0506

The study follows the procedures of Pesaran and Smith (1995) and Pesaran et al. (1999) to determine the appropriate estimator between the PMG and the mean group (MG) methods. As noted by Blackburne and Frank (2007), panels characterized by a relatively large number of cross-sectional units (N) and time periods (T) as well as non-stationarity and cross-sectional heterogeneity are well suited to the panel ARDL framework of Pesaran et al. (1999). The current study has large N and T features.

Model selection between the PMG and MG estimators is conducted using the Hausman (1978) specification test, which is computed on the vector of long-run slope coefficients. The test statistic H follows a chi-square distribution with k-degrees of freedom, where $H \sim \chi^2(k)$ with k = 10. The long-run coefficients are derived from the PMG and MG estimators on an ARDL (5, 4, 4, 4, 4, 4, 4, 4, 4, 4, 4) specification.

https://doi.org/10.3390/jrfm19020156

Table 7. Correlation matrix (continuation).

	HPR	UR	LDR	GDP	CASHR
HPR	1.00				
p-value	-----				
UR	−0.82	1.00			
p-value	0	-----			
LDR	−0.08	0.14	1.00		
p-value	0.0025	0	-----		
GDP	0.84	−0.74	−0.24	1.00	
p-value	0	0	0	-----	
CASHR	0.29	−0.37	−0.58	0.45	1.00
p-value	0	0	0	0	-----
LLR	−0.16	0.17	0.15	−0.12	−0.15
p-value	0	0	0	0	0

For the baseline specification with ten explanatory variables for the ROA model, the Hausman statistic equals 11.21 with a p-value of 0.341. This indicates the failure to reject the null hypothesis of common long-run coefficients. Consequently, the PMG model is selected. Using the same setup and applying it to the ROE models yields a H-statistic of 8.766, with a p-value of 0.554. The Hausman test fails to reject the null hypothesis of common long-run coefficients in the ROE model; therefore, the PMG model is preferred.

The presence of cross-sectional dependence is examined using Pesaran's (2004, 2021) cross-sectional dependence (CD) test and Friedman's (1937) rank-based test, which are employed as complementary diagnostics in line with the recommendations of De Hoyos and Sarafidis (2006). For the ROA model, the cross-sectional dependence tests provide no evidence of strong dependence across cross-sectional units. Specifically, Pesaran's CD test yields a Z-statistic of 0.287 with a p-value of 0.198, while Friedman's chi-square statistic equals 82.91 with a p-value of 0.178. Both tests fail to reject the null hypothesis of cross-sectional independence.

Similarly, for the ROE model, Pesaran's CD test produces a Z-statistic of 0.673 with a p-value of 0.501, and Friedman's test reports a chi-square statistic of 88.12 with a p-value of 0.100. Taken together, the results consistently indicate the absence of strong cross-sectional dependence. Accordingly, the analysis proceeds under the assumption of cross-sectional independence, supporting the application of the PMG–ARDL framework of Pesaran et al. (1999).

Bardi and Hfaiedh (2021) use panel macro econometric regression applying the PMG-ARDL approach without having a cross-dependent data concern since it is common the same macroeconomic variables to affect cross-sectional units. Bardi and Hfaiedh (2021) combine a mix of rates, ratios, numerical values, and monetary variables.

The following subsections of the Results and Discussion section presents the results of the long-run and short-run interdependencies of the applied PMG-ARDL approach of Pesaran et al. (1999).

4.1. Long-Run Equations

Table 8 provides the results of the error-correction equations revealed in current section. These cointegration equations reveal the long-run interdependence between the dependent and explanatory variables, following the methodology specified in the Section 3. Equation (4) reveals the long-term relationship between the dependent variable (ROA) and

https://doi.org/10.3390/jrfm19020156

the explanatory variables. All variables have p-value below 0.01 and are assumed to be significant at the 1% level of significance.

$$ROA_{it} = -0.005CIR_{it} + 0.683NIM_{it} + 1.352NFM_{it} + 0.359GYIELD_{it} - 0.077HPR_{it} - 0.177UR_{it} + 0.014LDR_{it} + 0.221GDP_{it} - 0.030CASHR_{it} - 0.266LLR_{it} + \eta_{it} \quad (4)$$

Table 8. Long-run equations (error-correction equations).

Variable	ROA		ROE	
	Coef.	Prob.	Coef.	Prob.
CIR	−0.005	0.00	−0.09	0.00
NIM	0.683	0.00	9.302	0.00
NFM	1.352	0.00	−24.35	0.04
GYIELD	0.359	0.00	6.268	0.00
HPR	−0.077	0.00	−1.357	0.00
UR	−0.177	0.00	−0.793	0.04
LDR	0.014	0.00	−0.067	0.34
GDP	0.221	0.00	4.30	0.00
CASHR	−0.030	0.00	0.202	0.03
LLR	−0.266	0.00	1.42	0.05

Note that all variables are significant at the 1% level of significance.

The other profitability measure approximated by the ROE dependent variables is presented in Equation (5). The equation reveals the long-term relationship between the dependent variable (ROE) and the explanatory variables. All variables are statistically significant at the 1% level, with the exception of NFM_{it}, LLR_{it}, URit, and $CASHR_{it}$, which do not reach significance at this threshold. In contrast, the LDR_{it} is not statistically significant, as its p-value exceeds 0.30.

$$ROE_{it} = -0.09CIR_{it} + 9.30NIM_{it} - 24.353NFM_{it} + 6.268GYIELD_{it} - 1.3575HPR_{it} - 0.793UR_{it} - 0.067LDR_{it} + 4.30GDPit + 0.202CASHR_{it} + 1.42LLR_{it} + \eta_{iit} \quad (5)$$

Note that all variables are significant at the 1% level of significance except NFM_{it}, $CASHR_{it}$, UR_{it}, LLR_{it}, which are significant at the 5% level of significance, while LDR_{it} and are insignificant at the 5% level, with p-values considerably above the 0.33 level.

The results of the ROA equation suggest that all coefficients are statistically significant. The dependent variable (ROA) relates negatively with the CIR variable, CASHR, LLR, and the UR and the HPR variable. The NIM, NFM, GYIELD, LDR, and the GDP are positively related to the dependent variables.

Using the same set of explanatory variables as in the ROA specification, with ROE as the dependent variable, largely confirms the findings obtained from the ROA model (see Table 8). The coefficients on NFM, UR, CASHR, and LLR are only weakly significant, reaching significance at the 5% level. In contrast, the LDR variable remains statistically insignificant, with p-values exceeding 0.30. The dependent variable (ROE) exhibits a negative relationship with the CIR variable at the 1% level of significance, with the UR variable at the 5% level, and with the HPR variable at the 1% level. In contrast, the LDR variable is statistically insignificant, with p-values exceeding 0.30. The coefficient on NFM is statistically significant at the 5% level but not at the 1% level. Although NFM is theoretically expected to enhance bank profitability, its negative sign and relatively low level of statistical significance suggest that this effect should be interpreted with caution, particularly as it contradicts the results obtained from the ROA model.

https://doi.org/10.3390/jrfm19020156

It is clear from these long-run findings that the NIM, GYIELD and the GDP have a positive relationship with the ROE (dependent) variables and confirm the findings of the ROA model.

It could be summarized that the negative association between CIR and the profitability measures indicates that inefficiency in operations deteriorates bank profitability.

NIM supports bank profitability, especially banks with a traditional business model, such as that of Bulgarian banks. NFM is the other main source for bank profitability for the case of the ROA model. However, the variable is statistically insignificant in the ROE model. For traditional banks, lending activity and charging fees and commissions are the main sources of bank income and profitability. Higher bond yields—GYIELD—improve ROE probably since bond yields are indicative of the rate on loans. On the other hand, higher house prices—HPR—may signal overheating in the housing market, increasing risk and realizing it leads to lower profitability. Higher UR significantly reduces ROE, and lower extends ROA, likely due to larger credit risk and lower economic activity. The GDP positively affects bank profitability in both models. The LDR variable has a positive relationship with the ROA dependent variable and has no relationship with the ROE model, indicating that risk-taking generates bank profitability and confirms the negative relationship between the CASHR variable and the ROA dependent variable.

The Kao (1999) residual-based cointegration test is applied to examine whether a long-run equilibrium relationship exists among the variables included in the ROA and ROE panel models. The results are summarized in Table 9 and indicate strong evidence of cointegration for both models, though the ROA model displays higher t-stat. The Kao cointegration test employs an Augmented Dickey–Fuller (ADF) statistic applied to the residuals from the panel regression. The p-value of the t-stat for the ROA and ROE models is significant at 1%. The negative coefficient of RESID(−1) and D(RESID(−1)) display the speed of adjustment toward the long-run equilibrium, i.e., 25% of the deviation is correct each quarter for the ROA model and 94% for the ROE model.

Table 9. Kao residual cointegration tests.

Variables	ROA Model		ROE Model	
	t-Statistic	Prob.	t-Statistic	Prob.
ADF	−7.03	0.00	3.35	0.00
Variable	Coefficient	Prob.	Coefficient	Prob.
RESID(−1)	−0.25	0.00	−0.94	0.00
D(RESID(−1))	−0.08	0.00	−0.09	0.00

4.2. Short-Term Interdependencies

The present sub-section analyzes the short-run error-correction models, revealed in Equations (6) and (7), together with Table 10.

The lag-lengths in the ARDL specification were determined using an automatic selection procedure based on the Akaike Information Criterion (AIC). Given the structure of the dataset, with a time dimension of T = 73 and N = 21 cross-sectional units and a relatively high number of explanatory variables (10 regressors), the Akaike Information Criterion (AIC) is the most appropriate choice for selecting lag lengths in a PMG-ARDL specification. AIC applies a lighter penalty for additional parameters than BIC or HQ, which is advantageous in dynamic models like PMG-ARDL (see Kripfganz & Schneider, 2023). The estimation routine evaluated 20 admissible ARDL(p, $q_1, \ldots, q_k$) combinations within these limits using a common selection sample, and selected the model with the lowest AIC, namely ARDL(5, 4, 4, 4, 4, 4, 4, 4, 4, 4, 4).

https://doi.org/10.3390/jrfm19020156

Table 10. Short-run models' results.

Dependent Variables	D(ROA)		D(ROE)	
Variable	Coefficient	Prob.	Coefficient	Prob.
COINTEQ01 (ECT)	−0.146	0.00	−0.284	0.03
D(ROA(-1))	0.125	0.00		
D(ROA(-2))	0.081	0.04		
D(CIR)	−0.005	0.00		
D(CIR(-1))	−0.004	0.00		
D(CIR(-2))	−0.004	0.02		
D(CIR(-3))	−0.006	0.00		
D(ROE(-1))			0.215	0.00
D(ROE(-2))			0.147	0.02
D(GYIELD)	−0.073	0.02		
D(CASHR(-2))	0.014	0.02		
D(LLR)	−0.467	0.00		
C	−0.278	0.00	−10.56	0.03

Equation (6) reveals the short-term dynamics between the change in ROA and its regressors, which are statistically significant at the 1% and 5% level of significance respectively.

$$\Delta ROA_{it} = -0.146ECT_{i,t-1} + 0.125\Delta ROA_{i,t-1} + 0.081\Delta ROA_{i,t-2} + 0.005\Delta CIR_{it} - 0.004\Delta CIR_{i,t-1} - 0.004\Delta CIR_{i,t-2} - 0.006\Delta CIRi_{,t-3} - 0.073\Delta GYIELD_{it} + 0.014\Delta CASHR_{i,t-2} - 0.466\Delta LLR_{it} - 0.278 + \eta_{it} \quad (6)$$

Note that all variables are significant at the 1% level of significance except D(ROA(-2)), D(CIR(-2)), D(GYIELD), and D(CASHR(-2)), which are significant at the 5% level of significance.

On the other hand, Equation (7) presents the short-term interdependencies between the change in ROE and its explanatory variables, which are statistically significant at the 1% and 5% level of significance, respectively.

$$\Delta ROE_{it} = -0.284ECT_{i,t-1} + 0.215\Delta ROE_{i,t-1} + 0.147\Delta ROE_{i,t-2} - 10.56 + \eta_{it} \quad (7)$$

Note that all variables are significant at the 5% level of significance except D(ROA(-1)), which is significant at the 1% level of significance.

The short-term models, where the dependent variables are the first differences of both profitability measures, ROA and ROE, reveal a strong interdependence between past values of the dependent variable and current values. This fact suggests that a strong momentum process is underway (see Table 10). Past values of profitability influence current profitability, but the effect fades away over time. A one percentage point (pp) change in the past value (one and two quarters lag) of the change in ROE leads to 21.5% (one quarter lag) and 14.7% (lag of two quarters) change in the change in ROE, respectively.

The CIR is negatively associated with the change in ROA, and one pp change in the D(CIR) variable leads to 0.5% decline in the dependent variable, while the D(CIR(-1)) variable leads to a 0.4% decline of the dependent variable. In similar magnitude is the effect of the second and third lag of the variable on the dependent variable (see Table 10). Operational inefficiencies in the short run harm short-term performance of commercial banks in Bulgaria.

The short-run results laid out in Table 10 reveal that a one pp increase in the change of loan losses-to-loans ratio (the LLR variable) reduces ROA by 46.7%, implying a strong negative impact. Loan loss impairments deteriorate bank profitability, as the logic states.

The rise in government bonds (the GYIELD variable) is inversely related to the short-term change in the profitability, possibly reflecting opportunity cost or channeling macroeconomic slowdown due to rising bond yields. Higher bond yields trigger down bond prices and the value of banks' bond portfolio, which might be a factor for overall lower profitability, especially for banks with large bond portfolios. A one pp change of the GYIELD rate leads to 7.3% decline in the change ROA in the short term (see Table 10).

The change in the liquidity measure CASHR with two lags supports short-term profitability but contradicts long-term results. A one pp change in the ratio leads to 1.2% increase in the short-run change of ROA.

Both ECT coefficients are negative and significant at the 1% level of significance for the ROA model and at the 5% for the ROE model. The ROA model corrects 14.6% of its disequilibrium each quarter, while the ROE model adjusts more strongly, with 28.4% disequilibrium corrected each quarter. The speed of adjustment is faster for the ROE model, even though the p-value for the ECT of the model is 0.03 in comparison to 0.00 for the ROA model.

The constant of the model is statistically significant at the 1% level of significance for the ROA model and at the 5% level of significance for the ROE model. Both coefficients are negative, and the value of −0.278 of the ROA model reveals small negative bias. The much larger negative constant for the ROE model of −10.56 may indicate structural downward pressure of omitted variables or even misspecification for the latter model.

More variables of the ROA model are significant in comparison to the ROE model, favoring the explanatory power of the ROA model.

As can be seen at Table 11, the log-Likelihood measure is much higher for the ROA model giving preferences for the higher goodness-to-fit of the model, almost twice as high as the ROE model's value. The value of the Akaike Info Criterion, Schwarz Criterion and Hannan–Quinn Criterion are times lower for the ROA model, justifying the model superiority. The ROA model has much tighter residuals, hinting it is more precise. On other hand, the ROE model has larger dispersion of the dependent variable and much higher overall error, measured through the sum squared residuals.

Table 11. Summarized statistics and goodness-to-fit stats.

Indicators	ROA Models	ROE Models
Mean dependent var	-8.33×10^{-5}	−0.001286
S.E. of regression	0.00	0.59
Sum squared resid	0.00	176.97
Log likelihood	7670.96	3936.96
S.D. dependent var	0.01	0.91
Akaike info criterion	−9.108	−4.028
Schwarz criterion	−5.595	−0.513
Hannan–Quinn criter.	−7.798	−2.712

4.3. Individual Banks' Short-Run Results

4.3.1. ROA Models (at the Bank Level)

The cointegration equation in the applied in the study PMG-ARDL Pesaran et al. (1999) model is common for all banks, while the approach allows for identifying individual short-term models for the banks comprising the panel. Short-term individual banks' ROA models are revealed in Tables A1 and A2 in Appendix A. Equation (4) represents the cointegration relationships and serves as the ECT.

All banks' ECTs exhibit a negative relationship with the dependent variable, reducing system disequilibrium each quarter except for ING Bank N.V.-Sofia Branch (bank ID 145), CHPB Texim (bank ID 545), and Allianz Bulgaria Commercial Bank (bank ID 561) (see

Table A1 in Appendix A). The latter three banks increase their disequilibrium with each quarter, justified by their positive coefficient. The average coefficient of the ECT accepts the value of −0.153, meaning that on average, 15.3% of banks' disequilibrium is reduced each quarter (for banks with available coefficients). The highest speed of adjustment is observed for the City Bank Europe-Bulgaria branch (ID: 250), TBI Bank (Former NLB Bank West-East) (ID: 310), and Bulgarian Development Bank (former Nastarchitelna Bank) (ID: 620), which correct between 46% and 52% of their disequilibrium each quarter.

The lagged ROA variables D(ROA (-1)), D(ROA(-2)), and D(ROA(-3)) reveal positive average effects (0.132, 0.089, and 0.052, respectively), implying that past profitability is a factor for current profitability, highlighting the momentum effect in profitability (see Table A1 in Appendix A). For some of the banks, one of the lagged variables may have a negative effect, but the mean and average values justify it. The D(ROA(-4)) has a negative coefficient value on average for all banks but is not invalidating the positive effects of previous three lags.

The average coefficients for D(CIR) and its lags range between approximately −0.006 and −0.004 (more precisely, from about −0.006 to −0.004, depending on the lag), with a high proportion of zero or negative values across banks. These results suggest that increases in operational inefficiency tend to have a modest negative impact on short-run performance, as can be seen at Table A1 in Appendix A. One unit change of the CIR ratio (current and lagged values) leads to about 0.4–0.6% decline in profitability on average across all presented lagged values.

The short-run impact of the change in the NIM variable on the profitability reveals that the change in the NIM variable in the current quarter (D(NIM)) and the first quarter has negative average values of −0.096 and −0.053, respectively, but the median values are positive (0.096 and 0.106, respectively), meaning that 7 out of 19 banks with available coefficients showed positive coefficients in the current quarter. Banks with following IDs have short-run negative effects: 120, 150, 250, 350, 470, 620, and 660. Almost the same seven banks demonstrate negative effects with the dependent variable in the one-quarter lag, while six banks experience negative effects in lag-two and five banks experience negative effects in lag three (out of the banks with available coefficients). For most of the banks, there is a positive association between the NIM variable and the dependent variable.

The NFM variable has a positive effect on the dependent variable in the current quarter and in the third quarter-lagged variable in the sense of positive average and median value. The NFM coefficients are statistically significant for much less banks, but the magnitude and the number of quarters with positive coefficients of the explanatory variable prevail considerably. Banks with the following IDs have short-run negative effects (in at least one of the reported quarters, where coefficients are available): 130, 145, 150, 240, 250, 350, 440, 545, and 920. It could be concluded, the NFM is in favor of higher short-term profitability.

The current change in government bond yields (D(GYIELD)) showed a predominantly negative impact, with an average coefficient of −0.094 and median of −0.051 and 13 out of 18 banks with available coefficients maintaining negative relationship with the dependent variable. This suggests that rising yields tend to reduce bank performance in the short run, potentially due to valuation losses on bond holdings or increased funding costs. The first lag of the variable has negative mean and positive median effects, with 11 banks showing positive coefficients and 9 experiencing negative interdependencies (out of banks with available coefficients). The second lag of the first-differenced government bond yield, D(GYIELD(-2)), demonstrates a positive relationship with the dependent variable based on its positive mean and median values. Conversely, the third lag, D(GYIELD(-3)), is characterized by negative mean (−0.021) and median (−0.048) values, suggesting an inverse relationship. Government bonds have mixed meaning for individual banks. Banks with predominantly negative effects are City Bank Europe-Bulgaria branch (ID 250), Tokuda Bank (ID 260), BNP Paribas S.A.—Sofia branch (ID 440), and Allianz Bulgaria Commercial Bank (ID 561), as can be seen from Table A2 in Appendix A. Banks that hold a large share of government bonds as their assets may experience lower profitability due to higher government bond yields, which move in the opposite direction with bond valuations.

The change in housing prices (D(HPR)) and its lags demonstrate relatively mild effects. The current quarter's change has a negative mean of −0.030 and negative median of −0.008 (see Table A2 in Appendix A). However, the lagged terms, D(HPR(-1)), D(HPR(-2)), and D(HPR(-3)), exhibit small average values (0.0002, 0.018, and 0.009, respectively), while most banks continue to display a positive relationship with the profitability dependent variable within the lagged framework. Higher house prices stimulated bank profitability in the short run, likely due to improved collateral values and reduced credit risk.

The unemployment rate, D(UR), demonstrates a negative effect on the dependent variable, in the current period and in lags D(UR(-1)) and D(UR(-2)). These findings indicate that rising unemployment tends to deteriorate bank performance, likely due to poorer credit quality and reduced loan demand. On the contrary, the third lag, D(UR(-3)), has a positive average value of 0.013 and a positive median value, as can be seen from Table A2 in Appendix A.

Lending growth outpacing deposit growth supports short-term profitability of banks, justified by the positive association between the change in ROA and current and lagged values of the D(LDR) variable. The LDR can also be considered as an indicator for risk-taking appetite, being positively related. The average and median coefficients for the current and first two lags are small but positive, as can be seen from Table A2 in Appendix A.

The short-run association between the GDP growth and the ROA varies and is heterogeneous among banks. The current change in the D(GDP) has a tiny positive mean coefficient, while D(GDP(-3)) has a near-zero mean (slightly negative). Economic activity stimulates bank profitability and reduces credit risk and loan loss impairments, but the size of the coefficients suggests a very small impact and an almost-balanced distribution of banks with positive and negative effects. The first and second lags of the economic growth variable D(GDP(-1)) and D(GDP(-2)) exhibit negative mean effects. The following banks have the largest negative short-term effects: TB Investbank (ID 120), City Bank Europe-Bulgaria branch (ID 250), TBI Bank (Former NLB Bank West-East) (ID 310), and Bulgarian Development Bank (Former Nastarchitelna Bank) (ID 620). The activity of these smaller and special case banks probably does not depend on the economic growth in the current period, and bank ID 250 and 310 especially may step in and increase their activity and profitability due to their specialty in the short run.

The liquidity indicator (D(CASHR)) and its lags predominantly demonstrate positive effects despite a smaller magnitude, judging by the small-coefficient values. This finding suggests that maintaining higher liquidity buffers tends to support profitability, contradicting the fact that cash holdings yield low returns. Higher liquidity triggers lower funding costs, increases shock absorption ability, and gives banks the opportunity to find good and effective lending opportunities. In general, one pp change in the ratio leads to about 1% change in the dependent variable. Largest positive effect comes from TBI Bank (Former NLB Bank West-East) (ID 310), Bulgarian Development Bank (ID 620), BNP PARIBAS S.A.—SOFIA branch (ID 440), Tokuda Bank (ID 260), and TE-DZHE Zirat Bank-Sofia branch (ID 350), while the largest negative effect exhibits CHPB Texim (ID545).

Loan loss impairments play a crucial role in the short term, according to the results of the ROA model. The D(LLR) exhibits a strong negative effect on the change in ROA, in the current, second (D(LLR(-2))), and the third lag (D(LLR(-3))). The current value of the variable has sharply negative effect, with a mean of −0.49 and median of −0.41. The

https://doi.org/10.3390/jrfm19020156

negative effect fades away with the second and third lag, with a mean of −0.09 and −0.02, respectively. The first lag (D(LLR(-1))) has a positive effect of 0.08 on average and a median value of 0.09. The results justify the hypothesis that losses related to materialized credit risk deteriorate profitability, but the effect weakens over time. This confirms that maintaining strong credit standards and early risk detection are essential for short-run bank profitability.

The negative intercept, with a mean of −0.29 and a median of −0.22 suggests that the short-run change in the ROA variable tends to be slightly negative in the short run, ceteris paribus. Structural factors in the banking sector such as narrow interest margins, high operational costs, or competitive pressures may be in force for deteriorating profitability if all else is kept equal. Without doing business and reporting net interest and fee incomes and without favorable macroeconomic imbalances, banks' ROA will shrink due to running costs. For three of the banks, there is positive constant, meaning that for their short-term profitability, it is better that their bank-specific and macroeconomic factors did not change. For those banks the positive intercept is associated with positive ECT, violating the cointegration justification.

The study also differentiates bank performance in terms of ROA by local and foreign ownership. Bulgarian-owned banks—including International Asset Bank, CHPB Texim, Central Cooperative Bank, Tokuda Bank, TB Investbank, Municipal Bank, First Investment Bank, Bulgarian American Credit Bank, and Bulgarian Development Bank—hold approximately 20% of banking system assets, while foreign-owned banks account for roughly 80%. Bulgarian-owned banks demonstrate slightly weaker adjustment dynamics compared to foreign-owned banks, although both groups follow similar general patterns.

Foreign-owned banks generally demonstrate larger ECT coefficients in absolute terms, indicating faster adjustment toward long-run equilibrium profitability. This reflects their stronger capitalization, superior access to funding, and more efficient risk management.

Short-run changes in NIM have a stronger positive impact on ROA in foreign-owned banks, especially in longer lags. This indicates that net interest income plays a more pronounced role in profitability for foreign-owned banks. These banks benefit from lower funding costs, stronger reputation, and access to international capital markets, allowing them to maintain more stable and wider interest spreads.

Changes in GYIELD and UR generally exert stronger adverse impact on ROA for Bulgarian-owned banks, implying that locally owned banks are more vulnerable to macroeconomic shocks. Similarly, changes in LLR exhibit stronger negative effects for Bulgarian-owned banks, reflecting greater sensitivity to credit risk materialization. This suggests that domestically owned banks are more exposed to local economic conditions and possess lower capacity to absorb credit risk shocks compared to foreign-owned institutions.

4.3.2. ROE Models (at the Bank Level)

The present section analyzes short-term results of the PMG-ARDL model applied in the study. The cointegration equation is common for all banks, while the approach allows for identifying individual short-term models for the banks comprising the panel. The short-term ROE models of individual banks are revealed in Tables A3 and A4 in Appendix B.

As in the ROA models discussed above, the error correction terms (ECTs) for almost all banks exhibit a negative relationship with the dependent variable, indicating a quarterly adjustment toward restoring long-run equilibrium. The only exceptions are Bulgarian-American Credit Bank (bank ID 160), CHPB Texim (bank ID 545), and Allianz Bulgaria Commercial Bank (bank ID 561), whose ECTs do not display this expected adjustment pattern (see Tables A3 and A4 in Appendix B). These three banks have positive ECT coefficients (+0.005, +0.013, and +0.045, respectively) and increase their disequilibrium

https://doi.org/10.3390/jrfm19020156

with each quarter passed. The average coefficient of the ECT accepts the value of −0.278, meaning that on average, 27.8% of banks' disequilibrium is reduced each quarter. The highest speed of adjustment is observed for the BNP Paribas S.A.—Sofia branch (ID: 440; ECT = −2.267), City Bank Europe-Bulgaria branch (ID: 250; ECT = −1.506), and ING Bank N.V.—Sofia branch (ID: 145; ECT = −0.960), which correct between 96% and 227% of their disequilibrium each quarter, indicating extremely fast adjustment toward equilibrium.

The short-term effect of lagged first differences of the return on equity (ROE) variable on the change in ROE in the current period is positive for the three lags. The average coefficients accept values of approximately 0.214, 0.152, and 0.071, respectively, implying that past profitability positively influences current profitability. Banks that increased ROE last quarter tend to experience continued short-run profitability improvements, though a few banks exhibit negative values, indicating temporary reversals. The positive effect is strongest in the first and second lags, but it starts fading away in the third quarterly lag. The dependent variable displays inertia since a +1 pp ROE shock currently increases future ROE cumulatively over the next quarters. The fifth-quarter lag of the dependent variable, D(ROE(-4)), demonstrates a weak and slightly negative average effect, with a mean coefficient of −0.027 and a median value of −0.086, based on 19 banks with available coefficients. This indicates that profitability shocks are largely absorbed within one year, and their persistence beyond four quarters becomes limited and unstable. The negative average coefficient suggests partial reversal of earlier profitability shocks, reflecting mean-reverting behavior in bank equity returns. Overall, the fifth-quarter lag confirms that ROE persistence weakens substantially after one year, supporting the conclusion that bank profitability adjusts toward equilibrium within four quarters.

The average coefficients for D(CIR) and its lags range between approximately −0.058 and −0.041, confirming that increases in operational inefficiency tend to have a negative impact on short-run performance, as can be seen at Tables A3 and A4 in Appendix B. A one pp increase in the CIR ratio leads to an approximately 0.4–0.6% decline in profitability, confirming the importance of operational efficiency for bank performance.

In comparison to the ROA models, the ROE models with significant NIM link are fewer, and the results vary considerably, as can be seen in Tables A3 and A4. In general, the changes in the net interest margin, D(NIM), generate large but inconsistent effects. Coefficients range from strongly negative to strongly positive values across banks. Banks exhibiting the strongest positive association include the BNP Paribas S.A.—Sofia branch (ID 440), the City Bank Europe-Bulgaria branch (ID 250), and TBI Bank (ID 310). Some banks exhibit negative association, indicating heterogeneity in interest income dynamics and balance sheet structures.

The first difference in government bond yields, D(GYIELD), along with its lagged terms, shows a predominantly negative relationship with D(ROE), with the contemporaneous explanatory variable having an average coefficient of −0.340. This suggests that increases in government bond yields might lead to higher interest rates on deposits and loans and can increase credit risk and profitability, probably also due to lower valuation of held bond portfolios or reducing loan demand. Banks with the strongest negative sensitivity include the BNP Paribas S.A.—Sofia branch (ID 440), the City Bank Europe-Bulgaria branch (ID 250), and Unicredit Bulbank (ID 660).

Changes in the Log of the House Price Rate (D(HPR)) and its lags have mixed effects on D(ROE). The current and first lag exhibit weak or slightly negative average effects, while the third lag demonstrates a positive impact, confirming that higher house prices support profitability through improved collateral values and reduced credit risk.

The change in the unemployment rate (D(UR)) shows a negative average effect across most lags, confirming that rising unemployment deteriorates profitability due to worsening credit quality and reduced economic activity. This relationship is particularly strong for smaller domestically owned banks such as TB Investbank (ID 120) and International Asset Bank (ID 470).

It could be summarized that in comparison to ROA, ROE models exhibit greater coefficient volatility and stronger sensitivity to bank-specific and macroeconomic shocks. This reflects the leverage nature of ROE and its higher sensitivity to financial and operational conditions.

The D(GDP) and its lags show mixed effects, with average coefficients close to zero. Current and first lags show weak positive association, while second and third lags demonstrate weak negative association. The largest negative effects are observed for TBI Bank (ID 310) and TB Investbank (ID 120), reflecting the specific business models of smaller banks.

Changes in CASHR and LDR generally show a mildly positive relationship with D(ROE), confirming that stronger liquidity and higher intermediation support profitability. However, the magnitude of coefficients remains small, indicating secondary importance relative to credit risk and efficiency factors.

Loan loss provisions (LLR) exert a strong and economically significant negative impact on short-run ROE. The contemporaneous coefficient D(LLR) has a large negative mean of −3.546 and median of −3.161, confirming that credit risk materialization immediately and substantially reduces profitability. The strongest negative effects are observed for Allianz Bulgaria Commercial Bank (ID 561; −8.086), Procredit Bank (ID 230; −6.936), and Eurobank Bulgaria (ID 920; −6.161). The first lag (D(LLR(-1)) shows a positive average effect (mean of 0.540), indicating partial recovery after initial provisioning, with the largest positive effect again for Allianz Bulgaria Commercial Bank (ID 561; +3.306), while CHPB Texim (ID 545; −2.336) shows the largest negative delayed impact. The second and third lags, D(LLR(-2)) and D(LLR(-3)), exhibit moderate negative average effects (−0.220 and −0.324, respectively), confirming that credit loss shocks gradually weaken but may persist up to one year. Overall, the results confirm that LLR is the most important short-run determinant of ROE, with large immediate negative effects followed by gradual adjustment and partial recovery and substantially higher sensitivity observed across domestically owned and higher-risk banks.

The intercept coefficient is significant for 13 out of 21 banks, and most intercepts are negative, averaging around −2.7, indicating that ceteris paribus, the profitability is set on a declining path. Only a few banks show slightly positive constants.

Comparing the ROA and ROE PMG-ARDL models reveals a clear divergence in how the two indicators respond to bank-specific and macroeconomic shocks. The ROA models exhibit lower volatility in coefficients and coefficients of lower value. In the ROE models, coefficients are more volatile and more sensitive to changes in macroeconomic and bank-specific factors.

ROE models to a larger extent support the conclusions for the ROA models for identifying differences between locally owned and foreign-owned banks' short-term dynamics. ROE models confirm the conclusions for the ROA models regarding ownership structure differences. Foreign-owned banks such as Unicredit Bulbank (ID 660), DSK Bank (ID 300), United Bulgarian Bank (ID 200), and BNP Paribas S.A. branch (ID 440) demonstrate faster adjustment toward equilibrium, justified by larger absolute ECT coefficients.

The change in CIR has a stronger negative impact on ROE for foreign-owned banks, reflecting their stronger operational efficiency discipline.

Short-run changes in NIM have stronger and more consistent positive effects for foreign-owned banks, reflecting their superior funding access and balance sheet management.

As in the ROA models, changes in GYIELD and UR exert stronger adverse impact on Bulgarian-owned banks, implying higher vulnerability to macroeconomic shocks. Simi-

https://doi.org/10.3390/jrfm19020156

larly, the change in LLR has a stronger negative impact on Bulgarian-owned banks' ROE, confirming their higher sensitivity to credit risk materialization and weaker shock absorption capacity.

5. Conclusions

This study investigates the determinants of profitability of Bulgarian commercial banks over the period from the first quarter of 2007 to the first quarter of 2025, using quarterly panel data and a dynamic econometric framework. The empirical analysis follows a structured methodological procedure, including descriptive analysis, panel unit root testing, cross-sectional dependence diagnostics, model selection using the Hausman test, and an estimation of long-run and short-run relationships using the pooled mean group autoregressive distributed lag (PMG-ARDL) estimator. This approach is particularly appropriate given the presence of both stationary and non-stationary variables and the need to jointly estimate long-run equilibrium relationships and heterogeneous short-run dynamics across banks.

The results confirm the existence of stable long-run equilibrium relationships between bank profitability and its determinants. In the long run, profitability, measured by both return on assets (ROA) and return on equity (ROE), is positively influenced by net interest margin, government bond yields, loan-to-deposit ratio, and economic growth, reflecting the importance of core banking income, favorable macroeconomic conditions, and efficient balance sheet utilization. Conversely, operational inefficiency, unemployment, higher cash holdings, house price dynamics, and loan loss provisions exert negative effects on profitability, highlighting the role of cost discipline, credit risk management, and macroeconomic stability.

The short-term dynamics reveal that a strong error correction is underway for both profitability models, ROA and ROE, respectively. Each quarter, the ROA model corrects for 14.61% of its disequilibrium, while the ROE model reduces the equilibrium by 28.4%. Short-run profitability dynamics also exhibit strong persistence, with past profitability exerting a positive and statistically significant influence on current profitability. At the same time, increases in operational costs, credit risk materialization, and adverse macroeconomic developments negatively affect short-run performance.

Importantly, the PMG-ARDL framework enables the identification of heterogeneous short-run dynamics at the individual bank level. Some banks demonstrate high sensitivity to costs or unemployment, others to bond yields or loan losses. A couple of banks show positive error-correction coefficients, showing their divergence from long-run equilibrium. The ECT divergence is likely caused by unique business models or structural characteristics. Coefficients of bank branches and smaller banks often are among the outliers, even diverging from the central tendencies for the panel. Larger banks demonstrate more consistent behavior. Overall, the ROA model reveals stronger explanatory power than the ROE model, confirmed by higher log-likelihood, lower information criteria, and residuals dynamics. Selected methodology also allows segregating short-term profitability by type of ownership. Foreign owned banks adjust faster to equilibrium and are more resilient to macroeconomic shocks and their profitability depends on the core banking income, namely the NIM. Local banks are more sensitive to materialized credit risk. Materialized credit risk has bigger negative impact on profitability for locally owned banks.

The findings in the study have practical implications for regulators, bank managers, analysts, and policymakers. The coefficients of the explanatory variables can help in calibrating the correct measures for supporting bank profitability. Banks with Bulgarian ownership must be subject to stricter supervision during boom times and larger support during economic challenging times. The higher sensitivity of the profitability of banks

https://doi.org/10.3390/jrfm19020156

with Bulgarian ownership to credit risk, cost inefficiencies, and macroeconomic conditions underline the need for improved cost controls, provisioning policies, and appropriate credit risk management.

Overall, the methodological framework applied in this study—combining panel unit root tests, cross-sectional dependence diagnostics, Hausman specification testing, and PMG-ARDL estimation—provides robust and consistent empirical evidence on the determinants of bank profitability in Bulgaria. The findings confirm that bank profitability is driven by a combination of structural bank-specific characteristics and macroeconomic conditions, with both long-run equilibrium relationships and heterogeneous short-run adjustment processes playing a critical role.

The analysis performed in present scientific article distinguishes from existing literature by providing new empirical evidence on the bank profitability dynamics across different phases of the business cycle. The novelty of the study is measured in several dimensions. The time span covers the structural breaks of global financial crisis, local banking crisis, the COVID-19 pandemic, global high-inflation period, and monetary tightening using quarterly data. The combination of bank-specific and macroeconomic variables is customized for the Bulgarian commercial banks, together with the applied methodology, and can be considered in the analysis of small and open economies. The identified long-term and short-run dynamic equations, together with analyzing individual bank dynamics through the PMG-ARDL framework, allows the study to stand out in empirical banking literature.

Despite the contributions, the study has the following limitations. First, the analysis is constrained by data availability. Banks without complete data for the whole period were excluded from the research. Second, the ARDL-PMG framework captures both short- and long-term dynamics, but it does not explicitly distinguish structural breaks caused by various national and international events. Third, the ownership classification is as of the end of the period and does not fully capture potential changes in ownership, control, and management over time.

Future research could address these limitations by explicitly testing for structural breaks at both the aggregate and individual bank levels, for example, through the inclusion of appropriately specified dummy variables. In addition, further investigation of the relationship between bank ownership structure, performance, and risk-taking behavior would provide valuable insights into the mechanisms underlying profitability dynamics. Expanding the sample period and incorporating additional banks excluded due to data constraints would also enhance the robustness and generalizability of the findings, allowing for a more comprehensive assessment of profitability determinants in the banking sector.

Funding: This work was financially supported by the UNWE Research Programme (Research Grant No. 29/2025/A).

Institutional Review Board Statement: Not applicable.

Informed Consent Statement: Not applicable.

Data Availability Statement: Data is available upon request.

Acknowledgments: Following the second revision of this manuscript, generative artificial intelligence tools (ChatGPT ver.5.2., OpenAI, San Francisco, CA, USA) were used to improve the clarity, coherence, and linguistic quality of selected parts of the text. The author retained full responsibility for the study's conception, research design, methodology, data collection, empirical analysis, interpretation of results, and conclusions. The AI tool was used solely for language editing and stylistic refinement.

https://doi.org/10.3390/jrfm19020156

Conflicts of Interest: The author declares no conflicts of interest. The funders had no role in the design of the study; in the collection, analyses, or interpretation of data; in the writing of the manuscript; or in the decision to publish the results.

Abbreviations

The following abbreviations are used in this manuscript:

ARDL	Autoregressive distributed lags
CASHR	Cash-to-assets ratio
CD	Cross-sectional Dependence
CEE	Central and Eastern European
CIR	Cost-to-income ratio
ECB	European Central Bank
ECT	Error-Correction Term
EU	European union
FE	Fixed effects
GDP	Gross domestic product
LDR	Loans-to-deposit ratio
LLR	Loan-loss-to-loans ratio
NIM	Net interest margin
NFM	Net fee and commission margin
PMG	Pooled Mean Group
pp	Percentage point
PMG-ARDL	Pooled Mean Group—Autoregressive Distributed Lag
QE	Quantitative easing
RE	Random effects
ROA	Return on Assets
ROE	Return on Equity
TTM	Twelve trailing months
UR	Unemployment rate

Appendix A. Short-Run ROA Models

Table A1. Short-run ROA models' coefficients.

VARIABLE\BANKID	120	130	145	150	160	200	230	240	250	260	300
COINTEQ01(ECT)	−0.234	−0.051	0.021	−0.149	−0.012	−0.155	−0.087	−0.137	−0.524	−0.146	−0.073
D(ROA(-1))	0.409	0.137	0.075	0.024		0.341	−0.116	0.145	0.043	0.110	0.064
D(ROA(-2))	0.060		−0.047	0.182	0.433	−0.038	0.045	0.143	0.181	0.079	0.042
D(ROA(-3))		0.302	0.055	−0.148	0.149	−0.047	−0.036	0.185	−0.281	−0.189	−0.05
D(ROA(-4))	−0.086	−0.209	−0.041	−0.16	−0.188	−0.068	0.033	0.046	−0.193	−0.114	−0.109
D(CIR)	−0.003	−0.004	−0.008	−0.017		−0.008	−0.011	−0.008		−0.002	−0.009
D(CIR(-1))		−0.001	−0.008	−0.02	−0.001	−0.011	−0.01	−0.007	−0.001	−0.005	−0.005
D(CIR(-2))			−0.006	−0.019		−0.007	−0.01	−0.009	−0.001	−0.001	−0.014
D(CIR(-3))	−0.001	0.001	−0.007	−0.019	−0.001	−0.005	−0.01	−0.008	−0.001	−0.004	−0.022
D(NIM)	−0.897	0.139	0.205	−0.14	0.116	0.373	0.028		−0.202	0.136	0.352
D(NIM(-1))	−0.586	0.166	0.114	−0.102	0.190	0.398	0.148	0.023	−0.088	0.163	0.329
D(NIM(-2))	−0.269	0.139	0.246	−0.18	0.259	0.421	0.194		−0.081	0.212	0.395
D(NIM(-3))	−0.3	0.091	0.208	−0.141	0.178	0.448	0.103	0.064	0.048	0.239	0.457
D(NFM)		0.354	−0.335				0.769	−0.339	−0.166		0.962
D(NFM(-1))		−0.328	−0.314	−0.899			0.291		−1.283	1.017	1.291
D(NFM(-2))							0.410	−0.516	−0.839	0.525	1.313
D(NFM(-3))		−0.87				0.990	0.900		−0.091	1.279	1.291
D(GYIELD)	−0.242	0.041	−0.016	−0.056	−0.057	−0.156	−0.065	0.018	−0.442	−0.109	
D(GYIELD(-1))		−0.015	0.022	0.057	0.115	0.079	−0.009	−0.017	−0.196	0.012	0.038
D(GYIELD(-2))	0.106		−0.055	−0.011	0.047	−0.04	0.013		−0.13	−0.087	0.011
D(GYIELD(-3))	0.107	−0.079	0.032	−0.082	−0.094	−0.063	0.005	−0.015	−0.309	−0.041	−0.048
D(HPR)	0.023	0.023	−0.015	−0.02	0.008	−0.014	0.003	−0.005	−0.068	0.006	−0.012
D(HPR(-1))	−0.003	−0.024	0.042	−0.005	0.024	−0.028	0.005	−0.014	−0.139	0.008	0.007
D(HPR(-2))	0.019	0.007	−0.005	0.011	−0.007	0.037		0.025	0.037	−0.02	0.002

Table A1. *Cont.*

VARIABLE\BANKID	120	130	145	150	160	200	230	240	250	260	300
D(HPR(-3))	−0.022	0.020	−0.004	−0.028	−0.027	−0.022	−0.005	−0.017	0.050	0.031	−0.004
D(UR)	−0.082	−0.061	0.036	−0.046	−0.01	0.049	−0.057	−0.004	0.364	0.079	0.027
D(UR(-1))		0.075	−0.061	−0.065	−0.113	−0.048	−0.016	0.093	−0.113	0.037	−0.019
D(UR(-2))	−0.201	0.066	0.007	−0.057	−0.104	0.022	−0.002		0.442	0.093	−0.018
D(UR(-3))	0.164	0.065	−0.026	−0.127	0.015	−0.038	0.040	0.046	−0.154	0.040	−0.069
D(LDR)	0.020	0.009	0.001	−0.006	0.014			−0.004	−0.003	0.025	
D(LDR(-1))	−0.006		0.008	−0.019	0.001	0.002	0.032	0.008	−0.006	−0.013	0.021
D(LDR(-2))	0.013	0.004	0.003	−0.031	0.001	−0.006	0.044		−0.016	−0.007	0.009
D(LDR(-3))	0.035	0.002	0.007	−0.012	−0.002	0.014	−0.022	−0.005	0.025	0.009	0.003
D(GDP)	−0.128	−0.038	−0.004	0.008	0.001	0.023	0.036	−0.009	0.068	−0.014	−0.006
D(GDP(-1))		−0.019	−0.018	0.023	−0.004	0.030	0.013	0.002	0.065	0.011	−0.005
D(GDP(-2))	−0.069	−0.031	0.008	−0.011	−0.016	−0.02	−0.023	0.002	−0.093	−0.004	−0.023
D(GDP(-3))	−0.02	0.037	0.004	0.039	0.024	0.001	−0.001	0.026	−0.076	0.015	−0.048
D(CASHR)	0.024	0.005	−0.001	0.001	0.020	0.002	−0.011	−0.001	0.014	0.040	
D(CASHR(-1))	0.019	0.015	0.009	−0.004	0.005	0.003	0.034	0.019	0.047	−0.014	0.012
D(CASHR(-2))	0.011	0.006	0.002	−0.002	0.029	−0.009	0.048	0.004	0.011	−0.001	0.001
D(CASHR(-3))	0.049	0.010	0.001		0.030	0.009	−0.032	−0.007	0.046	0.021	
D(LLR)	−0.176	−0.036	−0.614	−0.262	−0.684	−0.402	−0.78	−0.393		−0.424	−0.6
D(LLR(-1))	0.133	−0.015		−0.066		0.109	−0.08	0.050	1.098	0.181	−0.062
D(LLR(-2))	−0.03	−0.034	−0.115	0.027	0.132	0.031		0.069	−1.011	−0.029	−0.005
D(LLR(-3))	−0.116	0.012	0.061	−0.08	−0.073	−0.053		0.075	−0.421	−0.088	0.018
C	−0.445	−0.097	0.040	−0.284	−0.023	−0.296	−0.166	−0.261	−0.989	−0.279	−0.139

Note that all variables are statistically significant at conventional levels (1% or 5%), with p-values less than 0.01 or 0.05, respectively.

Table A2. Short-run ROA models' coefficients (continuation).

VARIABLE\BANKID	310	350	440	470	545	561	620	660	790	920
COINTEQ01(ECT)	−0.460	−0.330	−0.018	−0.090	0.144	0.044	−0.472	−0.251		−0.091
D(ROA(-1))	0.314	0.097	0.079	0.067	−0.377	0.116	0.499	0.119	0.092	0.392
D(ROA(-2))	0.211	0.257	0.178	0.274	0.274	−0.029	−0.421	0.084		−0.211
D(ROA(-3))	−0.076	0.191		0.241	0.256	−0.044	0.347	−0.148	0.076	0.205
D(ROA(-4))		0.063	−0.039	−0.094		−0.017	0.192	0.195	0.082	0.166
D(CIR)	0.003	−0.005	−0.004	−0.006	−0.002			−0.003	−0.007	−0.010
D(CIR(-1))	0.013	−0.008	−0.004	−0.008	−0.003		0.002		−0.006	
D(CIR(-2))	0.016	−0.008	−0.003	−0.007	−0.002		0.003	−0.002	−0.007	
D(CIR(-3))	−0.018	−0.007	−0.004	−0.006	−0.001		−0.004	−0.002	−0.007	−0.003
D(NIM)	0.076	−0.282	0.196	−0.187		0.338	−1.907	−0.392	0.132	0.096
D(NIM(-1))		−0.161	0.106	−0.228		0.334	−1.687	−0.339	0.161	0.043
D(NIM(-2))	0.335		0.230	−0.249	0.531	0.270	−0.639	−0.315	0.149	0.047
D(NIM(-3))	0.438	0.057	0.082	−0.290	0.928	0.237	−1.011	−0.210	0.121	0.138
D(NFM)				1.312		0.940			0.149	
D(NFM(-1))			−0.344	0.985				2.895	0.276	−1.713
D(NFM(-2))		−1.723	−0.194	1.692	−2.530	1.466				
D(NFM(-3))	1.984		−0.100	1.304	−2.330	1.057				1.677
D(GYIELD)		0.028		0.009	−0.186	−0.004	−0.410	0.014	−0.023	−0.045
D(GYIELD(-1))	−0.303	−0.035	−0.005	0.072	−0.185	−0.014	0.110	0.072	0.019	0.080
D(GYIELD(-2))	0.275	−0.024	−0.036	0.059	1.203	−0.007		0.012	0.022	−0.036
D(GYIELD(-3))	0.487	−0.100	−0.024	0.045		−0.063		−0.095	−0.004	−0.049
D(HPR)	−0.120	0.025	−0.013	−0.011	−0.145	0.002	−0.307	−0.008	0.007	0.002
D(HPR(-1))	0.111	0.061	0.015	−0.005	−0.144	0.002	0.106	0.006	−0.010	−0.009
D(HPR(-2))	0.182	0.030	0.004	−0.021	0.087	−0.001	0.009	−0.030	−0.003	0.008
D(HPR(-3))	−0.096	0.031	−0.008	0.005	0.180	−0.001	0.104	0.028	−0.006	−0.011
D(UR)	−0.445	0.126	−0.012	−0.033	0.387	−0.040	−0.445	0.101	−0.032	
D(UR(-1))	−0.251	0.087	−0.038	0.037	−1.264	0.012		0.040	0.024	−0.007
D(UR(-2))	−1.153	0.102	−0.026	−0.013	−0.391		−0.602	0.010	−0.014	−0.067
D(UR(-3))	0.254	0.070	0.002		−0.596	0.019	0.551	0.017	−0.004	−0.012
D(LDR)	0.072	0.015	0.046	0.004	−0.075	0.004	−0.010	−0.051	−0.002	−0.019
D(LDR(-1))	−0.033	0.019	0.050	0.037	−0.044		−0.016	−0.029	0.009	0.008
D(LDR(-2))	0.051	0.024	0.030	0.045	−0.009	0.008	0.008	−0.004	0.005	−0.008
D(LDR(-3))	0.034	0.013	0.028	0.012	−0.062	0.005	0.003		0.008	−0.015
D(GDP)	−0.122	−0.026	0.007	−0.024	0.296	0.003	−0.021	0.090	0.005	−0.011
D(GDP(-1))	−0.186	0.021	0.008	0.004	−0.258	0.006	−0.377	−0.037	0.030	−0.030
D(GDP(-2))	−0.461	0.050	−0.015	0.004	−0.053	0.007		−0.027	0.013	−0.005
D(GDP(-3))	−0.045	0.030	0.002	0.003		0.022	−0.053	−0.014	−0.004	0.008
D(CASHR)	0.103	0.038	0.047	−0.010	−0.043	−0.007	0.054	−0.036	−0.001	−0.023
D(CASHR(-1))	−0.042	0.048	0.056	0.036	−0.061	−0.017	0.054	−0.051	0.002	0.004
D(CASHR(-2))	0.080	0.055	0.029	0.042	−0.025	−0.011	0.021		0.004	−0.010
D(CASHR(-3))	0.069	0.032	0.034	0.010	−0.088	0.002	0.011	−0.020	0.008	−0.029
D(LLR)	0.017	−0.348	−0.996	−0.191	−0.698	−0.654	−1.175	−0.364	−0.346	−0.756
D(LLR(-1))	0.007	0.092	0.235	0.144	−0.722	0.143	−0.077	0.115	0.023	0.222
D(LLR(-2))	−0.130	0.075		0.113	−0.411		−0.321	−0.220	0.049	0.164
D(LLR(-3))	0.075	0.056	0.148	0.059	−0.188	0.027	−0.164	−0.031	−0.068	0.363
C	−0.873	−0.632	−0.035	−0.171	0.275	0.085	−0.899	−0.477		−0.173

Note that all variables are statistically significant at conventional levels (1% or 5%), with p-values less than 0.01 or 0.05, respectively.

https://doi.org/10.3390/jrfm19020156

Appendix B. Short-Run ROE Models

Table A3. Short-run ROE models' coefficients.

VARIABLE\BANKID	120	130	145	150	160	200	230	240	250	260	300
COINTEQ01(ECT)	−0.084	−0.261	−0.96	−0.106	0.01	−0.039	−0.062	−0.062	−1.506	−0.062	−0.113
D(ROE(-1))	0.39	0.13	0.00	0.04	0.17	0.28	−0.264	0.18	0.53	0.11	0.00
D(ROE(-2))	0.00	−0.21	0.00	0.18	0.23	−0.149	−0.021	0.08	0.36	0.00	−0.021
D(ROE(-3))	−0.08	0.13	0.11	−0.22	0.09	−0.137	0.00	0.02	0.17	−0.148	0.06
D(ROE(-4))	−0.201	−0.15	0.13	−0.12	−0.18	−0.081	0.00	−0.13	0.32	−0.121	−0.133
D(CIR)	−0.029	−0.04	0	−0.161	−0.002	−0.046	−0.079	−0.086	0.14	−0.031	−0.059
D(CIR(-1))	0.006	−0.006		−0.207	−0.002	−0.045	−0.076	−0.078	0.105	−0.059	−0.05
D(CIR(-2))	0.021	−0.055		−0.187	−0.001	−0.023	−0.082	−0.103	0.03	−0.028	−0.283
D(CIR(-3))	0	−0.057		−0.187	−0.003	−0.016	−0.089	−0.093	0.023	−0.052	−0.225
D(NIM)						3.541					
D(NIM(-1))						0	1.98				
D(NIM(-2))							2.266				
D(NIM(-3))						3.724	0				
D(NFM)						0					12.469
D(NFM(-1))											12.387
D(NFM(-2))											11.669
D(NFM(-3))											10.413
D(GYIELD)		−2.211				−0.884	−1.046			−0.79	0
D(GYIELD(-1))		−2.047		0.976	0.373	1.158	−0.519	−0.127		0.366	
D(GYIELD(-2))		−0.915		0	0.588	−0.404	−0.584	−0.142		−0.352	1.424
D(GYIELD(-3))		−2.319		−0.844	−0.501		−0.252	−0.327			−0.68
D(HPR)	0.318	−0.336		−0.197	0.233	−0.062	0.035	−0.137		0.039	−0.077
D(HPR(-1))	0	−0.673		−0.154			0	−0.127		0.058	−0.026
D(HPR(-2))	0.464	0.192		0.115	−0.226	0.183		0.165		−0.202	−0.035
D(HPR(-3))	−0.613	0.288		−0.341	0.019	−0.123	−0.02	−0.05		0.159	0.044
D(UR)		−0.836				0.318	−0.673	−0.528		0.581	1.215
D(UR(-1))		1.601			−0.887	−0.294		0.656			−1.304
D(UR(-2))	−2.841				−0.537			−0.182		0.631	
D(UR(-3))	1.874	1.023		−0.489	0.317	−0.58	0.458	0.812			−1.445
D(LDR)	0.242	0.226			0.194	0.027	−0.256	0.028		0.231	−0.024
D(LDR(-1))	−0.096	0.116		−0.174	−0.025			0.103		−0.142	0.263
D(LDR(-2))	0.214	0.218		−0.322	−0.07	0.049	0.415	0.066		0.088	−0.279
D(LDR(-3))	0.449	0.021		−0.062	0.06	0.134		0.008		0.139	0.298
D(GDP)	−1.51	−0.763			0.055	0.327	0.148	−0.058			−0.51
D(GDP(-1))				0.306		−0.078	0			0.198	0.347
D(GDP(-2))	−0.875	−0.847		−0.095			−0.203	−0.088			−0.248
D(GDP(-3))		−0.252		0.582	0.226	0.038		0.338		0.224	−0.799
D(CASHR)	0.294	−0.055		0.104	0.268	0.029	−0.317	0.022		0.359	−0.075
D(CASHR(-1))	0.142	0.171			0.056	−0.071		0.094		−0.152	0.296
D(CASHR(-2))	0.18	0.124		0.116	0.135	−0.043	0.46	0.067		−0.022	−0.388
D(CASHR(-3))	0.505	0.074		0.091	0.27	0.062	−0.125	−0.011		0.129	0.113
D(LLR)		−1.048		−2.651	−2.864	−3.247	−6.936	−3.482		−4.274	−3.935
D(LLR(-1))				−0.724						1.76	−0.796
D(LLR(-2))		−1.994						0.541			−0.17
D(LLR(-3))				−1.305		−0.761					−0.175
C		−9.818		−3.982		−1.467	−2.344	−2.326		−2.352	−4.245

Note that all variables are statistically significant at conventional levels (1% or 5%), with p-values less than 0.01 or 0.05, respectively.

Table A4. Short-run ROE models' coefficients (continuation).

VARIABLE\BANKID	310	350	440	470	545	561	620	660	790	920
COINTEQ01(ECT)	−0.066	−0.066	−2.267	−0.061	0.01	0.05	−0.059	−0.073	−0.021	−0.04
D(ROE(-1))	0.47	0.47	1.21	0.08	−0.096	0.22	0.38	0.13	0.05	0.22
D(ROE(-2))	0.25	0.25	0.96	0.16	0.74	0.15		0.22	0.02	−0.138
D(ROE(-3))			0.62	0.27	0.43	−0.219	0.29	−0.192	0.10	−0.087
D(ROE(-4))	0.04	0.04	0.18	−0.086	−0.143		−0.147	0.17	−0.02	0.13
D(CIR)	−0.001	−0.001		−0.08		−0.008	0.019	−0.03	−0.069	−0.069
D(CIR(-1))	−0.001	−0.001	4.346	−0.093	−0.003	−0.006	0.015	−0.005	−0.073	−0.015
D(CIR(-2))	−0.018	−0.018	4.48	−0.082		−0.005	0.019	−0.023	−0.071	−0.027
D(CIR(-3))	−0.017	−0.017	2.246	−0.065	−0.005	−0.004	0.013	−0.024	−0.08	−0.036
D(NIM)	−1.002	−1.002				3.707			0.77	
D(NIM(-1))						3.656			1.124	
D(NIM(-2))						3.143			0.985	
D(NIM(-3))						2.828				
D(NFM)	5.147	5.147								
D(NFM(-1))										
D(NFM(-2))										
D(NFM(-3))										
D(GYIELD)						−0.669	−0.492	0.575	−0.307	−0.367
D(GYIELD(-1))	−0.264	−0.264		0.41			0.445	0.748	0.338	0.716

https://doi.org/10.3390/jrfm19020156

Table A4. *Cont.*

VARIABLE\BANKID	310	350	440	470	545	561	620	660	790	920
D(GYIELD(-2))	−0.261	−0.261			3.95	−0.377		−0.357	0.263	−0.38
D(GYIELD(-3))	−0.319	−0.319			0	−1.031		−0.992	−0.193	−0.654
D(HPR)	−0.167	−0.167		−0.207	−0.469	0.227	−0.8	−0.089		
D(HPR(-1))	0.048	0.048		−0.085	−0.212	−0.105	0.413		−0.121	0.042
D(HPR(-2))	−0.068	−0.068		−0.208	0.448			−0.256	0.02	0.042
D(HPR(-3))	0.191	0.191			0.222	−0.015	0.07	0.18	−0.127	−0.079
D(UR)	0.382	0.382		−0.221		−0.322	−0.62	0.615	−0.383	−0.345
D(UR(-1))	0.547	0.547			−3.14	0.096	0.888		0.18	
D(UR(-2))	0.246	0.246			−1.788	−0.186	−0.943		−0.093	−0.458
D(UR(-3))	0.37	0.37				0.181	1.279			0.187
D(LDR)	−0.013	−0.013		−0.099	−0.231	0.009	−0.017	−0.323	−0.005	−0.077
D(LDR(-1))				0.293	−0.178	−0.057	−0.002	−0.139	0.04	−0.067
D(LDR(-2))	0.052	0.052		0.437	−0.175	0.022	0.019	0.055	0.091	−0.067
D(LDR(-3))	0.028	0.028		0.052	−0.142	0.046	0.017	0.123	0.066	
D(GDP)	−0.041	−0.041			0.85		0.163	0.869	0.033	−0.178
D(GDP(-1))	0.112	0.112		−0.085	−0.385	0.404	−0.345	−0.379	0.261	−0.234
D(GDP(-2))	0.332	0.332		−0.039	−0.204	0.084	0.503	−0.224	.1	
D(GDP(-3))	−0.16	−0.16		0.134		0.283	0.209	0.058		0.103
D(CASHR)	−0.003	−0.003		−0.258		−0.087	0.095	−0.263	0.04	−0.113
D(CASHR(-1))	−0.011	−0.011		0.247	−0.068	−0.163	0.115	−0.371	0.021	−0.13
D(CASHR(-2))	0.089	0.089		0.335	−0.187	−0.178	−0.112	0.083	0.063	−0.096
D(CASHR(-3))	0.028	0.028			−0.251	0.058	−0.09		0.058	−0.081
D(LLR)	−1.061	−1.061		−2.57	−3.075	−8.086	−2.519		−3.763	−6.161
D(LLR(-1))	0.379	0.379		1.356	−2.336	3.306	0.441	1.636		
D(LLR(-2))	−0.153	−0.153		0.799			0.418	−2	0.729	
D(LLR(-3))				0.52			0.543		−0.763	
C	−2.486	−2.486				1.689		−2.754	−0.782	−1.508

Note that all variables are statistically significant at conventional levels (1% or 5%), with *p*-values less than 0.01 or 0.05, respectively.

Appendix C. Figures

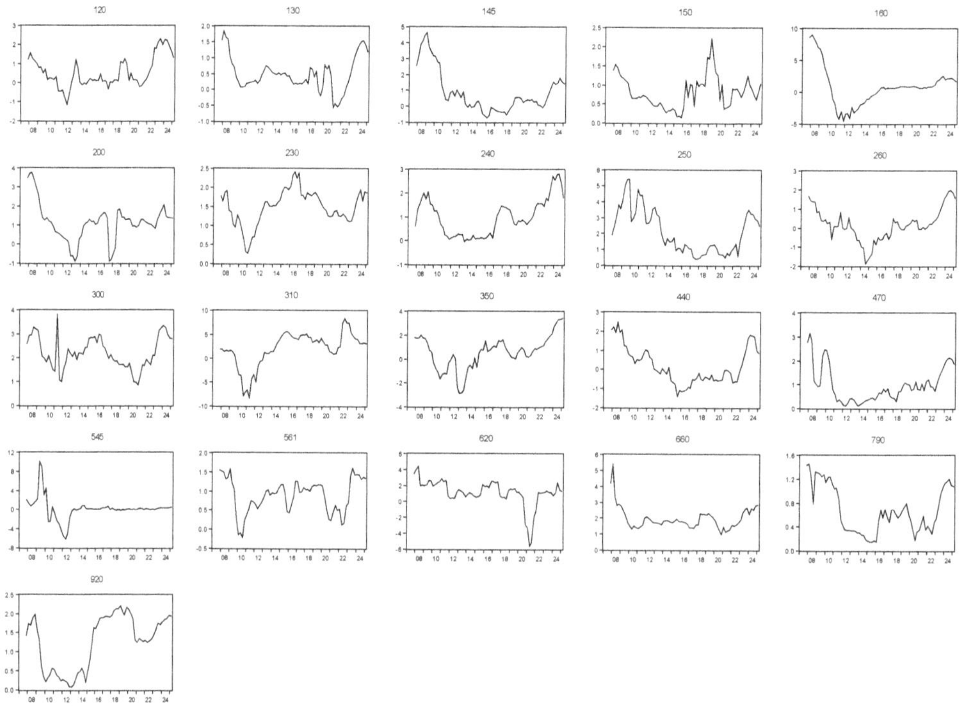

Figure A1. ROA (%).

https://doi.org/10.3390/jrfm19020156

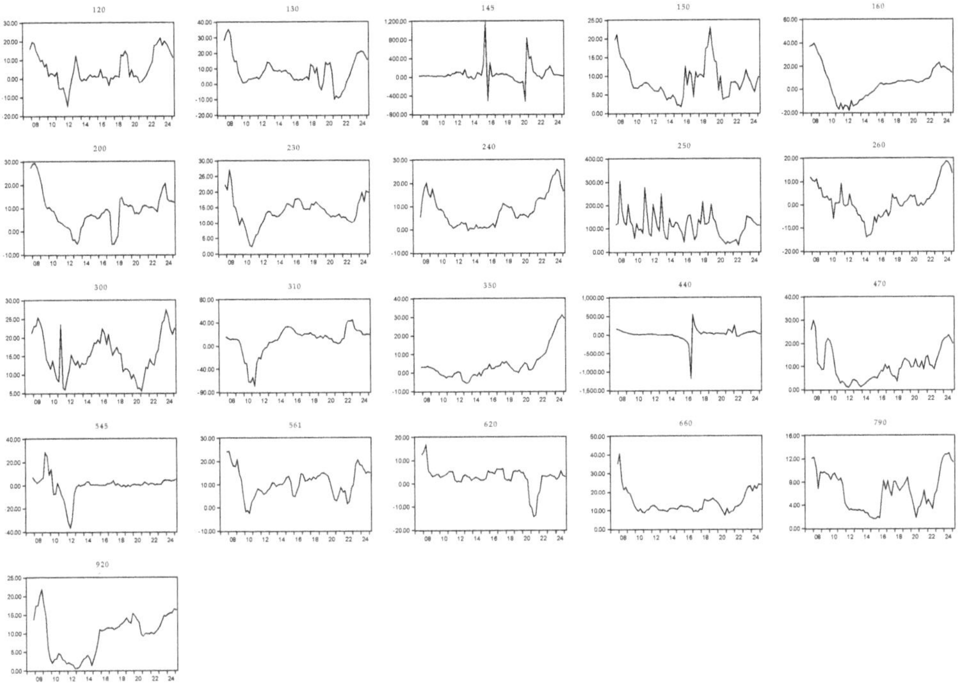

Figure A2. ROE (%).

References

Albertazzi, U., & Gambacorta, L. (2009). Bank profitability and the business cycle. *Journal of Financial Stability*, *5*(4), 393–409. [CrossRef]

Athanasoglou, B. P., Delis, M. D., & Staikouras, C. K. (2006). *Determinants of bank profitability in the South and Eastern European region, Bank of Greece* (Working Paper No. 47). Available online: https://papers.ssrn.com/sol3/papers.cfm?abstract_id=4163741 (accessed on 25 September 2025).

Athanasoglou, P. P., Brissimis, S. N., & Delis, M. D. (2008). Bank-specific, industry-specific and macroeconomic determinants of bank profitability. *Journal of International Financial Markets, Institutions and Money*, *18*(2), 121–136. [CrossRef]

Bardi, W., & Hfaiedh, M. A. (2021). International trade and economic growth: Evidence from a panel ARDL-PMG approach. *International Economics and Economic Policy*, *18*(4), 847–868. [CrossRef]

Blackburne, E. F., & Frank, M. W. (2007). Estimation of nonstationary heterogeneous panels. *Stata Journal*, *7*(2), 197–208. [CrossRef]

Borisov, L. (2017). Impact of mergers and acquisitions on the profitability and efficiency of the banks in Bulgaria. *VUZF Review*, *2017*(2), 16–30. [CrossRef]

Căpraru, B., & Ihnatov, I. (2014). Banks' profitability in selected Central and Eastern European countries. *Procedia Economics and Finance*, *16*, 587–591. [CrossRef]

Claeys, S., & Vander Vennet, R. (2008). Determinants of bank interest margins in Central and Eastern Europe: A comparison with the West. *Economic Systems*, *32*(2), 197–216. [CrossRef]

De Hoyos, R. E., & Sarafidis, V. (2006). Testing for cross-sectional dependence in panel-data models. *The Stata Journal: Promoting Communications on Statistics and Stata*, *6*(4), 482–496. [CrossRef]

Dietrich, A., & Wanzenried, G. (2011). Determinants of bank profitability before and during the crisis: Evidence from Switzerland. *Journal of International Financial Markets, Institutions and Money*, *2*, 307–327. [CrossRef]

Djalilov, K., & Piesse, J. (2016). Determinants of bank profitability in transition countries: What matters most? *Research in International Business and Finance*, *38*, 69–82. [CrossRef]

Dumicic, M., & Rizdak, T. (2013). Determinants of banks' net interest margins in Central and Eastern Europe. *Financial Theory and Practice*, *37*(1), 1–30. [CrossRef]

Endri, E., Sparta, S., Wiwaha, A., Karyatun, S., Oemar, F., & Setiawan, A. (2025). Banking profitability and COVID-19: Evidence from Indonesia. *Montenegrin Journal of Economics*, *21*(4), 115–128. [CrossRef]

Friedman, M. (1937). The use of ranks to avoid the assumption of normality implicit in the analysis of variance. *Journal of the American Statistical Association*, *32*(200), 675–701. [CrossRef]

García-Herrero, A., Gavilá, S., & Santabárbara, D. (2009). What explains the low profitability of Chinese banks? *Journal of Banking & Finance*, *33*(11), 2080–2092. [CrossRef]
Hausman, J. A. (1978). Specification tests in econometrics. *Econometrica*, *46*(6), 1251–1271. [CrossRef]
Horobet, A., Radulescu, M., Belascu, L., & Dita, S. M. (2021). Determinants of bank profitability in CEE countries: Evidence from GMM panel data estimates. *Journal of Risk and Financial Management*, *14*(7), 307. [CrossRef]
Im, K. S., Pesaran, M. H., & Shin, Y. (2003). Testing for unit roots in heterogeneous panels. *Journal of Econometrics*, *115*(1), 53–74. [CrossRef]
Kao, C. (1999). Spurious regression and residual-based tests for cointegration in panel data. *Journal of Econometrics*, *90*(1), 1–44. [CrossRef]
Karkowska, R., & Pawłowska, M. (2017). *The concentration and bank stability in Central and Eastern European countries* (NBP Working Paper No. 272, p. 30). Narodowy Bank Polski, Education & Publishing Department. Available online: https://nbp.pl/wp-content/uploads/2022/10/272_en.pdf (accessed on 5 October 2025).
Killins, R. N. (2000). Real estate prices and banking performance: Evidence from Canada. *Journal of Economics and Finance*, *44*, 78–98. [CrossRef]
Koetter, M., & Poghosyan, T. (2010). Real estate prices and bank stability. *Journal of Banking & Finance*, *34*(6), 1129–1138. [CrossRef]
Kripfganz, S., & Schneider, D. C. (2023). ardl: Estimating autoregressive distributed lag and equilibrium correction models. *The Stata Journal*, *23*(4), 983–1019. [CrossRef]
Mirzaei, A., Moore, T., & Liu, G. (2013). Does market structure matter on banks' profitability and stability? Emerging vs. advanced economies. *Journal of Banking & Finance*, *37*(8), 2920–2937. [CrossRef]
Niu, J. (2024). Liquidity hoarding and bank profitability: The role of economic policy uncertainty. *Finance Research Letters*, *68*, 106003. [CrossRef]
Onofrei, M., Bostan, I., Roma, A., & Firtescu, B. N. (2018). The determinants of commercial bank profitability in CEE countries. *Romanian Statistical Review*, (2), 33–46.
Pesaran, M. H. (2004). *General diagnostic tests for cross section dependence in panels*. University of Cambridge. [CrossRef]
Pesaran, M. H. (2007). A simple panel unit root test in the presence of cross-section dependence. *Journal of Applied Econometrics*, *22*(2), 265–312. [CrossRef]
Pesaran, M. H. (2021). General diagnostic tests for cross-sectional dependence in panels. *Empirical Economics*, *60*(1), 13–50. [CrossRef]
Pesaran, M. H., Shin, Y., & Smith, R. P. (1999). Pooled mean group estimation of dynamic heterogeneous panels. *Journal of the American Statistical Association*, *94*(446), 621–634. [CrossRef]
Pesaran, M. H., & Smith, R. (1995). Estimating long run relationships from dynamic heterogeneous panels. *Journal of Econometrics*, *68*(1), 79–113. [CrossRef]
Peshev, P. I., & Stamenova, R. A. (2025). Panel investigation of the factors determining the supply of bank loans in Bulgaria using microeconomic data. *Economics-Innovative and Economics Research Journal*, *13*(3), 493–520. [CrossRef]
Roodman, D. (2009). A note on the theme of too many instruments. *Oxford Bulletin of Economics and Statistics*, *71*(1), 135–158. [CrossRef]
Sufian, F., & Chong, R. R. (2008). Determinants of bank profitability in a developing economy: Empirical evidence from the philippines. *Asian Academy of Management Journal of Accounting & Finance*, *4*(2). Available online: https://ejournal.usm.my/aamjaf/article/view/aamjaf_vol4-no2-2008_5 (accessed on 28 January 2026).
Zajñac, J., & Paczos, W. (2025). *Euro adoption and banks profitability in Central and Eastern Europe* (No. E2025/17). Cardiff Economics Working Papers. Available online: https://www.econstor.eu/bitstream/10419/324444/1/1930668031.pdf (accessed on 11 October 2025).

https://doi.org/10.3390/jrfm19020156

Journal of
Risk and Financial Management

MDPI

Article

The Silver Economy and Fiscal Outcomes in Aging Europe: A Governance-Conditioned Panel Analysis

Ralitsa Veleva

Department of Public Administration, University of National and World Economy, Str. '8mi Dekemvri' 19, 1000 Sofia, Bulgaria; ralitsa.veleva@unwe.bg

Abstract

Population aging is widely regarded as a major fiscal risk for European welfare states and a central challenge to long-term fiscal sustainability. The article critically reexamines the deterministic assumption by assessing whether the fiscal implications of demographic aging in the European Union (EU) are mechanically driven or conditioned by policy context and institutional capacity. Using panel data for the EU-27 over the period 2014–2024, the study employs a two-way fixed-effects framework and interaction models to examine the relationship between demographic aging and key fiscal outcomes, including public pension expenditures, total social protection spending, and the general government balance. Furthermore, the analysis examines whether indicators associated with the silver economy, such as employment at older ages and digital inclusion, condition the fiscal effects of aging within countries over time. The results suggest that demographic aging does not exhibit a statistically significant association with pension or social protection expenditures once institutional heterogeneity and common shocks are controlled. In contrast to deterministic expectations, aging is positively associated with general government balance, suggesting the presence of policy-mediated fiscal adjustment dynamics rather than automatic fiscal deterioration. Interaction estimates further indicate that digital inclusion among older cohorts conditions the relationship between demographic aging and fiscal balance, while silver economy indicators do not display robust standalone fiscal effects. These findings should be interpreted as evidence of policy-mediated adjustment dynamics rather than as causal estimates of demographic effects. Building on these findings, the article advances a conceptual interpretation of the aging–fiscal nexus in which demographic pressures interact with institutional adaptation and policy capacity. Fiscal sustainability under demographic aging emerges as a policy-mediated outcome that may reflect broader institutional and governance contexts, rather than demographic structure alone. While governance quality is not directly estimated as an observable variable, the analysis interprets fiscal outcomes within a governance-conditioned institutional framework that emphasizes policy mediation rather than deterministic demographic effects. The findings contribute to ongoing debates on fiscal sustainability in aging societies by demonstrating that fiscal outcomes in the European Union are best understood as institutionally conditioned and policy-mediated rather than mechanically driven by demographic structure alone.

Keywords: demographic aging; fiscal sustainability; silver economy; governance; European Union

1. Introduction

The aging of the population has become one of the most widely discussed structural challenges to public finances in advanced economies. Across the European Union (EU), declining fertility rates and rising life expectancy are reshaping demographic structures and altering dependency ratios, prompting persistent concerns about the long-term sustainability of welfare states. In both academic and policy debates, demographic aging is frequently portrayed as an automatic source of fiscal pressure, expected to increase pension and social expenditure while simultaneously narrowing the tax base through a shrinking working-age population.

Despite the prominence of this deterministic narrative, empirical fiscal developments across EU Member States present a more complex picture. Countries that experience similar demographic trajectories often show markedly different fiscal outcomes, suggesting that the relationship between aging and public finances is neither uniform nor mechanically determined. Therefore, a growing body of research questions the assumption that demographic change translates directly into fiscal deterioration and instead highlights the importance of institutional arrangements, policy responses, and governance capacity in mediating fiscal outcomes under demographic pressure. However, much of the empirical literature continues to treat population aging primarily as an exogenous driver of fiscal stress, with comparatively limited attention to the role of administrative and policy capacity in shaping fiscal responses.

At the same time, the concept of the silver economy has gained increasing prominence as a policy framework for addressing aging societies. By emphasizing active aging, extended working lives, digital inclusion, and age-friendly innovation, the silver economy reframes older populations as economic participants rather than passive dependents. This perspective suggests that aging can create opportunities for growth, productivity, and participation that can mitigate some of the fiscal challenges associated with demographic change. However, the fiscal relevance of policies related to the silver economy remains empirically ambiguous. Although such policies are frequently presented as mechanisms for alleviating demographic pressure, evidence of their direct impact on public finances is limited and often context-dependent.

This article argues that the missing link in current debates lies in governance and policy capacity. Rather than conceptualizing demographic aging as a mechanical fiscal shock or the silver economy as an autonomous solution, the study advances the view that fiscal sustainability under aging is conditioned by the capacity of public administrations to design, coordinate, and implement effective policy responses. Governance and policy capacity shape how demographic pressures are translated into fiscal outcomes by influencing labor market participation at older ages, policy sequencing, institutional reform trajectories, and the effectiveness of social and economic adaptation measures. From this perspective, the fiscal implications of aging depend less on demographic structures alone and more on the institutional and policy context within which aging unfolds.

The central research question guiding this study is therefore:

Are the fiscal effects of demographic aging in the European Union mechanically determined, or are they conditioned by governance capacity and policy domains related to the silver economy?

Addressing this question requires moving beyond deterministic assumptions and examining whether fiscal outcomes under demographic aging vary systematically with policy context and institutional capacity.

To investigate these issues, the article conducts a comparative panel analysis of the 27 EU Member States over the period 2014–2024. Using fixed-effects regression models, the study examines the relationship between demographic aging and key fiscal outcomes, in-

https://doi.org/10.3390/jrfm19030212

cluding pension expenditure, social protection spending, and general government balance. It also incorporates interaction models to assess whether indicators associated with the silver economy, such as employment among older cohorts, active aging, and digital inclusion, condition the fiscal effects of aging. This empirical strategy focuses on within-country dynamics over time while controlling for time-invariant institutional characteristics and common shocks affecting all Member States.

The selected time period (2014–2024) is analytically relevant for examining the fiscal implications of demographic aging in the European Union. It captures the post-sovereign-debt-crisis policy environment, a decade marked by pension and labor market reforms aimed at improving fiscal sustainability, as well as major macroeconomic shocks including the COVID-19 pandemic and the subsequent fiscal policy responses across EU Member States. These developments provide a particularly informative context for assessing whether demographic aging translates into fiscal outcomes through deterministic mechanisms or through policy-mediated adjustment dynamics.

The study makes three main contributions to the literature. First, it advances new empirical evidence demonstrating that demographic aging does not exert a uniform or mechanically adverse effect on fiscal outcomes across the European Union once institutional heterogeneity and common macroeconomic shocks are appropriately accounted for. Second, it refines the fiscal interpretation of the silver economy by demonstrating that its relevance is primarily conditional rather than direct, emerging through interaction effects with demographic change rather than as a standalone driver of fiscal improvement. Third, the article advances a governance-centered conceptual framework that places administrative and policy capacity at the core of the aging–fiscal nexus, highlighting how institutional context shapes the translation of demographic pressures into fiscal outcomes.

By linking demographic change, fiscal sustainability, and governance capacity within a unified empirical framework, the article contributes to broader debates on public finance adaptation in aging societies. Its findings suggest that fiscal sustainability under demographic aging depends not only on demographic trends themselves but also on the ability of public administrations to anticipate demographic change and implement coordinated policy responses. These insights are particularly relevant for EU Member States facing rapid aging alongside constrained fiscal space, where strengthening governance and policy capacity may prove as important as demographic management itself. The contribution of the article is primarily interpretive and conceptual–empirical: it repositions demographic aging within a governance-conditioned fiscal framework using updated EU panel evidence.

2. Literature Review and Conceptual Model

2.1. Demographic Aging and Fiscal Sustainability: Deterministic and Conditional Perspectives

Population aging is widely recognized as one of the most significant structural transformations affecting advanced economies, particularly within the EU, where sustained declines in fertility and increasing life expectancy are reshaping demographic structures across Member States (European Commission, 2021; OECD, 2023a). In both academic and policy debates, demographic aging is frequently associated with concerns about fiscal sustainability, reflecting expectations that a growing share of older individuals will increase age-related public expenditure and place pressure on public budgets (European Commission, 2023; Rouzet et al., 2019).

A substantial strand of the literature conceptualizes the relationship between demographic aging and public finances in largely mechanical terms. From this perspective, aging is treated as an exogenous demographic process that predictably translates into fiscal stress through higher spending on pensions, health care, and long-term care, combined with a shrinking working-age population and a potentially narrower tax base (IMF, 2025;

https://doi.org/10.3390/jrfm19030212

Koutsogeorgopoulou & Morgavi, 2025). Such interpretations are particularly prominent in long-term fiscal projection exercises, which model future age-related expenditure trajectories under baseline demographic assumptions and frequently highlight substantial risks for fiscal sustainability in aging societies (European Commission, 2021). Within this deterministic framework, the demographic structure is often viewed as the main driver of long-term fiscal imbalance, and policy responses are considered to be largely reactive.

At the same time, an expanding body of empirical research offers important qualifications to this deterministic interpretation. Comparative analyses in EU and OECD Member States reveal considerable heterogeneity in fiscal outcomes among countries experiencing similar demographic aging patterns (Carone et al., 2016; Grech, 2010; Bieszk-Stolorz et al., 2024). Differences are observed not only in the level and growth of age-related expenditure but also in broader fiscal indicators such as budget balances and debt dynamics. These patterns suggest that demographic change alone does not fully account for observed fiscal trajectories and that fiscal outcomes under aging may be shaped by institutional arrangements and policy choices.

In response, a more conditional perspective has emerged, emphasizing the mediating role of institutional design, policy responses, and governance structures in shaping the fiscal implications of demographic change. From this point of view, aging is understood as a contextual demographic pressure whose fiscal effects depend on how welfare states, labor markets, and public finance systems are structured and adjusted over time (Natali, 2018; Rouzet et al., 2019). Therefore, it is not assumed that it responds automatically to changes in age structure, but rather reflects interactions between demographic trends and policy frameworks, including pension system design, labor market regulation, and fiscal governance arrangements.

Empirical evidence derived from panel data analyses is broadly consistent with this conditional interpretation. Studies employing within-country identification strategies typically reveal weak, heterogeneous, or statistically insignificant short- to medium-term relationships between shifts in the old age population share and core fiscal indicators once unobserved country-specific heterogeneity and common macroeconomic shocks are adequately controlled for (Rouzet et al., 2019; Guillemette & Turner, 2021). These findings do not negate the long-term fiscal relevance of demographic aging. Rather, they indicate that the observable fiscal manifestations of aging are mediated through institutional mechanisms and policy adjustments, particularly over the shorter horizons typically examined in comparative panel datasets.

The literature also underscores the importance of distinguishing between different types of fiscal results when assessing the fiscal implications of aging. Although age-related expenditure components, such as public pensions, are often assumed to be closely linked to demographic structure, aggregate fiscal indicators, including the general government balance, reflect a broader set of policy decisions and macroeconomic interactions (Auerbach & Lee, 2011; Rouzet et al., 2019). Governments facing demographic pressures may respond through revenue-side measures, expenditure reallocation, or structural reforms, resulting in fiscal outcomes that do not mirror demographic change in a simple or uniform manner. Consequently, the relationship between demographic aging and fiscal sustainability cannot be fully understood without considering the institutional and policy context within which demographic change occurs.

This distinction is particularly relevant in the EU, where most Member States have implemented extensive reforms in the pension and labor market over the past two decades. Increases in statutory retirement ages, restrictions on early retirement pathways, and adjustments to benefit indexation have altered the relationship between demographic structure and pension expenditure dynamics (Carone et al., 2016; European Commission,

https://doi.org/10.3390/jrfm19030212

2018a; OECD, 2021). As a result, the sensitivity of fiscal results to short-term demographic change has become increasingly dependent on institutional design rather than demographic structure alone.

Building on the conditional perspective, this study examines within-country fiscal dynamics in the EU-27 over 2014–2024 using a two-way fixed-effects framework. The empirical strategy further evaluates whether silver economy domains, captured through labor market participation at older ages and digital inclusion, act as conditioning factors in the association between demographic aging and fiscal outcomes.

2.2. Theoretical Foundations of Fiscal Sustainability in Aging Societies

The relationship between demographic aging and fiscal sustainability has been extensively analyzed within several foundational theoretical frameworks in public finance, macroeconomics, and political economy. Although demographic change is frequently portrayed as a direct driver of fiscal pressure, theoretical research consistently emphasizes that the fiscal implications of aging depend not only on demographic structure but also on institutional arrangements, policy design, and governance capacity. Four strands of theory are particularly relevant for understanding the fiscal consequences of demographic change: life-cycle and overlapping-generations models, theories of intertemporal fiscal sustainability, welfare state adjustment perspectives, and institutional approaches to fiscal governance.

Recent research has further emphasized that population aging is becoming one of the most important structural drivers of fiscal dynamics in advanced economies. Long-term fiscal projections for the European Union indicate that age-related public expenditures, particularly pensions, healthcare, and long-term care, are expected to increase significantly over the coming decades (European Commission, 2021, 2024). These projections have intensified academic and policy debates about the sustainability of public finances in aging societies.

- Life-cycle theory and overlapping-generations models

The analytical foundations of the aging–fiscal nexus originate in life-cycle theory and overlapping-generations (OLG) models, which examine how demographic structure influences saving, taxation, and intergenerational transfers. In these frameworks, individuals allocate consumption and savings over the life course, while governments finance age-related social programs through intergenerational transfers embedded in public pension and social protection systems. Population aging alters the balance between contributors and beneficiaries in pay-as-you-go welfare systems and may generate fiscal pressures if the growth of age-related expenditures exceeds the growth of the tax base (Auerbach & Lee, 2011).

OLG models demonstrate that demographic shifts such as declining fertility and increasing longevity can significantly affect public finances through changes in dependency ratios and intergenerational transfer mechanisms. In aging societies, a rising share of retirees relative to the working-age population increases the fiscal burden associated with pension and health expenditures while simultaneously reducing the number of contributors financing these systems. As a result, demographic aging can create structural pressures on public budgets and long-term fiscal sustainability (Auerbach & Gorodnichenko, 2012).

However, these models also emphasize that fiscal outcomes depend critically on policy parameters embedded in social protection systems, including retirement age rules, contribution rates, benefit formulas, and indexation mechanisms. Consequently, demographic aging does not automatically translate into fiscal imbalance; rather, the magnitude and timing of fiscal pressures depend on how pension systems and social protection institutions are designed and reformed over time.

https://doi.org/10.3390/jrfm19030212

- Intertemporal fiscal sustainability and the government budget constraint

A second theoretical strand focuses on intertemporal approaches to fiscal sustainability rooted in public finance theory. In this perspective, fiscal sustainability is evaluated through the intertemporal government budget constraint, which requires that current public debt be matched by future primary surpluses over the long run. Recent empirical research confirms that demographic change interacts with macroeconomic conditions and policy responses in shaping fiscal sustainability. Studies examining long-term fiscal projections in advanced economies show that demographic aging affects both the expenditure side of public budgets and the dynamics of economic growth, labor supply, and productivity (Bloom et al., 2010; Maestas et al., 2023). Fiscal sustainability therefore depends on the capacity of governments to maintain fiscal policies consistent with long-term solvency conditions (Chalk & Hemming, 2000; Bohn, 1998).

From this perspective, demographic aging affects fiscal sustainability primarily through its influence on long-term expenditure commitments and the evolution of public debt dynamics. Age-related expenditures, particularly pensions, health care, and long-term care, may increase substantially as populations age, thereby affecting the trajectory of government budgets and long-term debt sustainability. Aging societies therefore pose challenges for maintaining the intertemporal balance between public revenues and expenditures (Ramos-Herrera & Sosvilla-Rivero, 2020).

At the same time, intertemporal approaches emphasize that fiscal sustainability is not determined solely by demographic factors. Macroeconomic variables such as economic growth, interest rates, productivity dynamics, and labor market participation also play a crucial role in shaping long-term fiscal trajectories. As a result, demographic change interacts with broader macroeconomic and policy conditions in determining fiscal outcomes.

- Welfare state adjustment and the political economy of aging

A third theoretical strand emphasizes welfare state adaptation and the political economy of demographic change. Comparative political economy research demonstrates that welfare states respond to demographic pressures through institutional reforms, policy recalibration, and changes in labor market participation across the life course. Pension systems in particular have undergone extensive reforms across advanced economies, including increases in statutory retirement ages, tighter eligibility rules, and stronger links between contributions and benefits (N. Barr & Diamond, 2008; Grech, 2010). Recent policy analyses also emphasize the growing importance of labor market adaptation in aging societies. Policies that extend working lives, promote lifelong learning, and support age-inclusive labor markets are increasingly viewed as key instruments for maintaining fiscal sustainability in the context of demographic change (OECD, 2020, 2023b).

Within this perspective, demographic aging represents a structural constraint, but the fiscal consequences depend on how governments redesign social policies and adjust institutional arrangements in response to demographic change. Welfare states are not passive recipients of demographic pressures; instead, they actively adapt through reforms aimed at stabilizing public finances and maintaining the sustainability of social protection systems. Such reforms may involve extending working lives, adjusting pension indexation rules, modifying contribution structures, or introducing mixed pension financing models that combine pay-as-you-go and funded elements.

Political economy research further emphasizes that fiscal responses to demographic change are shaped by institutional configurations, electoral incentives, and intergenerational distributional conflicts. As populations age, the political weight of older cohorts may increase, potentially influencing fiscal policy choices and the design of welfare state reforms.

https://doi.org/10.3390/jrfm19030212

These dynamics illustrate that fiscal outcomes under demographic aging are mediated by institutional and political processes rather than determined solely by demographic structure.

- Fiscal governance and institutional capacity

A fourth theoretical perspective focuses on fiscal governance and institutional capacity. Research on fiscal institutions highlights that budgetary outcomes are strongly influenced by governance structures, fiscal rules, and the effectiveness of public administration (Hallerberg et al., 2010). More recent research on fiscal institutions also highlights the role of fiscal rules, independent fiscal councils, and institutional transparency in strengthening governments' ability to respond to long-term fiscal pressures (Eyraud et al., 2017).

Institutional frameworks shape governments' ability to anticipate long-term fiscal pressures, implement reforms, and maintain budgetary discipline over time.

Countries with stronger fiscal governance systems, characterized by credible fiscal rules, transparent budgeting procedures, and effective administrative coordination, are generally better able to adopt timely policy adjustments and manage long-term fiscal challenges, including those associated with demographic aging. Conversely, weaker institutional capacity may delay necessary reforms and amplify fiscal vulnerabilities. In this sense, governance structures influence not only the level of fiscal sustainability but also the capacity of governments to respond to structural pressures arising from demographic change.

- Implications for the empirical analysis

These theoretical perspectives suggest that demographic aging does not translate mechanically into fiscal deterioration. While demographic trends may generate structural pressures on public finances, the fiscal outcomes observed in practice depend on how governments respond through policy adaptation, institutional reforms, and labor market adjustments. Fiscal sustainability therefore emerges as the result of an interaction between demographic dynamics, macroeconomic conditions, policy design, and institutional frameworks.

From this perspective, the relationship between demographic aging and fiscal outcomes is unlikely to be deterministic. Instead, fiscal dynamics may reflect conditional adjustment processes, in which policy choices and institutional contexts mediate the fiscal implications of demographic change. This theoretical insight motivates the empirical approach adopted in this study. Rather than assuming a direct demographic effect on fiscal outcomes, the analysis examines whether fiscal developments in the European Union reflect deterministic demographic pressures or policy-mediated adjustment mechanisms associated with labor market participation, digital inclusion, and broader institutional contexts.

2.3. *Pension Expenditure as an Institutionally Mediated Fiscal Outcome*

Although demographic aging provides the structural background for the expansion of public pension systems, the literature on pension finance increasingly emphasizes that observed pension expenditure dynamics cannot be inferred directly from demographic structure alone. Unlike aggregate fiscal indicators, pension expenditure is governed by a dense set of statutory rules, eligibility criteria, and long-term policy commitments that substantially constrain its short- and medium-term responsiveness to demographic change (N. Barr & Diamond, 2008; Natali, 2018). As a result, the relationship between demographic aging and pension spending is mediated by characteristics of institutional design and reform trajectories, rather than acting as a direct mechanical link.

Public pension systems in EU Member States exhibit a high degree of legal and institutional codification. Eligibility conditions, contribution requirements, benefit formulas, and indexation rules are typically embedded in primary legislation and modified only through explicit reform processes. Consequently, pension expenditure evolves along relatively stable institutional trajectories, with demographic pressures translated into fiscal outcomes primarily through their interaction with existing policy parameters (Carone et al., 2016; Grech, 2010). This institutional embeddedness distinguishes pension expenditures from other components of public spending that may respond more flexibly to changing economic or social conditions.

A central implication of this institutional structure is the presence of substantial adjustment delays. Demographic aging affects pension systems primarily through cohort replacement processes that unfold over extended periods rather than within short time frames. Increases in life expectancy, for example, may lengthen the duration of benefit receipt, but their fiscal impact depends critically on retirement age rules, accrual rates, and indexation mechanisms that determine how longevity gains are distributed between working life and retirement (OECD, 2021, 2023a). As a result, contemporaneous changes in the share of the population aged 65 and over do not necessarily correspond to immediate shifts in pension expenditure within the time horizons typically examined in comparative panel analyses.

The European experience further illustrates the importance of institutional mediation. Since the early 2000s, most EU Member States have implemented successive rounds of pension reforms aimed at improving long-term sustainability. These reforms have included increases in statutory retirement ages, tighter restrictions on early retirement, stronger links between lifetime contributions and benefits, and the introduction of automatic adjustment mechanisms linked to demographic or macroeconomic indicators (Carone et al., 2016; European Commission, 2018a). Many of these reforms were explicitly designed to delink the dynamics of short-term pension expenditure from demographic fluctuations by embedding adjustment rules within the institutional architecture of pension systems. As a result, pension expenditure has increasingly become a policy-managed outcome rather than a purely demographic one.

Empirical research supports this interpretation. Studies examining pension expenditure dynamics in advanced economies often find that, following major reforms, the marginal effect of changes in demographic structure on observed pension expenditure ratios tends to weaken, particularly in within-country analyses that control for time-invariant institutional characteristics (Grech, 2010; Rouzet et al., 2019). In such contexts, pension spending trajectories frequently reflect the legacy of past reforms, indexation choices, and benefit rules more strongly than contemporaneous demographic variation.

Macroeconomic conditions introduce an additional layer of mediation. Pension expenditure is commonly expressed as a share of GDP, implying that short-term fluctuations in economic growth, inflation, and labor market performance can influence pension expenditure ratios independently of changes in the number of beneficiaries (Auerbach & Lee, 2011). Periods of strong economic growth can reduce pension expenditure ratios through denominator effects, whereas economic downturns may increase them even in the absence of significant demographic change. This further reinforces the interpretation of pension expenditure as an observed fiscal outcome shaped by institutional and macroeconomic context rather than as a direct demographic indicator.

From a normative perspective, the institutional rigidity of pension expenditure reflects deliberate policy choices. Pension systems are designed to provide predictability, income security, and social adequacy for older cohorts, objectives that often constrain rapid fiscal adjustment (N. A. Barr, 2012; Grech, 2010). Governments can prioritize stability and credibility over short-term fiscal responsiveness, accepting gradual adjustment paths even under conditions of demographic pressure. This trade-off further limits the extent to which pension expenditure can be expected to respond contemporaneously to demographic aging or to policy domains external to the pension system itself.

https://doi.org/10.3390/jrfm19030212

The literature supports treating pension expenditure as an institutionally mediated fiscal outcome. Although demographic aging represents a fundamental long-term challenge for pension systems, the observable evolution of pension spending is primarily shaped by statutory design features, reform trajectories, and macroeconomic conditions. Pension expenditure therefore reflects institutional parameters such as retirement age rules, benefit indexation mechanisms, and contribution structures, which often evolve gradually through policy reforms. As a result, short-term fluctuations in pension spending may be only weakly associated with contemporaneous demographic change or with policy domains associated with the silver economy.

This conceptualization has important implications for empirical analyses of fiscal outcomes in aging societies. It suggests that pension expenditure should be analyzed separately from broader fiscal indicators such as overall fiscal balance or public debt dynamics. In institutionalized welfare systems, pension spending trajectories often reflect the cumulative effects of past reforms and structural policy parameters rather than immediate demographic pressures. Consequently, weak or statistically insignificant short-term relationships between demographic aging and pension expenditure in panel data should not necessarily be interpreted as empirical anomalies, but rather as outcomes consistent with the institutional characteristics of contemporary European pension systems.

2.4. The Silver Economy and Fiscal Adaptation: A Conditional Perspective

The concept of the silver economy has gained increasing prominence in academic and policy debates as a framework for reinterpreting the economic and social implications of demographic aging. Rather than viewing older populations primarily as fiscal dependents, the perspective of the silver economy emphasizes their role as workers, consumers, and contributors to economic and social life (Klimczuk, 2016; European Commission, 2018b). From a broader European perspective, the silver economy is increasingly conceptualized as a strategic policy and economic framework that repositions older individuals as active participants in production, consumption, and social innovation, rather than solely as beneficiaries of welfare systems (Veleva, 2025b). This reframing shifts analytical attention from demographic burden to adaptive capacity and policy-mediated opportunity in aging societies.

The silver economy is typically understood as the aggregate of economic activities and policy domains that respond to the needs, preferences, and productive potential of older adults. These domains span labor markets, health and care systems, housing, digital technologies, and age-related innovation (European Commission, 2018b; Bieszk-Stolorz et al., 2024). Active aging is widely conceptualized as a multidimensional process shaped by health, social, and economic determinants that influence participation, independence, and quality of life at older ages, thus affecting the economic and fiscal role of older cohorts in aging societies (Pavlova et al., 2021). Empirical comparative analyses across EU Member States reveal substantial differences in demographic structure, employment among older cohorts, fiscal expenditures on pensions and healthcare, poverty risks, and digital inclusion, highlighting the heterogeneous development of the silver economy across Europe (Veleva, 2025a). Importantly, the silver economy does not constitute a single sector or policy instrument. Rather, it represents a multidimensional policy space that transcends traditional sectoral boundaries and involves complex interactions between public policy, market dynamics, and social innovation. As such, its development depends not only on demographic demand but also on institutional coordination and governance capacity.

A central insight emerging from the literature is that the expansion of the silver economy is neither automatic nor demographically predetermined. Although population aging generates potential demand for age-related goods, services, and forms of participation,

https://doi.org/10.3390/jrfm19030212

the degree to which this potential is realized varies significantly between countries and depends on policy design, institutional frameworks, and governance quality (Klimczuk, 2016; Peine & Neven, 2019). Differences in labor market regulation, lifelong learning systems, digital infrastructure, and social protection arrangements contribute to divergent silver economy trajectories even among countries facing similar demographic pressures. Consequently, demographic change alone does not ensure the emergence of economically productive aging; policy context and institutional capacity play a central mediating role.

These considerations have important implications for fiscal analysis. Although silver economy-related policy domains are often invoked as mechanisms to mitigate the fiscal challenges of aging, the literature provides limited support for the notion that they generate direct and immediate fiscal improvements. Instead, its relevance for public finances is typically indirect and mediated through broader economic channels, including labor market participation at older ages, productivity dynamics, and the efficiency of public service delivery (Rouzet et al., 2019; Scott, 2021). Policies that promote active aging, digital inclusion, and lifelong learning are generally not designed with short-term budgetary objectives in mind; instead, they aim to enhance participation, autonomy, and long-term economic resilience (Beard et al., 2016; Zaidi et al., 2017). Therefore, any fiscal effects that arise are contingent on how these policies interact with existing labor market institutions, tax systems, and social protection arrangements.

The literature on social innovation in aging societies further reinforces this conditional interpretation. Initiatives such as integrated care models, community services and digital health solutions are frequently promoted as cost-effective responses to aging-related needs (Phills et al., 2008; Klimczuk, 2017). However, empirical evidence on their fiscal impact remains mixed and context-dependent. Although such initiatives may improve service coordination and user outcomes, their budgetary implications depend on scale, institutional embedding, and complementarities with existing public systems (Ghiga et al., 2020; Peine & Neven, 2019). As a result, social innovation within the silver economy is better understood as a factor that influences the efficiency and adaptability of public spending than as a direct driver of expenditure reduction.

From a broader political–economic perspective, the rise of the silver economy reflects changing policy narratives around aging. The transition from viewing older populations as passive beneficiaries to recognizing their productive and social potential aligns with the broader evolution of welfare states toward social investment and life-course-oriented policy models (Morel et al., 2011; Hemerijck, 2017). Within these frameworks, policies targeting older cohorts are justified primarily in terms of long-term economic resilience, social inclusion, and intergenerational balance, with fiscal outcomes viewed as downstream consequences of broader policy strategies rather than as immediate policy objectives.

At the same time, the literature cautions against overestimating the fiscal agency of the silver economy. Although policies promoting active aging, digital inclusion, and age-related innovation can support higher employment among older cohorts and facilitate productivity gains, their ability to offset demographic pressures is highly dependent on governance quality and policy coherence (Klimczuk, 2016; Rouzet et al., 2019). Fragmented implementation, weak administrative capacity, or limited coordination across policy domains can substantially reduce the potential fiscal relevance of silver economy initiatives, even in demographically aging societies.

Existing research supports conceptualizing the silver economy as a conditional policy domain whose fiscal significance is inherently context dependent. Rather than exerting strong standalone effects on public finances, policies related to the silver economy shape the institutional and economic environment in which demographic aging interacts with fiscal systems. Their relevance lies primarily in conditioning how demographic pressures

https://doi.org/10.3390/jrfm19030212

are translated into employment, productivity, and public finance outcomes rather than directly determining expenditure or fiscal balance dynamics.

From a theoretical perspective, the fiscal relevance of silver economy policies is therefore largely indirect. Policies promoting active aging, later-life employment, and digital inclusion are typically examined within human capital and endogenous growth frameworks, where their primary effects operate through labor supply, productivity, and economic resilience. In this sense, fiscal implications emerge through mediated channels such as increased labor participation among older cohorts, higher tax revenues, and changes in dependency ratios rather than through immediate budgetary adjustments.

This interpretation provides the theoretical basis for empirical strategies that focus on conditional relationships and interaction effects rather than direct causal links. By treating silver economy indicators as conditioning variables, it becomes possible to examine whether the policy context modifies the relationship between demographic aging and fiscal outcomes. The empirical analysis developed in this study therefore evaluates whether indicators associated with active aging, employment at older ages, and digital inclusion condition the relationship between demographic change and fiscal sustainability across EU Member States.

2.5. Governance and Policy Capacity as Conditioning Factors in Aging Societies

Beyond demographic structure and policy domains associated with the silver economy, a growing body of research emphasizes the importance of governance quality and policy capacity in shaping economic and fiscal outcomes in advanced economies. In the context of demographic aging, governance and administrative capacity influence how effectively public institutions anticipate demographic change, design appropriate policy responses, and coordinate reforms across policy domains. As a result, the fiscal implications of aging may depend not only on demographic and economic factors but also on the institutional capacity of states to manage structural transformation.

The concept of policy capacity encompasses the analytical, operational, and political resources available to governments for the formulation and implementation of public policy (Wu et al., 2015). Administrative capacity refers more specifically to the ability of public administrations to coordinate complex reforms, ensure policy coherence across sectors, and sustain long-term policy commitments (Painter & Pierre, 2005). In aging societies, these dimensions of capacity become particularly salient as demographic change interacts with pension systems, labor markets, health care provision, and social protection arrangements in ways that require coordinated and sustained policy responses. The effectiveness of public administration in carrying out complex policy activities depends on a set of organizational, institutional, and procedural conditions that shape implementation capacity and administrative coherence across sectors (Krusteva & Lulanski, 2025).

The literature on fiscal governance further underscores the role of institutional quality in shaping public finance outcomes. Comparative studies demonstrate that fiscal performance varies systematically with governance indicators such as government effectiveness, regulatory quality, and institutional stability (Hallerberg et al., 2010; Rouzet et al., 2019). Countries with stronger fiscal institutions and higher administrative capacity are generally better able to implement reforms, maintain budget discipline, and adapt to structural pressures, including those associated with demographic aging. In contrast, weaker governance capacity can amplify fiscal vulnerabilities by limiting the effectiveness of policy responses and causing the necessary adjustments.

In the European context, governance capacity has played a central role in shaping responses to demographic change. Many EU Member States have implemented pension and labor market to improve long-term sustainability, but the timing, sequence, and effective-

https://doi.org/10.3390/jrfm19030212

ness of these reforms have varied considerably between countries (Natali, 2018; European Commission, 2021). Differences in administrative coordination, political consensus, and institutional continuity help explain why similar demographic pressures have translated into divergent fiscal trajectories. Public trust represents a critical institutional resource that underpins the legitimacy, compliance, and the effectiveness of long-term reforms of policies, particularly in contexts that require sustained adjustment of fiscal and social policy (Valcheva, 2025). These variations suggest that governance capacity functions as a conditioning factor that influences how demographic aging is translated into fiscal outcomes rather than as a direct determinant of fiscal performance. Evidence from Bulgaria suggests how differences in forecasting frameworks, fiscal modeling approaches, and institutional assumptions across national and international institutions can lead to divergent expectations regarding fiscal performance and macroeconomic stability, underscoring the role of governance and analytical capacity in shaping fiscal outcomes (Hristozov et al., 2025).

Governance also plays a crucial role in the development and effectiveness of policy domains related to the silver economy. Policies that promote active aging, digital inclusion, and extended working lives typically require coordination across multiple policy sectors, including employment, education, health, and social protection. Effective implementation depends on the capacity of public administrations to design integrated strategies, mobilize resources, and ensure policy coherence over time (Klimczuk, 2016; Rouzet et al., 2019). Where governance capacity is strong, such policies can contribute to higher employment in older ages, improved productivity, and more efficient public service delivery. Where it is weak, similar initiatives can produce limited or fragmented effects.

Importantly, governance and policy capacity are often difficult to capture through single observable indicators in cross-country panel analyses. Institutional effectiveness and administrative coordination are multidimensional and can be reflected indirectly in reform trajectories, policy outcomes, and the effectiveness of sectoral initiatives rather than in discrete quantitative measures. As a result, several studies adopt an indirect approach, treating governance capacity as an underlying contextual factor that shapes observed policy outcomes and economic performance (Hemerijck, 2017; Rouzet et al., 2019). This approach allows governance to be incorporated conceptually without requiring direct measurement in econometric models, particularly when the focus lies on understanding conditional relationships rather than estimating the causal impact of governance itself.

Within this conceptual framework, governance and policy capacity can be understood as conditioning factors that shape how demographic pressures and policy domains interact to influence fiscal outcomes. Effective governance can enable countries to translate challenges into opportunities through timely reforms, coordinated policy responses, and efficient delivery of public service delivery. On the contrary, limited administrative capacity can constrain the ability of governments to implement such responses, allowing demographic pressures to translate more directly into fiscal strain.

By situating governance and policy capacity at the center of the aging–fiscal nexus, the present study contributes to an emerging strand of literature that views fiscal sustainability under demographic aging as fundamentally policy-mediated. Instead of treating governance as an additional explanatory variable, the analysis conceptualizes it as an underlying institutional condition that shapes the effectiveness of policy domains and the broader fiscal response to demographic change. This governance-centered perspective provides the conceptual foundation for examining whether the fiscal implications of demographic aging in the EU are conditioned by policy domains associated with active aging, participation in the labor market at older ages, and digital inclusion.

For this reason, the present study adopts an indirect institutional interpretation in which governance capacity is treated as an underlying contextual condition captured through within-country policy outcomes and adjustment patterns rather than through single governance indicators. This approach is consistent with comparative political economy research emphasizing institutional mediation without relying on potentially noisy cross-country governance indices.

2.6. Research Gaps and Contribution of the Study

The existing literature provides extensive information on the demographic, economic, and institutional dimensions of population aging in Europe. However, several analytical and empirical gaps remain regarding the relationship between demographic aging, policy domains related to the silver economy, and fiscal sustainability. Addressing these gaps requires a more integrated analytical framework that links demographic dynamics, institutional capacity, and fiscal outcomes within a unified empirical perspective.

First, much of the empirical literature that examines the fiscal implications of demographic aging continues to treat aging primarily as an exogenous driver of fiscal pressure. Although a growing number of studies acknowledge institutional mediation, relatively few explicitly analyze how policy domains associated with the silver economy interact with demographic change to shape fiscal outcomes. Research on the fiscal impact of aging often focuses on expenditure projections or long-term sustainability indicators without incorporating potential moderating effects arising from active aging, digital inclusion, or extended working lives (Rouzet et al., 2019). In contrast, studies on the silver economy and social innovation frequently emphasize economic participation, well-being, and innovation outcomes without systematically examining their implications for public finances (Klimczuk, 2016; Peine & Neven, 2019). This fragmentation has limited the development of integrated empirical analyses linking the dynamics of the silver economy with fiscal sustainability.

Second, comparative panel analyses that jointly examine demographic change, policy adaptation, and fiscal outcomes remain relatively limited in scope and temporal coverage. Rapid developments in the past decade, including pension reforms, digital transformation, and policy responses to major economic shocks such as the COVID-19 pandemic, have altered the institutional and macroeconomic context in which aging unfolds. As a result, earlier empirical findings may not fully capture the evolving relationship between demographic structure and fiscal outcomes in contemporary EU economies. Recent studies highlight the need for updated cross-country analyses that incorporate post-2014 developments and capture the interaction between demographic change and evolving policy environments (Bieszk-Stolorz et al., 2024).

Third, although governance and policy capacity are widely recognized as essential for effective policy adaptation in aging societies, they are rarely integrated into empirical analyses of fiscal sustainability. Existing research shows that institutional quality and administrative capacity shape the effectiveness of pension reforms, labor market policies, and social investment strategies (Hemerijck, 2017; Rouzet et al., 2019). However, empirical models of the aging–fiscal nexus often omit governance considerations or treat them only indirectly, limiting understanding of how institutional capacity conditions fiscal responses to demographic change. A governance-centered analytical perspective remains underdeveloped in quantitative studies that examine fiscal outcomes under demographic aging.

Fourth, the literature provides limited empirical evidence on the fiscal relevance of social innovation and silver economy-related initiatives. Although qualitative studies document the potential of community-based services, digital health solutions, and age-friendly innovation to improve service delivery and well-being, quantitative assessments of their implications for public expenditure and fiscal balance are comparatively scarce (Ghiga et al., 2020). In particular, there is a lack of panel-based analyses that examine whether

https://doi.org/10.3390/jrfm19030212

such policy domains condition the fiscal effects of demographic aging across countries and over time.

The present study addresses these gaps by developing an integrated empirical framework that links demographic aging, policy domains related to the silver economy, and fiscal outcomes within a governance-centered perspective. Using panel data for the EU-27 during the period 2014–2024, the analysis examines whether the fiscal implications of demographic aging are mechanically determined or conditioned by policy context and institutional capacity. By incorporating interaction models that capture the conditional role of active aging, employment in older ages, and digital inclusion, the study goes beyond deterministic interpretations of demographic pressure and assesses the extent to which fiscal outcomes under aging are policy-mediated.

In doing so, the article makes three main contributions to the literature. First, it provides updated panel evidence on the relationship between demographic aging and fiscal outcomes in the EU, focusing on within-country dynamics over the past decade. Second, it refines the fiscal interpretation of the silver economy by conceptualizing it as a conditional policy domain whose fiscal relevance emerges primarily through interaction effects rather than direct impacts. Third, it advances a governance-centered conceptual framework that places administrative and policy capacity at the core of the aging–fiscal nexus, highlighting how institutional context shapes the translation of demographic pressures into fiscal sustainability outcomes.

These contributions establish the theoretical and empirical basis for the conceptual framework and hypotheses developed in the following section, which formalize the expected relationships between demographic aging, policy domains related to the silver economy, governance capacity, and fiscal outcomes in the European Union.

In addition to addressing these conceptual gaps, the present study contributes empirically by providing updated panel evidence for the EU-27 over the period 2014–2024. This period captures important institutional and macroeconomic developments, including the post-sovereign debt crisis policy environment, the fiscal and economic disruptions associated with the COVID-19 pandemic, and the ongoing digital transformation affecting older cohorts. Empirically, the study departs from earlier EU and OECD panel analyses by focusing on within-country dynamics through a two-way fixed-effects framework and by introducing interaction models that treat silver economy indicators as conditioning factors rather than as direct fiscal drivers. This approach allows the analysis to examine whether demographic pressures translate into fiscal outcomes differently depending on the development of selected policy domains.

3. Conceptual Framework and Hypotheses

3.1. Reframing the Aging–Fiscal Nexus: From Demographic Pressure to Policy-Conditioned Outcomes

Demographic aging is commonly associated with increased fiscal pressure through increased age-related expenditure, particularly on pensions, health care, and social protection, alongside potential constraints on revenue growth due to a shrinking working-age population (Rouzet et al., 2019; European Commission, 2020). This conventional perspective treats demographic structure as the primary driver of fiscal sustainability risks, implying a largely mechanical transmission from population aging to fiscal imbalance. Within such a framework, a higher share of older individuals is expected to increase public expenditure ratios and place downward pressure on fiscal balances unless offset by structural reforms or revenue adjustments.

However, the literature reviewed in the previous section suggests that this deterministic interpretation may be overly simplistic. Fiscal outcomes under demographic aging

https://doi.org/10.3390/jrfm19030212

are shaped not only by demographic structure, but also by institutional design, policy responses, and governance capacity. Pension systems are embedded in statutory frameworks that constrain short- and medium-term expenditure dynamics, while aggregate fiscal indicators reflect broader policy choices and macroeconomic interactions. At the same time, policy domains associated with the silver economy, such as active aging, extended working lives, and digital inclusion, can influence how demographic pressures translate into economic participation, productivity, and public finance outcomes.

This study adopts a non-deterministic conceptualization of the aging–fiscal nexus. Rather than assuming a direct and uniform relationship between demographic aging and fiscal outcomes, the analysis treats demographic change as a structural pressure whose fiscal implications are conditioned by the policy context and institutional capacity. Within this framework, fiscal sustainability under aging depends on how effectively governments adapt through policy design, institutional reform, and coordination across relevant policy domains.

Two distinctions are central to this conceptualization. First, the analysis differentiates between institutionally constrained fiscal outcomes and aggregate fiscal indicators. Pension expenditure, governed by statutory rules and long-term commitments, is expected to exhibit limited short-term responsiveness to demographic change and to policy domains external to the pension system. By contrast, aggregate fiscal outcomes, such as the general government balance, reflect a broader set of policy adjustments and may therefore respond more flexibly to demographic pressures and policy interventions.

Second, the study conceptualizes the policy domains not as direct fiscal instruments, but as conditioning mechanisms that shape how demographic change interacts with fiscal systems. Policies that promote active aging, digital inclusion, and employment in older ages are expected to influence fiscal outcomes indirectly by supporting labor market participation, productivity, and revenue capacity. Therefore, their fiscal relevance depends on how they interact with the demographic structure and institutional context, rather than on their standalone effects.

Governance and policy capacity provide the overarching institutional context within which these interactions unfold. Although governance capacity is not measured directly in empirical models, it is conceptualized as an underlying condition that shapes the design, coordination, and implementation of policy responses to demographic change. Therefore, differences in administrative effectiveness, reform sequencing, and policy coherence between countries can influence how demographic pressures and policies related to the silver economy translate into fiscal results.

Within this integrated framework, demographic aging, silver economy-related policy domains, and governance capacity are understood as interacting elements that shape fiscal sustainability. Figure 1 illustrates the conceptual model, linking the demographic structure with fiscal results, while highlighting the conditioning role of the policy domains associated with the silver economy and embedded within broader governance contexts.

The conceptual framework implies that the fiscal implications of demographic aging cannot be assessed solely by examining direct relationships between age structure and fiscal indicators. Instead, they must be evaluated in relation to the policy and institutional environment within which demographic change occurs. This perspective provides the basis for the empirical strategy adopted in the following sections and for the formulation of the study's hypotheses.

https://doi.org/10.3390/jrfm19030212

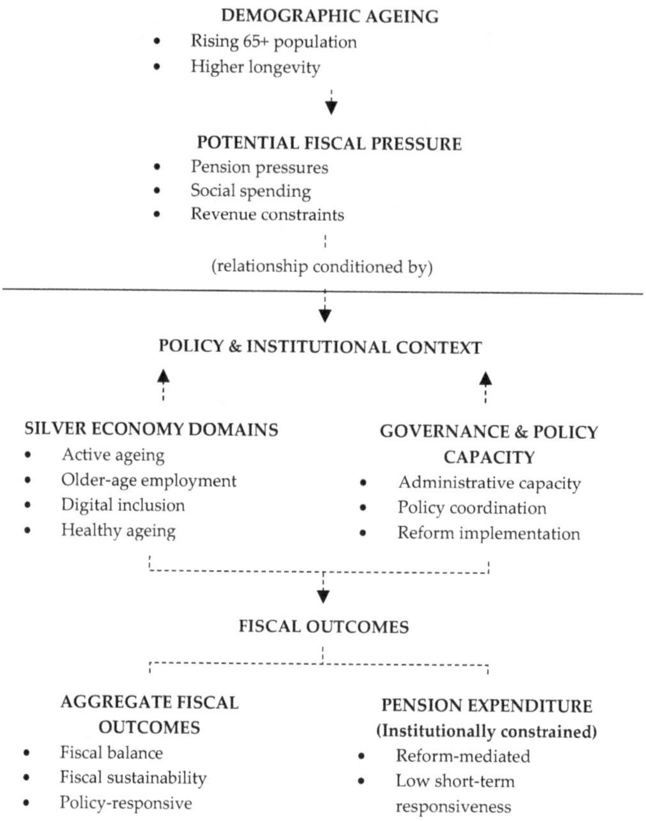

Figure 1. Governance-conditioned conceptual framework of the aging–fiscal nexus. Source: Author's own elaboration.

3.2. Hypotheses

The hypotheses derive from the theoretical perspectives outlined in the previous section, particularly life-cycle and overlapping-generations models of fiscal sustainability, welfare state adjustment theories, and institutional approaches emphasizing fiscal governance and policy capacity.

Based on the theoretical arguments and empirical findings reviewed above, the study formulates four hypotheses on the relationship between demographic aging, policy domains related to the silver economy, and fiscal outcomes in the European Union.

H_1: Demographic aging and age-related public expenditure

The conventional expectation in the literature is that demographic aging increases age-related public expenditure, particularly pension spending. Therefore, a higher share of the population aged 65 and over is expected to be associated with higher pension expenditures as a share of GDP. Broader social protection expenditures are examined as a complementary outcome to assess whether demographic pressure extends beyond pension spending.

H_1: *Demographic aging is associated with higher age-related public expenditures, particularly pension expenditures as a share of GDP.*

H_2: Demographic aging and aggregate fiscal outcomes

https://doi.org/10.3390/jrfm19030212

Although demographic aging is often assumed to weaken fiscal balances, institutional mediation and policy responses can alter this relationship. The aggregate fiscal results reflect not only demographic pressures, but also policy adjustments, including pension reforms, revenue measures, and reallocation of expenditures. Therefore, the relationship between demographic aging and the general government balance is treated as an empirical question rather than as a predetermined negative association.

H_2: *Demographic aging is associated with changes in aggregate fiscal outcomes, measured by the general government balance, reflecting policy-mediated rather than purely mechanical fiscal effects.*

H_3: Silver Economy-Related Policy Domains as Standalone Fiscal Factors

Drawing on theoretical perspectives emphasizing indirect fiscal transmission through labor supply, productivity, and human capital accumulation, the fiscal effects of silver economy policies are expected to operate primarily through mediated channels rather than through direct budgetary impacts.

Policies associated with the silver economy, such as active aging, older ages, and digital inclusion, are often expected to support fiscal sustainability. However, their fiscal effects are likely to be indirect and mediated through broader economic and institutional channels. As a result, they may not have robust standalone relationships with fiscal outcomes once the demographic structure and macroeconomic conditions are considered.

H_3: *The indicators associated with the silver economy do not exert strong standalone effects on fiscal outcomes but operate primarily through indirect and conditional channels.*

H_4: Conditional effects of silver economy-related policy domains

The central hypothesis of the study is that the fiscal implications of demographic aging are conditioned by policy domains associated with the silver economy. In particular, higher levels of employment at older ages, active aging, and digital inclusion are expected to moderate the relationship between demographic aging and aggregate fiscal outcomes by supporting participation, productivity, and revenue capacity. On the contrary, such conditioning effects are expected to be weaker or absent for pension expenditure, which remains largely determined by institutional design characteristics.

H_4: *The fiscal implications of demographic aging are conditioned by policy domains related to the silver economy, with stronger conditioning effects expected for aggregate fiscal outcomes than for pension expenditure.*

4. Data and Methodology

4.1. Data

This study uses an unbalanced panel dataset covering the 27 Member States of the European Union (EU-27) during the period 2014–2024. The data set combines annual country-level observations drawn from publicly available international statistical sources, including Eurostat, the AMECO database of the European Commission, the OECD and the World Bank. The resulting panel is largely complete, with a maximum of 297 country-year observations (27 countries over 11 years), although data availability varies across indicators and years, particularly at the beginning of the sample period.

The core demographic variable is the share of the population aged 65 and older (age65_share), which captures the evolution of population aging within countries over time. Fiscal outcomes are measured using three dependent variables. Public pension expenditure, expressed as a percentage of GDP (pensions_gdp), reflects age-related fiscal pressure through statutory pension systems. Total fiscal sustainability is represented by the general government balance as a percentage of GDP, defined as net lending (+) or

https://doi.org/10.3390/jrfm19030212

net borrowing (−). In addition, total social protection expenditure as a share of GDP (social_protection_gdp) is employed as a broader robustness measure encompassing non-pension social spending.

Silver economy-related policy domains and social innovation are represented through indicators that capture labor market participation, digital inclusion, health capacity, and social vulnerability among older cohorts. These include employment rates for individuals aged 55–64 and 65–74 years, Internet use among individuals aged 55–74 years, healthy life years at age 65, and the at-risk of poverty or social exclusion rate for persons 65 and older (AROPE 65+). Macroeconomic conditions are controlled using annual real GDP growth.

Although observations for 2024 are available for most key variables, data availability is not uniform across all indicators, particularly for social variables in the early years of the sample. Consequently, the number of observations varies slightly depending on the model specifications. This unbalanced structure is explicitly accommodated within the fixed-effects estimation framework and does not affect the identification of within-country relationships over time, which constitute the primary focus of the empirical analysis.

4.2. Variables and Measurement

The empirical specification focuses on demographic aging as the main source of fiscal pressure and examines whether factors related to the silver economy, particularly active aging and social innovation, are associated with more favorable fiscal outcomes. The key demographic indicator is the share of the population 65 and older, which is widely used in the literature as a proxy for age-related expenditure pressures. Population aging is typically associated with higher pension and social spending and, ceteris paribus, with weaker fiscal balances. According to this expectation (H_1), it is assumed that a higher share of the older population exerts upward pressure on pension and social protection expenditure and downward pressure on the general government balance.

To capture the potential mitigating role of active aging, two labor market indicators are included: the employment rate for people 55–64 years old and the employment rate for individuals 65–74 years old, both obtained from the Eurostat labor force survey. These variables reflect the extent to which older individuals remain economically active. Higher employment at older ages can reduce the fiscal burden associated with aging by supporting tax revenues and postponing retirement, thus alleviating pressure on pension systems. Consequently, higher employment among older cohorts is expected to be associated with lower pension expenditure and improved fiscal balances (H_2).

Digital inclusion among older cohorts is introduced as a proxy for social innovation and technological integration in aging societies. This is measured by the share of 55–74 year olds who have used the Internet in the last 12 months, according to the Eurostat ICT usage survey. Greater digital participation may improve access to services, improve productivity, and support more efficient delivery of public services, including e-government and digital health services. Therefore, higher digital inclusion is expected to be associated with more favorable fiscal outcomes, including lower expenditure pressures and better fiscal balances (H_3).

The health dimension of aging is captured through healthy life years at 65 years of age, a health-adjusted life expectancy indicator derived from Eurostat. Higher values may either alleviate fiscal pressure if healthier older individuals remain economically active and require less care or increase it through longer benefit duration. The working hypothesis of this study is that healthier aging contributes to fiscal sustainability by extending working lives and reducing health-related expenditure pressures, implying a negative association with pension and social protection expenditures.

Socioeconomic vulnerability among older individuals is proxied by the at risk of poverty or social exclusion for people 65 years and over (AROPE 65+), derived from the

EU-SILC survey. This variable captures the broader social conditions of older populations. The lower risk of poverty among older cohorts may reflect more generous pension and social transfers, while higher poverty rates may signal inadequate social protection. The inclusion of this variable allows for controlling for differences in the socioeconomic position of older individuals and their potential fiscal implications.

Finally, real GDP growth (year on year) is included to control for the macroeconomic environment. Economic growth influences fiscal outcomes through both revenue and denominator effects. Stronger growth typically improves fiscal balances and reduces expenditure-to-GDP ratios, while weak or negative growth may intensify fiscal pressures. All variables are measured annually.

Table A1 in Appendix A summarizes variable definitions, data sources, and expected directional relationships within the conceptual framework. The selected indicators form a panel data set that captures both the fiscal challenges associated with population aging and the potential mitigating role of active aging and social innovation in EU Member States.

4.3. Empirical Strategy and Model Specification

The study adopts a panel data econometric approach to examine the relationship between demographic aging, silver economy-related factors, and fiscal sustainability in the 27 EU Member States over the period 2014–2024. Fiscal pressure and sustainability are operationalized through three dependent variables: public pension expenditure as a percentage of GDP, the general government balance as a percentage of GDP, and total social protection expenditure as a share of GDP. Explanatory variables capture demographic structure, participation in the labor market among older cohorts, digital inclusion, health capacity, and broader socioeconomic conditions.

Although the conceptual framework of the study emphasizes governance and policy capacity as important contextual factors shaping fiscal adjustment in aging societies, governance is not directly operationalized as an observable variable in the econometric specification. Instead, the empirical model focuses on demographic structure and selected policy-related indicators associated with the silver economy.

The two-way fixed-effects framework absorbs time-invariant institutional heterogeneity across EU Member States, including persistent characteristics of welfare regimes, fiscal institutions, and administrative capacity. However, fixed effects do not constitute a direct empirical test of governance mechanisms. Accordingly, governance is treated in this study as a conceptual institutional context that informs the interpretation of the empirical results, rather than as a variable whose causal effect is estimated econometrically.

The empirical analysis proceeds in two stages. First, baseline fixed-effects models are estimated to assess the direct association between demographic aging and fiscal outcomes, conditional on indicators related to the silver economy and macroeconomic controls. Second, interaction models are estimated to evaluate whether the relationship between population aging and fiscal outcomes varies systematically with the level of development of selected policy domains, including active aging and digital inclusion.

All baseline specifications are estimated using a two-way fixed-effects framework, incorporating both country and year fixed effects. Fixed-effects control for time-invariant differences between countries in institutional design, welfare regimes, demographic structures, and administrative capacity. Fixed effects capture common shocks and developments that affect fiscal outcomes in a given year. This specification ensures that the estimated coefficients reflect variation over time rather than cross-sectional differences between countries.

The fixed-effects framework is particularly appropriate for this analysis given the heterogeneity of EU Member States and the relatively short time dimension of the panel. By focusing on changes within the country, the estimation strategy mitigates bias arising

https://doi.org/10.3390/jrfm19030212

from unobserved time-invariant factors and allows for a more precise assessment of the association between demographic and policy variables and fiscal outcomes.

4.3.1. Panel Estimation Framework

To empirically assess the relationship between demographic aging, policy domains related to the silver economy and fiscal outcomes, the study employs a of linear fixed-effects panel model of the following general form.

$$Y_{it} = \alpha + \beta_1 Age65_{it} + \beta_2 SocInno_{it} + \beta_3(Age65_{it} \times SocInno_{it}) + \beta_4 X_{it} + \mu_i + \lambda_t + \varepsilon_{it}$$

where Y_{it} denotes the fiscal outcome of interest in country i and year t, μ_i, represents country fixed effects, λ_t represents year fixed effects, and ε_{it} is the idiosyncratic error term. The fixed-effects estimator accounts for unobserved heterogeneity across countries and potential omitted variables that are time invariant. All models use robust standard errors at the country level (27 clusters) to correct for autocorrelation and heteroskedasticity.

4.3.2. Model Specifications

Model 1: Pension Expenditure

Model 1 evaluates the fiscal implications of population aging using public pension expenditure as a percentage of GDP as the dependent variable. The specification includes demographic aging (share of population aged 65+), participation among older cohorts (employment rates for 55–64 and 65–74), digital inclusion, healthy life years at 65 and socioeconomic vulnerability among older individuals (AROPE 65+). Real GDP growth is included to control for macroeconomic conditions. Fixed effects by country and year are incorporated to account for time-invariant institutional factors and common temporal shocks. Standard errors are clustered at the country level.

$$Pensions_{it} = \alpha + \beta_1 Age65_{it} + \beta_2 SilverEconomy_{it} + \beta_3 X_{it} + \mu_i + \lambda_t + \varepsilon_{it}$$

Model 2: Fiscal Sustainability

Model 2 shifts the focus to aggregate fiscal sustainability by using the general government balance as a dependent variable. The explanatory variables mirror those of Model 1, allowing for direct comparison of the estimated coefficients between fiscal outcomes based on expenditures and balances. This specification allows for an assessment of whether silver economy-related factors are associated not only with expenditure dynamics but also with broader fiscal performance. Fixed effects by country and year and clustered standard errors are retained.

$$\begin{aligned} Balance_{it} = {} & \alpha + \beta_1 Age65_{it} + \beta_2 Emp55_{64_{it}} + \beta_3 Emp65_{74_{it}} + \beta_4 Digital_{it} + \beta_5 Health_{it} + \\ & \beta_6 Poverty_{it} + \beta_7 GDPgrowth_{it} + \mu_i + \lambda_t + \varepsilon_{it} \end{aligned}$$

Model 3: Interaction Models

Models 3A (pension expenditure) and 3B (fiscal balance) extend the baseline specifications by including interaction terms between demographic aging and selected indicators related to the silver economy. These interaction terms capture potential conditioning effects, testing whether the association between aging and fiscal outcomes varies systematically with the level of active aging, digital inclusion, or health capacity. The inclusion of interaction terms allows the analysis to move beyond average effects and to examine whether the policy and social innovation domains moderate the fiscal implications of demographic change.

$$Fiscal_{it} = \alpha + \beta_1 Silver_{it} + \beta_2 Age65_{it} + \beta_3(Age65_{it} \times Silver_{it}) + \beta_4 X_{it} + \mu_i + \lambda_t + \varepsilon_{it}$$

https://doi.org/10.3390/jrfm19030212

Model 4: Robustness Specification

As a robustness check, the baseline specification is re-estimated using total public expenditure on social protection as a percentage of GDP as the dependent variable. This alternative dependent variable provides a broader measure of age-related and social expenditure and allows verification of whether the main findings extend beyond pension systems. The specification retains the same set of explanatory variables, fixed effects, and clustered standard errors to ensure comparability between models.

$$SocialProtection_{it} = \alpha + \beta_1 Age65_{it} + \beta_2 Silver_{it} + \beta_3 X_{it} + \mu_i + \lambda_t + \varepsilon_{it}$$

Although the conceptual framework of the study emphasizes governance and policy capacity as important contextual factors shaping fiscal adjustment in aging societies, governance is not directly operationalized as an observable regressor in the empirical specification. Instead, the econometric analysis focuses on demographic and policy-related indicators whose relationships with fiscal outcomes can be evaluated within a fixed-effects framework.

Country fixed effects absorb time-invariant institutional differences between EU Member States, including persistent characteristics of welfare regimes, administrative capacity, and fiscal institutions. However, they do not constitute a direct empirical test of governance mechanisms. Accordingly, governance is treated in this study as a conceptual institutional context that motivates the interpretation of conditional fiscal adjustment patterns, rather than as a variable whose causal impact is estimated econometrically. Future research could investigate these mechanisms more directly by incorporating explicit governance indicators or complementary institutional analyses.

4.4. Estimation Approach and Robustness

All regressions are estimated using a fixed-effects panel estimator with country-specific intercepts and a full set of annual time dummies. The within (fixed effects) estimator is implemented in Stata 19 MP (StataCorp LLC, College Station, TX, USA) using the xtreg, fe procedure, which removes country-specific means, and thereby controls for all time-invariant characteristics of EU Member States, including institutional design, welfare regime features, and persistent structural differences.

To address potential heteroskedasticity and serial correlation within countries, standard errors are computed as cluster-robust at the country level (27 clusters). This approach allows for statistically valid inference in the presence of within-country error dependence, which is typical in macropanel datasets covering EU Member States. The inclusion of year-fixed effects further captures common shocks and EU-wide developments affecting fiscal outcomes in a given year, including major macroeconomic and policy events during the sample period.

For specifications that include interaction terms (Models 3A and 3B), conditional effects are estimated using the Stata factor variable notation. This approach ensures a consistent estimate of the main effects and interactions within a unified specification and allows the interpretation of the coefficients as conditional associations between demographic aging and fiscal outcomes at different levels of indicators related to the silver economy. Therefore, the interaction framework facilitates the evaluation of whether the fiscal implications of population aging vary systematically with the development of active aging, digital inclusion, or health capacity.

Several robustness considerations were applied to assess the stability of the empirical results. First, although the panel data set is largely complete, it remains unbalanced due to variable-specific data availability, with an average of approximately ten annual observations

https://doi.org/10.3390/jrfm19030212

per country. Sensitivity checks were carried out to verify that the main findings are not driven by individual countries or by observations at the endpoints of the sample period, where missing values are more frequent for some social indicators. The qualitative pattern of the results remains stable across specifications.

Second, standard diagnostic checks were performed to assess the potential multicollinearity among the regressors. Variance inflation factors (VIFs) were calculated and did not indicate problematic levels of collinearity. Considerations related to heteroskedasticity and serial correlation further motivated the use of robust standard errors. Alternative ways of expressing fiscal outcomes, including interpreting the general government balance in terms of deficits versus surpluses, were also considered, with no substantive change in the interpretation of results.

In general, the adopted estimation strategy and robustness procedures support the reliability of the reported panel regression findings. The results should be interpreted as conditional associations over time rather than as evidence of strict causal relationships, but provide consistent empirical insights into the fiscal implications of demographic aging and the dynamics related to the silver economy in EU Member States.

The empirical strategy is not designed to establish strict causal identification, but to evaluate whether demographic and policy variables exhibit systematic within-country associations consistent with a governance-conditioned interpretation of fiscal sustainability. Within the institutional context, where fiscal outcomes are strongly shaped by policy coordination and reform sequencing, such conditional associations provide meaningful evidence on policy-mediated adjustment dynamics even in the absence of explicit causal instruments.

The empirical strategy adopted in this study is not intended to establish strict causal identification. Instead, the fixed-effects framework is designed to capture within-country conditional associations over time, controlling for time-invariant country characteristics and common year-specific shocks. Given the relatively short time dimension of the panel and the focus on contemporaneous relationships, the empirical specification does not introduce dynamic structures such as lagged dependent variables or distributed-lag models.

It is also important to acknowledge that several variables related to the silver economy, particularly employment rates among older cohorts and indicators of digital inclusion, may be partly endogenous to policy environments and fiscal conditions. For example, improvements in digital inclusion or labor market participation at older ages may themselves reflect broader policy reforms or institutional developments that simultaneously influence fiscal outcomes. Although the inclusion of country and year fixed effects mitigates some sources of bias, it cannot fully eliminate potential reverse causality or time-varying omitted variables.

Accordingly, the estimated coefficients should be interpreted as conditional empirical associations rather than as causal effects. Future research could address these issues more directly through alternative identification strategies or by incorporating additional institutional indicators and longer time series.

5. Results

This section presents empirical results on the relationship between demographic aging, silver economy indicators, and fiscal results in the EU-27 over the period 2014–2024. The analysis is carried out sequentially. First, fixed-effects baseline models assess the association between aging and pension expenditure and fiscal balance (Models 1–2). Second, the interaction models evaluate whether these associations vary with the indicators (Model 3). Third, robustness is examined using total social protection expenditure as an alternative dependent variable (Model 4).

https://doi.org/10.3390/jrfm19030212

5.1. Population Aging and Pension Expenditure (Model 1)

Table 1 presents estimates for public pension expenditure as a percentage of GDP in EU-27 Member States over the period 2014–2024. All specifications include fixed effects for the country and year and cluster-robust standard errors at the country level (27 clusters). The estimation sample comprises 241 country-year observations. The model explains a substantial share of the variation in pension expenditure (within $R^2 = 0.5039$), and the joint significance of the regressors is confirmed by the F test (F (15,26) = 43.15, $p < 0.001$).

Table 1. Fixed-effects estimates of pension expenditure in the EU-27 (2014–2024). Dependent variable: Public pension expenditure (% of GDP). Estimator: Fixed effects (within). Standard errors: Robust clusters at the country level (27 clusters).

Variable	Coefficient	Robust SE	t-Stat	*p*-Value
Share of the population aged 65+ (age65_share)	−0.102	0.186	−0.55	0.587
Employment rate 55–64 (emp_55_64)	0.057	0.037	1.55	0.133
Employment rate 65–74 (emp_65_74)	−0.036	0.029	−1.06	0.299
Internet use 55–74 (net_use_55_74)	−0.007	0.011	−0.65	0.524
Healthy life years (hlth_hlye)	0.014	0.008	1.88	0.072 *
At-risk-of-poverty 65+ (arope_65)	0.038	0.022	1.71	0.099 *
GDP growth (gdp_growth)	−0.050	0.022	−2.28	0.028 **
Year fixed effects			Yes	
Country fixed effects			Yes	
Observations			241	
Number of countries			27	
Within R^2	0.5039, F-test (15,26) = 43.15 ($p < 0.001$)			

Notes: Cluster-robust standard errors at the country level. * $p < 0.10$, ** $p < 0.05$.

Demographic Aging

The coefficient on the share of the population aged 65 and over is negative and statistically indistinguishable from zero (β = 0.102, SE = 0.186, $p = 0.587$). The estimated magnitude is small and imprecise, and the confidence interval includes both negative and positive values. Within the fixed-effects specification, the estimates do not indicate a statistically detectable association between within-country changes in the elderly population share and pension expenditure ratios over the sample period.

Labor market participation of older cohorts

Employment rates among individuals 55–64 and 65–74 enter with negative coefficients but are not statistically significant at conventional levels. The coefficient on the employment rate for ages 55–64 is −0.057 (SE = 0.037, $p = 0.133$), while the coefficient for ages 65–74 is −0.036 (SE = 0.029, $p = 0.299$). In both cases, the confidence intervals include zero, indicating limited precision in the estimated marginal effects.

Digital Inclusion

The coefficient on Internet use among individuals 55–74 years is negative and statistically non-significant (β = −0.007, SE = 0.011, $p = 0.524$). The estimated magnitude is close to zero and the confidence interval spans both negative and positive values.

Health capacity and socioeconomic vulnerability

The years of healthy life at 65 years of age enter with a positive coefficient that is marginally significant at the 10% level (β = 0.014, SE = 0.008, $p = 0.072$). The rate of poverty or social exclusion at risk among 65 year olds and over is also positive and marginally

https://doi.org/10.3390/jrfm19030212

significant at the 10% level (β = 0.038, SE = 0.022, $p = 0.099$). Both estimates are moderate in magnitude and are not accurately estimated.

Macroeconomic Conditions

The real GDP growth is negative and statistically significant at the 5% level (β = −0.050, SE = 0.022, $p = 0.028$). Higher economic growth is associated with lower pension expenditure as a share of GDP within countries over time.

Time effects

Fixed effects capture common temporal dynamics in pension expenditure ratios across EU Member States. Positive coefficients are observed for the pandemic period, particularly for 2020 and 2021, indicating an upward shift in pension expenditure ratios relative to the omitted base year. The inclusion of year-fixed effects ensures that common shocks are absorbed in the estimation of within-country relationships.

Figure 2 shows the predicted values of pension expenditure in the observed range of the population 65 and older, based on the fixed-effects specification of fixed effects and the control variables in the sample means. The confidence intervals remain wide throughout the range of the demographic variable, consistent with the statistically non-significant coefficient reported in Table 1.

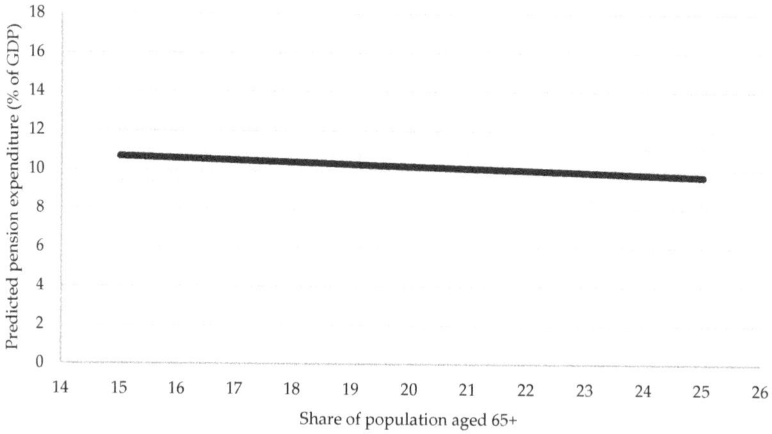

Figure 2. Predicted pension expenditure over the observed range of the population aged 65+, with 95% confidence bands. Source: Author's own elaboration.

5.2. *Fiscal Sustainability: General Government Balance (Model 2)*

Table 2 reports estimates for fiscal sustainability measured by the balance of the general government balance as a percentage of GDP in the 27 Member States of the EU during the period 2014–2024. All specifications include fixed effects for the country and year and cluster-robust standard errors at the country level (27 clusters). The estimation sample consists of 241 country-year observations. The model explains a substantial share of variation in fiscal balance (within $R^2 = 0.693$), and the joint significance of the regressors is confirmed by the F test ($F(15,26) = 60.42$, $p < 0.001$).

Demographic Aging

The coefficient in the 65- and over-age share is positive and statistically significant at the 5% level (β = 1.282, SE = 0.475, $p = 0.012$). The magnitude indicates a measurable association between changes in the share of the elderly population and the balance of the

https://doi.org/10.3390/jrfm19030212

general government balance over the sample period. The confidence interval excludes zero and remains positive throughout its range.

Table 2. Fixed-effects estimates of fiscal balance in the EU-27 (2014–2024). Dependent variable: General government balance (% of GDP). Estimator: Fixed effects (within). Standard errors: Robust clusters at the country level (27 clusters).

Variable	Coefficient	Robust SE	t-Stat	*p*-Value
Share of the population aged 65+ (age65_share)	1.282	0.475	2.70	0.012
Employment rate 55–64 (emp_55_64)	−0.101	0.117	−0.86	0.397
Employment rate 65–74 (emp_65_74)	0.114	0.076	1.49	0.147
Internet use 55–74 (net_use_55_74)	−0.061	0.038	−1.62	0.118
Healthy life years (hlth_hlye)	0.078	0.207	0.38	0.709
At-risk-of-poverty 65+ (arope_65)	0.019	0.035	0.55	0.590
GDP growth (gdp_growth)	0.031	0.060	0.51	0.616
Year fixed effects			Yes	
Country fixed effects			Yes	
Observations			241	
Number of countries			27	
Within R^2	0.693, F-test (15,26) = 60.42 ($p < 0.001$)			

Notes: Cluster-robust standard errors at the country level. * $p < 0.10$, ** $p < 0.05$.

Labor market participation of older cohorts

Employment rates among 55–64 and 65–74 are not statistically significant at conventional levels. The employment rate for the 55–64 age group 55–64 is −0.101 (SE = 0.117, $p = 0.397$), while the age group coefficient for the 65–74 age group is 0.114 (SE = 0.076, $p = 0.147$). In both cases, the confidence intervals include zero, indicating limited precision in the estimated marginal effects.

Digital Inclusion

The coefficient of Internet use among individuals 55–74 is negative and is not statistically significant at conventional levels ($\beta = -0.061$, SE = 0.038, $p = 0.118$). The confidence interval includes zero, and the magnitude remains moderate.

Health capacity and socioeconomic vulnerability

Healthy life years at 65 years of age and those at risk of poverty or social exclusion among individuals 65 years and older do not display statistically significant coefficients in this specification. The estimated coefficient for healthy years of life is 0.078 (SE = 0.207, $p = 0.709$), while the coefficient for the AROPE 65+ variable is 0.019 (SE = 0.035, $p = 0.590$). Both estimates are imprecise and cannot be distinguished from zero at conventional significance levels.

Macroeconomic Conditions

The real GDP growth is entered with a positive but statistically non-significant coefficient ($\beta = 0.031$, SE = 0.060, $p = 0.616$). The estimated confidence interval includes zero.

Time effects

Fixed effects capture common temporal variation in fiscal balances across EU Member States. Positive coefficients are observed for several pre-pandemic years relative to the omitted base year, whereas the pandemic period exhibits pronounced negative coefficients. In particular, the coefficients for 2020 and 2021 are negative and statistically significant, indicating a marked shift in fiscal balances during these years. The inclusion

https://doi.org/10.3390/jrfm19030212

of year-fixed effects ensures that these common shocks are absorbed in the estimation of within-country relationships.

Figure 3 presents the predicted values of the general government balance in the observed range of the population 65 and older, based on the specification and the control variables in the sample means. The predicted profile follows the positive association reported in Table 2, with confidence bands reflecting the uncertainty of the estimation.

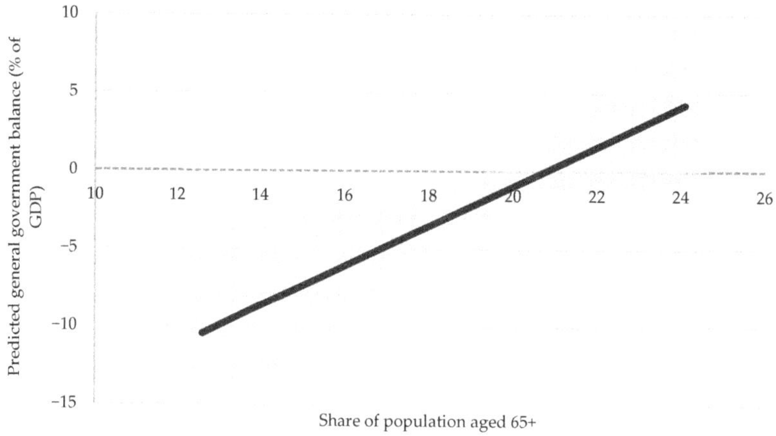

Figure 3. Predicted general government balance (% of GDP) over the observed range of the 65+ population share, based on Model 2, with 95% confidence bands. Source: Author's own elaboration.

5.3. Interaction Models: Conditional Effects of Aging (Models 3A–3B)

Table 3 reports two-way fixed-effect interaction models examining whether the association between demographic aging and fiscal outcomes varies with selected silver economy indicators. Both specifications include fixed effects for the country and year and cluster-robust standard errors at the country level (27 clusters). Model 3A uses public pension expenditure (% of GDP) as the dependent variable, while Model 3B uses the general government balance (% of GDP). The interaction structure is identical across models, allowing for direct comparison of conditional relationships across fiscal outcomes.

Table 3. Interaction Models of Aging and Silver Economy Channels. Model (3A): Pension expenditure (% of GDP). Model (3B): General government balance (% of GDP). Estimator: Fixed effects (within). Standard errors: Cluster robust at country level.

Variable	(3A) Pension Expenditure	(3B) Fiscal Balance
Share of the population aged 65+ (age65_share)	−0.103 (0.358)	0.750 (0.885)
Employment rate 55–64 (emp_55_64)	0.018 (0.116)	−0.668 (0.373)
Internet use 55–74 (net_use_55_74)	−0.076 * (0.044)	0.292 * (0.152)
Age65 × Emp55–64	−0.004 (0.006)	0.030 (0.020)
Age65 × NetUse55–74	0.004 (0.003)	**−0.020** (0.009)
Employment rate 65–74 (emp_65_74)	−0.021 (0.028)	0.053 (0.077)
Healthy life years (hlth_hlye)	0.057 (0.046)	0.200 (0.195)
At-risk-of-poverty 65+ (arope_65)	−0.038 * (0.022)	0.023 (0.041)
GDP growth (gdp_growth)	**−0.055** (0.019)	0.052 (0.052)
Constant	16.56 ** (5.65)	−8.32 (15.44)
Year fixed effects	Yes	Yes
Country fixed effects	Yes	Yes

https://doi.org/10.3390/jrfm19030212

Table 3. *Cont.*

Variable	(3A) Pension Expenditure	(3B) Fiscal Balance
Observations	241	241
Number of countries	27	27
Within R^2	0.515	0.706
F-test	60.47 ***	62.17 ***

Notes: Cluster-robust standard errors in parentheses. * $p < 0.10$, ** $p < 0.05$, *** $p < 0.01$. Interaction terms of primary interest are shown in bold.

5.3.1. Model 3A: Pension Expenditure

In Model 3A, the interaction between the share of the population and the employment rate for individuals aged 55–64 is not statistically significant (β = −0.004, SE = 0.006, $p > 0.10$). The estimated coefficient is small in magnitude, and the confidence interval includes zero.

The interaction between demographic aging and internet use among individuals aged 55–74 years is positive, but not statistically significant at conventional levels (β = 0.004, SE = 0.003, $p > 0.10$). The confidence interval includes zero, indicating limited precision in the estimated conditional effect.

Among the main effects, the use among the older cohorts is negative and marginally significant (β = −0.076, SE = 0.044, $p < 0.10$). The at-risk rate of poverty or social exclusion among 65- and over-aged individuals is also negative and marginally significant (β = −0.038, SE = 0.022, $p < 0.10$). The real GDP growth remains negative and statistically significant at conventional levels (β = 0.055, SE = 0.019, $p < 0.05$).

Other covariates, including the employment rate for individuals aged 65–74 years and healthy life years at age 65, do not show statistically significant coefficients. The coefficient on the share of the population aged 65 and over remains statistically non-significant in the interaction specification.

Figure 4 presents the predicted values of pension expenditure in the observed range of the population aged 65 and over at different levels of employment between people aged 55–64. The predicted profiles remain broadly similar across the range of the moderating variable, consistent with the non-significant interaction coefficients.

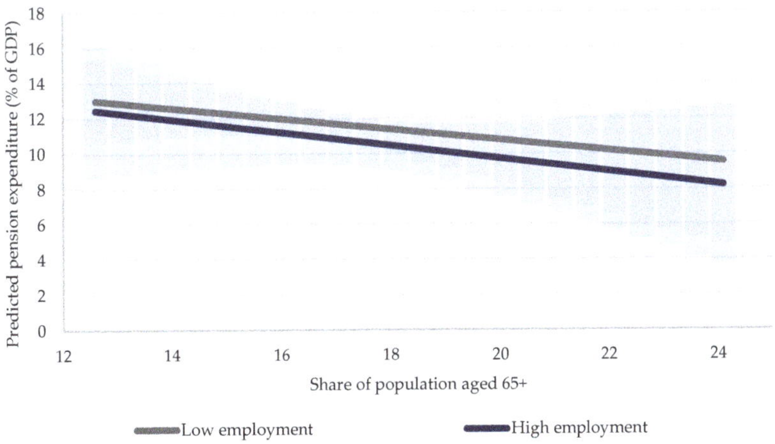

Figure 4. Interaction between Population Aging and Older Age Employment. Note: Predicted pension expenditure (% of GDP) in the observed range of population aging for low (50%) and high (67%) employment rates among individuals aged 55–64 years. Shaded areas denote 95% confidence intervals. Source: Author's own elaboration.

https://doi.org/10.3390/jrfm19030212

5.3.2. Model 3B: Fiscal Balance

Model 3B reports interaction estimates for the general government balance. The interaction between demographic aging and the employment rate for 55–64 year olds is positive but not statistically significant (β = 0.030, SE = 0.020, $p > 0.10$). The confidence interval includes zero.

The interaction between demographic aging and internet use among individuals aged 55–74 years is negative and statistically significant at the 5% level (β = −0.020, SE = 0.009, $p < 0.05$). The estimated coefficient indicates that the marginal association between aging and fiscal balance varies with the level of digital inclusion among older cohorts within countries over time. This interaction should be interpreted cautiously. The estimated coefficient indicates that the marginal association between demographic aging and fiscal balance differs depending on the level of digital inclusion among older cohorts. However, the result reflects conditional correlations within the fixed-effects framework rather than a causal mechanism linking digitalization and fiscal outcomes.

The main effects of employment rates and digital inclusion are not statistically significant at conventional levels in this specification. The coefficients on healthy life years, elderly poverty risk, and GDP growth are also not statistically distinguishable from zero. The coefficient on the share of the population aged 65 and over remains positive, but becomes statistically non-significant once interaction terms are included.

In interaction models, the coefficient on the interaction term represents how the marginal effect of demographic aging on fiscal balance changes with the level of digital inclusion. Accordingly, the predicted profiles reported in Figure 5 illustrate the estimated association between aging and fiscal balance evaluated at different levels of Internet use among individuals aged 55–74.

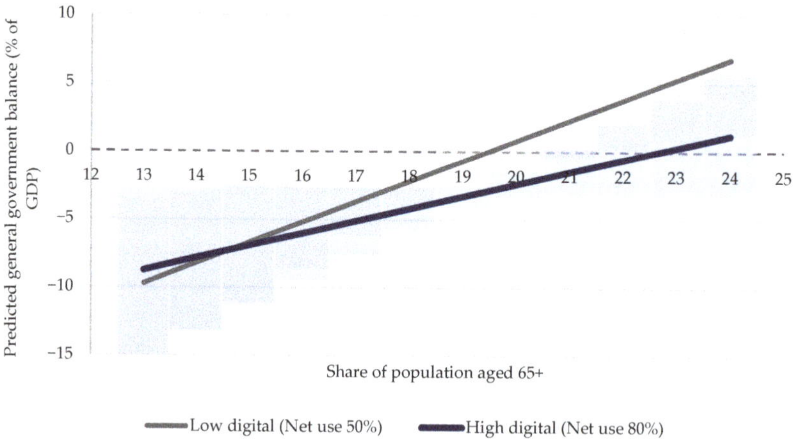

Figure 5. Predicted general government balance (% of GDP) by population aging at low and high levels of digital inclusion. Note: Figure reports predicted general government balance as a function of population aging, evaluated at low (50%) and high (80%) levels of digital inclusion among people aged 55–74 years, with shaded areas denoting 95% confidence intervals. Source: Author's own elaboration.

Figure 5 presents the balance of the predicted values of the general government in the observed range of the population 65 years and older at different levels of digital inclusion among 55–74 year olds. The predicted profiles differ between the levels of the moderating variable, consistent with the statistically significant interaction term reported in Table 3.

https://doi.org/10.3390/jrfm19030212

Given that several interaction relationships are explored in the empirical specification, the statistically significant interaction identified in this model should be interpreted as indicative rather than definitive evidence of conditional fiscal dynamics.

5.4. Social Protection Expenditures (Model 4)

Table 4 reports estimates of two-way fixed effects for total social protection expenditures as a percentage of GDP across the EU-27 Member States over the period 2014–2024. All specifications include fixed effects for the country and year and cluster-robust standard errors at the country level (27 clusters). The estimation sample comprises 241 country-year observations. The model explains a substantial share of the variation in social protection expenditure (within $R^2 = 0.608$), and the joint significance of the regressors is confirmed by the F test ($F(15,26) = 29.86$, $p < 0.001$).

Table 4. Fixed-effects estimates of social protection expenditure in the EU-27 (2014–2024). Dependent variable: Social protection expenditures (% of GDP). Estimator: Fixed effects (within). Standard errors: Robust clusters at the country level (27 clusters).

Variable	Coefficient	Robust SE	t-Stat	*p*-Value
Share of the population aged 65+ (age65_share)	0.075	0.319	0.24	0.816
Employment rate 55–64 (emp_55_64)	−0.088	0.070	−1.26	0.218
Employment rate 65–74 (emp_65_74)	−0.016	0.074	−0.22	0.831
Internet use 55–74 (net_use_55_74)	0.030	0.026	1.17	0.254
Healthy life years (hlth_hlye)	0.139	0.107	1.29	0.208
At-risk-of-poverty 65+ (arope_65)	−0.038	0.032	−1.20	0.242
GDP growth (gdp_growth)	−0.071	0.044	−1.63	0.116
Year fixed effects			Yes	
Country fixed effects			Yes	
Observations			241	
Number of countries			27	
Within R^2	0.608, F-test (15,26) = 29.86 ($p < 0.001$)			

Notes: Cluster-robust standard errors at the country level. * $p < 0.10$, ** $p < 0.05$.

Demographic Aging

The coefficient on the share of the population aged 65 and over is positive, but statistically indistinguishable from zero ($\beta = 0.075$, SE = 0.319, $p = 0.816$). The estimated magnitude is small and imprecise, and the confidence interval includes both negative and positive values.

Labor market participation of older cohorts and digital inclusion

Employment rates among individuals 55–64 and 65–74 do not show statistically significant coefficients in this specification. The coefficient for 55–64 is −0.088 (SE = 0.070, $p = 0.218$), while the coefficient for ages 65–74 years is −0.016 (SE = 0.074, $p = 0.831$).

The coefficient of Internet use among individuals aged 55–74 is positive but not statistically significant ($\beta = 0.030$, SE = 0.026, $p = 0.254$). All confidence intervals include zero, indicating limited precision in the estimated marginal effects.

Health capacity and socioeconomic vulnerability

Healthy life years at 65 years and the rate of at risk of poverty or social exclusion among people 65 and over are not statistically significant. The estimated coefficient for healthy years of life is 0.139 (SE = 0.107, $p = 0.208$), while the coefficient for AROPE 65+ is −0.038 (SE = 0.032, $p = 0.242$).

Macroeconomic Conditions

The real GDP growth is entered with a negative coefficient that does not reach conventional significance levels (β = 0.071, SE = 0.044, $p = 0.116$). The confidence interval includes zero.

Time effects

Fixed effects capture common temporal dynamics in social protection expenditures across EU Member States. Positive and statistically significant coefficients are observed for the pandemic period, particularly for 2020 and 2021, indicating an upward shift in social protection expenditure ratios relative to the omitted base year. The inclusion of year-fixed effects ensures that these common shocks are absorbed in the estimation of within-country relationships.

Figure 6 presents the predicted values of social protection expenditures in the observed range of the population 65 years and older, based on the specification of fixed effects of the fixed effects and the control variables in the sample means. The predicted profile remains relatively flat across the demographic range, with wide confidence intervals consistent with the statistically non-significant coefficient reported in Table 4.

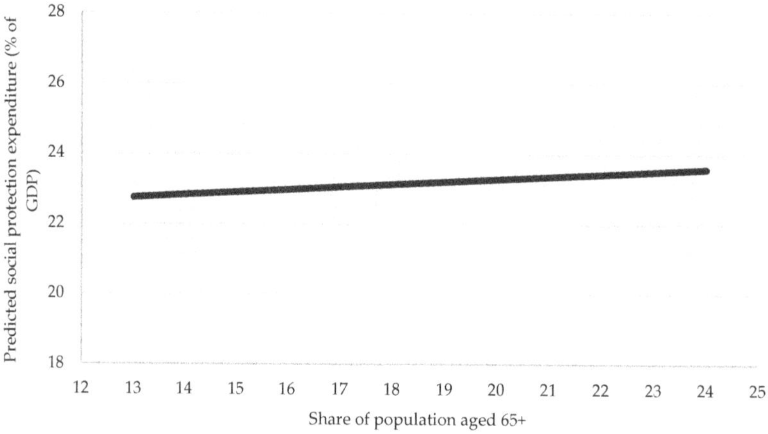

Figure 6. Predicted social protection expenditure (% of GDP) in the observed range of the 65+ population share, based on Model 4, with 95% confidence bands. Note: The figure shows predicted social protection expenditures as a share of GDP across the values of population aging, with shaded areas representing 95% confidence intervals based on fixed-effects estimates. Source: Author's own elaboration.

6. Discussion

Although governance quality and policy capacity are not directly modeled as observable variables in the empirical specifications, they emerge as central conditioning factors shaping the relationships identified in the analysis. Fixed-effects results indicate that demographic aging does not translate mechanically into fiscal deterioration across EU Member States. Instead, the fiscal implications of aging appear to be mediated by institutional adaptation, administrative capacity, and the broader policy environment within which domains related to the silver economy operate.

This section synthesizes the empirical results for the EU-27 over 2014–2024 and interprets them within the study's conditional institutional framework. While the empirical analysis focuses on demographic and policy-related indicators, the discussion situates the results within the broader institutional context in which fiscal adjustment under demo-

https://doi.org/10.3390/jrfm19030212

graphic aging takes place. The discussion highlights two empirical takeaways: (1) demographic aging is not systematically associated with pension or social protection expenditure ratios once country heterogeneity and common year shocks are controlled; and (2) aging is positively associated with the general government balance in the baseline specification, while the interaction evidence suggests that this association varies with digital inclusion among older cohorts. Throughout, the results are interpreted as within-country conditional patterns rather than causal estimates.

6.1. *Reassessing the Demographic–Fiscal Nexus*

A central result of the empirical analysis is the absence of a statistically significant within-country relationship between the share of the population aged 65+ and either pension expenditure or total social protection expenditure. Once time-invariant institutional characteristics and common shocks are controlled, demographic aging does not exhibit a systematic direct association with these expenditure ratios.

This pattern does not imply that aging is fiscally neutral. Rather, it is consistent with the view that age-related expenditure ratios in the short-to-medium run are shaped by institutional design and policy adjustment. Over 2014–2024, EU Member States implemented or operated within established pension-reform trajectories (e.g., parametric adjustments and statutory age increases), which can weaken the contemporaneous link between demographic structure and expenditure outcomes in within-country estimates. Accordingly, the results are more consistent with conditional, policy-mediated adjustment than with a mechanical demographic–expenditure relationship.

6.2. *Aging and Fiscal Sustainability: Adjustment Dynamics*

The positive association between population aging and the general government balance identified in Model 2 is consistent with the non-mechanical character of the demographic–fiscal relationship. Within-country estimates indicate that increases in the share of the population aged 65+ coincide with improvements in the fiscal balance after controlling for time-invariant institutional characteristics and common shocks.

This pattern may reflect that demographic change is closely related to the dynamics of fiscal adjustment. Rather than operating solely as a direct expenditure pressure, aging appears to be associated with policy responses that affect aggregate fiscal outcomes. Governments facing rising old-age dependency ratios have implemented a combination of expenditure reforms, entitlement adjustments, and fiscal consolidation measures, often within the framework of EU fiscal governance.

Accordingly, the observed association is best interpreted as reflecting the interaction between demographic pressures and policy responses, rather than a direct fiscal benefit of aging. Fiscal sustainability emerges not as a mechanical function of the age structure, but as an outcome shaped by institutional adaptation and policy capacity. This distinction clarifies the relationship between demographic trends and fiscal performance and highlights the importance of policy-mediated adjustment processes.

6.3. *The Silver Economy as a Conditioning Mechanism*

The empirical results also provide a more differentiated view of the fiscal role of the silver economy. The indicators of active aging, employment in older age, and digital inclusion do not show robust standalone effects on fiscal outcomes in the baseline models. This suggests that silver economy variables do not operate as independent drivers of fiscal performance within the fixed-effects framework.

However, the results of the interaction indicate that digital inclusion among older cohorts conditions the relationship between demographic aging and the general government balance. The statistically significant interaction identified in Model 3B implies that the fiscal

https://doi.org/10.3390/jrfm19030212

association of aging varies systematically with the level of digital inclusion. This finding points to the relevance of social innovation and technological adoption as contextual factors shaping the dynamics of fiscal adjustment.

The absence of comparable interaction effects for pension expenditure highlights the institutional specificity of pension systems. Pension expenditures are largely determined by formal eligibility rules, benefit formulas, and indexation mechanisms, which are less sensitive to short- and medium-term variation in social innovation indicators. In contrast, aggregate fiscal outcomes remain more responsive to broader policy and institutional adjustments.

These findings position the silver economy as a conditioning domain whose fiscal relevance depends on the institutional and policy context in which it operates. Its effects are not captured by isolated marginal coefficients but emerge through interactions with demographic and policy dynamics.

6.4. Governance and Policy Capacity as Mediating Conditions

Although governance quality and policy capacity are not directly included as observable variables in empirical models, the results point to their implicit mediating role. Similar demographic trajectories are associated with different fiscal outcomes across EU Member States, indicating that institutional and administrative factors shape how demographic pressures translate into fiscal performance.

Policy capacity can be understood as the ability of public administrations to anticipate demographic change, design coherent reform packages, and implement adjustments in multiple policy domains. Differences in reform sequencing, administrative coordination, and implementation effectiveness help explain why aging does not produce uniform fiscal outcomes across countries.

This interpretation aligns with the broader comparative literature on welfare state adaptation and fiscal governance. It suggests that demographic change operates within an institutional context in which governance quality influences the translation of structural pressures into fiscal outcomes. Fiscal sustainability under aging therefore reflects not only demographic trends, but also the capacity of public institutions to respond to them effectively.

6.5. Policy Implications: From Demographic Determinism to Governance-Centered Strategies

The findings have several implications for fiscal policy in aging societies. First, they caution against deterministic narratives that portray demographic aging as an automatic driver of fiscal deterioration. Empirical results indicate that fiscal outcomes under aging are contingent on institutional and policy responses rather than mechanically determined by demographic structure.

Second, the results highlight the importance of governance and policy capacity in shaping fiscal resilience. The ability to coordinate pension reform, participation in the labor market at older ages, and digital inclusion strategies appear to be central to managing demographic pressures within sustainable fiscal frameworks.

Third, the silver economy emerges as a conditional domain whose fiscal relevance depends on its integration into broader policy strategies. Measures that support active aging, digital inclusion, and participation in the labor market among older cohorts can contribute to fiscal sustainability when embedded in coherent institutional and policy frameworks. These considerations are particularly relevant for Member States facing rapid demographic aging and constrained fiscal space, where institutional capacity may play a decisive role in shaping fiscal adjustment paths.

https://doi.org/10.3390/jrfm19030212

6.6. An Empirically Informed Governance-Centered Framework

Based on empirical evidence from Models 1–4, the analysis supports a governance-centered interpretation of the relationship between demographic aging and fiscal sustainability. The results indicate that demographic change does not exert a uniform or mechanical effect on public finances in EU Member States. Instead, the fiscal results reflect the interaction between demographic pressures, institutional structures, and policy responses over time.

Empirical findings show that increases in the share of the population aged 65+ are not associated with systematic within-country growth in pension or total social protection expenditure once institutional heterogeneity and common shocks are controlled. At the same time, the positive association between aging and general government balance suggests that demographic pressures are closely related to fiscal adjustment dynamics rather than to automatic fiscal deterioration. Together, these results indicate that demographic change operates through institutional and policy channels rather than as a direct fiscal driver.

Figure 7 synthesizes this interpretation by positioning administrative and policy capacity as a central coordinating element through which demographic aging affects fiscal outcomes. Pension expenditure is characterized as institutionally restricted, reflecting the role of formal entitlement rules and indexation mechanisms. Aggregate fiscal outcomes, particularly the general government balance, appear more adaptive and responsive to policy adjustments and administrative coordination.

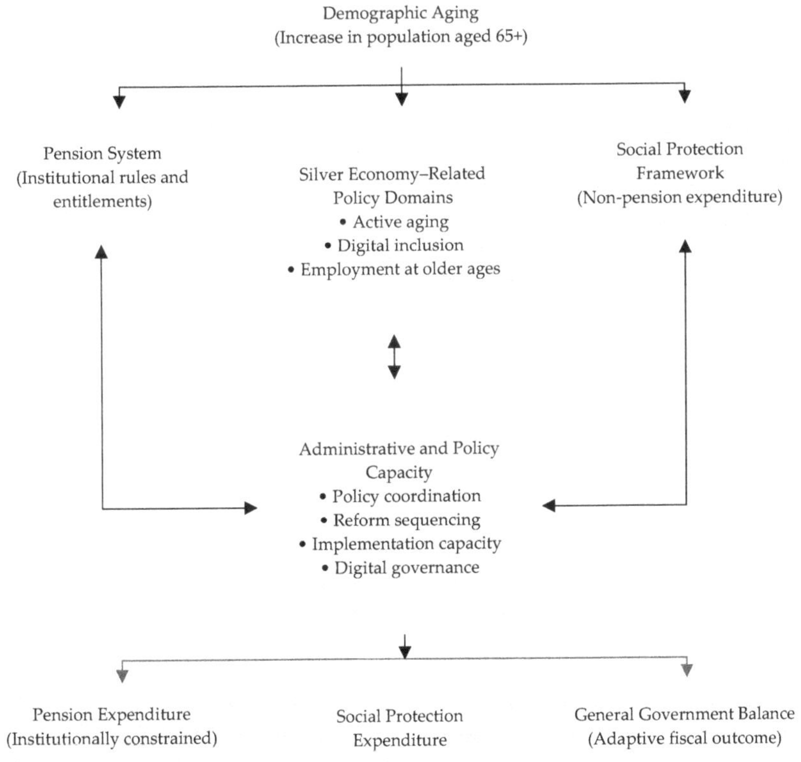

Figure 7. An empirically informed governance-centered conceptual framework. Source: Author's own elaboration.

https://doi.org/10.3390/jrfm19030212

Within this framework, silver economy-related domains, such as active aging, digital inclusion, and employment at older ages, are conceptualized as conditioning channels rather than autonomous fiscal drivers. Their relevance emerges through interaction with institutional settings and policy strategies, rather than through direct marginal effects. Differences in policy coordination, implementation capacity, and reform sequencing help explain why similar demographic trends are associated with divergent fiscal outcomes between countries.

By distinguishing between institutionally constrained expenditure components and adaptive fiscal aggregates, the framework reconciles the absence of a direct aging effect on pension and social protection expenditures with the observed association between aging and fiscal balance. Fiscal sustainability under demographic change thus emerges as an outcome shaped by governance capacity and policy adaptation, with the silver economy representing a context-dependent component of this broader adjustment process.

6.7. Limitations and Scope of the Analysis

Several limitations of the present analysis should be acknowledged. First, the empirical results are based on associations and are not intended to establish strict causal identification. The objective of the empirical design is interpretive and comparative, focusing on conditional relationships rather than on causal estimation of policy effects.

Second, governance and policy capacity are conceptualized as underlying institutional conditions shaping fiscal outcomes rather than as directly observable variables included in econometric models. This approach reflects the multidimensional nature of governance capacity and its indirect manifestation through policy coordination, reform trajectories, and administrative effectiveness across EU Member States.

Third, the time horizon of the analysis (2014–2024) captures short- to medium-term fiscal adjustment dynamics in the context of demographic change but does not fully address long-term demographic fiscal projections. Fiscal sustainability under population aging remains inherently a long-term issue that extends beyond the temporal scope of the present panel data set.

These limitations do not weaken the analytical contribution of the study; rather, they clarify its interpretive scope and reinforce the central argument advanced throughout the article. Empirical evidence consistently indicates that fiscal outcomes under demographic aging in the European Union cannot be adequately understood through deterministic demographic mechanisms alone. Instead, they are more convincingly interpreted as policy-mediated and institutionally conditioned processes shaped by reform trajectories, administrative coordination, and the broader governance environment within which demographic change unfolds. By situating demographic pressures within this governance-conditioned framework, the analysis highlights the central role of institutional adaptation in shaping observable fiscal dynamics across EU Member States and challenges simplified narratives of automatic demographic fiscal deterioration.

More broadly, the findings support a re-evaluation of demographic change in advanced welfare states and its implications for fiscal sustainability. Rather than treating population aging primarily as an exogenous fiscal shock, the results underscore the extent to which fiscal trajectories in aging societies reflect institutional resilience, policy sequencing, and governance capacity. Fiscal sustainability under demographic aging therefore appears less a function of the demographic structure itself than of the ability of public institutions to anticipate, coordinate, and implement adaptive policy responses over time. This perspective aligns with contemporary research in comparative political economy and public finance that emphasizes policy-mediated adjustment and institutional adaptation as central determinants of fiscal outcomes in aging European economies.

https://doi.org/10.3390/jrfm19030212

It is important to note that governance is not directly estimated in the empirical specification. Instead, the governance perspective adopted in this study provides a conceptual framework for interpreting heterogeneous fiscal adjustment patterns observed across EU Member States. The empirical analysis identifies conditional relationships between demographic aging, policy-related indicators, and fiscal outcomes, while the governance dimension helps contextualize these patterns within broader institutional environments.

7. Conclusions

The objective of this article is to examine whether the fiscal implications of demographic aging in the European Union are mechanically determined or conditioned by the policy context and institutional capacity. Using panel data for the EU-27 during the period 2014–2024 and fixed-effects regression models, the analysis evaluated the relationship between demographic aging, silver economy-related policy domains, and key fiscal outcomes, including pension expenditure, social protection spending, and general government balance.

Empirical results provide little support for deterministic interpretations of the aging–fiscal nexus. Within-country estimates indicate that demographic aging does not exhibit a statistically significant direct association with pension or total social protection expenditure once time-invariant institutional characteristics and common shocks are controlled. These findings suggest that age-related expenditure dynamics in contemporary European welfare states are shaped primarily by institutional design and policy adjustments rather than by demographic structure alone.

At the same time, the analysis identifies a positive association between demographic aging and the general government balance. This pattern indicates the presence of policy-mediated fiscal adjustment dynamics, indicating that demographic pressures are accompanied by institutional and fiscal responses that influence aggregate fiscal outcomes. Rather than reflecting an automatic fiscal benefit of aging, the observed relationship highlights the role of reform trajectories, fiscal governance frameworks, and administrative capacity in shaping fiscal sustainability under demographic change.

The results also refine the fiscal interpretation of the silver economy. Indicators of employment at older ages, digital inclusion, and related policy domains do not display robust standalone associations with fiscal outcomes in the baseline models. Their relevance emerges primarily through interaction effects, particularly in the case of digital inclusion, which conditions the relationship between demographic aging and fiscal balance. These findings suggest that silver economy-related policies function less as autonomous fiscal instruments and more as contextual factors shaping how demographic pressures interact with fiscal systems.

The findings support a governance-centered interpretation of fiscal sustainability in aging societies. Demographic change constitutes a structural background condition for fiscal policy, but its observable fiscal implications depend on the capacity of public institutions to anticipate, coordinate, and implement policy responses in multiple domains. Fiscal sustainability under demographic aging, therefore, may reflect a policy-mediated outcome shaped by institutional adaptation and administrative capacity rather than by demographic structure alone.

Several limitations should be acknowledged. The analysis focuses on within-country dynamics over a relatively short time horizon and does not directly measure governance quality or policy capacity as observable variables. Instead, governance is treated as an underlying conditioning factor reflected in observed fiscal and policy dynamics. Future research could extend this approach by incorporating explicit governance indicators, longer time series, or alternative identification strategies to further examine the institutional mediation of demographic–fiscal relationships.

https://doi.org/10.3390/jrfm19030212

Despite these limitations, the study contributes to ongoing debates on public finance adaptation in aging societies by providing up-to-date panel evidence for the EU-27 and by integrating demographic change, silver economy dynamics, and governance capacity within a unified empirical framework. The findings underscore that fiscal sustainability under demographic aging depends not only on demographic trends themselves, but also on the institutional and policy capacity of states to manage structural transformation. In this sense, demographic aging should be interpreted less as a deterministic fiscal threat and more as a policy-conditioned structural transformation that requires coordinated institutional adaptation.

An important avenue for future research concerns the explicit empirical examination of governance and institutional capacity. While the present study interprets the results within a governance-conditioned conceptual framework, future analyses could incorporate observable indicators of fiscal institutions, government effectiveness, or administrative capacity in order to examine these mechanisms more directly. Such extensions would allow a more explicit empirical assessment of how governance structures shape fiscal adjustment dynamics in aging societies.

Funding: This article presents results from the project No. КП-06-ПН85/17 "Research and assessment of the capacity of the state administration in Bulgaria and guidelines for good governance", funded by the Bulgarian National Science Fund. Comparative evidence contributes to the project by highlighting the role of governance and policy capacity in managing demographic and fiscal risks.

Institutional Review Board Statement: Not applicable.

Informed Consent Statement: Not applicable.

Data Availability Statement: Data used in this study are publicly available from official international databases, including Eurostat, the European Commission (AMECO), the OECD, and the World Bank. All data supporting the reported results can be accessed directly from these sources. No new primary data were created in this study.

Acknowledgments: The author expresses sincere gratitude to Eugenia Penkova-Pantaleeva for her creative insights and the enthusiasm with which she has encouraged the author to engage with research questions that remain underexplored in Bulgarian academic practice and theory. Her intellectual support and motivation have been invaluable in shaping the broader conceptual orientation of this study. During the preparation of this study, the author used ChatGPT (OpenAI, San Francisco, CA, USA; GPT-5.3) for language editing and stylistic refinement, since English is not the author's native language, and to verify the syntax and logical consistency of the Stata commands used in the empirical analysis. The author reviewed and edited all AI-assisted output and assumes full responsibility for the content of this publication.

Conflicts of Interest: The author declares no conflicts of interest.

Appendix A

Table A1. Summary of variables: definitions, sources, and expected effects.

Variable	Description and Measurement	Source	Expected Effect (Hypothesis)
Public Pension Expenditure (% of GDP)	Dependent variable (Model 1). General government expenditure on pensions for old age and survivors, expressed as a percentage of GDP. Reflects the age-related pension burden on public finances.	Eurostat (ESSPROS/COFOG; national accounts)	+ (Aging of the larger population leads to higher pension spending—H_1).

https://doi.org/10.3390/jrfm19030212

Table A1. *Cont.*

Variable	Description and Measurement	Source	Expected Effect (Hypothesis)
Budget Balance (Deficit) (% of GDP)	Dependent variable (Model 2). Net lending from the general government (+)/borrowing (−) as % of GDP (negative values indicate fiscal deficits). Measures overall fiscal balance or sustainability.	Eurostat (AMECO; ESA 2010 gov. finance)	− (Population aging worsens fiscal balance, i.e., larger deficits—H_1).
Social Protection Expenditure (% of GDP)	Dependent variable (Model 4). Total public social protection outlays (all functions: pensions, health care, disability, etc.) as % of GDP, based on COFOG classification. Indicates a broad level of welfare expenditure.	Eurostat (COFOG; national budgets)	+ (Population aging increases overall social spending—aligned with H_1).
Population Age 65+ (% of total population)	Share of the population aged 65 years and older. Key demographic aging indicator, rising over time (EU average 21% in 2024). Higher values indicate greater aging pressure.	Eurostat (demo_pjan)	+ on spending; − on fiscal balance; (Aging raises expenditure needs and strains budgets—H_1).
Employment Rate 55–64 (%)	Employment rate of persons 55–64 (percentage of that age group in employment). Captures active aging through late-career labor participation (preretirement).	Eurostat (LFS)	− (An older employment is expected to reduce pension spending and improve fiscal balance by reducing early retirements—H_2).
Employment Rate 65–74 (%)	Employment rate of persons 65–74 years of age. Measures postretirement employment/engagement in the workforce. Typically, much lower than the 55–64 rate, but indicative of silver economy activity (e.g., part-time work, encore careers).	Eurostat (LFS)	− (Similarly, more people working past 65 should alleviate pension and social transfer pressures—H_2).
Internet Use by Seniors (55–74) (%)	Percentage of people aged 55–74 who have used the internet in the last 12 months. Proxy of digital inclusion and tech adoption among older adults, reflecting the development of the silver economy and e-participation.	Eurostat (ICT usage survey)	− (A greater digital inclusion is hypothesized to reduce age-related costs and improve fiscal sustainability via efficiency gains—H_3).
Healthy Life Years at 65 (years)	Number of years that a person at 65 is expected to live in good health (disability-free life expectancy). Indicates health quality of the elderly (i.e., "healthy aging"). Higher values may enable longer working lives and lower care needs.	Eurostat (EHLEIS; EU-SILC)	− (Healthier aging is expected to ease pressure on pension/health systems and improve fiscal outcomes by enabling active aging—expected negative effect).

https://doi.org/10.3390/jrfm19030212

Table A1. *Cont.*

Variable	Description and Measurement	Source	Expected Effect (Hypothesis)
AROPE 65+ (% of 65+ population)	At-risk-of-poverty or social exclusion rate for people aged 65 years or older. Definition as the share of elderly people who face income poverty, severe material deprivation, or very low intensity of work in the household. Signals the adequacy of pensions and social support for the elderly.	Eurostat (EU-SILC)	– (Inversely related to generosity of pension systems: higher elderly poverty tends to coincide with lower social spending; included as a control, without strong prior hypothesis).
GDP Growth (% annual)	Annual growth rate of real GDP. Controls for macroeconomic conditions (business cycle effects on budgets and spending ratios). Positive growth improves revenues and denominators, while recessions worsen deficits.	World Bank; AMECO	– (Higher growth is associated with lower social spending ratios and smaller deficits, whereas low or negative growth has the opposite effect).

References

Auerbach, A. J., & Gorodnichenko, Y. (2012). Measuring the output responses to fiscal policy. *American Economic Journal: Economic Policy*, *4*(2), 1–27. [CrossRef]

Auerbach, A. J., & Lee, R. (2011). Welfare and generational equity in sustainable unfunded pension systems. *Journal of Public Economics*, *95*(1–2), 16–27. [CrossRef] [PubMed]

Barr, N., & Diamond, P. (2008). *Reforming pensions: Principles and policy choices*. Oxford University Press.

Barr, N. A. (2012). *The economics of the welfare state* (5th ed.). Oxford University Press.

Beard, J. R., Officer, A., de Carvalho, I. A., Sadana, R., Pot, A. M., Michel, J. P., Lloyd-Sherlock, P., Epping-Jordan, J. E., Peeters, G. M. E. E. G., Mahanani, W. R., Thiyagarajan, J. A., & Chatterji, S. (2016). The world report on ageing and health: A policy framework for healthy ageing. *The Lancet*, *387*(10033), 2145–2154. [CrossRef] [PubMed]

Bieszk-Stolorz, B., Dmytrów, K., & Frąckiewicz, E. (2024). Multivariate analysis of the sustainable development of the silver economy in the European Union countries. *Sustainability*, *16*(23), 10703. [CrossRef]

Bloom, D. E., Canning, D., & Fink, G. (2010). Implications of population ageing for economic growth. *Oxford Review of Economic Policy*, *26*(4), 583–612. [CrossRef]

Bohn, H. (1998). The behavior of U.S. public debt and deficits. *Quarterly Journal of Economics*, *113*(3), 949–963. [CrossRef]

Carone, G., Eckefeldt, P., Giamboni, L., Laine, V., & Pamies Sumner, S. (2016). *Pension reforms in the EU since the early 2000's: Achievements and challenges ahead* (European Economy Discussion Paper No. 042). European Commission, Directorate-General for Economic and Financial Affairs. [CrossRef]

Chalk, N., & Hemming, R. (2000). *Assessing fiscal sustainability in theory and practice* (IMF Working Paper). International Monetary Fund. Available online: https://www.imf.org/external/pubs/ft/wp/2000/wp0081.pdf (accessed on 2 March 2026).

European Commission. (2018a). *The 2018 ageing report: Economic and budgetary projections for the EU member states (2016–2070)* (European Economy Institutional Paper No. 079). Publications Office of the European Union. Available online: https://economy-finance.ec.europa.eu/publications/2018-ageing-report-economic-and-budgetary-projections-eu-member-states-2016-2070_en (accessed on 15 November 2025).

European Commission. (2018b). *The silver economy: Executive summary*. Publications Office of the European Union. Available online: https://publications.europa.eu/resource/cellar/2dca9276-3ec5-11e8-b5fe-01aa75ed71a1.0002.01/DOC_1 (accessed on 15 November 2025).

European Commission. (2020). *Report on the impact of demographic change*. Publications Office of the European Union. Available online: https://commission.europa.eu/system/files/2020-06/demography_report_2020_n.pdf (accessed on 15 November 2025).

European Commission. (2021). *The 2021 ageing report: Economic and budgetary projections for the EU Member States (2019–2070)* (European Economy Institutional Paper No. 148). Publications Office of the European Union. Available online: https://economy-finance.ec.europa.eu/document/download/58bcd316-a404-4e2a-8b29-49d8159dc89a_en?filename=ip148_en.pdf (accessed on 15 November 2025).

European Commission. (2023). *The 2024 ageing report: Underlying assumptions and projection methodologies* (European Economy Institutional Paper). Publications Office of the European Union. Available online: https://economy-finance.ec.europa.eu/publications/2024-ageing-report-underlying-assumptions-and-projection-methodologies_en (accessed on 15 November 2025).

European Commission. (2024). *The 2024 ageing report: Economic and budgetary projections for the EU member states (2022–2070)*. Publications Office of the European Union. Available online: https://economy-finance.ec.europa.eu/publications/2024-ageing-report-economic-and-budgetary-projections-eu-member-states-2022-2070_en (accessed on 3 March 2026).

Eyraud, L., Gaspar, V., & Poghosyan, T. (2017). *Fiscal politics in the Euro area* (IMF Working Paper). International Monetary Fund. Available online: https://www.imf.org/-/media/files/publications/wp/wp1718.pdf (accessed on 3 March 2026).

Ghiga, I., Pitchforth, E., Lepetit, L., Miani, C., Ali, G. C., & Meads, C. (2020). The effectiveness of community-based social innovations for healthy ageing in middle- and high-income countries: A systematic review. *Journal of Health Services Research & Policy, 25*(3), 202–210. [CrossRef]

Grech, A. G. (2010). *Assessing the sustainability of pension reforms in Europe* (CASE paper No. 140). Centre for Analysis of Social Exclusion, London School of Economics and Political Science. Available online: https://ideas.repec.org/p/cep/sticas/case140.html (accessed on 13 November 2025).

Guillemette, Y., & Turner, D. (2021). *The long game: Fiscal outlooks to 2060 underline need for structural reform* (OECD Economic Policy Papers No. 29). OECD Publishing. [CrossRef]

Hallerberg, M., Strauch, R., & von Hagen, J. (2010). *Fiscal governance in Europe*. Cambridge University Press. [CrossRef]

Hemerijck, A. (Ed.). (2017). *The uses of social investment*. Oxford University Press.

Hristozov, Y., Kasabov, D., & Miteva, D. (2025). The Bulgarian economy—Trends and signals in the context of global challenges. *Economic Alternatives, 31*(4), 1026–1059. [CrossRef]

International Monetary Fund (IMF). (2025). *World economic outlook: A critical juncture amid policy shifts*. Available online: https://www.imf.org/-/media/files/publications/weo/2025/april/english/text.pdf (accessed on 23 December 2025).

Klimczuk, A. (2016). Comparative analysis of national and regional models of the silver economy in the European Union. *International Journal of Ageing and Later Life, 10*(2), 31–59. Available online: https://ijal.se/article/view/1309 (accessed on 10 November 2025). [CrossRef]

Klimczuk, A. (2017). Welfare state. In B. S. Turner, P. Kivisto, W. Outhwaite, C. Kyung-Sup, C. Epstein, & J. M. Ryan (Eds.), *The Wiley-Blackwell encyclopedia of social theory* (pp. 1–5). Wiley-Blackwell. [CrossRef]

Koutsogeorgopoulou, V., & Morgavi, H. (2025). *Ageing populations, their fiscal implications and policy responses* (OECD Economics Department Working Papers No. 1844). OECD Publishing. [CrossRef]

Krusteva, D., & Lulanski, P. (2025). *Conditions for carrying out activities in the state administration: Prerequisites, state, and parametric resonance*. UNWE Publishing House.

Maestas, N., Mullen, K. J., & Powell, D. (2023). The effect of population aging on economic growth, the labor force, and productivity. *American Economic Journal: Macroeconomics, 15*(2), 306–332. [CrossRef]

Morel, N., Palier, B., & Palme, J. (2011). Social investment: A paradigm in search of a new economic model and political mobilization. In N. Morel, B. Palier, & J. Palme (Eds.), *Towards a social investment welfare state? Ideas, policies and challenges* (pp. 353–376). Policy Press.

Natali, D. (2018). Recasting pensions in Europe: Policy challenges and political strategies to pass reforms. *Swiss Political Science Review, 24*(1), 53–59. [CrossRef]

OECD. (2020). *Promoting an age-inclusive workforce: Living, learning and earning longer*. OECD Publishing. [CrossRef]

OECD. (2021). *Pensions at a glance 2021: OECD and G20 indicators*. OECD Publishing. [CrossRef]

OECD. (2023a). *OECD economic outlook* (Vol. 2023, Issue 2). OECD Publishing. [CrossRef]

OECD. (2023b). *Pensions at a glance 2023: OECD and G20 indicators*. OECD Publishing. [CrossRef]

Painter, M., & Pierre, J. (Eds.). (2005). *Challenges to state policy capacity: Global trends and comparative perspectives*. Palgrave Macmillan. [CrossRef]

Pavlova, V., Tosheva, E., Murgova, M., Pandurska, R., & Dimov, A. (2021). *Active aging—Health, social and economic determinants*. UNWE Publishing Complex.

Peine, A., & Neven, L. (2019). From intervention to co-constitution: New directions in theorizing about aging and technology. *The Gerontologist, 59*(1), 15–21. [CrossRef] [PubMed]

Phills, J. A., Jr., Deiglmeier, K., & Miller, D. T. (2008). Rediscovering social innovation. *Stanford Social Innovation Review, 6*(4), 34–43. [CrossRef]

Ramos-Herrera, M. C., & Sosvilla-Rivero, S. (2020). Fiscal sustainability in aging societies: Evidence from Euro area countries. *Sustainability, 12*(24), 10276. [CrossRef]

Rouzet, D., Sánchez, A. C., Renault, T., & Roehn, O. (2019). *Fiscal challenges and inclusive growth in ageing societies* (OECD Economic Policy Papers No. 27). OECD Publishing. [CrossRef]

Scott, A. J. (2021). The longevity economy. *The Lancet Healthy Longevity, 2*(12), e828–e835. [CrossRef] [PubMed]

https://doi.org/10.3390/jrfm19030212

Valcheva, K. (2025). *The state of trust*. UNWE Publishing House.
Veleva, R. (2025a). Indicators for the development of the silver economy: Differences between Bulgaria and the European Union. *Economic and Social Alternatives*, *31*(3), 82–97. [CrossRef]
Veleva, R. (2025b). The silver economy in a European perspective. *Economic and Social Alternatives*, *31*(2), 47–63. [CrossRef]
Wu, X., Ramesh, M., & Howlett, M. (2015). Policy capacity: A conceptual framework for understanding policy competences and capabilities. *Policy and Society*, *34*(3–4), 165–171. [CrossRef]
Zaidi, A., Gasior, K., Zolyomi, E., Schmidt, A., Rodrigues, R., & Marin, B. (2017). Measuring active and healthy ageing in Europe. *Journal of European Social Policy*, *27*(2), 138–157. [CrossRef]

https://doi.org/10.3390/jrfm19030212

Journal of
Risk and Financial Management

MDPI

Article

Fiscal Decentralization as a Strategic Risk-Management Tool: Institutional Threshold Effects on EU Output Volatility

Ahmet Münir Gökmen

Department of E-Commerce and Marketing, Vocational School, Istanbul Kent University, Merkez Mah., Cendere Cad. No:24, Kagithane, 34406 Istanbul, Turkey; ahmetmunir.gokmen@kent.edu.tr; Tel.: +90-533-5210113

Abstract

This study examines whether fiscal decentralization operates as a strategic macroeconomic risk-management instrument and whether its effectiveness depends on institutional quality. Using a balanced panel of 27 European Union member states over 2008–2023, a composite fiscal decentralization index combining expenditure and revenue autonomy is constructed, and a dynamic specification is estimated using a two-step System-GMM estimator. Output volatility is measured as a five-year rolling standard deviation of real GDP growth. The results indicate that fiscal decentralization exhibits a statistically significant effect on volatility whose direction depends on governance quality. Institutional quality directly reduces volatility, and the interaction between decentralization and institutional quality is negative and highly significant. A critical institutional threshold of 1.865 (WGI estimate scale), above which decentralization reduces output volatility, is identified. These findings indicate that decentralization functions as a conditional risk-management mechanism embedded within institutional capacity. The results provide policy-relevant insights into EU fiscal architecture design in an era of recurrent macroeconomic shocks.

Keywords: fiscal decentralization; institutional quality; strategic risk management; output volatility; macro-financial stability; System-GMM; European Union

1. Introduction

Over the past decade, the European Union has faced a sequence of systemic shocks, including the sovereign debt crisis, the COVID-19 pandemic, and the energy price surge. These episodes have exposed vulnerabilities in fiscal frameworks and renewed interest in the design of public finance architecture capable of enhancing macroeconomic resilience. In this context, fiscal decentralization, the allocation of expenditure and revenue authority across levels of government has moved beyond an administrative reform question and increasingly represents a strategic governance instrument with potential implications for macro-financial stability.

Classical fiscal federalism theory emphasizes allocative efficiency gains arising from decentralization, arguing that local governments possess superior information regarding regional preferences and economic conditions (Oates, 1972; Tiebout, 1956). Musgrave (1959) further distinguished the stabilization, allocation, and redistribution functions of public finance, suggesting that macroeconomic stabilization has traditionally been viewed as a centralized responsibility. Empirical evidence also indicates that fiscal institutions and government structures influence macroeconomic stabilization capacity (Fatás & Mihov, 2001). However, subsequent research highlights that decentralization may influence stabilization indirectly through institutional channels. On one side, decentralization may generate coordination failures, soft budget constraints, and pro-cyclical local fiscal behavior, potentially amplifying volatility (Rodden, 2002). On the other side, decentralized systems may enhance adaptability, diversify fiscal responses, and enable policy experimentation tailored to local conditions, thereby strengthening economic resilience (Rodríguez-Pose & Ezcurra, 2011; Lessmann, 2012).

Recent empirical studies further suggest that the macroeconomic consequences of fiscal decentralization depend strongly on institutional and structural contexts. Meta-analytic evidence indicates that the growth and stability effects of decentralization vary across governance environments (Baskaran et al., 2016). Similarly, revenue decentralization and expenditure decentralization may generate different macroeconomic outcomes depending on the degree of fiscal autonomy and institutional oversight (Canavire-Bacarreza & Martinez-Vazquez, 2013). Recent empirical research also emphasizes that the macroeconomic implications of fiscal decentralization depend on governance capacity and fiscal institutions across countries (Bahl et al., 2021; Dougherty & Phillips, 2021). These findings highlight the importance of examining the institutional conditions under which fiscal decentralization operates effectively.

A central limitation of existing empirical work is the insufficient attention paid to institutional quality as a conditioning factor. The effectiveness of decentralized fiscal authority is unlikely to be uniform across governance environments. Strong institutions characterized by accountability, transparency, and rule-based decision-making can ensure disciplined subnational budgeting and strategic allocation of public resources. Conversely, weak institutional frameworks may transform decentralization into a source of fiscal fragmentation and instability. Thus, decentralization may operate not as an unconditional stabilizer, but as a conditional macroeconomic risk-management mechanism embedded within institutional capacity. Recent studies further highlight that improvements in governance quality and fiscal accountability strengthen the effectiveness of decentralized fiscal systems (Rodríguez-Pose, 2022; Onofrei et al., 2022).

The conditioning role of institutional quality can be understood through two complementary mechanisms. First, high-quality institutions ensure fiscal discipline and coordination across levels of government, reducing the risk of soft budget constraints and pro-cyclical subnational behavior. Second, strong governance frameworks enhance the efficiency of decentralized decision-making by improving accountability, transparency, and policy credibility. In this context, fiscal decentralization can contribute to macroeconomic stabilization only when embedded within institutional environments capable of enforcing fiscal rules and coordinating policy responses.

To formalize these expectations, two hypotheses are tested:

H1. *Fiscal decentralization significantly affects macroeconomic output volatility.*

H2. *The stabilizing effect of fiscal decentralization emerges only when institutional quality exceeds a critical threshold.*

This paper advances the argument that fiscal decentralization functions as a strategic risk-management tool only when institutional quality surpasses a critical threshold. Using a balanced panel of 27 European Union member states over the period 2008–2023, the dynamic relationship between fiscal decentralization, institutional quality, and output volatility is examined. Output volatility is measured as the five-year rolling standard deviation of real GDP growth, capturing macroeconomic instability rather than short-term cyclical fluctuations. Macroeconomic volatility has become a central concern for policymakers, as fiscal structures influence both shock transmission and stabilization capacity (Aghion et al., 2019).

https://doi.org/10.3390/jrfm19050322

Fiscal decentralization is operationalized through a composite index combining subnational expenditure shares and revenue autonomy. Institutional quality is measured using the Worldwide Governance Indicators, focusing on Government Effectiveness, Rule of Law, and Control of Corruption. Institutional quality plays a critical role in shaping the effectiveness of decentralized fiscal systems (Rodríguez-Pose & Gill, 2020).

To address endogeneity, persistence, and unobserved heterogeneity, a two-step System Generalized Method of Moments (System-GMM) estimator is employed. This approach allows us to account for the dynamic nature of volatility, potential reverse causality between stability and fiscal structure, and country-specific effects. The empirical results yield three central findings. First, output volatility exhibits strong persistence, confirming the importance of dynamic modeling. Second, institutional quality directly reduces volatility, reinforcing the macro-stabilizing role of governance. Third, and most importantly, the interaction between fiscal decentralization and institutional quality is negative and statistically significant. This indicates that decentralization becomes stabilizing only when governance quality is sufficiently high.

A critical institutional threshold of 1.865 on the WGI estimate scale is identified. Above this level, fiscal decentralization reduces macroeconomic volatility; below it, decentralization fails to generate stabilizing effects. This nonlinear mechanism demonstrates that fiscal architecture operates as a conditional stabilization device rather than a universally beneficial reform. Ongoing debates on European fiscal governance highlight the importance of institutional coordination across multi-level fiscal systems (Darvas et al., 2018). Fiscal structures and institutional arrangements also influence the transmission of macroeconomic shocks and stabilization capacity within integrated economies (Eyraud et al., 2020). The results are robust to alternative instrument specifications within the System-GMM framework.

This study contributes to literature in three main ways. First, it provides dynamic causal evidence on the relationship between fiscal structure and macroeconomic risk within the European Union. Second, it quantifies an institutional threshold governing the stabilizing effectiveness of decentralization, offering a measurable benchmark for policy design. Third, it reframes fiscal decentralization within a strategic risk-management perspective, integrating fiscal federalism theory with macro-financial stability analysis.

Unlike prior studies focusing on average effects, this study introduces a quantifiable institutional threshold, providing a measurable benchmark for policy evaluation.

In an era characterized by recurrent and overlapping shocks, fiscal architecture design must be approached as a risk-governance problem rather than solely an efficiency-enhancing reform. By demonstrating that decentralization's stabilizing capacity depends on institutional quality, this paper provides indicative policy insights subject to empirical limitations for policymakers seeking to strengthen macroeconomic resilience within multi-level governance systems.

The remainder of the paper is structured as follows. Section 2 describes the data, variable construction, and econometric methodology. Section 3 presents empirical results and marginal effect analysis. Section 4 discusses policy implications and robustness checks. Section 5 concludes.

2. Literature Review

The relationship between fiscal decentralization and macroeconomic performance has been extensively examined within the framework of fiscal federalism and public finance. Classical contributions emphasize efficiency gains arising from decentralized governance structures, arguing that subnational governments possess superior information regarding local preferences and economic conditions (Oates, 1972; Tiebout, 1956). In this

https://doi.org/10.3390/jrfm19050322

context, decentralization is expected to enhance allocative efficiency and responsiveness of public policy. However, its implications for macroeconomic stability remain theoretically ambiguous and empirically contested.

Early empirical research highlights the role of fiscal institutions in shaping macroeconomic fluctuations. For example, government structure and fiscal size influence the strength of automatic stabilizers and the transmission of shocks (Fatás & Mihov, 2001). At the same time, decentralization may introduce coordination failures, soft budget constraints, and pro-cyclical fiscal behavior at the subnational level, potentially amplifying volatility (Rodden, 2002). These contrasting perspectives suggest that the macroeconomic impact of decentralization is not uniform but depends on broader institutional arrangements.

Recent empirical literature increasingly supports the view that decentralization outcomes are conditional on governance environments. Meta-analytic evidence shows that the effects of fiscal decentralization on growth and stability vary significantly across institutional contexts (Baskaran et al., 2016). Similarly, different forms of decentralization—such as revenue and expenditure autonomy—may generate heterogeneous macroeconomic effects depending on fiscal discipline and oversight mechanisms (Canavire-Bacarreza & Martinez-Vazquez, 2013). These findings highlight the importance of moving beyond average effects and examining the conditions under which decentralization becomes beneficial.

A growing body of research emphasizes the central role of institutional quality in shaping fiscal outcomes. Strong governance frameworks characterized by accountability, transparency, and rule-based decision-making are associated with improved public sector performance and macroeconomic stability (Rodríguez-Pose & Gill, 2020; Rodríguez-Pose, 2022). Empirical studies further indicate that fiscal decentralization contributes to economic performance only when supported by adequate institutional capacity and governance mechanisms (Bahl et al., 2021; Dougherty & Phillips, 2021). In this perspective, decentralization operates as a conditional policy instrument whose effectiveness depends on the quality of institutions.

In the European context, fiscal governance and institutional coordination have become increasingly important in the aftermath of successive macroeconomic shocks. Studies on EU fiscal frameworks emphasize the importance of institutional arrangements for managing fiscal risks and ensuring macroeconomic resilience (Darvas et al., 2018; Eyraud et al., 2020). At the same time, broader structural dynamics such as innovation cycles and economic transformation contribute to volatility patterns, highlighting the need for adaptive fiscal systems (Aghion et al., 2019). These dynamics suggest that fiscal architecture must be analyzed within a macro-financial stability framework.

Recent contributions extend this perspective by linking fiscal decentralization to broader economic resilience and risk management. For instance, decentralization has been associated with improved efficiency outcomes when institutional quality is sufficiently high (Afonso & Kazemi, 2022), while empirical evidence also suggests that decentralization contributes to macroeconomic stability under strong governance conditions (Bushashe, 2023). These findings reinforce the argument that institutional quality acts as a key moderating factor in the decentralization–stability relationship.

Beyond macroeconomic stabilization, studies on fiscal autonomy and local governance provide additional insights into decentralized systems. Empirical evidence indicates that fiscal autonomy is closely linked to local economic performance and efficient resource allocation, although outcomes vary across institutional environments (Prodanov & Naydenov, 2020; Sabitova et al., 2020). These results suggest that decentralization effectiveness depends not only on fiscal structure but also on the capacity of subnational governments to manage resources within coherent institutional frameworks.

https://doi.org/10.3390/jrfm19050322

Recent interdisciplinary research further highlights the role of governance structures in shaping economic resilience and macro-financial stability. Economic systems undergoing structural transformation—such as the transition toward circular and sustainable production models—demonstrate that adaptive institutional frameworks are essential for managing systemic risks and enhancing resilience (Roleders et al., 2024). Similarly, sectoral financial dynamics are highly sensitive to external shocks, emphasizing the importance of institutional and market conditions in determining economic stability (Zaharieva et al., 2022).

From a macro-financial perspective, fiscal sustainability and public debt management are also closely linked to institutional capacity and economic stability. Advanced analytical approaches reveal that effective governance plays a critical role in mitigating fiscal risks and maintaining macroeconomic balance (Zahariev et al., 2020). In parallel, recent studies employing data-driven and machine learning techniques demonstrate the importance of robust institutional environments in improving the projection and management of public indebtedness (Zarkova et al., 2023). These findings reinforce the need to integrate fiscal policy analysis with modern risk assessment frameworks.

In addition, research on economic security and global financial challenges highlights the importance of governance strategies in strengthening resilience against systemic shocks. Institutional quality and policy coordination mechanisms are key determinants of economic stability in increasingly complex and interconnected environments (Ushenko et al., 2023). These insights further support the view that fiscal systems must be understood within a broader risk-governance framework.

Despite this growing body of research, a critical gap remains in the literature. Most empirical studies focus on average effects of fiscal decentralization without explicitly identifying the conditions under which decentralization becomes stabilizing or destabilizing. In particular, limited attention has been paid to quantifying threshold effects in the interaction between fiscal decentralization and institutional quality. This study addresses this gap by introducing a dynamic panel framework that explicitly models the interaction between fiscal decentralization and institutional quality and identifies a quantifiable institutional threshold governing macroeconomic volatility. By integrating insights from fiscal federalism, institutional economics, and macro-financial stability literature, the study contributes to a more comprehensive understanding of fiscal decentralization as a conditional risk-management mechanism.

Unlike prior studies focusing on average effects, this study explicitly identifies a quantifiable institutional threshold governing the decentralization–stability relationship, thereby providing a measurable contribution to the fiscal federalism literature.

3. Materials and Methods

To test these hypotheses, a quantitative research design suitable for causal inference in public economics is employed.

3.1. Data and Sample

A balanced panel dataset covering 27 European Union member states over the period 2008–2023 is constructed. The time frame is determined by data availability and ensures comparability across fiscal and governance indicators following the global financial crisis.

Macroeconomic and fiscal data are obtained from Eurostat, including real GDP growth rates and subnational government finance statistics. Institutional quality indicators are drawn from the World Bank's Worldwide Governance Indicators (WGI) database.

The analysis is conducted at the country level, consistent with the availability of harmonized fiscal decentralization indicators across EU member states.

https://doi.org/10.3390/jrfm19050322

Data for 2024–2025 are not included due to limited availability and revision status in Eurostat databases, which may affect comparability. The dataset covers the period up to 2023, ensuring consistency and reliability. Eurostat data were obtained from general government finance statistics (gov_10a_exp and gov_10a_taxag), while GDP growth data were retrieved from national accounts (nama_10_gdp).

3.2. Variables

Dependent Variable

Output volatility is measured as the five-year rolling standard deviation of annual real GDP growth:

$$\text{Volatility}_{i,t} = \text{SD}(\text{GDP growth i, t} - 4\text{:t})$$

This measure captures macroeconomic instability and medium-term exposure to shocks rather than short-run cyclical fluctuations.

Fiscal Decentralization (FDI)

Fiscal decentralization is operationalized through a composite index combining:

1. Subnational expenditure share in total general government expenditure;
2. Subnational revenue share in total general government revenue.

The index captures both fiscal autonomy and spending responsibility, reflecting the degree of vertical fiscal dispersion.

The composite index assigns equal weights to expenditure and revenue decentralization components, following standard practice in the literature. This specification is preferred as it captures both fiscal autonomy and spending responsibility, while avoiding over-reliance on a single dimension of decentralization.

Institutional Quality (INST)

Institutional quality is measured as the average of three WGIs:

- Government Effectiveness;
- Rule of Law;
- Control of Corruption.

The WGI estimate scale (approximately −2.5 to +2.5) is used. Higher values indicate stronger governance quality.

While the composite index captures overall governance quality, additional robustness considerations regarding individual WGI components are acknowledged and discussed in the robustness section.

Interaction Term

To test the conditional stabilization hypothesis, an interaction term between fiscal decentralization and institutional quality is included:

$$\text{FDI}_{i,t} \times \text{INST}_{i,t}$$

This specification allows the marginal effect of decentralization on volatility to vary with governance quality.

3.3. Econometric Strategy

Given the dynamic nature of macroeconomic volatility and potential endogeneity between fiscal structure and stability, a two-step System Generalized Method of Moments (System-GMM) estimator is employed (Blundell & Bond, 1998). All estimations were performed using R statistical software R 4.5.1 (R Core Team, 2024) within the RStudio integrated development environment (Posit Team, 2024).

https://doi.org/10.3390/jrfm19050322

The baseline dynamic specification is:

$$\text{Volatility}_{i,t} = \alpha + \beta 1\text{Volatility}_{i,t} - 1 + \beta 2\text{FDI}_{i,t} + \beta 3\text{INST}_{i,t} + \beta 4(\text{FDI} \times \text{INST})_{i,t} + \mu_i + \varepsilon_{i,t}$$

where

μ_i captures unobserved country-specific effects,

$\varepsilon_{i,t}$ is the idiosyncratic error term.

The System-GMM is appropriate for three reasons:

1. It addresses potential reverse causality between fiscal decentralization and macroeconomic stability by using internal instruments (lagged levels and differences).
2. It accounts for the persistence of volatility through inclusion of the lagged dependent variable.
3. It controls unobserved heterogeneity across countries.

Instrument validity is evaluated using the Sargan test of overidentifying restrictions and Arellano–Bond tests for serial correlation in first and second differences. The Arellano–Bond test is used to detect serial correlation in the error terms (Arellano & Bond, 1991).

The instrument matrix includes lagged levels for differenced equations and lagged differences for level equations, following Blundell and Bond (1998). To mitigate potential instrument proliferation, the lag depth of instruments is restricted, and alternative specifications with reduced instrument sets are estimated. The number of instruments remains below the number of cross-sectional units, consistent with recommended practice.

4. Empirical Results

4.1. Descriptive Statistics and Correlation Analysis

Table 1 reports the descriptive statistics of the main variables. Output volatility exhibits substantial variation across EU member states, reflecting heterogeneous exposure to macroeconomic shocks over the sample period. Institutional quality also displays meaningful dispersion, with WGI scores ranging from negative values in lower-governance environments to values exceeding 2 in high-quality institutional systems. Fiscal decentralization indicators similarly vary across countries, confirming sufficient cross-sectional heterogeneity for identification.

Table 1. Descriptive Statistics.

Variable	Mean	SD	Min	Max
Volatility	4.462	3.469	0.131	20.641
Fiscal decentralization (FDI)	0.228	0.133	0.011	0.656
Institutional quality (INST)	1.040	0.654	−0.324	2.166
Revenue decentralization	0.234	0.132	0.012	0.661
Expenditure decentralization	0.222	0.134	0.010	0.668
GDP growth	3.967	5.880	−23.811	30.555

Notes: EU sample (27 countries), 2008–2023. Volatility is the 5-year rolling standard deviation of GDP growth. FDI is the composite fiscal decentralization index based on revenue and expenditure decentralization. INST is the WGI-based institutional quality index (average of Government Effectiveness, Rule of Law, and Control of Corruption; estimate scale).

Table 2 presents the pairwise correlation matrix. Institutional quality is negatively correlated with output volatility, suggesting that stronger governance environments are associated with more stable growth dynamics. Fiscal decentralization does not exhibit excessively high correlations with institutional quality, alleviating concerns of multicollinearity in the interaction specification. Overall, the correlation structure supports proceeding with dynamic panel estimation.

https://doi.org/10.3390/jrfm19050322

Table 2. Correlation Matrix.

Variable	Volatility	FDI	INST	rev_decent	exp_decent	gdp_growth
volatility	1.000	0.018	−0.270	0.035	0.001	−0.031
FDI	0.018	1.000	0.302	0.998	0.998	−0.087
INST	−0.270	0.302	1.000	0.278	0.325	−0.036
rev_decent	0.035	0.998	0.278	1.000	0.992	−0.101
exp_decent	0.001	0.998	0.325	0.992	1.000	−0.072
gdp_growth	−0.031	−0.087	−0.036	−0.101	−0.072	1.000

Note: Pairwise correlations for the main variables used in the baseline System-GMM estimations.

4.2. Baseline Dynamic Panel Results

Table 3 reports the baseline two-step System-GMM estimates.

Table 3. Baseline System-GMM Estimates.

Variable	Coefficient	Std. Error
lag(volatility, 1)	0.743 ***	(0.028)
FDI	7.651 ***	(1.379)
INST	0.591 ***	(0.176)
I(FDI × INST)	−4.101 ***	(0.804)

*** $p < 0.001$. Notes: Two-step System-GMM (Blundell–Bond). Robust standard errors in parentheses. AR(1) $p = 0.0009$; AR(2) $p = 0.0509$; Sargan $\chi^2(43) = 25.507$ ($p = 0.9843$). Significance levels: *** $p < 0.01$.

The lagged dependent variable is positive and highly significant ($\beta_1 \approx 0.74$–0.78, $p < 0.01$), confirming strong persistence in output volatility. This justifies the dynamic specification. Fiscal decentralization (FDI) enters with a statistically significant coefficient. However, its marginal effect cannot be interpreted independently due to the presence of the interaction term with institutional quality. Institutional quality (INST) exhibits a negative and significant coefficient, indicating that stronger governance environments directly reduce output volatility. Most importantly, the interaction term between fiscal decentralization and institutional quality is negative and highly significant ($p < 0.01$). This indicates that the effect of decentralization on volatility becomes more stabilizing as governance quality improves.

Model diagnostics support the validity of the specification. The Arellano–Bond test for first-order serial correlation is significant, as expected in differenced models, while the test for second-order serial correlation is not significant at conventional levels (AR(2) $p \approx 0.05$). The Sargan test does not reject the null hypothesis of instrument validity, suggesting that the instrument set is appropriate. These findings provide empirical support for the institutional contingency hypothesis.

4.3. Institutional Threshold and Marginal Effects

To interpret the interaction term, the marginal effect of fiscal decentralization on volatility is computed as:

$$\partial Volatility \div \partial FDI = \beta 2 + \beta 4 INST$$

Setting the marginal effect equal to zero yields the institutional threshold:

$$INST* = -\beta 2 \div \beta 4$$

Table 4 reports the estimated institutional threshold and its confidence interval. To further interpret the interaction effect, the institutional threshold at which fiscal decentralization changes its impact on volatility is calculated as $-\beta_1/\beta_3$. Using the estimated

https://doi.org/10.3390/jrfm19050322

coefficients, the turning point is 1.865. The 95% confidence interval derived via the delta method is [1.756, 1.975], indicating that fiscal decentralization contributes to macroeconomic stabilization only when institutional quality exceeds this level.

Table 4. Institutional Quality Threshold for Stabilizing Effect.

Statistic	Value
Estimated Threshold (INST*)	1.865
95% Confidence Interval	[1.756, 1.975]

Notes: INST* denotes the estimated institutional quality threshold at which the marginal effect of fiscal decentralization on output volatility changes sign. Confidence interval computed using the delta method.Threshold computed as $-\beta\_FDI/\beta\_FDI \times INST$. Confidence interval derived using the delta method with robust variance–covariance matrix.

This result implies that fiscal decentralization reduces output volatility only in countries whose institutional quality exceeds this threshold. Below this level, decentralization does not generate stabilizing effects and may even be associated with higher volatility.

Figure 1 visualizes the marginal effect of fiscal decentralization across different levels of institutional quality. The marginal effect curve crosses zero at the estimated threshold and becomes negative in high-governance environments. The confidence bands confirm statistical significance of the stabilizing effect beyond the critical value.

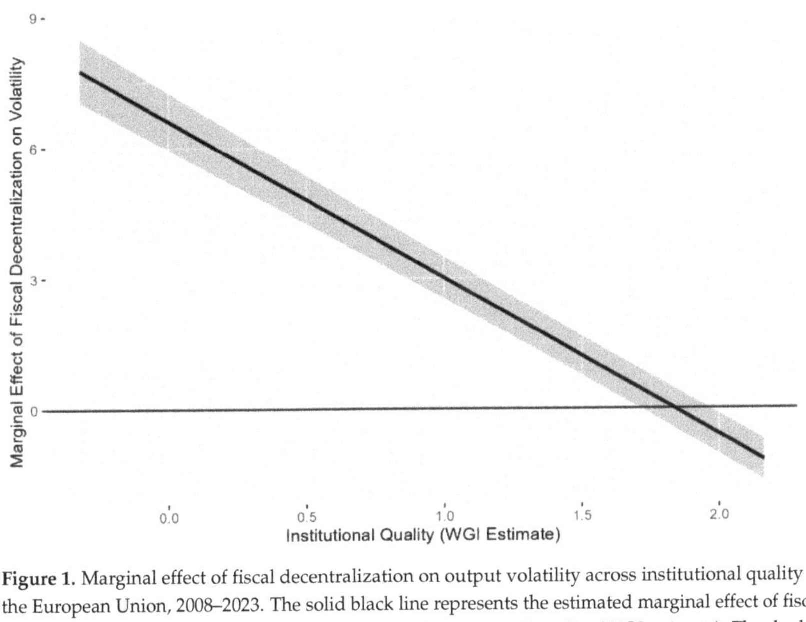

Figure 1. Marginal effect of fiscal decentralization on output volatility across institutional quality in the European Union, 2008–2023. The solid black line represents the estimated marginal effect of fiscal decentralization on output volatility as a function of institutional quality (WGI estimate). The shaded gray area indicates the 95% confidence interval derived using the delta method. The horizontal line at zero denotes the threshold at which the effect changes sign, indicating the level of institutional quality above which fiscal decentralization contributes to macroeconomic stabilization.

The figure plots the marginal effect of fiscal decentralization (FDI) on output volatility as a function of institutional quality (WGI estimate scale). Shaded bands denote 95% confidence intervals computed using the delta method based on the System-GMM variance–covariance matrix. The effect becomes negative when institutional quality exceeds 1.865 (95% CI: 1.756–1.975).

https://doi.org/10.3390/jrfm19050322

The threshold is derived from interaction effects rather than estimated using a formal nonlinear threshold model. Therefore, it should be interpreted as an indicative turning point rather than a strict structural threshold. These findings demonstrate that fiscal decentralization functions as a conditional stabilization mechanism rather than a universally beneficial reform.

4.4. Robustness Analysis

Table 5 reports robustness checks using an alternative instrument specification that incorporates year indicators in the instrument matrix.

Table 5. Robustness Checks.

Variable	Baseline System-GMM	System-GMM + Year IV
lag(volatility, 1)	0.743 ***	0.783 ***
	(0.028)	(0.019)
FDI	7.651 ***	6.609 ***
	(1.379)	(1.071)
INST	0.591 ***	0.560 ***
	(0.176)	(0.157)
FDI × INST	−4.101 ***	−3.600 ***
	(0.804)	(0.561)

*Notes: Two-step System-GMM. Robust standard errors in parentheses. Baseline: AR(1) p = 0.0009; AR(2) p = 0.0509; Sargan $\chi^2(43) = 25.507$ (p = 0.9843). Year-IV: AR(1) p = 0.0016; AR(2) p = 0.0521; Sargan $\chi^2(582) = 26.946$ (p = 1.0000). Significance levels: *** p < 0.01.*

The main coefficients retain their signs and statistical significance across specifications. The interaction term remains negative and significant, confirming that the conditional stabilizing effect of decentralization is robust to alternative instrument choices. Although the inclusion of year instruments increases the number of instruments substantially, the qualitative conclusions remain unchanged. This reinforces the interpretation that institutional quality governs the volatility impact of fiscal decentralization. Overall, the robustness results strengthen confidence in the baseline findings.

5. Discussion

The empirical results provide empirical support for the institutional contingency hypothesis in fiscal federalism. Fiscal decentralization does not operate as a universally stabilizing reform; rather, its macroeconomic impact depends critically on the quality of governance. The identification of an institutional threshold at 1.865 on the WGI estimate scale reveals that decentralization becomes stabilizing only in sufficiently strong institutional environments.

This threshold mechanism explains the conflicting findings in the existing literature. Studies that report stabilizing effects of decentralization may implicitly capture high-governance environments, whereas those documenting destabilizing or neutral effects may reflect weaker institutional contexts. International policy analyses emphasize that successful decentralization reforms require strong institutional capacity and clear fiscal rules (OECD, 2022). By explicitly modeling the interaction between fiscal structure and governance quality, this study reconciles these divergent empirical outcomes within a unified framework.

From a macro-financial perspective, the results suggest that fiscal decentralization contributes to stability through two channels when embedded in strong institutions. First, decentralization enhances policy responsiveness. Subnational governments with well-defined fiscal autonomy can tailor expenditure and revenue decisions to local economic conditions, enabling quicker adjustment during downturns. Second, decentralization

https://doi.org/10.3390/jrfm19050322

diversifies fiscal decision-making across jurisdictions, reducing the systemic risk associated with centralized policy errors. This diversification effect resembles portfolio risk dispersion in financial systems, where distributed decision-making can mitigate aggregate volatility. Structural economic dynamics and innovation cycles may contribute to volatility patterns across advanced economies (Aghion et al., 2019).

However, these stabilizing mechanisms rely on institutional discipline. In weak governance environments, decentralization may amplify coordination failures, encourage fiscal pro-cyclicality, and increase fragmentation. Without effective oversight, transparent budgeting, and credible fiscal rules, subnational autonomy may lead to soft budget constraints and inefficient allocation. In such cases, decentralization does not function as a risk-management tool but instead introduces additional instability.

The robustness analysis reinforces this interpretation. The conditional stabilizing effect remains statistically significant across alternative instrument specifications, suggesting that the threshold mechanism is not driven by model specification choices. Although instrument proliferation must be monitored carefully in dynamic panel settings, the qualitative stability of the interaction coefficient strengthens confidence in the findings.

Recent interdisciplinary research also highlights the importance of adaptive institutional and organizational interactions in shaping economic performance and resilience (Bezgin et al., 2022).

The results carry several policy implications. First, decentralization reforms should be sequenced with institutional strengthening. Enhancing governance quality—through improved transparency, accountability mechanisms, and rule-of-law enforcement—appears to be a prerequisite for achieving macroeconomic stabilization benefits. Second, supranational monitoring frameworks, particularly within the European Union, should incorporate governance quality indicators when evaluating fiscal architecture risks. Focusing exclusively on deficit and debt aggregates may overlook structural vulnerabilities associated with institutional capacity. Third, fiscal rules designed for multi-level governance systems should consider institutional heterogeneity across member states, recognizing that identical decentralization reforms may yield different macroeconomic outcomes depending on governance quality.

Recent empirical evidence also links fiscal decentralization to broader public sector efficiency outcomes and macroeconomic performance when supported by strong governance frameworks (Afonso & Kazemi, 2022). Overall, the findings shift the debate from whether decentralization is stabilizing to when it becomes stabilizing. Fiscal architecture should, therefore, be understood as a conditional component of macroeconomic risk governance rather than a uniformly beneficial structural reform.

Additional research highlights that fiscal decentralization can contribute to macroeconomic stability when institutional coordination mechanisms are well established (Bushashe, 2023).

6. Conclusions

This study examines whether fiscal decentralization functions as a strategic macroeconomic risk-management mechanism and whether its effectiveness depends on institutional quality. Using a dynamic panel of 27 European Union member states over 2008–2023 and a two-step System-GMM estimator, the analysis identifies a critical governance threshold governing the volatility effects of decentralization. The results indicate that fiscal decentralization becomes stabilizing only when institutional quality exceeds 1.865 on the WGI estimate scale. Below this threshold, decentralization does not reduce output volatility. These findings demonstrate that fiscal structure and institutional capacity interact in shaping macroeconomic stability outcomes.

https://doi.org/10.3390/jrfm19050322

The contribution of this paper is threefold. First, it provides dynamic causal evidence on the relationship between fiscal architecture and macroeconomic risk in advanced economies. Second, it quantifies an institutional threshold that can inform reform sequencing and governance assessment. Third, it integrates fiscal federalism theory with macro-financial stability analysis by framing decentralization as a conditional risk-management instrument. The findings are specific to European Union economies and may differ in developing countries with weaker institutional frameworks.

In an environment characterized by recurrent economic shocks, policymakers should approach fiscal decentralization not merely as an efficiency-enhancing reform but as part of a broader institutional strategy for macroeconomic resilience. Strengthening governance quality appears to be a necessary condition for decentralized fiscal systems to deliver stabilization benefits. Future research may extend this framework by examining subnational heterogeneity within countries, disaggregating expenditure categories, or exploring nonlinear dynamics in greater detail.

Funding: This research received no external funding.

Institutional Review Board Statement: Not applicable.

Informed Consent Statement: Not applicable.

Data Availability Statement: Publicly available datasets were analyzed in this study. Data are available at Eurostat (https://ec.europa.eu/eurostat) and the Worldwide Governance Indicators provided by the World Bank (https://www.worldbank.org/en/publication/worldwide-governance-indicators, accessed on 1 January 2026).

Acknowledgments: During the preparation of this manuscript, the author used ChatGPT (OpenAI, 2025 version) for language refinement and formatting guidance. The author reviewed and edited the output and takes full responsibility for the content of this publication.

Conflicts of Interest: The author declares no conflicts of interest.

Abbreviations

The following abbreviations are used in this manuscript:

EU	European Union
FDI	Fiscal Decentralization Index
GDP	Gross Domestic Product
GMM	Generalized Method of Moments
OECD	Organisation for Economic Co-operation and Development
WGI	Worldwide Governance Indicators

References

Afonso, A., & Kazemi, M. (2022). Fiscal decentralization and public sector efficiency. *Economic Modelling, 111*, 105833. [CrossRef]

Aghion, P., Akcigit, U., & Howitt, P. (2019). Innovation, growth and macroeconomic volatility. *Journal of Economic Literature, 57*(3), 647–721.

Arellano, M., & Bond, S. (1991). Some tests of specification for panel data: Monte Carlo evidence and an application to employment equations. *Review of Economic Studies, 58*(2), 277–297. [CrossRef]

Bahl, R., Bird, R. M., & Gendron, P. (2021). Fiscal decentralization and governance. *Public Finance Review, 49*(3), 385–412.

Baskaran, T., Feld, L. P., & Schnellenbach, J. (2016). Fiscal federalism, decentralization and economic growth: A meta-analysis. *Economic Inquiry, 54*(3), 1445–1463. [CrossRef]

Bezgin, K., Zahariev, A., Shaulska, L., Doronina, O., Tsiklashvili, N., & Wasilewska, N. (2022). Coevolution of education and business: Adaptive interaction. *International Journal of Global Environmental Issues, 21*(2–4), 259–275. [CrossRef]

Blundell, R., & Bond, S. (1998). Initial conditions and moment restrictions in dynamic panel data models. *Journal of Econometrics, 87*(1), 115–143. [CrossRef]

https://doi.org/10.3390/jrfm19050322

Bushashe, M. A. (2023). Fiscal decentralization and macroeconomic stability nexus: Evidence from developing economies. *Cogent Economics & Finance*, *11*(1), 2244353. [CrossRef]

Canavire-Bacarreza, G., & Martinez-Vazquez, J. (2013). Fiscal decentralization and economic growth: An empirical analysis. *World Development*, *53*, 105–120. [CrossRef]

Darvas, Z., Martin, P., & Ragot, X. (2018). *European fiscal rules require a major overhaul* (Bruegel Policy Contribution No. 18). Bruegel.

Dougherty, S., & Phillips, L. (2021). Fiscal decentralisation and inclusive growth. *OECD Economic Studies*, *2021*(1), 59–83.

Eyraud, L., Gaspar, V., & Poghosyan, T. (2020). Fiscal politics in the euro area. *IMF Working Papers*, *20*(181). [CrossRef]

Fatás, A., & Mihov, I. (2001). Government size and automatic stabilizers: International and intranational evidence. *Journal of International Economics*, *55*(1), 3–28. [CrossRef]

Lessmann, C. (2012). Regional inequality and decentralization: An empirical analysis. *Regional Studies*, *46*(1), 91–104.

Musgrave, R. A. (1959). *The theory of public finance: A study in public economy*. McGraw-Hill.

Oates, W. E. (1972). *Fiscal federalism*. Harcourt Brace Jovanovich.

OECD. (2022). *Fiscal decentralisation and regional development*. OECD Publishing.

Onofrei, M., Oprea, F., & Tudose, M. B. (2022). Fiscal decentralization and economic growth: An analysis for European Union countries. *Sustainability*, *14*(5), 3065. [CrossRef]

Posit Team. (2024). *RStudio: Integrated development environment for R with version 2025.05.1+513* [Computer software]. Posit Software, PBC. Available online: https://posit.co (accessed on 1 January 2026).

Prodanov, S., & Naydenov, L. (2020). Theoretical, qualitative and quantitative aspects of municipal fiscal autonomy in Bulgaria. *Economic Studies*, *29*(2), 126–150.

R Core Team. (2024). *R: A language and environment for statistical computing* (Version 4.5.1) [Computer software]. R Foundation for Statistical Computing. Available online: https://www.r-project.org/ (accessed on 1 January 2026).

Rodden, J. (2002). The dilemma of fiscal federalism: Grants and fiscal performance around the world. *American Journal of Political Science*, *46*(3), 670–687. [CrossRef]

Rodríguez-Pose, A. (2022). The economic returns of decentralisation: Government quality and regional growth. *Environment and Planning A: Economy and Space*, *54*(6), 1031–1048. [CrossRef]

Rodríguez-Pose, A., & Ezcurra, R. (2011). Is fiscal decentralization harmful for economic growth? Evidence from the OECD countries. *Journal of Economic Geography*, *11*(4), 619–643. [CrossRef]

Rodríguez-Pose, A., & Gill, N. (2020). Fiscal decentralisation and the quality of government. *Regional Studies*, *54*(5), 676–691.

Roleders, V., Oriekhova, T., Zaharieva, G., Sysoieva, I., Dobizha, V., Pidhaiets, V., & Kucher, L. (2024). Economic justification of recycling in the processing industry. *Cleaner and Responsible Consumption*, *13*, 100195. [CrossRef]

Sabitova, N. M., Shavaleyeva, C. M., Lizunova, E. N., Khairullova, A. I., & Zahariev, A. (2020). Tax capacity of the Russian Federation constituent entities: Problems of assessment and unequal distribution. In S. L. Gabdrakhmanov (Ed.), *Regional economic developments in Russia* (pp. 79–86). Springer. [CrossRef]

Tiebout, C. M. (1956). A pure theory of local expenditures. *Journal of Political Economy*, *64*(5), 416–424. [CrossRef]

Ushenko, N., Likhonosova, G., Zahariev, A., Shaulska, L., Kęsy, M., & Hurochkina, V. (2023). Strategies for strengthening business economic security with account to global financial challenges. *Financial and Credit Activity: Problems of Theory and Practice*, *6*(53), 300–317. [CrossRef]

Zahariev, A., Zveryakov, M., Prodanov, S., Zaharieva, G., Angelov, P., Zarkova, S., & Petrova, M. (2020). Debt management evaluation through support vector machines: On the example of Italy and Greece. *Entrepreneurship and Sustainability Issues*, *7*(3), 2382–2393. [CrossRef] [PubMed]

Zaharieva, G., Tarakchiyan, O., & Zahariev, A. (2022). Market capitalization factors of the Bulgarian pharmaceutical sector in pandemic environment. *Business Management*, *32*(4), 35–51.

Zarkova, S., Kostov, D., Angelov, P., Pavlov, T., & Zahariev, A. (2023). Machine learning algorithm for mid-term projection of the EU member states' indebtedness. *Risks*, *11*(4), 71. [CrossRef]

https://doi.org/10.3390/jrfm19050322

MDPI AG
Grosspeteranlage 5
4052 Basel
Switzerland
Tel.: +41 61 683 77 34

Journal of Risk and Financial Management Editorial Office
E-mail: jrfm@mdpi.com
www.mdpi.com/journal/jrfm

www.ingramcontent.com/pod-product-compliance
Lightning Source LLC
LaVergne TN
LVHW070453061126
851858LV00011B/231
9783725881499